# GLOBAL POLITI

CASS SERIES: ISRAELI HISTORY, POLITICS AND SOCIETY
Series Editor: Efraim Karsh
ISSN: 1368-4795

This series provides a multidisciplinary examination of all aspects of Israeli history, politics and society, and serves as a means of communication between the various communities interested in Israel: academics, policy-makers, practitioners, journalists and the informed public.

1. *Peace in the Middle East: The Challenge for Israel,* edited by Efraim Karsh.
2. *The Shaping of Israeli Identity: Myth, Memory and Trauma,* edited by Robert Wistrich and David Ohana.
3. *Between War and Peace: Dilemmas of Israeli Security,* edited by Efraim Karsh.
4. *U.S.-Israeli Relations at the Crossroads,* edited by Gabriel Sheffer.
5. *Revisiting the Yom Kippur War,* edited by P. R. Kumaraswamy.
6. *Israel: The Dynamics of Change and Continuity,* edited by David Levi-Faur, Gabriel Sheffer and David Vogel.
7. *In Search of Identity: Jewish Aspects in Israeli Culture,* edited by Dan Urian and Efraim Karsh.
8. *Israel at the Polls, 1996,* edited by Daniel J. Elazar and Shmuel Sandler.
9. *From Rabin to Netanyahu: Israel's Troubled Agenda,* edited by Efraim Karsh.
10. *Fabricating Israeli History: The 'New Historians',* second revised edition, by Efraim Karsh.
11. *Divided Against Zion: Anti-Zionist Opposition in Britain to a Jewish State in Palestine, 1945–1948,* by Rory Miller.
12. *Peacemaking in a Divided Society: Israel After Rabin,* edited by Sasson Sofer.
13. *Israeli-Egyptian Relations: 1980–2000,* by Ephraim Dowek.
14. *Global Politics: Essays in Honour of David Vital,* edited by Abraham Ben-Zvi and Aharon Klieman.
15. *Parties, Elections and Cleavages; Israel in Comparative and Theoretical Perspective,* edited by Reuven Y. Hazan and Moshe Maor.
16. *Israel and the Polls 1999,* edited by Daniel J. Elazar and M. Ben Mollov.
17. *Public Policy in Israel,* edited by David Nachmias and Gila Menahem.

**Israel: The First Hundred Years** (*Mini Series*), edited by Efraim Karsh.
1. *Israel's Transition from Community to State,* edited by Efraim Karsh.
2. *From War to Peace?* edited by Efraim Karsh.
3. *Politics and Society Since 1948,* edited by Efraim Karsh.
4. *Israel in the International Arena,* edited by Efraim Karsh.
5. *Israel in the Next Century,* edited by Efraim Karsh.

# Global Politics

*Essays in Honour of David Vital*

Edited by
ABRAHAM BEN-ZVI and AHARON KLIEMAN

FRANK CASS
LONDON • PORTLAND, OR

*First published in 2001 in Great Britain by*
FRANK CASS PUBLISHERS
Crown House, 47 Chase Side
London N14 5BP

*and in the United States of America by*
FRANK CASS PUBLISHERS
c/o ISBS, 5824 N. E. Hassalo Street
Portland, Oregon 97213-3644

*Website:* http://www.frankcass.com

British Library Cataloguing in Publication Data:

Global politics: essays in honour of David Vital. –
(Israeli history, politics and society)
1. Jews – Politics and government – 1948– 2. Israel – Foreign
relations 3. Israel – Politics and government – 1993–
I. Ben-Zvi, Abraham II. Klieman, Aaron S.
320.9′5694

ISBN 0-7146-5174-5 cloth
ISBN 0-7146-8181-4 paper
ISSN: 1368-4795

Library of Congress Cataloging-in-Publication Data:

Global politics: essays in honour of David Vital/edited by Abraham
Ben-Zvi and Aharon Klieman.
p. cm. – (Cass series–Israeli history, politics, and society,
ISSN 1368-4795; 14)
Includes bibliographical references and index.
ISBN 0-7146-5174-5 (cloth) – ISBN 0-7146-8181-4 (pbk.)
1. Jews–History–19th century. 2. Jews–History–20th century. 3.
Zionism—History. 4. Israel–Foreign relations. 5.
Diplomacy–History–20th century. I. Vital, David. II. Ben-Zvi,
Abraham. III. Klieman, Aaron S. IV. Series.
DS125 .G56 2001
909′.04924–dc21

2001028003

Typeset in Palatino in 10.5/13pt by FiSH Books, London.
Printed in Great Britain by MPG Books Ltd, Bodmin, Cornwall

# Contents

**Part Three   Zionism and Modern Jewish History**

# Contributors' Biographies

**Abraham Ben-Zvi** is Senior Research Associate professor in the Department of Political Science at Tel Aviv University, head of the Security Studies Programme and Senior Research Associate at the Jaffee Centre for Strategic Studies. His most recent books are: *The United States and Israel: The Limits of the Special Relationship* (Columbia University Press, 1993); and *Decade of Transition: Eisenhower, Kennedy and the Formation of the American–Israeli Alliance* (Columbia University Press, 1998).

**Neil Caplan** teaches in the Humanities Department at Vanier College in Montreal, Canada. His publications include: *Palestine Jewry and the Arab Question, 1917–1925; The Lausanne Conference, 1949: A Case Study in Middle East Peacemaking; Futile Diplomacy,* a multi-volume documentary history of the Arab–Israeli conflict; and (with Laura Zittrain Eisenberg) *Negotiating Arab–Israeli Peace: Patterns, Problems, Possibilities.* His recent research includes the early role of United Nations peacemaking in the Arab–Israeli conflict.

**Eyal Chowers** is assistant professor in the Political Science Department at Tel Aviv University. He received his PhD from McGill University. His current research probes into the political philosophy of Zionism.

**Alan Dowty** is professor of Government and International Studies and Fellow of the Joan B. Kroc Institute for International Peace Studies at the University of Notre Dame. He has also taught in the Department of International Relations at the Hebrew University and the Department of Political Science at the University of Haifa. His most recent book is *The Jewish State: A Century Later* (University of California Press, 1998).

**Yehezkel Dror** is Professor Emeritus of Political Science and Wolfson Chair in Public Administration at the Hebrew University of Jerusalem. He is a member of the Club of Rome and an international counsellor on statecraft, security affairs and policy-planning, having occupied senior positions in the Office of the Prime Minister and the Ministry of Defence in Israel, the RAND Corporation in the USA and the European Institute of Public Administration in Maastricht. His most recent book is *The Capacity to Govern: A Report to the Club of Rome*, to be published in 2001.

**Eytan Gilboa** is professor of Government and chair of the Department of Social Sciences at the Holon Academic Institute of Technology, Israel, and is affiliated with the Department of Political Studies at Bar-Ilan University. He is the author and editor of several books. His scholarly journal articles have appeared most recently in *Communication Theory*, *The Harvard International Journal of Press/Politics*, *Gazette*, *Political Science Quarterly* and *International Negotiation*.

**Tamar Hermann** is senior lecturer in Political Science at the Open University of Israel and director of the Tami Steinmetz Centre for Peace Research, Tel Aviv University. Her main fields of academic research are extra-parliamentary politics, political protest, peace movements, domestic influences on foreign policy-making and Israeli public opinion. With Professor Ephraim Yaar she heads the Peace Index project which, since 1994, has followed Israeli public opinion about the various aspects of the regional peace process.

**Arie M. Kacowicz** is senior lecturer in International Relations at the Hebrew University of Jerusalem. He is the author of *Peaceful Territorial Change* (1994) and *Zones of Peace in the Third World: South America and West Africa in Comparative Perspective* (1998), and co-editor of *Stable Peace among Nations* (2000). He is currently completing a book on the impact of international norms in the Latin American subsystem.

**Efraim Karsh** is professor and head of Mediterranean Studies at King's College, University of London. He has held teaching and/or research positions at the Sorbonne, Columbia University, the London School of Economics, the International Institute for Strategic Studies (London), the Kennan Institute for Advanced Russian Studies (Washington, DC) and the Jaffee Centre for Strategic Studies at Tel Aviv University. Professor Karsh has published extensively on Middle Eastern affairs, Soviet foreign policy, strategic issues and European neutrality. His books include: *Empires of the Sand: The Struggle for Mastery in the Middle East, 1789–1922* (Harvard University Press, 1999; with Inari Karsh); *Fabricating Israeli History: The 'New Historians'* (Frank Cass, 1997; second revised edition 2000); *The Gulf Conflict 1990–1991: Diplomacy and War in the New World Order* (Princeton University Press, 1993; with Lawrence Freedman); *Saddam Hussein: A Political Biography* (The Free Press, 1991; with Inari Karsh); *Soviet Policy towards Syria Since 1970* (Macmillan, 1991); *Neutrality and Small States* (Routledge, 1988); *The Soviet Union and Syria* (Routledge, 1988); and *The Cautious Bear: Soviet Military Engagement in Middle East Wars in the Post-1967 Era* (Westview, 1985).

**David Kimche** is president of the Israel Council for Foreign Affairs, is a member of the board of governors of the Hebrew University and of the Truman Research Institute for the Advancement of Peace. A member of the steering committee of the International Alliance for Arab–Israel Peace and senior executive vice-president for a leading telecommunications group, Dr Kimche was a senior official in the Office of the Prime Minister until 1980, director-general of the Ministry for Foreign Affairs (1980–87) and Ambassador-at-large (1987).

**Aharon Klieman** is the Nahum Goldmann Professor of Diplomacy in the Political Science Department at Tel Aviv University, where he is deputy director of the Peres Institute for Diplomacy and Regional Cooperation and Senior Research Associate in the Jaffee Centre for Strategic Studies. His latest book is *Compromising Palestine: A Guide to Final Status Negotiations* (Columbia University Press, 2000).

**Zeev Maoz** is professor of Political Science and head of the School of Government and Public Policy at Tel Aviv University, specializing in international politics, strategy and Middle East international affairs. He is the author of several books, including, most recently: *International Hate Affairs: The Evolution of Enduring International Rivalries* (University of Michigan Press, forthcoming; with Ben D. Mor); *Domestic Sources of Global Change* (University of Michigan Press, 1996); *National Choices and International Processes* (Cambridge University Press, 1990); and *Paradoxes of War: On the Art of National Self-Entrapment* (Unwin Hyman, 1990).

**Gil Merom** is assistant professor of Political Science at Tel Aviv University, and U2000 Fellow of International Relations, the University of Sydney. His recent publications include articles on: 'Exceptionalism and Israel's National Security' (*Political Science Quarterly*, 1999); 'Charles de Gaulle and the End of the Algerian War' (*Armed Forces and Society*, 1999); and '1962 American National Intelligence Estimate of Cuba' (*Intelligence and National Security*, 1999). His book *The Failure of Democracies in Small Wars* is scheduled for publication by Cambridge University Press in 2001.

**Itamar Rabinovich**, Israel's former ambassador to the United States (1993–96), is President of Tel Aviv University. The Yona and Dina Ettinger Professor of Contemporary Middle Eastern History, he is also Senior Research Fellow in the Moshe Dayan Centre for Middle Eastern and African Studies. His two latest books are: *The Brink of Peace: Israel and Syria, 1992–1994;* and *Waging Peace: Israel and the Arabs at the End of the Century.*

**Yossi Shain** is currently the Aaron and Cecile Goldman Visiting Israeli Professor of Government at Georgetown University. He received his PhD from Yale University in 1988 and since 1989 has taught Political Science at Tel Aviv University, where he served as head of the department from 1996 to 1999. He is the author of: *The Frontier of Loyalty: Political Exiles in the Age of the Nation-State* (1989); *Between States: Interim Governments and Democratic Transitions* (1995; with Juan J. Linz); and *Marketing the American Creed Abroad: Diasporas in the U.S. and Their Homelands* (1999).

**Yaacov Shavit** teaches modern Jewish history and the history of *Eretz-Israel* (Palestine) at Tel Aviv University. His latest books in English are: *The New Hebrew Nation: A Study in Israeli Heresy and Fantasy* (1987); *Jabotinsky and the Revisionist Movement, 1925–1948* (1988); *Athens in Jerusalem: Classical Antiquity and Hellenism in the Making of the Modern Secular Jew* (1997); and *History in Black: African-Americans in Search of a Past* (2000).

**David Tal** is Lecturer in the Department of History at Tel Aviv University. His first book, *Israel's Conception of Current Security – Origins and Development, 1949–1956*, was published in 1998 by Be'ersheba University Press. Dr Tal has published articles dealing with the history of Israel's security and foreign affairs, and is currently completing a book on the 1948 Arab–Israeli war.

# David Vital:
# An Appreciation

## ABRAHAM BEN-ZVI AND AHARON KLIEMAN

Any attempt at categorizing David Vital's career-long scholarly contribution risks oversimplification in the face of its depth and scope. Nonetheless, thanks to its coherence and continuity (both conceptual and historical), there are several dominant themes linking each monograph, book, multi-volume enterprise, essay, review and journal article to the other.

It is fair to say that the major thread representing Vital's core approach to history and politics is closely patterned on Max Weber's distinction between pragmatic and charismatic leadership. However, Vital's juxtaposition between the charismatic/utopian and the pragmatic/realistic is not limited solely to the realm of political leadership. Nor does it exclusively evolve around the distinction between the cognitive or psychological environment of the individual actor, and the operational environment which he or she seeks to shape according to preconceived beliefs and preferences. Indeed, in extending Weber's individualism to the broader level of collective social movements and political entities, Vital predicates his entire intellectual enterprise on the irreconcilable gap between, on the one hand, apocalyptic and passionate ideologies largely oblivious to constraints on Man's latitude of choice, and, on the other hand, a more pragmatic issue-oriented approach.

Against the backdrop of this paradigmatic incompatibility between the ideal and the real, between the revolutionary and the evolutionary, and between the sweeping and the incremental, Vital's preferences are clear. Whether addressing the security predicaments of small or tertiary states (as he defines them) in confronting great powers (in *The Survival of Small States*[1]), or analysing the origins of the Zionist movement, Vital's argumentation is firmly rooted in the logic of the achievable and the possible. Thus, while Zionism can certainly be defined in revolutionary terms as a sharp departure from traditional patterns of diasporic Jewish life in Eastern Europe, Vital's narrative in *The Origins of Zionism*[2] consistently differentiates between ideas and dreams periodically articulated by a few isolated intellectuals with no impact whatsoever on their environment in contrast to the effective spread of *political* Zionism's programmatic message. By focusing on the institutional and organizational means for mobilizing broad segments of Jewish society, leaders like Theodor Herzl and Yehuda Leib Pinsker – Vital's heroes in the Zionist drama – successfully managed to transform Diaspora yearning for the land of Zion into a concrete, operational programme.

This emphasis on (a) structure and (b) organization as necessary prerequisites for converting the Jewish national idea into a reality capable of adapting to changing international dynamics is similarly evident in *Zionism: The Formative Years*.[3] It is even more pronounced in Vital's analysis of the forces continuously shaping British foreign policy. As Vital makes abundantly clear throughout the pages of *The Making of British Foreign Policy*,[4] there is no such thing as 'foreign policy' in the abstract, nor can it ever be isolated from ever-present domestic and external constraints inevitably reducing the decision-maker's freedom of action and range of options.

While it is seemingly confined to a specific, limited English historical and political context, Vital's careful reconstruction of the processes by which decisions in British external affairs were actually made sheds light on foreign-policy behaviour in general. In the never-ending debate between Plato and Aristotle, Woodrow Wilson and Henry Kissinger, the optimal and the possible, Vital's preferences and policy prescriptions reflect his keen sense of empiricism and awareness that only on the basis of acknowledging limits to the possible can a route to heaven, the promised land or the millennium be safely navigated.

David Vital's overriding sensitivity to specific contexts and his early interest in British foreign policy and small-state behaviour provides us with the crucial groundwork for a bureaucratic theory of decision-making without the cumbersome jargon afflicting latter-day political science theory.

Through its identification of a broad cluster of bureaucratic constraints upon the Foreign Office's latitude of choice, which originated in the competing interests and priorities of such departments and organizations as the Ministry of Defence and the Board of Trade, *The Making of British Foreign Policy* deserves to be viewed as one of the pioneering applications of a bureaucratic approach to the study of decision-making, predating Allison, Destler and Halperin[5] in vividly reconstructing skirmishes and 'decision games' between rival bureaucratic actors constantly engaged in pushing and shoving. So, too, have many of Vital's other observations and insights preceded their time.

Although more than three decades have elapsed since the publication of *The Inequality of States*, its lessons and findings remain valid today. Particularly impressive in this respect is Vital's capacity to look beyond the current and the superficially salient. Indeed, he has consistently been able to identify sources of vulnerability in the thinking and behaviour of nominally strong, seemingly omnipotent powers. His recognition that power is always contextual and relative, that domestic attributes such as a high level of solidarity and cohesion may actually enable small powers to prevail, and that sanctions by primary actors against dependents or weak adversaries may not guarantee their surrender or acquiescence are but three observations made during a period characterized by so many other observers as a Cold War era of overwhelming and unquestionable superpower preponderance.

In the end, David Vital emerges from his cumulative writings as a true iconoclastic thinker in the best Socratic tradition. He has always been prepared to challenge conventional wisdom and to reexamine long-standing axioms and norms in cold, unsentimental fashion and from new, unorthodox perspectives. He remains – in all his thought and work – a staunch advocate of partial, relativist, empirically sound and incremental policies and courses of action. Highly sceptical of the human capacity to simultaneously tackle a variety of issues head-on, and equally unimpressed with the promise of grand theories and paradigms to provide definitive explanations and 'solutions' to human behaviour in the international sphere, Vital remains an indefatigable proponent of the inductive tradition, as manifested in Isaiah Berlin's parallel work. History rather than abstraction is his anchor.

Notwithstanding that Vital's entire approach is strictly conditioned upon rigorous, meticulous procedures and rules of inference and proof, there is no doubt that at least some of the ideas and themes at the heart of his thinking reflect personal and family experiences and lessons drawn from cataclysmic events to which he has been witness. His undisguised abhorrence of all forms of ideological and political radicalism is only one illustration of the profound impact Nazism, fascism and communism had in shaping his *Weltanschauung*. After all, his father, Meir Grossman, narrowly escaped a Bolshevik execution squad because of his Zionist activity in Russia.

In this respect, no attempt at appraising Vital's overall scholarly contributions can be divorced from these larger forces affecting his belief system. More specifically, beneath his clinical observations and interpretations there exists another stratum in Vital's writings – a layer permeated with concern for the future of the Zionist move- ment and of the Jewish state.

Clearly, if there is one major undercurrent organically linking most facets of Vital's scholarship, it is his abiding fear that the Zionist option may not guarantee the long-term future of the Jewish people. This concern is particularly acute in *The Future of the Jews*,[6] patterned on his belief that Jews of late are losing their pre-state unity, cohesion and ethnic solidarity. Cognizant that contemporary Jewish life has become increasingly divisive, Vital's vision of Jewish prospects is fraught with an unbounded fear of this growing bifur- cation:

> Where there was once a single, if certainly a scattered and far from monolithic people – indeed a nation – there is now an archipelago of discrete islands composed of rather shaky communities of all qualities, shapes and sizes, in which the island of Israel, as it were, is fated increasingly to be in a class by itself.[7]

For Vital, the sharp, merciless observer, this shrinking of the Zionist dream into one small political entity while the majority of the Jewish people becomes increasingly susceptible to assimilation and intermarriage implies that *all* responsibility for preserving the essence of the Zionist dream now falls exclusively upon Israel's shoulders.

For Vital, the uncompromising Zionist, who made *aliyah* (emigrated to Israel) from England in 1934, and whose father devoted much of his life to the promotion of Vladimir Jabotinsky's interpretation of Zionism, this recognition of the growing tension between the Diaspora and Israeli Jewry (combined with the grow- ing fragmentation of diasporic life) is acutely alarming. Anything but a merely intellectual or purely scholarly predicament, the existential dilemma embedded in *The Future of the Jews* is, for Vital, both personal and immediate. It pertains to nothing less than the survival of the very core of Judaism, namely, Jewish nationalism and its future identity.

It is hardly surprising, therefore, that David Vital has chosen to devote so much of his energy and talent to analysing this core and to examining those preconditions which might ensure Israel's continued survival as an independent, viable political entity. His brilliant study 'Israel: The Contemporary Paradigm',[8] and his careful delineation of the boundaries between permissible and forbidden patterns of small-state behaviour, unmistakably originate in this abiding concern for the survival of one particular small state.

Given the traumatic destruction of European Jewry and the bankruptcy of all major alternatives to Zionism, the only remaining option left for Vital – the avowedly Zionist scholar as outlined in his seminal volume: *A People Apart: The Jews in Europe, 1789–1939*[9] – is to see to it, in his own unique way, that the Jewish state does not overextend its limited capabilities by pursuing courses of action that might ultimately endanger its own existence.

Thus, although they are couched in objective rather than affective terms, contingencies which Vital develops as ideologically derived policy goals[10] are best viewed as tripwires designed to warn Israel's leaders of the dangers in either ignoring or downplaying the possible and the achievable:

> The results of the 1967 war did not merely confront the nation with a fresh and unanticipated set of problems. It initiated a fresh debate ... which raised ... radically conflicting notions of what constituted the true and proper nature and ethos of the state. And the result was a reversal of the rules that normal, rational practice seems to prescribe. Instead of options being chosen by reference *inter alia* to established goals, goals were effectively multiplied by the creation of new options; and most attempts to set them were made by reference to these new options.[11]

Painfully aware of modern Jewish history's sobering lessons, this English-born, cosmopolitan Zionist nationalist Russian Jew, and insightful historian, has really never abandoned the battle his father waged for a territorial and political solution to the Jewish problem by creating conditions necessary for the rehabilitation of the Jews. Whether on the military front in the Israel Defence Forces, on the diplomatic front in the Israeli Prime Minister's Office, or in his numerous scholarly efforts, David Vital has continuously been driven by his undiminished desire to guarantee that the fulfillment of his father's dream – Jewish statehood – never be compromised.

For all its centrality, this cluster of beliefs, hopes and convictions inextricably linked to the very core of Vital's psychological environment does not in the least infringe upon the internal consistency of his scientific arguments, but only reinforces them. Which is yet another tribute to his intellectual gifts, in particular his capacity to build a conceptual bridge between the actual and the perceived.

The following essays contributed by those who have benefited most from his insights and counsel – friends, colleagues in the Department of Political Science at Tel Aviv University and former students – aim at further developing the three pillars comprising the essence of David Vital's academic work: modern diplomacy and interstate behaviour (Part One); the State of Israel and its foreign relations (Part Two); and issues relating to modern Jewish history and to the Zionist movement in particular (Part Three).

Our hope is that these chapters augment some of the themes articulated so clearly and lucidly by David Vital and, in so doing, will inspire further exploration of the central questions which have preoccupied him so intensively, and so productively, for the last half-century.

## NOTES

1. David Vital, *The Survival of Small States* (Oxford: Oxford University Press, 1971).
2. David Vital, *The Origins of Zionism* (London: Oxford University Press, 1975).
3. David Vital, *Zionism: The Formative Years* (London: Oxford University Press, 1982).
4. David Vital, *The Making of British Foreign Policy* (London: Allen and Unwin, 1968).
5. Graham T. Allison, *Essence of Decision: Explaining the Cuban Missile Crisis* (Boston: Little, Brown, 1971); I. M. Destler, *Presidents, Bureaucrats, and Foreign Policy: The Politics of Organizational Reform* (Princeton: Princeton University Press, 1974); Morton Halperin, *Bureaucratic Politics and Foreign Policy* (Washington, DC: The Brookings Institution, 1974); John D. Steinbrunner, *The Cybernetic Theory of Decision* (Princeton: Princeton University Press, 1974).
6. David Vital, *The Future of the Jews* (Cambridge: Harvard University Press, 1990).
7. Ibid., p. 147. See also Gideon Shimoni, 'The Future of the Jews: A Review', *Jewish Political Studies Review*, Vol. 6 (autumn 1994), 209–10.
8. Vital, *The Survival of Small States*, Chapter 4, passim.
9. David Vital, *A People Apart: The Jews in Europe, 1789–1939* (New York: Oxford University Press, 1999).
10. See, for example, David Vital, 'The Definition of Goals in Foreign Policy', in Asher Arian (ed.), *Israel – A Developing Society* (Assen: Van Gorcum Press, 1980), pp. 21–7.
11. Ibid., p. 22.

# PART ONE

# Modern Diplomacy and International Relations

# 1 The Traditional and the Transitional in Statecraft

DAVID KIMCHE

'The old order changeth, leading place to new', wrote the poet Lord Alfred Tennyson at the turn of the nineteenth century. At the time, startling and dramatic changes were, indeed, challenging the old order – not least, the classic conduct of diplomacy. Recalling that period of change, a senior Norwegian diplomat not too long ago quoted a fellow countryman, Hendrik Ibsen, who asked provocatively whether diplomacy would survive in the modern world:

> Why should countries maintain expensive ambassadors in faraway places, writing long informative reports to be mailed to their ministers at home, when recent inventions such as the express train and the telegraph are able to send news messages and even people home before the ambassadorial letter reaches the foreign minister?

The Norwegian diplomat was quoting from an article by Ibsen written 100 years ago.[1]

Contrary to such dire warnings, nineteenth-century diplomacy survived by adapting itself to the major, dramatic changes. It had to do so again, at an ever-increasing pace throughout the twentieth century, a century characterized by continuous change – political, socio-economic, technological. All of which has had a profound bearing on the conduct of diplomacy.

The last 50 years in particular have witnessed a world convulsed by political upheavals and transformed by technological revolution. World wars, the demise of colonialism, the advent of the Cold War and its eventual collapse, the growth of multinational bodies both in the form of world organizations and regional groupings, and the gradual transition to universalism and to the concept of the 'global village' have all been part of the political metamorphosis of the last 50 years which has inspired concomitant change in diplomatic activity. At the same time, the transformation of our lives by continuous technological advances has had a similar effect. If Ibsen could wonder whether the advent of the express train and the telegraph made diplomats redundant, what would he have said of such features of our daily lives as air travel, the CNN or the Internet?

Many definitions of the word 'diplomacy' have been volunteered. Suffice it, for our purposes, to use the *Oxford English Dictionary* definition quoted by Harold Nicolson in his classic book *Diplomacy*: diplomacy is 'the management of international relations by negotiation; the method by which these relations are adjusted and managed by ambassadors and envoys; the business or art of the diplomatist'.[2] Similarly, much has been written about the differences between 'old' and 'new' diplomacy.[3] 'New' diplomacy, however, was originally defined as 'open' or 'public' as opposed to the 'secret' or 'discreet' which had been the hallmark of classic diplomacy, a change which occurred after the First World War, and is mirrored in the first of the Fourteen Points of President Wilson, which insisted that henceforth there be 'open covenants openly arrived at, after which there should be no private understandings of any kind, but diplomacy shall proceed always frankly and in the public view'.[4] Diplomacy having failed to prevent that war, it is hardly surprising that after it was over a strong reaction set in against the 'old, secretive diplomacy', which acted as a backdrop to President Wilson's new 'open covenant'.[5]

However, since then, the world, and diplomatic activity with it, has changed almost beyond recognition. Classic diplomacy is characterized not only by the secrecy, or discretion, with which it is conducted; it has been largely bilateral, pertaining principally to political and security matters. Ambassadors and embassies have been the tools with which it is executed. As Abba Eban pointed out, 'meetings between heads of state and heads of government before World War Two were so rare as to create a sensation when they occurred'.[6]

The situation today is vastly different. Meetings of heads of state, of premiers and of foreign ministers have become almost everyday occurrences and have largely superseded ambassadorial activity in dealing with vital matters of state. Moreover, an ever-growing number of diplomatic encounters take place in a multilateral environment, and the subjects discussed concern economy, environment, and social and humanitarian issues much more than politics and security, about which diplomacy in the past had been principally concerned. Also, many of the subjects discussed are highly specific in nature. The diplomats concerned have little or no knowledge of the subject matter being discussed, and act as chaperons to qualified experts who conduct talks with experts from other countries. Long and protracted negotiations were held, for example, within the framework of the European Union on how to deal with the so-called mad-cow disease, a subject which certainly had not formed part of the training of the diplomats taking part in those negotiations![7]

The end of the Cold War changed, to a very large extent, the *modus operandi* of diplomatic activity. For 35 years the daily deeds of diplomats had been largely fashioned by their affiliation to one of the three world blocs dominating world politics after the Second World War. The subject matter of diplomatic activity revolved largely around issues pertaining to the Cold War, politics and security. The disappearance of the blocs led to the process of globalization, which so characterized the twilight years of the twentieth century; so, too, has it brought to the fore problems not defined within the boundaries of politics or within political boundaries: such problems as demography, environment, human rights, poverty and hunger, fundamentalism and international terrorism, organized crime and drug trafficking, nuclear proliferation and the danger of non-conventional weapons. Just as the list is long, so does its international – or global – nature necessitate international, multilateral treatment.

Yet side by side with this new universalism we are witnessing outbursts of tension and strife of a virulent national, ethnic or religious character – potential conflicts which the Cold War had suppressed and swept under the carpet.

Classic diplomacy has no easy answer to either situation – the universalism of the global village or particularistic conflicts as seen in Bosnia, Chechnya, Kosovo, the Sudan, Rwanda, Congo, Sierra Leone, East Timor, South Lebanon and elsewhere. The formula for ending such conflicts has not been discreet, bilateral diplomacy at the ambassadorial level, but rather open, multilateral diplomatic activity pursued by ministers or special envoys. This pattern has occurred in former Yugoslavia – Bosnia, Kosovo; in Angola, where a troika composed of Russian, American and Portuguese diplomats brought the warring parties to the negotiation table in Lusaka; *inter alia*, in South Lebanon, where a body composed of representatives from the US, France, Syria, Lebanon and Israel formed to oversee arrangements agreed after a particularly violent flare-up in 1996.

Similarly, the new global dimensions of the problems besetting world leaders in the wake of the Cold War demand open, multilateral treatment for an entire range of subjects that transcend national frontiers. A typical case of this need for multilateral cooperation is the fight against terrorism. The need to coordinate, pool resources and share information becomes all but self-evident in response to the international character of terrorism. Largely at the behest of Israel, an apparatus was established in the early 1970s under which information on terrorism was disseminated instantaneously to a group of 13 countries which began to cooperate closely on diplomatic and intelligence levels in an effort to curb terrorist activity.

Nowadays, multilateral activity exists in virtually every facet of life in modern society. Indeed, much more emphasis is placed on economic development, preserving the global environment and maintaining human rights and physical well-being than on the classic, traditional subjects which in the past filled the agendas of diplomats.[8]

All these changes have naturally affected the work of the foreign ministry of Israel and of Israeli diplomats. Yet in many ways Israel's diplomatic activity is different from that of other countries. The fact that Israel was beleaguered – militarily and politically – throughout most of its history naturally had an effect both on foreign-policy postulates and on the *modus operandi* of Israel's diplomats. Thus they were not among the first to join colleagues throughout the world who were moving to the multilateral track and placing greater emphasis on economic and social matters than on security and political issues. Quite simply, force of circumstance did not allow Israel's diplomats to do so.

Throughout its history, Israel's most basic national goals have been to attain peace and security, to consolidate and strengthen its political position in the world, to bolster its economy and to fulfil Zionist aspirations by offering a haven and a home to Diaspora Jews.[9] These goals have remained constant, and have guided Israel's foreign service throughout. Emphasis was placed primarily on the first two of these aims, namely security and political, which is hardly surprising in view of the constant threat of political isolation and delegitimization which faced Israel, and because of the ever-present danger of renewed military conflict. These aims have been pursued in countless meetings, usually held in a discreet manner, and in bilateral frameworks, because the very nature of the sensitive subject matter of these meetings invariably necessitates both discretion and the bilateral milieu. However, bilateral meetings for Israel's diplomats are hardly ever a matter of choice. One of the few countries in the world excluded from regional associations of countries, Israel has been largely excluded from multilateral activities. Even in those international bodies that did include the Jewish state, Israel was largely constrained from taking an active role because of its isolated position.[10]

There has, however, been an additional factor setting Israel's foreign service apart from those of most Western countries. Israeli diplomacy is the child of Jewish, and particularly Zionist, attitudes and aspirations. Long before the State of Israel was established Zionist policy prescribed the need for the fledgling *Yishuv* to rely on a strong outside ally as a constant prerequisite, and this has been the case throughout: from the Ottoman Empire to Great Britain in the early days of Zionist settlement, through France to the United States in more recent decades. Yet paradoxically a deep, underlying suspicion of the gentile world – the natural outcome of centuries of persecution – proscribed reliance on outside factors. This built-in hesitancy gave birth to deep undercurrents of rejection of, and even disdain for, the need for sound international relations, especially with international bodies such as the United Nations.[11] Jewish and particularly Zionist history was the backdrop to the development of a policy giving precedence to physical action over diplomacy. In the words of David Ben-Gurion:

> Foreign policy and defense policy...both served the same purpose...if explanations do not persuade, use is made of force...a change in relative strength in practice comes before friendly relations. Our foreign policy is nothing but an auxiliary tool of secondary importance, not as in an established, stable country.[12]

Suspicion of the outside world, with its concomitant self-reliance, the need to buttress the strength of the nascent state in the face of a constant threat to its existence and the domestic obligation to forge one nation from the massive, diverse flood of immigrants who poured into Israel – all three factors profoundly influenced the moulding of foreign-policy postulates in the first years of Israel's existence. They conspired to demand an inward-looking, national-ist attitude at precisely the time when the trend in most Western countries was towards a more international, global orientation, particularly after the end of the Cold War. In the words of Professor Sasson Sofer, 'the attempt to combine nationalism with the univer-salism of western civilization has succeeded only partially'.[13]

Likewise, Zionist realities, superimposed on the innate distrust of the gentile world, led to strong emphasis being placed on rela-tions with the Jewish Diaspora. Appearing before Israeli foreign ministry personnel in 1950, Ben-Gurion declared: 'If we do not learn how to add the influence of all the Jews throughout the world to our strength we sabotage our diplomacy: world Jewry is a great political, economic and moral factor.'[14] Indeed, the adviser to the minister of diaspora affairs has been an important function in the foreign ministry throughout the years of Israel's existence.[15] The foreign ministry's first director-general, Walter Eytan, described the ministry's relationship with the Diaspora in the following manner:

> It is commonplace of our Foreign Service that every Envoy Extraordinary and Minister Plenipotentiary of Israel has a dual function. He is Minister Plenipotentiary to the country to which he is accredited – and Envoy Extraordinary to its Jews.[16]

However, Israel's diplomacy has been most affected by the coun-try's physical and military security needs. For these, of necessity, must take precedence over every other issue. Security and defence requirements have actually been the first priority of Israel's foreign service since its first days in 1948. In the words of another of the foreign ministry's director-generals, Gideon Rafael: 'The access to sources of arms supplies and the effort to secure their unimpeded flow…determined more than any other factor [Israel's] interna-tional conduct',[17] as did also the necessity to prevent sophisticated weaponry reaching Israel's neighbours.

One of the subjects that occupied my attention almost more than any other during my second year as director-general was the campaign we waged against the supply of sophisticated spy planes (AWACS) by the US to Saudi Arabia. The issue was of such impor-tance that the prime minister, together with the foreign and defence ministers, travelled to Washington on 6 September 1981 in an effort to dissuade President Reagan from implementing the transaction.[18]

In effect, security and defence requirements on the one hand, and the necessity to prevent Israel's isolation on the other, were the major tasks of Israel's diplomats. The combined pressure placed upon Israel by the Arab and Muslim countries, by the communist bloc and by the non-aligned states forced Israel's diplomats to devote a major part of their time and skill to discreet, bilateral meetings in an ongoing effort to avoid condemnation, delegitimization and complete isolation in the dozens of international bodies which, in the second half of the twentieth century, comprised an imposing mosaic of diplomatic activity encompassing every possible subject about which countries have dealings with each other. In the United Nations, for example, more resolutions condemning Israel were tabled than against any other country. Every such attempt necessitated renewed general mobilization of Israel's diplomats in a determined, concerted effort to prevail on individual and key UN member states not to vote in favour of those resolutions. Time and again, Israel's ambassadors were sent to foreign ministries around the world to cajole and persuade their hosts not to support a decidedly anti-Israeli resolution. With such a political agenda, there is no wonder that our overseas envoys could not, and did not, spend their time and talents on economics, for example, or on other ostensibly non-political subjects increasingly commanding the attention of their colleagues in the diplomatic world, and especially those representing countries of the progressive, Western world.[19]

Moreover, efforts to isolate Israel and blacken her name were not confined to international organizations. In the 1970s, when the price of oil topped $40 a barrel, many countries found it expedient to limit their contacts with Israel. Other countries chose to do so either for ideological reasons or because of political allegiance to blocs or organizations hostile to Israel. Isolation, from Israel's point of view, meant not only the severing of diplomatic relations, as happened throughout Africa after the Yom Kippur War in 1973, but also no less damaging, the minimizing of contacts, for example, not promoting cultural cooperation, or not allowing ministerial visits, or restricting imports and trade exports.[20] Thus, to take another example, in the 1970s and early 1980s not many countries would gladly have agreed to a state visit by the president of Israel.

The Arab economic, political and diplomatic onslaught against Israel actually received added impetus in the early 1980s. Counterintuitively, even while the 1979 peace treaty between Egypt and Israel may have lessened the dangers of renewed military conflict, if anything, it led the other Arab states to redouble their efforts against Israel in the diplomatic and economic arena. The Lebanese war of 1982 added further fuel to the fire, and to the competition worldwide, for the war cast Israel in a negative light, yet again providing further incentive to Israel's detractors.[21]

Thus, in an era when world diplomacy was moving away from the classic tenets defining diplomatic activity, Israel's diplomats were still engaged primarily in the traditional methods of maintaining narrow, minimalist political and security interests. When I became director-general of the foreign ministry in 1980, very little multilateral activity was taking place, and the ministry's economic division was still a quiet backwater. Rather, overall emphasis was placed on the need to negate hostile moves to isolate us, moves which foreign ministry personnel were instructed to counter by broadening the field of activity. Accordingly, clandestine meetings were held with heads of state in Africa in an endeavour to renew diplomatic relations with countries of that continent.[22] Missions previously closed for budgetary reasons in Hong Kong and Paraguay were reopened. Countries which for many years had not sent any ministers to visit Israel and had not received Israeli ministerial visits were singled out for special attention, as were countries that had no diplomatic relations with Israel, such as Spain and Ireland. A senior Israeli diplomat was sent to Madrid as head of a government tourist office with instructions to foster relations with Spanish leaders; another was sent to Dublin in an economic guise but with a similar mission. At the same time, delegates were sent to every possible conference with instructions to do whatever possible to prevent our expulsion from international organizations, large and small. In this manner Israel sought, again by traditional diplomatic means, to counter hostile moves from whatever quarter.

Israel's diplomacy has acquired an additional aim, however: the attainment of peace. Clandestine relations with Morocco, King Hussein of Jordan and others in the Arab world were directed, *inter alia*, at this objective. The Moroccan initiative to bring together an emissary of Egypt and Israel's foreign minister on Moroccan soil would never have happened if Israel had not for years impressed upon the Moroccans its desire that Rabat act as a midwife for peace between Israel and its Arab neighbours.[23] Indeed, secret meetings between Arabs and Jews seeking to overcome the enmity between the two peoples had been a feature of Israeli diplomatic activity from the first days of the establishment of the state, and, indeed, there is a rich precedent for this in the very beginnings of the Zionist movement.[24] Of necessity, all these activities had to be conducted secretly and far from the public eye.

Secret diplomacy reached its apex with the negotiations conducted in Oslo in 1993, leading to the signing of the Declaration of Principles by Israelis and Palestinians on the White House lawn on 13 September 1993. We must ask ourselves why the secret diplomacy of Oslo was so successful, while parallel formal negotiations conducted at the same time between Israelis and Palestinians in Washington were an abject failure. Surely one compelling explanation is that the Washington negotiations were so public that, in the words of Shimon Peres, they resembled a permanent press conference. With the media pouncing on every idea raised, there was no possibility in Washington to undertake intellectual exercises, to float ideas and create a meeting of minds. Any such ideas were immediately leaked to the press with concomitant repercussions.

In short, the complete antithesis of President Wilson's famous dictum on transparency and openness was needed both for Oslo and for the Camp David negotiations between Egyptians and Israelis to succeed.[25] The primary lesson of the Oslo negotiating format is that the greater the sensitivity and complexity of the subject matter at hand, the more does secrecy have to be maintained during the critical phase of negotiations. With the end of the Cold War, this necessity may be becoming less acute in other parts of the world, but, for as long as full peace has not been attained with its neighbours, Israel cannot, and dare not, afford the luxury of transparent diplomacy. Nor can it forgo the imperatives of political and security considerations.

For the present, the *modus operandi* of Israel's diplomacy remains, stylistically and even substantively, different from that of most other countries. It can only be hoped that circumstances will permit this anomaly to be corrected, and in the not-too-distant future.

### NOTES

1. Jan Egeland, *Diplomacy in Transition* (Jerusalem, 1995), p. 14.
2. Harold Nicolson, *Diplomacy* (London, 1950), p. 15.
3. See, for example, Herbert Butterfield and Martin Wright (eds.), *Diplomatic Investigations* (London, 1966), pp. 181ff.; Henry Kissinger, *Diplomacy* (New York, 1994), pp. 218ff.; Abba Eban, *The New Diplomacy: International Affairs in the Modern Age* (New York, 1983), pp. 330ff.

4. Eban, *The New Diplomacy*, p. 345.
5. Butterfield and Wright, *Diplomatic Investigations*, p. 181.
6. Eban, *The New Diplomacy*, p. 344.
7. Similarly, after the peace treaty between Egypt and Israel was signed, Israeli foreign ministry officials chaperoned experts from other ministries who negotiated with the Egyptians some 40 normalization agreements.
8. For a precise description of the development of multilateral diplomacy, see the contribution of Antonio Monteiro, director-general for foreign policy of the Portuguese foreign ministry, in Egeland, *Diplomacy in Transition*, p. 33.
9. There have been different definitions of Israel's basic foreign-policy goals. See, for instance, Aaron S. Klieman, *Israel and the World After 40 Years* (Washington, 1990), p. 6.
10. Speaking before an audience of the Israel Council on Foreign Relations and the UN Association of Israel, the Secretary-General of the United Nations, Kofi Annan, declared on 28 March 1998: 'I know that Israelis see hypocrisy and double standards in the intense scrutiny given to some of its actions while other situations fail to elicit the world's outrage and condemnations...I believe it is time to usher in a new era of relations between Israel and the United Nations...one way to write that new chapter would be to rectify an anomaly: Israel's position as the only Member State that is not a member of one of the regional groups, which means it has no chance of being elected to serve on main organs such as the Security Council or Economic Social Council. This anomaly should be corrected.' See Kofi Annan, *Israel and the United Nations* (Jerusalem, 1998).
11. See Sasson Sofer, *Zionism and the Foundations of Israeli Democracy* (Cambridge, 1998), p. 380: 'Throughout its history the Zionist Movement displayed an inclination to cultivate extensive relations with the world power that dominated the Middle East as the only – and sometimes preferred – course open to it.' As for the United Nations, Ben-Gurion's famous *'Oom-Shmoom'* expression comes to mind – Oom being the Hebrew for UN.
12. *Ben-Gurion's Diary*, Sde Boker, 22 July 1950, quoted by Uri Bialer, 'Facts and Pacts: Ben-Gurion and Israel's International Orientation 1948–1956', in Ronald W. Zweig (ed.), *David Ben-Gurion: Politics and Leadership in Israel* (London, 1991), pp. 216–17. See also Sofer, *Zionism*: Professor Sasson writes of 'activism and the use of military means for obtaining political ends', p. 380.
13. Sasson, *Zionism*, p. 360.
14. Bialer, 'Facts and Pacts', p. 218.
15. For a detailed description of relations between Israel and the Diaspora – a two-way traffic of help – see Klieman, *Israel and the World*, pp. 171ff.
16. Walter Eytan, *The First Ten Years – Israel between East and West* (London, 1958), p. 179.
17. Gideon Rafael, *Destination Peace – Three Decades of Israeli Foreign Policy* (London, 1981), p. 377.
18. On 20 September 1981, a cabinet communiqué was issued voicing 'unreserved opposition to the sale of sophisticated weapons to Saudi Arabia including offensive equipment for F-15 planes and the most sophisticated intelligence planes'. See *Israel's Foreign Relations – Selected Documents, 1981–1983* (Jerusalem, 1988), p. 148.
19. The secretary-general of the ministry of foreign affairs of the Netherlands, D. J. Van den Berg, had this to say on the need for diplomats to spend more time on economic subjects: 'classical diplomats somehow rank economics at the low end of the spectrum of activities in international affairs. I think they are dead wrong. Economics is a very important determining factor in the assessment of trends in the international order. If only for that reason, economics should be an integral part of political work in the ministry of foreign affairs.' See Egeland, *Diplomacy in Transition*, p. 61.
20. There were a number of countries which, although maintaining diplomatic relations, had not for many years sent a minister or senior official to visit Israel, or invited Israeli ministers or officials to visit them. Japan, Greece, Sweden and Brazil were among such countries.
21. On 2 June 1982, Israel's ambassador in London was shot and critically wounded in a terrorist attack engendering a spiral of violence culminating in Israel's offensive against the PLO in Lebanon. This was a particularly trying time for Israel's diplomats. The war also created a unique situation for Israeli diplomacy, as a *de facto*

embassy was established in Beirut – in a country that was technically at war with Israel and in a city in which terrorist organizations considered the diplomatic post and Israeli diplomats their primary target. As an illustration of the anomaly of the situation, I held a meeting with the director-general of the Lebanese ministry of foreign affairs in an apartment in West Beirut, which, at the time of the meeting in December 1982, was still a stronghold of elements hostile to Israel.

22. In the 1980s I held secret meetings with Presidents Mobutu, Mbia Houphouet-Boigny, Moi and Kaunde in an effort to persuade them to renew diplomatic relations. The head of the African department of the foreign ministry, Avi Primor, visited other heads of state in Africa in a well-planned diplomatic offensive.

23. Moshe Dayan and Hassan Tohami met in Rabat on 16 September 1977. The outcome of that meeting brought about the visit of President Anwar al Sadat to Jerusalem later that year.

24. Though many of these endeavours have been chronicled there are still numerous contacts, carried out mainly by the Mossad, which must remain secret. Among some of the more noteworthy publications on this subject are: David Ben-Gurion, *My Talks with Arab Leaders* (New York, 1973); Itamar Rabinovich, *The Road not Taken: Early Arab–Israeli Negotiations* (New York, 1991); Charles Enderlin, *Paix ou Guerre: Les Secrets des Negociations Israelo-Arabes 1917–1997* (Paris, 1997).

25. For an analysis of the Oslo secret negotiations as opposed to the open negotiations held in New York, see Karin Aggestam, 'Two-Track Diplomacy: Negotiations between Israel and the PLO through Open and Secret Channels', *Davis Papers on Israel's Foreign Policy* (Jerusalem, 1996). For a full description of the Oslo negotiations, see Uri Savir, *The Process: 1100 Days That Changed the Middle East* (New York, 1998).

# 2 Diplomacy in the Age of Global Communication

## EYTAN GILBOA

### INTRODUCTION: 'THE NEW DIPLOMACY'

The communication and information revolutions of the twentieth century have fundamentally and irreversibly changed the conduct of diplomacy, including, in particular, the making of policy in defence and foreign affairs. Scholars and diplomats agree that exposing diplomacy to the media and public opinion plus the emergence of global television have challenged policy-makers and negotiators by creating a 'new diplomacy' that operates under new rules and techniques. Abba Eban, former Israeli ambassador and minister of foreign affairs, has recently written that

> nothing has done more to revolutionize the diplomatic craft than the current vogue of persistent media attention...[and] there is no way of putting the clock back to an era in which negotiations were sheltered from domestic constituencies.[1]

Former British foreign secretary Douglas Hurd also observes that 'public debate is no longer run by events, but by the coverage of events'.[2] From a scholarly perspective, Hamid Mowlana argues that

> the technologies and institutions of communication that have become so central to world politics and economics over the past couple of decades have fundamentally altered the nature and sources of power and influence, both domestically and internationally.[3]

Interrelated revolutionary changes in politics, international relations and mass communication have immensely expanded the media's multiple roles in diplomacy. The revolution in politics has generated growing mass participation in political processes and transformation of many societies from autocracy to democracy. The revolution in communication technologies – the capability to broadcast, often live, almost every significant development in world events, to almost every place on the globe – has led to the globalization of electronic journalism and to substantial growth in networks, stations and communication consumers worldwide.[4] The revolutionary change in international relations refers to the gradual replacing of military and economic power with 'soft power', and to the emergence of non-state actors and worldwide attention to global issues.[5]

Politicians and journalists indicate that the convergence of this dual revolution in politics and communication is creating a new media-dominated governing system. US Senator Richard Lugar calls this system 'Medialism', and David Gergen, a media adviser to Presidents Ronald Reagan and Bill Clinton, calls it 'Teledemocracy'.[6] A few observers insist that in foreign policy this transformation in media power has inspired a phenomenon known as the CNN (Cable News Network) effect or factor.[7]

All these terms refer to various effects of the media on governments and diplomacy, primarily to decision-makers' loss of control to the news media. For example, Johanna Neuman describes the CNN effect in the following way: 'When CNN floods the airwaves with news of foreign crisis, policymakers have no choice but to redirect their attention to the crisis at hand',[8] and to change to a course that perhaps otherwise they would not have pursued. The CNN-effect theory claims that at least in crisis situations global television has become the dominating actor in the conduct of foreign policy and diplomacy, replacing elected and appointed policy-makers.

This study raises serious questions about the validity of the CNN-effect theory. Exposing diplomacy to the media and public opinion certainly increases the influence of mass communication on both the domestic and external environments of policy-making in defence and foreign affairs and on negotiation processes.[9] Domestically, the media and the public are more aggressively examining policy issues and voicing opinions on them. In modern democracies it has become almost impossible to conduct effective diplomacy across time without sufficient public support. Although peace is always seen as a highly desirable and worthy cause, peacemaking often requires painful concessions and could become very controversial, as can clearly be seen in recent efforts to resolve the Arab–Israeli conflict and confrontations in Northern Ireland as well as in the former Yugoslavia. The more controversial the diplomatic moves, the greater the public pressure on negotiators, and the greater the need of governments to respond with effective communication campaigns. Governments pursuing peacemaking with enemies and rivals must ensure they have enough public support or else risk public punishment at the next elections.

Exposing diplomacy to the media and to public opinion has also generated a major debate among practitioners and scholars since the beginning of the twentieth century as to whether this hinders or helps diplomacy.[10] In his famous 1918 'Fourteen Points' speech, President Woodrow Wilson blamed secret diplomacy as one of the major causes of the First World War and advocated 'open covenants of peace, openly arrived at, after which there shall be no private international understandings of any kind, but diplomacy shall proceed always frankly and in the public view'.[11] One year later, however, Wilson failed to follow his own principle when he negotiated the 1919 Versailles Treaty in secrecy. In seeking to explain the contradiction between word and deed, Wilson insisted that by advocating 'open diplomacy' he only meant that agreements must be revealed to the public, but that the negotiations to achieve them might legitimately be conducted in secrecy.[12]

Diplomats and officials since then have had serious reservations about 'open diplomacy'.[13] Eban argued that this format endangers the chance to achieve international agreements. 'The hard truth', he wrote, 'is that the total denial of privacy even in the early stages of a negotiation has made international agreements harder to obtain than ever in past history.'[14] Hurd agreed with Eban, stating in 1993 that open diplomacy 'doesn't work on matters of high importance... If you want to arrive at it openly, you are unlikely to arrive at all.'[15] Michael Ledeen, a special adviser in the State Department and the National Security Council, also claimed that 'if secrets – of various sorts – cannot be kept, good policy and good relations are impossible'.[16] In the age of global television and extensive coverage of world affairs by other media, it has become increasingly difficult to conduct negotiations in secrecy, although sometimes policymakers do find innovative ways to protect sensitive talks, as in the cases of Henry Kissinger's 1971 secret negotiations in China and the 1993 secret Israeli–PLO talks in Oslo.[17]

Following rather than leading the public is yet another reason for having reservations about open diplomacy. 'Too often in recent years', observes Gergen, 'U.S. officials have substituted the power of television for the power of their own reasoning, believing that successful policies must first and foremost please the Great God of Public Opinion.'[18] He adds that what too often counts is how well the policy will 'play' on television and not whether the policy promotes America's long-term interests. Based on his recent practical experience, former Secretary of State Henry Kissinger confirms this observation by commenting that diplomats seeking his advice used to ask him what they should *do*, but now ask him what they ought to *say*.[19]

Although there is wide consensus that the media has transformed diplomacy, the question remains whether the media are functioning today primarily as an independent dominating actor, as suggested by the CNN-effect theory, or are more a sophisticated tool in the hands of officials. This study now turns to investigate the CNN-effect theory as well as the other related influences and effects global television is having on diplomacy and the formulation of foreign policy, and shows that television both constrains diplomats and provides them with opportunities to advance their goals.

## THE CNN-EFFECT THEORY

The CNN-effect theory, which suggests that global television has become a direct and perhaps even dominant actor in the formulation of policies in defence and foreign affairs, results from reflections made on the roles played by global television, particularly CNN, in major violent crises of the post-Cold War era. These include coverage of the Chinese government crackdown on the student-led protest in Beijing's Tiananmen Square in June 1989; the 1990–91 Persian Gulf crisis and war following Iraq's occupation of Kuwait; the Russian attempted coup of August 1991; and the civil wars in Somalia, Rwanda, northern Iraq, Bosnia and Kosovo. CNN was given special credit for directly affecting and channelling the Russian attempted coup while it was happening,[20] and for the subsequent humanitarian interventions in Somalia, Bosnia and Kosovo.[21]

The end of the Cold War effectively removes any rationale, ostensibly, for American military intervention abroad except in clear cases of direct threat to vital American economic and strategic interests, such as the Iraqi invasion and occupation of Kuwait in August 1990. Even then, the United States went to war only after it had negotiated for several months with Saddam Hussein, built a large international coalition and received authorization from the United Nations to use force. American policy-makers were extremely reluctant to intervene in civil wars in Somalia, Rwanda and Bosnia but said they felt pressured to send soldiers abroad because of pictures of massacres and starvation shown repeatedly on CNN and other global networks.

Rozanne Ridgway, an assistant secretary of state, describes this effect as CNN's ability to prompt popular demands for action by displaying images of starvation or other tragedy, only to reverse this sentiment when Americans are killed while trying to help.[22] Clinton's adviser, George Stephanopoulos, too, says CNN has long since become a universal and immediate actor, and that 'we're often forced to respond to them as much as to actual activity'.[23] The veteran diplomat George Kennan added his opinion, claiming there was no rational reason for the US humanitarian intervention in Somalia except Congressional and public emotional reactions aroused by television coverage.[24] These perceptions were not held only by Americans. Officials from international organizations and other countries have described the power and influence of global television in a similar way. Former UN Secretary General Boutros Boutros-Ghali has complained that 'CNN is the sixteenth member of the Security Council'.[25] In 1993, Hurd blamed foreign correspondents covering the Bosnian war for advocating military intervention by being the founding members of the 'something must be done' school.[26]

These statements by senior officials imply loss of policy control to global television, as if major policy-makers no longer make decisions on the basis of interests but are driven by emotional public opinion aroused by television coverage. On the other hand, several empirical studies using a variety of research methods applied to one or several specific case studies have raised serious questions about the validity of this theory. Nik Gowing, for example, agrees that CNN coverage has drawn attention to crises and may have evoked emotional public reactions. But based on interviews with policy-makers in several countries, he concluded that they resisted pressure to act solely in response to television news reports. He noted that in 1991 the United States and Western governments refrained from intervention in the Bosnia crisis despite substantial news coverage of atrocities. Gowing sees the CNN effect as a necessary but insufficient condition for intervention.[27] Using careful content analysis and interviews with decision-makers in Washington and Africa, Steven Livingston and Todd Eachus conclude that the US decision to intervene militarily in Somalia for humanitarian reasons 'was the result of diplomatic and bureaucratic operations, with *news coverage coming in response to those decisions*' (emphasis added).[28]

Several foreign policy-makers have offered a more complex view of the CNN effect by considering global network coverage as only *one factor* weighed against other considerations. President Clinton's former national security adviser, Anthony Lake, said, for example, that public pressure driven by televised images was only one factor in decision-making on humanitarian engagement.[29] Other considerations were cost, feasibility, the willingness of regional and international bodies to do their part, and the likelihood that actions will generate broader security benefits for the people of the region in question.

Peter Jakobsen has followed by examining the role of some of the factors mentioned by Lake in the initiation of peace-enforcement operations in five crises: Kuwait, northern Iraq, Somalia, Rwanda and Haiti. He investigated the following factors: the CNN effect itself, a strong and clear legal or humanitarian case, national interest, prospects for success and domestic support. Jakobsen basically confirmed Lake's statement and Gowing's conclusions. He found CNN coverage to have been an important factor in four of the five crises because it placed them on the agenda; but still the *ultimate decision to intervene was made on the basis of perceived chances for success*.[30] At a more general level, W. Lance Bennett suggested that as a rule reporters tend to 'index' the slant of their coverage to reflect the range of opinion that exists within the government.[31] John Zaller and Dennis Chiu used Bennett's theory of press indexing to examine US press coverage of 39 foreign-policy crises between 1945 and 1991, and found that in general the coverage supported US policy.[32] In other words, the media's decisions to slant news follows the lead of government officials, although other independent situational factors – such as whether the foe was communist or the United States has suffered a setback – also affect the slant direction. In any case, the findings of these studies essentially contradict the popular notion of officials losing policy control to the media.

## REAL-TIME DIPLOMACY

While there is insufficient evidence to support the claim that global television is becoming the dominant actor in the formulation of foreign policy, indirectly it certainly affects many important dimensions of diplomacy, primarily through high-speed global communication.[33] Tran Van Dinh notes that the speed of diplomatic messages has in this century gone from weeks to minutes.[34] This speed has challenged both policy-makers and diplomats. In traditional diplomacy, ambassadors and state representatives had a monopoly over the following important areas of diplomacy: representing their countries, communicating their government's positions, negotiating and concluding agreements, gathering information about the countries to which they were posted, and recommending actions to policy-makers back home. But the communication and information revolutions have substantially eroded the ambassadors' central position in all the above areas. In the 1992 US presidential elections Ross Perot made the following observation about the effects of the 'new diplomacy' on embassies and ambassadors:

> Embassies are relics of the days of sailing ships. At one time, when you had no world communication, your ambassador spoke for you in that country. But now, with instantaneous communication around the world, the ambassador is primarily in a social role.[35]

Indeed, policy-makers, including heads of state and ministers, talk and negotiate directly, in secrecy or in public, with their counterparts. Their negotiations are conducted primarily through official and unofficial visits but also via much simpler means such as secured phone lines. The media call this particular use of high-level direct conversations and negotiations 'Rolodex diplomacy'. In 1990, for example, President Bush used this method to cultivate support among world leaders for his policy towards the Iraqi invasion and occupation of Kuwait. Similarly, in 1999, President Clinton achieved an agreement to resume Israeli–Syrian peace talks through intensive, highly personal secret phone conversations with Israeli Prime Minister Ehud Barak and Syrian leader Hafez al-Assad. Veteran diplomats are appalled by the idea that a leader might make a significant commitment to another leader on the basis of a phone conversation alone.

Diplomats and scholars alike have expressed reservations about the possible consequences of fast and direct diplomatic exchanges. A former veteran American diplomat, David Newsom, said he has 'always trembled when a president picks up the phone to talk to his counterparts'. He worried because 'the idea of solving difficult international issues through personal rapport is a very risky one'.[36] Michael Beschloss also suggests that the fast speed of diplomatic exchanges on global television may force hurried responses based on intuition rather than on careful extensive policy deliberation, and this may lead to dangerous policy mistakes. He asked whether under the pressure of global television President Kennedy would have the time to consider carefully options to resolve the highly inflammable Cuban missile crisis.[37]

If this is the case, why do policy-makers participate in a 'game' considered to be so dangerous? The answer is that they face a difficult dilemma. If they respond immediately without taking the time to carefully consider policy options, they may make a mistake. But if they insist they need more time to think, or have no comment for the time being, they create the impression, both at home and abroad, of confusion, that they do not know what to do, or have lost control over events and the immediate problem at hand. Officials often tend to resolve this dilemma by providing some response rather than asking for additional time to deliberate a decision. Yet time in itself is not the only significant factor in decision-making, and the relationship between the amount of time available for reviewing options and the quality of decisions is not necessarily clear. Mistakes occur even if policy-makers have sufficient time to discuss options, while good decisions are often made despite severe time constraints.

Certainly, the faster pace of diplomatic communication alters standard decision-making processes particularly in acute crisis situations. Valuable information, observations and suggestions from overseas diplomatic and intelligence sources may no longer arrive in time to have the desired influence on decisions. Several senior officials admitted that when information does arrive in time, it can hardly compete with dramatic television images and ongoing reportage of crises and foreign-policy issues. In many recent crises global television coverage has supplemented ambassadors and experts as the authoritative sources of critical information and evaluation on what is happening in the world.

An American official acknowledged that 'diplomatic communications just can't keep up with CNN'.[38] Bush's press secretary, Marlin

Fitzwater, said that in international crises 'we virtually cut out the State Department and the desk officers...Their reports are still important, but they don't get here in time for the basic decisions to be made...The normal information flow into the oval office was vastly altered by video images.'[39] President Bush himself admitted during the 1990–91 Gulf crisis: 'I learn more from CNN than I do from the CIA'.[40]

Soviet leaders also used global television as a fast source of information on other countries. In December 1988, Alexander Bessmertnykh, then the Soviet first deputy foreign minister, congratulated Colin Powell in a meeting at the United Nations on being promoted that day to a four-star general. Powell thanked the Soviet official and added: 'I'm surprised you learned about it so quickly. Yuri [the Soviet ambassador to the United States] must be reporting more quickly than he usually does, or maybe you're using the new fax machine you guys put in.' 'No', laughed Bessmertnykh, 'I saw it on CNN...I have it in my office and I watch it all day long.' Powell said he did too, joking that the two countries could save a lot on communication and intelligence just by relying on CNN.[41]

Sometimes conventional diplomatic messages, regardless of their depth and sophistication, do not have the same effect on policy-makers as do televised images from the field. Hurd acknowledged that 'when it comes to distant but important events, even all the Foreign Office cables do not have the same impact as a couple of minutes of news video'.[42] Fitzwater recalled that during the violence in Tiananmen Square they were getting reports and cables from the American embassy in Beijing, 'but they didn't have the sting, the demand for a government response that the television pictures had'.[43] The US response in this case was based almost entirely on what the administration's officials saw on television. A similar phenomenon occurred during the 1991 Russian attempted coup. In the absence of Mikhail Gorbachev, who was seized by rebels, Boris Yeltsin's phone messages to Washington did not impress Bush until the actual arrival of photos from Moscow showing Yeltsin's visible and viable resistance. Only then did the US administration become convinced the resistance was serious, and proceed to take action to support Gorbachev.[44] Owing to this CNN coverage President Bush felt Gorbachev's government had a chance to survive, and that when he spoke out at news conferences in support of the democratic forces in Moscow, his words 'would travel much swifter by global TV than by any diplomatic channel. These facts, in addition to the pictures of resistance inside and outside the Russian Parliament building, energized the resisters.'[45]

In addition, policy-makers now bypass established diplomatic channels, using the new technologies of global television to transmit non-secret messages directly to leaders of state and non-state actors as well as to their respective publics. For example, on hearing about the attempted coup in Russia, the first consideration of the Bush administration was not how to cable instructions to American diplomats, but how to get a statement on CNN that could shape the response of America's allies. Likewise, during the 1990–91 Gulf crisis and war, Saddam Hussein proposed a peace plan. Perceived in Washington as a false proposal, President Bush proceeded to inform all 26 members of the international coalition confronting Iraq of this American view. Fitzwater later recalled how the quickest and most effective way of transmitting this evaluation was CNN, because 'all countries in the world had it and were watching it on a real-time basis...and 20 minutes after we got the proposal...I went on national television...to tell the 26 members...that the war was continuing'.[46]

Similarly, global television has altered the traditional roles of diplomats, experts and intelligence officers, even replacing them in certain critical situations as the main source of information and recommendations for actions.[47] Friedland concluded that 'as is evident from events such as the Gulf War and the Tiananmen Square massacre, the world television system has begun to supplement traditional diplomatic activity... By the end of 1992, CNN was seen to be the foreign policy tool of choice'.[48] The fast speed of global communication has applied pressure on policy-makers to respond ever faster to world events, while allowing them to send significant messages that, in turn, and in general, have favourably affected the outcomes of these events.


MEDIA DIPLOMACY

Today, officials extensively use the media, particularly global television, for yet another cardinal diplomatic function: advancing negotiation and conflict resolution. These uses have come to be known as *media diplomacy*.[49] In this study, media diplomacy refers to uses of the mass media by officials to communicate with state and non-state actors, to build confidence and advance negotiations as well as to mobilize public support for agreements. Media diplomacy is pursued through various routine and special media activities including press conferences, interviews and leaks, as well as visits by heads of state and mediators in rival countries, and spectacular media events organized to usher in a new era.

Signalling has been discussed in early studies of media diplomacy.[50] In the absence of adequate direct channels of communication, or when one side is unsure how the other side might react to conditions for negotiations or to proposals for conflict resolution, officials prefer to use the media, with or without attribution, in order to send messages to leaders of rival states and non-state actors. After the 1973 Arab–Israeli war, Kissinger perfected the use of the media for signaling and pressure purposes during his famous and highly successful 'shuttle diplomacy'. His relentless efforts to achieve disengagement and interim agreements between Israel and its neighbours, Egypt and Syria, included the extensive use of senior American correspondents aboard his plane.[51] He would often give them background reports, information and leaks mostly intended (a) to extract concessions from the negotiating parties and (b) to break deadlocks.[52] British foreign secretaries employ a similar technique called by John Dickie 'travelling diplomacy'.[53]

Sometimes officials signal interest in negotiation through gestures towards journalists of the other side. In January 1994, for example, Syrian leader Hafez al-Assad met with President Clinton in Geneva primarily to convey Syria's interest in peace. Assad barred Israeli reporters from participating in the press conference he held with Clinton at the end of the meeting, thus indicating Syria's lack of sincere intentions.[54] In September 1994, by contrast, this attitude was reversed when Syrian Foreign Minister Farouq al-Shara, for the first time, answered a question from an Israeli reporter at a press conference in London and later gave a first-ever interview to Israeli television. Although the contents of these interviews were disappointing to Israel, Syria's seemingly new conciliatory attitude towards Israeli journalists was seen for a moment as an attempt by Syria to build the confidence required for peace with Israel.

Sometimes during severe international crises the media provide the sole unblocked channel for communication and negotiation between rival actors. During the first phase of the 1979–81 Iran hostage crisis, the United States communicated exclusively through the press with terrorists holding the embassy hostages.[55] A similar case occurred in the 1985 hijacking of a TWA jetliner to Beirut.[56] In recent years, officials more frequently use global television rather than traditional diplomatic channels to deliver messages. During the 1990–91 Gulf crisis that preceded the war, Secretary of State James Baker delivered the last ultimatum to Saddam Hussein through CNN, and not through the US ambassador to Iraq.[57] Baker chose CNN not only to save time but also to persuade the entire international community that the United States was exhausting peaceful means to resolve the crisis and was determined to use force only if Saddam Hussein ignored the ultimatum. Similarly, in January 1998, the newly elected moderate Iranian president, Mohammed Khatami, chose CNN to send a conciliatory message to the United States.[58]

As mentioned earlier, two principal components of the 'new diplomacy' are exposure of negotiations to the media, and the conduct of talks directly between high-level leaders. Perhaps more than any other phenomenon, summit meetings between protagonist leaders seeking an opening for conflict resolution and possibly even longer-term reconciliation vividly demonstrate the combination of these two components. Depending on context and conditions, many of these summits such as the US–USSR summit meetings and celebrations of peace agreements signed between former enemies are primarily media events. Dramatic media events after all represent media diplomacy at its best. These events are broadcast live, organized outside the media, pre-planned, and presented with reverence and ceremony.[59] Live coverage of media events interrupts scheduled broadcasting and attracts wide audiences around the world.

Daniel Dayan and Elihu Katz identify several direct effects of media events on diplomacy: (1) trivializing the role of ambassadors; (2) breaking diplomatic deadlocks and creating a climate conducive to negotiations; and (3) creating a favourable climate for sealing an accord.[60] The distinction between the last two effects is significant because media events can be used at the onset of negotiations to build confidence and facilitate negotiations, or at the end of negotiations to mobilize public support for an agreement that has already been achieved.

There are also an intermediary and a third-phase effect that occur in the interim: when officials use media events to cultivate public support for a peace process *after* the conclusion of the initial phase but *before* moving on to the next phase. This typically appears in cases where a breakthrough has been achieved, but the sides still have a long way to go before translating a declaration of principle into a permanent legal peace agreement. Such an intermediary effect can help in mobilizing sufficient public support inside the societies involved for the next phase in the negotiations. All three effects of media events gained vivid expression in chapters of international 'summit diplomacy' and in Arab–Israeli peacemaking running from President Sadat's televised journey in 1977 to the Israel–Egypt peace treaty of 1979 and, more recently, in post-Oslo (1993) talks between Israel and the Palestinians.

Gorbachev's summits with Presidents Reagan and Bush demonstrate how both superpowers became adept at exploiting the media in the transition from the Cold War to the post-Cold War era. Their summits above all reflected the dramatic changes in superpower relations. As media events, they motivated individuals, groups and nations 'to reassess their relations with each other in light of the actions taking place live in front of their eyes'.[61] The first Gorbachev–Reagan summit in 1985 demonstrated the initial effect: the use of a media event to begin a process of conciliation. The next summits demonstrated the intermediary effect, where each event represented a step forward in the movement from confrontation to cooperation. The climactic Gorbachev–Bush summit held in Washington in May 1990 then officially ended the Cold War. Gorbachev for his part used the summits with Reagan and Bush to cultivate public support at home and abroad for his major political and economic reforms. Reagan, on the other hand, used the summits to legitimize the dramatic shift in his attitudes towards the Soviet Union, which at the beginning of his presidency was branded as 'the evil empire'.

Media events became increasingly popular and were frequently used in Arab–Israeli peacemaking. Sadat's historic visit to Jerusalem in November 1977[62] and the 1991 Madrid peace conference demonstrate the initial effect of the use of a media event to facilitate negotiations.[63] The signing ceremonies of three major documents represent the intermediary effect: the Camp David Accords of September 1978, the PLO–Israel Declaration of Principles of September 1993, and the Israel–Jordan Washington Declaration of July 1994. The signing ceremonies of two peace treaties demonstrate the 'sealing effect' of media events: the

Israeli–Egyptian Peace Treaty of March 1979, and the Israeli–Jordanian Peace Treaty of October 1994.

According to the typology of media events suggested by Dayan and Katz, the initial Arab–Israeli media events and the US–USSR summit meetings belong to the category of conquests where a great leader is able to overcome decades of hatred, conflict and war and to replace them with negotiations, cooperation and peace. It should be emphasized, however, that media events are fully controlled by politicians and officials, who determine when, where and how they are to be played out before the television cameras. The officials thus serve as the prime producers and directors of television coverage while journalists are reduced to more of a secondary and supporting role. For the sake of balance, it is necessary to note that media events are not always successful, as was the case with the US-sponsored Arab–Israeli Madrid peace conference. Such ploys become far less effective when employed too frequently, but are nonetheless considered extremely useful in confidence-building and for mobilizing domestic public support for difficult peacemaking processes involving painful concessions.

## CONCLUSIONS

The several parallel transforming revolutions in communication, politics and international affairs directly challenge policy-makers and diplomats alike. The media, particularly global television, are increasingly becoming a source of rapid real-time information for policy-makers; have accelerated the pace of diplomatic communication; and focused world attention on crises in places such as Bosnia, Rwanda, Somalia and Kosovo. Global television also provides a stage for new actors in international politics, primarily non-state actors like the proliferating NGOs (non-governmental organizations concerned with global problems such as nuclear proliferation, global warming and human rights). Yet the CNN effect, defined in terms of decision-makers' loss of control, has not been sufficiently validated. Nor has the media's role in diplomacy rendered the role of ambassadors obsolete.

All those who debate the CNN-effect theory agree that global television becomes a far more powerful independent actor either in periods of leadership vacuum or at times of grave crisis. When the House Foreign Affairs Committee in the United States Congress summoned Ted Koppel of *ABC News Nightline* to 'a friendly lecture' on television coverage of crises in places such as Somalia and Bosnia, he replied by criticizing both Presidents Bush and Clinton for failing to design policies for guiding the television cameras: 'When an administration fails to set forth a clear agenda of its own, it will become the prisoner of somebody else's.'[64] Furthermore, James Hoge Jr, the editor of *Foreign Affairs*, wrote:

> If policy-makers want to set the agenda and not leave it to the media, they must have an agenda. The existence of policy that can command public support against emotional swings stirred up by television imagery is key. In the absence of persuasive government strategy, the media will be catalytic.[65]

Warren Strobel,[66] Larry Minear, Colin Scott and Thomas Weiss[67] and Johanna Neuman[68] reached similar conclusions. On the other hand, as shown in the previous section, when policy-makers adopt a clear diplomatic strategy they can successfully harness the growing power of global television to achieve their goals.

Even if the CNN effect helps to explain US actions in certain humanitarian crises, it is certainly not a valid, let alone comprehensive, theory of media–government relations in security and foreign affairs. The extreme opposite approach,[69] which suggests that the media blindly serve governments' national interests in world affairs or staunchly protect the liberal–capitalist system and have no interest or standing of their own, is also highly questionable.

Patrick O'Heffernan adopts a more realistic and balanced assessment of the relations between media and diplomacy that incorporates elements from the two extreme polar approaches. His 'mutual exploitation model' suggests that both sides incorporate 'each other into their own existence, sometimes for mutual benefit, sometimes for mutual injury, often both at the same time'. He explains that 'policymaking cannot be done without the media, nor can the media cover international affairs without government cooperation'.[70]

This study shows that diplomats, foreign-policy experts and intelligence officers indeed have lost many of their traditional functions to journalists who are assuming some of these roles, and to spokespersons and communication experts, who are increasingly influential in inner government circles. I also suggest that successful coping with the challenges of global television and efficient utilization of new and innovative media technologies require two sets of reforms: first, in the training of high-level policy-makers and diplomats; second, in the planning and implementation of policies.

Policy-makers must be prepared to handle the rapid pace of global communication and to avoid serious policy mistakes deriving from global television's demands for fast effective responses, particularly in crisis situations. Thus, in addition to traditional and conventional diplomatic considerations, sophisticated policy-making in defence and foreign affairs today requires a sensitive understanding of possible media effects, reinforced by an efficient media strategy for dealing with them.

## NOTES

1. Abba Eban, *Diplomacy for the Next Century* (New Haven and London: Yale University Press, 1998), p. 75.
2. P. Taylor, *Global Communications, International Affairs and the Media Since 1945* (London: Routledge, 1997), p. 92.
3. Hamid Mowlana, 'Toward a NWICO for the Twenty First Century', *Journal of International Affairs*, 47 (summer 1993).
4. Hamid Mowlana, *Global Information and World Communication*, 2nd edition (London: Sage, 1997).
5. J. S. Nye Jr., 'Soft Power', *Foreign Policy*, XX (1990), pp. 153–71; J. S. Nye Jr. and W. A. Owens, 'America's Information Edge', *Foreign Affairs*, 75 (1996), pp. 20–36.
6. David Gergen, 'Diplomacy in a Television Age: The Dangers of Teledemocracy', in S. Serfaty (ed.), *The Media and Foreign Policy* (New York: St Martin's Press, 1991).
7. N. Gowing, *Real-Time Television Coverage of Armed Conflicts and Diplomatic Crises: Does It Pressure or Distort Foreign Policy Decisions?* (Cambridge, MA: The Joan Shorenstein Center on the Press, Politics and Public Policy, John F. Kennedy School of Government, Harvard University, Working Paper 94–1, 1994); J. F. Hoge Jn., 'Media Persuasiveness', Foreign Affairs, 73 (1994), pp. 136–44.
8. Johanna Neuman, *Lights, Camera, War: Is Media Technology Driving International Politics?* (New York: St Martin's Press, 1996), pp. 15–16.
9. Eytan Gilboa, 'Mass Communication and Diplomacy: A Theoretical Framework', *Communication Theory*, 10 (August 2000).
10. H. G. Nicolson, *Diplomacy*, 3rd edition (London: Oxford University Press, 1963); D. Newsom, *The Public Dimension of Foreign Policy* (Bloomington, IN: Indiana University Press, 1996); R. P. Barston, *Modern Diplomacy*, 2nd edition (London: Longman, 1997).
11. W. Wilson, *War and Peace: Presidential Messages, Addresses, and Public Papers, 1917–1924*, Vol. 1 (New York: Harper, 1927), p. 159.
12. I. Claude Jn., *The Impact of Public Opinion Upon Foreign Policy and Diplomacy: Open Diplomacy Revisited* (The Hague: Mouton, 1995), pp. 5–7.
13. E. May, 'The News Media and Diplomacy', in G. Craig and F. Loewenheim (eds), *The Diplomats, 1939–1979* (Princeton: Princeton University Press, 1994); D. Pearce, *Wary Partners: Diplomats and the Media* (Washington, DC: Congressional Quarterly Press, 1995); D. Newsom, *The Public Dimension of Foreign Policy* (Bloomington, IN: Indiana University Press, 1996).
14. Abba Eban, *The New Diplomacy* (New York: Random House, 1983), p. 347.
15. K. Hindell, 'The Influence of the Media on Foreign Policy', *International Relations*, 12 (1995), p. 82.
16. Michael Ledeen, 'Secrets', in S. Sefaty (ed.), *The Media and Foreign Policy* (New York: St Martin's Press, 1991), p. 121.

17. Eytan Gilboa, 'Secret Diplomacy in the Television Age', *Gazette: The International Journal for Communication Studies*, 60 (1998), pp. 211–25.
18. Gergen, *Diplomacy in a Television Age*, pp. 48–9.
19. Neuman, *Lights, Camera, War*, p. 270.
20. L. Friedland, *Covering the World: International Television News Services* (New York: Twentieth Century Fund Press, 1992), p. 42.
21. W. Goodman, 'Critic's Notebook'; Re Somalia: How Much Did TV Shape Policy?, *New York Times*, 8 December 1992, p. C20; J. F. Hoge Jnr., 'The End of Predictability', *Media Studies Journal*, 7 (1993), pp. 1–9; J. Anderson, 'Delivering the Message: The Press as an Instrument of Diplomacy', *Foreign Service Journal*, 71 (1994), pp. 32–6.
22. W. Strobel, *Late-Breaking Foreign Policy: The News Media's Influence on Peace Operations* (Washington, DC: United States Institute of Peace Press, 1997), pp. 4–5.
23. Neuman, *Lights, Camera, War*, p. 15.
24. George Kennan, 'If TV Drives Foreign Policy, We're in Trouble', *New York Times*, 24 October 1993, p. A14.
25. L. Minear, C. Scott and T. Weiss, *The News Media, Civil War, and Humanitarian Action* (Boulder: Lynne Rienner, 1996), p. 4.
26. Hindell, 'The influence of the Media', p. 73.
27. Gowing, *Real-Time Television Coverage*.
28. Steven Livingston and Todd Eachus, 'Humanitarian Crises and U.S. Foreign Policy. Somalia and the CNN Effect Reconsidered', *Political Communication* 12 (1995), pp. 413–29.
29. Hoge, 'Media Persuasiveness', 138–9.
30. P. Jakobsen, 'National Interest, Humanitarianism or CNN: What Triggers UN Peace Enforcement After the Cold War?', *Journal of Peace Research*, 33 (1996), pp. 205–15.
31. W. Lance Bennett, 'Toward a Theory of Press–State Relations', *Journal of Communication*, 40 (1990), pp. 103–25.
32. J. Zaller and D. Chiu, 'Government's Little Helper: US Press Coverage of Foreign Policy Crises, 1945–1991', *Political Communication*, 13 (1996), pp. 385–405.
33. Steven Livingston, 'Beyond the "CNN Effect": The Media–Foreign Policy Dynamic', in P. Norris (ed.), *Politics and the Press: The News Media and Their Influences* (Boulder, CO: Lynne Rienner, 1997).
34. Tran Van Dingh, *Communication and Diplomacy in a Changing World* (Norwood, NJ: Ablex, 1987), p. 32.
35. Neuman, *Lights, Camera, War*, pp. 270–1.
36. Ibid., p. 5.
37. Michael Beschloss, *Presidents, Television, and Foreign Crises* (Washington, DC: The Annenberg Washington Program, 1993).
38. D. Hoffman, 'Global Communications Network Was Pivotal in Defeat of Junta', *Washington Post*, 23 August 1991, p. A27.
39. T. McNulty, 'Television's Impact on Executive Decision Making and Diplomacy', *The Fletcher Forum of World Affairs*, 17 (winter 1993).
40. Friedland, *Covering the World*, pp. 7–8.
41. B. Woodward, *The Commanders* (New York: Simon and Schuster, 1991), p. 53.
42. N. Hopkinson, *The Media and International Affairs After the Cold War* (London: HMSO, Wilton Park Paper 74, 1993), p. 11.
43. Hoge, 'Media Persuasiveness', p. 140.
44. Friedland, *Covering the World*, p. 44.
45. R. Donovan and R. Scherer, *Unsilent Revolution: Television News and American Public Life, 1948–1991* (Cambridge: Cambridge University Press, 1992), p. 317.
46. W. Wriston, 'Bits, Bytes, and Diplomacy', *Foreign Affairs*, 76 (1997), p. 174.
47. M. Fitzwater, *Call the Briefing: A Decade with Presidents and the Press* (New York: Times Books, 1995).
48. Friedland, *Covering the World*, p. 41.
49. Y. Cohen, *Media Diplomacy* (London: Frank Cass, 1986); Gilboa, 'Secret Diplomacy'.
50. P. Davison, 'Mass Communication and Diplomacy', in J. Rosenau, K. Thompson and G. Boyd (eds.), *World Politics* (New York: The Free Press, 1976); R. Cohen, *Theater of Power: The Art of Diplomatic Signaling* (London: Longman, 1987).

51. M. Kalb and B. Kalb, *Kissinger* (Boston: Little, Brown, 1974); R. Valeriani, *Travels with Henry* (Boston: Houghton Mifflin, 1979).
52. W. Isaacson, *Kissinger: A Biography* (New York: Simon and Schuster, 1992), pp. 573–86).
53. John Dickie, *The Boys on the Bongo Bus: The Media and Travelling Diplomacy* (Luton: University of Luton Press, 1997).
54. M. Maoz, *Israel and Syria: From War to Peacemaking* (Tel Aviv: Ma'ariv Book Guild, 1996), pp. 211–13 (in Hebrew); Itamar Rabinovich, *The Brink of Peace, Israel and Syria, 1992–1996* (Tel Aviv: Miskal–Yediot Ahronoth Books, 1998), pp. 168–9 (in Hebrew).
55. J. Larson, 'Television and U.S. Foreign Policy: The Case of the Iran Hostage Crisis', *Journal of Communication*, 36 (1986), pp. 108–30; David Newsom, *Diplomacy and American Democracy* (Bloomington, IN: Indiana University Press, 1988), p. 56.
56. Eytan Gilboa, 'Effects of Televised Presidential Addresses on Public Opinion: President Reagan and Terrorism in the Middle East', *Presidential Studies Quarterly*, XX (1990), pp. 43–53; P. O'Heffernan, *Mass Media and American Foreign Policy: Insider Perspectives on Global Journalism and the Foreign Policy Process* (Norwood, NJ: Ablex, 1991), p. 49.
57. Neuman, *Lights, Camera, War*, p. 2.
58. *International Herald Tribune*, 9 January 1998, p. 10.
59. Daniel Dayan and Elihu Katz, *Media Events: The Live Broadcasting of History* (Cambridge, MA: Harvard University Press, 1992), pp. 4–9.
60. Ibid., pp. 204–5.
61. R. Negrine, *The Communication of Politics* (London: Sage, 1996), p. 172.
62. M. Bagnied and S. Schneider, 'Sadat Goes to Jerusalem: Televised Images, Themes, and Agendas', in W. Adams (ed.), *Television Coverage of the Middle East* (Norwood, NJ: Ablex, 1982).
63. E. Bentsur, *The Road to Peace Crosses Madrid* (Tel Aviv: Miskal–Yediot Ahronoth Books, 1997) (in Hebrew).
64. M. Kortanek, 'When Pictures Make Policy', *Congressional Quarterly*, 1078, 30 April 1994.
65. Hoge, 'Media Persuasiveness', p. 138.
66. Strobel, *Late-Breaking Foreign Policy*.
67. Minear, Scott and Weiss, *The News Media*.
68. Neuman, *Lights, Camera, War*.
69. T. Carpenter, *The Captive Press: Foreign Policy Crises and the First Amendment* (Washington, DC: Cato Institute, 1995).
70. Patrick O'Heffernan, 'Mass Media and U.S. Foreign Policy: A Mutual Exploitation Model of Media Influence in U.S. Foreign Policy', in R. Spitzer (ed.), *Media and Public Policy* (Westport, CT: Praeger, 1993).

# 3 Studying International Norms

## ARIE M. KACOWICZ*

### INTRODUCTION: THE NORMATIVE DIMENSION(S) OF INTERNATIONAL RELATIONS

This chapter explores the study of international norms by suggesting several different perspectives and foundations for a much-needed dialogue on the normative dimension or dimensions of international politics. I suggest that while the definition of international norms presupposes a shared or inter-subjective social reality, one does not have to be an *explicit* Constructivist scholar in order to study and examine international norms. Constructivism is not a specific paradigm of international relations, but rather a general approach to social sciences and social life. In this chapter, I examine alternative approaches to international relations that partially overlap with Constructivism and might be equally effective in the *empirical* study of international norms, including international law and the Grotian approach to international relations (the so-called English school of international relations) and ethical approaches to international relations.

There is a vast body of literature in the social sciences in general and in political science and international relations in particular that copes with the subject of social norms. It includes the war convention; the democratic peace; the long peace; alliance dynamics; and

* I am grateful for the comments and suggestions of Emanuel Adler, Orly Kacowicz, Galia Press-Natan, Patrick James, Robert Johansen, Nicholas Onuf and Kathryn Sikkink; the research assistance of Lea Gedalia in Jerusalem; the insights and incisive suggestions of Micha Bar; the hospitality of both the Kellogg and Kroc Institutes at the University of Notre Dame; and the financial support of the Leonard Davis Institute of International Relations at the Hebrew University of Jerusalem.

international regimes.[1] However, this literature is disparate and not sufficiently systematic. To rearrange this literature in a logical sequence, two distinctions are warranted:

## (1) Philosophical distinctions

Norms can be considered moral (ethical) artifacts, stressing their deontological character; or social and legal conventions, emphasizing their utilitarian character. In other words, norms may or may not emphasize an ethical condition.[2]

## (2) Epistemological distinctions

According to a rationalist or positivist logic, international norms are social institutions subordinated to the actors' interests, as in the case of international regimes. Positivists share a clear disadvantage in studying international norms, since it is difficult (though not impossible) to be a positivist and at the same time to study social facts such as norms.[3] Norms are rules, identifiable as such on linguistic grounds. If you cannot state it, it is not a norm. Thus, mental states and cognitive dispositions are not norms. If norms are considered elusive and invisible as opposed to material facts, it is because they are informal.[4] Alternatively, international norms can be *understood* according to a Constructivist or reflectivist approach, positing a more interactive, inter-subjective relationship among norms, actors and interests.

   Despite the existence of a booming industry in international relations that has established empirical and even causal links between specific norms and international behaviour (that is, 'democratic peace'), this literature is under-developed with respect to theoretical formulations of international norms (that is, how do they originate and why?; how do they evolve and why?), and even more in the empirical testing of their impact and evolution. Only a few exceptions can be mentioned.
   Gary Goertz, in an intriguing study on contexts of international politics, elaborates a 'pre-theory' of international norms and tests it in the context of decolonization. Similarly, Judith Goldstein and Robert O. Keohane have edited a stimulating volume on the role of ideas in the framing of foreign policy, geared more towards the empirical evidence than towards a strict theoretical formulation (in which ideas and norms are close relatives, but not twins). In the last

few years, several scholars in the Constructivist approach have addressed theoretical issues regarding the origins and influence of norms in the international society, including Klotz, Finnemore, Adler, Ruggie and the edited volumes by Katzenstein on the culture of national security, and by Adler and Barnett on security communities. Moreover, there has been an important legalist/ Constructivist tradition to the study of norms in international relations, initiated by Kratochwil and Onuf, which transcended the English school because of its limitation to norms in the international society and the lack of reference to agents as actors.

Yet there is a further need in the literature to build bridges between the philosophical, legal and theoretical discussion of the role of international norms, and the empirical evidence of their actual impact upon the international society. The bridging of this theory–practice gap can take place, but only after superseding the current and quite sterile debate between positivist (that is, Realist and Liberal approaches) and post-positivist (mainly Constructivist approaches).

We should focus upon more practical or empirically oriented approaches to the study of international norms: international ethics, international law and, in more general terms, the Grotian approach to international relations. Thus, we should switch our focus of inquiry from meta-theoretical debates back to problem-oriented and real-life issues, recognizing that *both* norms and interests impinge upon and affect international behaviour.

In empirical terms, one of the major problems we face in the study of international norms is to identify their effects upon the behaviour of states in international society in general, and particularly in a regional context. There is a reality of international norms that has an indeterminate qualitative and even quantitative impact that should be addressed and elucidated. Thus, I contend in this study that international norms can be recognized as a distinctive phenomenon in international relations quite independent of actors' self-interests. Furthermore, that norms do make a difference to the quality of life in international society can be empirically assessed. Finally, international norms are a dynamic variable that evolve and change across time and space.

## DEFINITION AND CLASSIFICATION OF INTERNATIONAL NORMS

Norms pose serious analytical problems because of their elusive nature, in contrast to clearer concepts of rational choice (although they do not necessarily contradict rational choice). In the first place, it is important to draw distinctions between ideas, norms and ideologies; and between norms and institutions. Norms are social institutions by definition, while ideas and ideologies create or wish to create norms. While ideas can be assessed on a subjective, personal basis, norms are inter-subjective by definition, to the extent that they are a *social*, collective phenomenon. Thus, for example, while on an individual, personal basis we can sustain different worldviews and ideologies regarding the best form of political system in a given country, there has been an evolving normative consensus in the last two decades that democratization and democracy are (and should be) the best political system for most, if not all, of the countries of the world.

In the second place, there is a myriad of definitions of norms and of international norms, which converge and overlap stemming from different philosophical traditions and theoretical approaches.

(a) From a *Constructivist* perspective, norms are considered *a set of collective expectations, regarding the proper behaviour of states (and other actors), in a given context or identity*. In this sense, norms are directly related to collective identities.[5]

(b) From a *Positivist* perspective, norms are defined as *standards of behaviour, defined in terms of rights and obligations.*[6] In this sense, they are general prescriptions of behaviour, which regulate intentions and effects.

(c) From an *ethical* perspective, norms are *moral (normative) prescriptions* – in other words, theories of justice and rights express themselves through (moral or ethical) norms of behaviour, assuming the possibility of moral choice.[7]

(d) From a *sociological* perspective, norms imply *normal practices in the international system*: what the normal, usual and customary practices are. Whether these practices reflect normative beliefs, habit, fear or acquiescence to leadership is a separate analytical issue.[8] Hence, whether norms reflect an ethical perspective or not, they all define what is considered 'normal practices' or behaviour.

(e) From a *rational choice* perspective, norms act as a *sanction system*: 'A norm exists in a given social setting to the extent that individuals usually act in a certain way and are often punished when seen not to be acting in this way.'[9]

(f) In terms of *international law*, international norms *regulate the mutual behaviour of states, the specific subjects of international law*.[10] International law is considered law to the extent that it incorporates some form of coercive order, by attaching certain coercive acts (sanctions) to certain facts. From this perspective, this definition encompasses many other aspects that were mentioned above, such as collective expectations, standards of behaviour, moral prescriptions, normal practices and a sanction system.

This partial list of definitions conveys the need to classify norms, so we can identify different types with different functions, from competing and sometimes overlapping theoretical and philosophical approaches. First, we should differentiate between 'moral' or 'normative' norms (stemming from an international ethics perspective), and 'non-normative' or 'non-moral' perspectives (stemming mainly from positivist approaches). Hence, not all norms necessarily entail moral commitments, though all norms define accepted behaviour within a certain social environment. Only norms that can be considered *evaluative*, sustaining a deontological dimension related to the possibility of choice, stress questions of morality and moral commitment.

Second, in functional terms (according to the roles they play and functions they fulfil) norms can be classified as *constitutive, regulative* and *practical*, though the same norm can be at the same time constitutive, regulative *and* practical:[11]

## (a) Constitutive norms

They operate like rules that define the identity of an actor; hence, they define the essence of the game and the parameters of the possible interactions. For instance, in international relations the norm of sovereignty has been deemed the 'constitutive norm' of international society since the Westphalia Treaty of 1648.

## (b) Regulative norms

They operate as standards that specify the proper enactment of an already defined identity. In other words, they establish the rules of the game in terms of rights and obligations. Most of the rules of peaceful coexistence, and even those of conflict interaction (such as the 'rules of war'), are examples of regulative norms, which comprise a substantial part of international law.

### (c) Practical norms

They focus on commonly accepted notions of 'best solutions', as epitomized by custom and recurrent behaviour. Over time, constitutive norms (such as the principle of sovereignty) and regulative norms (such as reciprocity) have become practical norms, part and parcel of the practices and common interactions among states (and other actors of the international society).

In addition to this functional classification (that is, constitutive, regulative and practical norms) the study of international norms is complicated by the fact that norms are embedded in alternative, and at times contradictory, approaches to their origins, evolution and dynamics.

## APPROACHES TO THE STUDY OF INTERNATIONAL NORMS

Norms can be defined and classified as a function of several variables: (a) egoistic interests (functionalist approaches, neo-Liberal institutionalism and to a certain extent Realism); (b) power (Realism and neo-Realism); (c) knowledge (cognitive approaches, including Constructivism); and (d) a societal framework (the Grotian approach, Constructivism, international law and international ethics). Some of the differences between these schools of thought reflect discrepancies in their perceptions of international norms.

### (a) Egoistic interests: the Liberal view

According to the Liberal, and especially the neo-Liberal approach, compliance with norms takes place in terms of cost–benefit analysis. Neo-Liberals stress the institutional framework of individual (rational) choice. According to this institutionalist–microeconomic approach (that is, methodological individualism), collective/societal rules (norms) constrain and enable individual choice, though actor identities and interests are still considered to be pre-existing and fixed. Hence, norms derive from rational egoistic choice.

From this perspective, norms overlap with rational choice calculations and serve the egoistic interests of individual, rational actors. In this sense, norms serve as intervening variables, being the epiphenomena or the formalization of a given, pre-existing reality. For instance, the norms articulated in international regimes (such as trade, finance, Antarctica or, even, nuclear non-proliferation) promote and regulate the common interests of the members of that particular regime. Over time, however, norms and regimes can acquire a 'life of their own,' shaping institutions and even the behaviour of the actors that created them in the first place.

## (b) Power: the Realist view

Conventional structural–materialist theories, including Realism and especially neo-Realism, regard norms as the powerless product of interests, reflecting any given power distribution. Thus, if norms matter at all, they do so at the discretion of the power structure (that is, hegemony, balance of power, bipolar or multi-polar). This view is rather deterministic: norms reflect the underlying material forces as dependent variables. At the same time, even Realists cannot live without norms, since the behaviour they propose is presented and depicted as 'normative': for instance, acting to preserve the balance of power and the promotion of peace is based upon non-moral norms such as prudence.[12] Moreover, the Realist world is premised on the constitutive norm of a system of independent, sovereign states.

## (c) Knowledge and Cognition: the Constructivist turn[13]

The social Constructivist approach regards norms as crucial elements of society and the social construction of reality. Norms shape both the goals of state actors – their perceptions of their interests – and the means they use to achieve those goals. Overall, norms help to determine the articulation of preferences by states.

For Constructivists, norms are *constitutive* components of both the international system and of states' interests. Norms are not simply an ethical alternative to, or a constraint on, self-interest. They play a broader role in world politics, shaping both trends of cooperation and conflict in ways that are invisible to theories that focus either on material structural forces or on individual (rational) choice. In sum, norms act as independent variables: they shape identities and partially define the interests of states, and they might even teach individual and collective actors (both states and political élites) how to behave and act under certain circumstances.

### (d) Society; the Grotian approach; international society, law and ethics[14]

According to the 'English school of international relations' (the Grotian approach), the international system is considered a 'society' in which states adhere to shared norms and rules in a variety of issue areas. Material power matters, but its effect should be assessed within a framework of normative expectations, embedded in a set of public and customary international law and incorporating certain elements of international (but not necessarily world or global) morality.

In the international society, the sense of common interests about the elementary goals of social life (such as security, freedom and peaceful coexistence) does not in itself provide precise guidance as to what behaviour should be consistent with these elementary goals. That is precisely the function of norms (as rules). Hence, norms establish behaviour.[15]

Since norms act as independent variables, while international law and practices shape both behaviour and interests, one can notice a *great overlap* between the (older) Grotian approach and the (more recent) Constructivist approach. Both schools refer to international law much more than structural realists and rationalist (neo-Liberal) institutionalists do.[16] International legal rules are socially constructed; they have inter-subjective meaning; and they constitute the non-material structure of the international system. The advantage of the Grotian approach in general, and of international law in particular, compared with other approaches, is that the rules can be *empirically tested* through the perusal of legal instruments.[17] Thus, one can take law very seriously, as both a crystallization of state expectations and as a vehicle for transforming state understandings and practices, though in a rather specific area of human activity.[18]

## THE DYNAMICS AND IMPACT OF INTERNATIONAL NORMS

So far we have established that there are different ways to define, classify and study international norms. Although the Constructivist approach has become a very fashionable and sensible way of assessing the dynamics and impact of international norms, it is neither essential nor the most effective way to do so. In fact, we should build upon the tenets of some of Constructivism's insights and *combine* them with other, older traditions in international relations, such as international ethics and international law, to obtain better answers to the questions and issues related to the dynamics and impact of international norms, as follows:

1. *The genealogy and evolution of norms.* Where do norms come from? How do they evolve and change over time? How and when are norms codified?

2. *The impact of norms.* How do norms affect the foreign policy of individual countries in a given region? How do they impinge upon the intra-regional international relations in a region in general?

3. *The methodology of international norms.* How should we study international norms? What is the *empirical* evidence for the impact of norms?

## 1. The genealogy and evolution of international norms

There are a variety of mechanisms that explain the origins and evolution of international norms, including: (a) social practices; (b) ecological processes; (c) social and internal processes; and (d) historical evolution and evolutionary models.

### (a) Social practices

International norms are based upon pre-existing cultural knowledge and institutions, including other norms. From an international-law/international-society perspective, as well as from a Constructivist viewpoint, norms can be embedded in and derived from pre-existing practices and customs (for instance, codification of international law based upon custom and commonplace rules of behaviour). There would be a greater impact for these social practices if powerful actors, such as the superpowers or the great powers in a given historical period, sustained and upheld them. This is true for both 'normative' (ethical) and 'non-moral' norms of behaviour as well.

### (b) Ecological processes

An ecological process implies an explicit interaction between actors and their environment. In this sense, norms can be the result of the conscious promotion of actors (so-called 'moral entrepreneurs'); they can be negotiated between the different actors; or they can be imposed from a hegemonic position, as in the initial establishment of economic international regimes after the Second World War.[19] In all these cases, norms arise and have an impact whether they are 'needed' or simply considered 'functional'.

### (c) Social and internal processes

Similarly, the etiology and evolution of international norms are linked to social processes such as social diffusion, transgovernmental networks, epistemic communities and transnational movements. Some of these processes are international and transnational (they spill over borders), while some are domestic (within the borders of a given state). Yet, ultimately the adoption of international norms is an *internal* process, characterized by the *internalization* of the norm at the domestic (state) and individual (cognitive and psychological) level. For example, in terms of international law, international norms of behaviour are adopted and implemented once they become *internalized* as national (domestic) laws, given the pre-eminence and supra-national essence of international law.

### (d) Historical evolution and evolutionary models

Norms constitute a dynamic phenomenon; they may evolve and change over time. There are alternative evolutionary models in this regard. There is a model that posits an analogy between norms and genes; hence, norms are transmitted from one individual to another through similar processes of *inheritance*.[20] Another different evolutionary model stresses the importance of dominance, reputation and prestige.[21] In both cases, norms should be researched in tandem with the study of change, as both causes and consequences of momentous transformations over the course of time across time and space.

## 2. The impact of norms upon foreign policy and international relations

If norms can be considered an independent, rather than intervening variable, then they sustain a certain impact and policy relevance for the formulation and implementation of foreign policies in the contemporary system. Because of the discrepancies between several approaches to the study of norms in international relations, one can suggest several answers regarding the effect international norms might have upon international relations, including:

(a) The normative context (regional or international) affects international and domestic politics in direct or indirect ways, through the shaping of foreign and domestic policies, or at least its structural normative constraining. In more specific terms, norms can set the regional or international agenda of the relevant actors by 'teaching' them how to behave under specific conditions, both in domestic and in international politics. For instance, without ruling out competing explanations of *Realpolitik* and self-interest, it is clear that norms of peaceful settlement have explained the maintenance of regional peace in different sub-systemic settings, such as South America since 1883, West Africa since 1957 and South-East Asia since 1967.

(b) International norms may become salient in the domestic political discourse when (1) they influence the beliefs and values of decision-makers within the state; (2) they become part of domestic law, and the standard operational procedures (SOPs) of bureaucratic agencies. Hence, the impact of international norms is usually mediated through domestic (political and economic) structures.

(c) According to rationalist approaches, norms are exogenously determined coordinating mechanisms that enable actors to overcome problems of collective action. In other words, norms arise and have an impact when they are 'needed' or are 'functional'. Hence, they introduce a modicum of predictability in world politics, such as their institutionalization through international regimes.

(d) According to Constructivist approaches, the impact of international norms is twofold: (1) *norms shape state interests* (norms either define identities in the first place, or prescribe or proscribe ('regulate') behaviours for already constituted identities, generating expectations about how these identities will shape behaviours); and/or (2) *norms shape state identities* (norms may also constitute or shape the basic identitites of states; that is, the features of state 'actorhood' or national identity (that is, decolonization and juridical sovereignty)).[22]

(e) International norms affect the foreign policy of individual countries in a given region and the intra-regional international
relations in a region in general through their *institutionalization*
in the international society, usually through multilateral instruments of regional law. In other words, through the different
institutions of the international society – the states themselves,
international diplomacy, international law, mechanisms of
balance of power and, even, the waging and limitating of wars –
international norms shape and affect individual foreign policies
and regional international relations.

(f) In more specific terms of international law, international legal
norms (or rules) constitute the non-material structure of the
international system by enshrining the doctrine of sovereignty;
establishing the criteria for membership of the international society; providing rules that determine when other legal rules will
be binding; providing a language for diplomacy; and giving
normative value to actions and claims made by international
actors, state and non-state actors alike.[23]

Charles Kegley and Gregory Raymond have shown persuasively that when states accept international norms such as *pacta sunt
servanda* and alliance commitments, then the incidence of war is
reduced.[24] Hence, the maintenance of peace is associated with periods in which the dominant tradition in international law considers
alliance norms binding and the unilateral abrogation of international commitments and treaties as illegitimate.[25] In the same vein,
Peter Wallensteen refers to 'norms of universalism' by which the
major powers of a region or the system as a whole have tried to
stabilize the territorial status quo by enhancing their normative
consensus regarding conflict management and resolution.[26] Thus, if
a mechanism of normative consensus to cope with international
conflict is well established and entrenched, international norms that
enable political decisions to take place might fulfill a function
equivalent to that of war.[27]

To illustrate the impact of international norms in a regional
setting we can turn to the example of the evolution and development of a Latin American international society since the beginning
of the nineteenth century. Since their independence, the Latin
American countries have gradually built up a sophisticated and
highly developed system of regional international law and institutions, including a series of regional norms that have regulated their

international and domestic behaviour. The norms and principles of international law adopted by this society since independence include: (1) sovereignty and equality of states; (2) *uti possidetis* (recognition of the former colonial borders); (3) peaceful settlement of international disputes, including the principles of peaceful international coexistence (*convivencia*) and harmonization (*concertación*); (4) arms control and collective security; and (5) political legalism and commitment to democracy and the protection of human rights.[28]

In more specific terms, *three* clear influences can be traced from these common norms on the international relations of the region: first, regional norms and institutions have contributed to the maintenance of the 'long peace' in South America since 1883; second, they have reshaped the definition of state interests in terms of their foreign relations; third, in some cases they have moved and 'upgraded' peaceful relations in Latin America in the direction of a pluralistic security community. There are several examples of these positive influences:

- Between 1851 and 1922 at least 14 peaceful cessions and exchanges of territory took place in South America. Eight of these disputes were resolved following arbitration, the rest through direct negotiations, good offices and mediation. Moreover, the Latin American nations seem to have preferred the continuation of the status quo, even if it led to continuing tensions, rather than escalating their disputes into full-scale wars.
- Similarly, it can be argued that norms of peaceful settlement and *convivencia* have had a restraining effect in the direction of de-escalation and resolution of international conflicts and civil wars. This has been evident in the cases of the Leticia dispute in 1932–34 (between Peru and Colombia); the resolution of the Beagle Channel crisis in 1978 and the subsequent negotiations between Argentina and Chile (1979–84); the regional initiatives of Contadora (1984) and Esquipulas (1987) to resolve the civil wars in El Salvador and Nicaragua; and, more recently, the final and peaceful resolution of the long conflict between Peru and Ecuador in October 1998.
- In the Southern Cone of South America, the return to democracy in Argentina (1983), Brazil (1985) and Chile (1989) has clearly affected and 'upgraded' the quality of the peace among these

three countries and the level of *rapprochement* and security cooperation between Argentina and Brazil since 1985, and Argentina
and Chile since 1990.

In sum, the effects of these regional norms upon Latin American
politics can be considered both constitutive and regulative, both
shaping interests and identities and reflecting them. Moreover, the
effects have had a 'double' or combined impact, both domestic and
international, or what might be called *inter-mestic*. After all, it is
only through their (domestic) internalization within the different
Latin American states, and their institutionalization at bilateral and
multilateral levels, that these norms have become effective, if at all.

## 3. The methodology of international norms

Assuming that norms are a dynamic and elusive phenomena, which
have a certain effect and impact upon foreign policy and international
relations, how should we study them? In other words, what is the
empirical evidence for the impact of norms? How do we know that
norms are not an ideal or idealistic personification of egoistic interests?

Sometimes we only have circumstantial evidence for the existence of a given norm. For instance, if we find a regulative norm,
somewhere there should also be the 'parent' constitutive, formative
norm.[29] Where should we look for the latter? My personal suggestion is to shy away from the methodological/formal traps of an
obscure post-Positivist language (or 'discourse') while accepting
many of its meta-theoretical/epistemological claims, which actually
derive and overlap with the older English school of international
relations. Hence, adopting a Grotian (or neo-Grotian) approach to
the study of international norms implies also accepting the basic
framework of international law, at least a minimalist recognition of
the existence of ethics in international affairs, and a positivist or
empiricist focus upon the practical, real, down-to-earth manifestations of this normative dimension. In this context, we should also
distinguish between regional specific norms and universal norms
such as sovereignty.

In methodological terms, the preliminary answer(s) to the question 'How do we recognize a *relevant* international norm when we
actually see one?' reads as follows:

(a) *Through written recognition*, such as reading documents of international law;

(b) *They are embedded in formal institutions*; norms become institutionalized through multilateral mechanisms of cooperation involving states and other actors in the international society;

(c) *They are part of customs and practices*, as evidenced in international law and in the formation of several international regimes;

(d) *By tracing the deontological (moral) history of the norm*, as embodied in public documents, treaties and philosophical works.

(e) *Through the study of the behaviour of states*, and how that behaviour relates, refutes or corroborates the prescribed norm(s).

## CONCLUSIONS: NEEDED – PLURALISM AND MODESTY

The five methodological rules presented above lead us to focus any research on international norms upon their empirical evidence, through the analysis of international law and practices. At the same time, this is a challenging theoretical and methodological exercise since we should beware of counterfactual validity. No single counterfactual occurrence refutes the existence of a norm. Thus, even when a norm is violated, that does not mean that it is insignificant, or that it does not have any political effect at all. In that case, we still need the insights of the sociological/interpretative approaches, whether they are found in the late Hedley Bull's writings or in more recent Constructivist explorations. In any case, we cannot study empirically international norms without knowing the instruments of international law and at least being aware of the ethical ('normative') dimension of norms, quite neglected in the cacophony of the meta-theoretical debates between Rationalists and Constructivists.

Malign tendencies in the field of international relations to draw lines, form camps, celebrate new and old fads, and constantly reinvent old and forgotten wheels have led in the last decade to a 'third debate' confronting Positivists (or Rationalists) with Constructivists that has been exacerbated and taken to absurd extremes. Constructivists and other post-Positivist approaches were insightful enough in denouncing Realism (and especially the neo-Realist version of Kenneth Waltz's theory) as the hegemonic and distorted paradigm of international relations until the late 1980s. Thus, the major contribution of Constructivism to international relations has been to readdress the existing distorted balance between interests and norms in the direction of ideas, culture, norms and identities.

Yet in an interesting reversal of fortune typical of the study of political science and particularly of international relations, Constructivism has become the new 'fad' and almost the new hegemonic 'ism' and ideological (even dogmatic) magnet for the new legions of PhD students in search of new areas of exploration. The focus on norms and identities, essential for Constructivism, becomes in itself distorted when it is isolated from international law and from international ethics, wrapped sometimes in obscure if not incomprehensible language. The absurdity resides in the fact that sometimes, in the process of applying the Constructivist approach, the study of international norms seems to be a pretext or subservient to justify sterile meta-theoretical and epistemological debates such as the agent-structure or the material/ideational divides. It seems that our discipline is suffering from an overdose of 'epistemologism'.[30] What about the *problematique* related to the content and impact of international norms? How can we turn those norms into more effective instruments of foreign policy for the international community as a whole in order to improve the world we all share?

Nobody will dispute that international relations is socially constructed, as nobody will argue with Mr Jordan in Molière's comedy who realized that all his life he had been 'talking prose'. But just being aware of having talked prose all our lives (or socially constructing our reality) in itself will not improve our normative condition, in ethical and non-ethical terms, or ameliorate our practical condition.

The example of the Latin American international society can illustrate some of these theoretical claims. One can speculate that the Latin American countries, through a gradual historical and learning process, have managed to establish a unique Latin 'diplomatic culture' that has helped their governments to resolve their international conflicts short of war. If that is the case, it can be argued that the Latin American nations, especially the South American ones, have succeeded in developing a theory and practice of Latin American exceptionalism regarding their recourse to international law – arbitration of disputes, mediation, bilateral negotiations and other techniques for the peaceful settlement of international disputes, rather than the use of force in their international relations. it should be pointed out, however, that this normative and legal reluctance to engage in war against fellow Latin American nations never implied the lack of serious inter-state disputes throughout the region. And yet the predilection of peaceful settlement carries with it a clear ethical consideration in favour of 'norms of peace,' at least at the international level. All the regional norms mentioned above – *uti possidetis*; peaceful international coexistence; non-intervention and mutual respect of national sovereignties; peaceful settlement of international disputes; and commitment to liberalism and political democracy – embody a formidable normative consensus that seems to explain the peaceful predisposition of the South American nations in the last 100 years.

Considering the fact that most of the time most of the Latin American political regimes *have not* been democratic (with the exceptions of Chile, Uruguay and Costa Rica), it is striking to observe that norms of *convivencia*, peaceful settlement and arms control have flourished in a regional system characterized by authoritarian regimes. In other words, the Latin American experience has proved that non-democratic states can share some of the normative perspectives and institutional restraints that characterize democracies. In this sense, the Latin American international regional society has been a successful Grotian laboratory for testing the presence, effect and impact of regional norms.

From a methodological standpoint, the evidence for this normative impact can be traced through the regional documents of international law, including arbitration and bilateral treaties; the common practices of peaceful settlement of disputes; and the behaviour of the individual states in the region. The result is an empirical assessment that reconciles Realist and Liberal approaches through the middle ground of a Grotian approach, incorporates the recent Constructivist insights in a more practical and applied fashion, and elevates the maintenance and diffusion of peace to an ethical category beyond the mere self-interests of the countries involved.

Hence, by adopting an eclectic approach, I suggest that we take the best of these schools and reconcile them through the analysis of the instruments of international law. This will help us to closely examine the impact of international norms in the international society in general, and in a regional context in particular. And this will bring back, helpfully and hopefully, the ethical aspects of the normative dimension of international relations, under-studied if not neglected, by mainstream scholars of international relations, including Constructivists.

## NOTES

1. See Gregory A. Raymond, 'Problems and Prospects in the Study of International Norms', *Mershon International Studies Review*, 41 (Supplement 2, November 1997), pp. 208–13.
2. According to Nicholas Onuf, norms as social and legal conventions are always deontological because agents encounter them in the form of ought-statements (personal correspondence with the author, 30 July 1999).
3. I thank Emanuel Adler for his comments in this regard.
4. I thank Nicholas Onuf for his insights and comments on this issue.
5. See Peter J. Katzenstein, 'Introduction: Alternative Perspectives on National Security', in Peter J. Katzenstein (ed.), *The Culture of National Security: Norms and Indentity in World Politics* (New York: Columbia University Press, 1996), pp. 1–32.
6. This is a typical positivist definition which belongs to Stephen D. Krasner, 'Structural Causes and Regime Consequences: Regimes as Intervening Variables', *International Organization*, 36, 2 (spring 1982), pp. 185–205. Norms act as rules, guiding us on what to do and how to do it, irrespective of moral (normative) considerations.
7. See Gary Goertz, *Contexts of International Politics* (Cambridge: Cambridge University Press, 1994), p. 229. In this sense, deontological criteria define and justify norms and normative action. For other references to international norms in terms of international ethics see James Turner Johnson, 'International Norms and the Regulation of War', in Charles W. Kegley (ed.), *The Long Postwar Peace: Contending Explanations and Projections* (New York: HarperCollins, 1991), pp. 290–303; Charles R. Beitz, *Political Theory and International Relations* (Princeton, NJ: Princeton University Press, 1979); Mervyn Frost, *Ethics in International Relations: A Constitutive Theory* (Cambridge: Cambridge University Press, 1996); Stanley Hoffmann, *Duties Beyond Borders: On the Limits and Possibilities of Ethical International Politics* (Syracuse, NY: Syracuse University Press, 1981); Robert W. McElroy, *Morality and American Foreign Policy* (Princeton, NJ: Princeton University Press, 1992); Terry Nardin, *Law, Morality, and the Relations of States* (Princeton, NJ: Princeton University Press, 1983); Terry Nardin, 'Ethical Traditions in International Affairs', in Terry Nardin and David R. Mapel (eds), *Traditions of International Ethics* (Cambridge: Cambridge University Press, 1992), pp. 1–22; Kimberly Hutchings, 'The Possibility of Judgement: Moralizing and Theorizing in International Relations', *Review of International Studies*, 18, 1 (January 1992), pp. 51–62; Chris Brown, 'International Theory and International Society: The Viability of the Middle Way?', *Review of International Studies*, 21, 2 (April 1995), pp. 185–96; Andrew Linklater, *The Transformation of Political Community* (Columbia, SC: University of South Carolina Press, 1998).
8. See Janice E. Thompson, 'Norms in International Relations: A Conceptual Analysis', *International Journal of Group Tensions*, 23, 1 (1993), p. 67. This is more of a 'sociological' definition, which tries to distinguish between moral and non-moral aspects of the normative dimension.
9. Robert Axelrod, 'An Evolutionary Approach to Norms', *American Political Science Review*, 80, 4 (1986), p. 1097. Notice the convergence between the normative dimension and a rational-choice approach to norms.
10. Hans Kelson, 'The Essence of International Law', in Karl Deutsch and Stanley Hoffmann (eds), *The Relevance of International Law* (New York: Doubleday, 1971), p. 115. The identification of 'norms' with law presumes: (1) a statement of a prescribed pattern of behaviour; (2) an obligational basis usually approved by the society; and (3) a process for punishing illegal behaviour. See William D. Coplin, *The Functions of International Law: An Introduction to the Role of International Law in the Contemporary World* (Chicago: Rand McNally, 1966), p. 1.
11. According to Nicholas Onuf, *World of Our Making: Rules and Rule in Social Theory and International Relations* (Columbia, SC: University of South Carolina Press, 1989), all norms (rules) are always, simultaneously, constitutive and regulative. It is exactly this property that accounts for the co-constitution of structures and agents as a continuous and pervasive process. Moreover, all norms are always practical: they cease to exist if they are never put to use.
12. See, for instance, the last chapter in Hans J. Morgenthau and Kenneth W. Thompson,

*Politics among Nations: The Struggle for Power and Peace*, 6th edition (New York: Alfred A. Knopf, 1985).

13. For reviews of the Constructivist approach and the use of international norms see, *inter alia*, Jeffrey T. Checkel, 'The Constructivist Turn in International Relations Theory: A Review Essay', *World Politics*, 50, 2 (January 1998), pp. 324–48; Alexander Wendt, 'Anarchy is What States Make of It: The Social Construction of Power Politics', *International Organization*, 46, 2 (spring 1992), pp. 391–425; Alexander Wendt, 'Constructing International Politics', *International Security*, 20, 1 (summer 1995), 71–81; Alexander Wendt, 'Identity and Structural Change in International Politics', in Yosef Lapid and Friedrich Kratochwil (eds), *The Return of Culture and Identity in International Relations Theory* (Boulder, CO: Lynne Rienner, 1996), pp. 47–64; Audie Klotz, 'Reconstituting Interest: Interpretive Analysis of Norms in International Relations', unpublished manuscript, November 1992, Center for International Studies, University of Southern California; Nina Tannenwald, 'Dogs that Don't Bark: The United States, the Role of Norms, and the Non-Use of Nuclear Weapons in the Post WWII Era', unpublished PhD manuscript, Department of Government, Cornell University, 1992; Emanuel Adler, 'Seizing the Middle Ground: Constructivism in World Politics', *European Journal of International Relations*, 3, 3, pp. 319–63; Christian Reuss-Smith, 'The Constitutional Structure of International Society and the Nature of Fundamental Institutions', *International Organization*, 51, 4 (autumn 1997), pp. 555–89; Katzenstein, 'Alternative Perspectives'; Ronald L. Jepperson, Alexander Wendt and Peter J. Katzenstein, 'Norms, Identity and Culture in National Security', in Katzenstein, *The Culture of National Security*, pp. 33–75; Martha Finnemore, 'Constructing Norms of Humanitarian Intervention', in Katzenstein, *The Culture of National Security*, pp. 153–85; Martha Finnemore, *National Interests in International Society* (Ithaca, NY: Cornell University Press, 1996); Martha Finnemore, 'Norms, Culture, and World Politics: Insights from Sociology's Institutionalism', *International Organization*, 50, 2 (autumn 1996), pp. 325–47; Paul Kowert and Jeffrey Legro, 'Norms, Identity, and Their Limits: A Theoretical Reprise', in Katzenstein, *The Culture of National Identity*, pp. 451–97; Klotz, 'Reconstituting Interest'; Klotz, 'Norms Reconstituting Interests: Global Racial Equality and U.S. Sanctions against South Africa', *International Organization*, 49, 3 (summer 1995), pp. 451–78; Friedrich Kratochwil and John G. Ruffie, 'International Organization: A State of the Art on an Art of the State', *International Organization*, 40, 4 (autumn 1986), pp. 753–75; Robert O. Keohane, 'International Institutions: Two Approaches', *International Studies Quarterly*, 32 (1988), pp. 379–96; John G. Ruggie, *Constructing the World Polity: Essays on International Institutionalization* (London: Routledge, 1998); Ted Hopf, 'The Promise of Constructivism in International Relations Theory', *International Security*, 23, 1, pp. 171–200; Thomas Risse-Kappen, 'Democratic Peace – Warlike Democracies? A Social Constructivist Interpretation of the Liberal Argument', *European Journal of International Relations*, 1, 4 (December 1995), pp. 491–517; Checkel, 'The Constructivist Turn'; and especially Matha Finnemore and Kathryn Sikkink, 'International Norm Dynamics and Political Change', *International Organization*, 50, 2 (autumn 1998), pp. 887–917.

14. For reviews of the English school of international relations (the Grotian approach) see, *inter alia*, Barry Buzan, 'From International System to International Society: Structural Realism and Regime Theory Meet the English School', *International Organization*, 47, 3 (summer 1993), pp. 327–52; Robert H. Jackson and Mark W. Zacker, 'Westphalian Liberalism and the International Territorial Order', paper presented at the ISA/JAIR Joint Convention, Japan, 20–22 September 1996; Hedley Bull, 'The Grotian Conception of International Society', in Herbert Butterfield and Martin Wight (eds), *Diplomatic Investigations: Essays in the Theory of International Politics* (London: Allen and Unwin, 1966), pp. 51–73; Hedley Bull, *The Anarchical Society: A Study of Order in World Politics* (London: Macmillan, 1977); Martin Wight, 'Western Values in International Relations', in Butterfield and Wight, *Diplomatic Investigations*, pp. 89–131; Adam Watson, *The Evolution of the International Society* (London: Routledge, 1992); Robert H. Jackson, *Quasi-states: Sovereignty, International Relations and the Third World* (Cambridge: Cambridge University Press, 1990); Robert H. Jackson, 'Pluralism in International Political Theory'; Robert H. Jackson, 'The

Weight of Ideas in Decolonization: Normative Change in International Relations', in Judith Goldstein and Robert O. Keohane (eds), *Ideas and Foreign Policy* (Ithaca, NY: Cornell University Press, 1993), pp. 111–38; Nardin, *Law, Morality*; Sheila Grader, The English School of International Relations: Evidence and Evaluation', *Review of International Studies*, 14 (1988), pp. 29–44; Roy E. Jones, 'The English School of International Relations: A Case for Closure', *Review of International Studies*, 7 (1981), pp. 1–13; Peter Wilson, 'The English School of International Relations: A Reply to Sheila Grader', *Review of International Studies*, 15 (1989), pp. 49–58; Hermann Mosler, *The International Society as a Legal Community* (Alphen ann den Rijn: Sijthoff & Noordhoff, 1980); Brown, 'International Theory and International Society'; Martin Griffiths, 'Order and International Society: The Real Realism?', *Review of International Studies*, 18, 3 (July 1992), pp. 217–40; A. Claire Cutler, 'The "Grotian Tradition" in International Relations', *Review of International Studies*, 17, 1 (January 1991), pp. 41–65; Richard Little, 'Neorealism and the English School: A Methodological, Ontological, and Theoretical Assessment', *European Journal of International Relations*, 1, 1 (March 1955), pp. 9–34. For a direct link between the English school and the recent Constructivist school see especially Timothy Dunne, 'The Social Construction of International Society', *European Journal of International Relations*, 1, 3 (September 1995), pp. 367–89.

International law and international norms are considered in the following works: Inis L. Claude, 'Collective Legitimization as a Political Function of the United Nations', *International Organization*, 20 (summer 1966), pp. 367–79; Friedrich Kratochwil, 'Thrasymmachos Revisited: On the Relevance of Norms and the Study of Law for International Relations', *Journal of International Affairs*, 37, 2 (winter 1984), pp. 343–56; Anne-Marie Slaughter Burley, 'Law and the Liberal Paradigm in International Relations Theory', *American Society of International Law, Proceedings of the 86th Annual Meeting* (Washington, DC, 1–4 April 1992), pp. 180–5; Anne-Marie Slaughter Burley, 'International Law and Intrenational Relations Theory: A Dual Agenda', *American Journal of International Law*, 87, 2 (April 1983), pp. 205–39; Sonya Brown, 'The Changing Nature of International Legal Instruments'; Stephen A. Kocs, 'Explaining the Strategic Behaviour of States: International Law as System Structure', *International Studies Quarterly*, 38, 4 (December 1994), pp. 535–56; Anthony C. Arend, 'Toward an Understanding of Legal Rules', in Robert J. Beck, Anthony C. Arend and Robert D. Vander Lugt (eds), *International Rules: Approaches from International Law and International Relations* (Oxford: Oxford University Press, 1996), pp. 289–310; Anthony C. Arend, 'Legal Rules and International Conflicts: A Constructivist Approach', paper presented at the ISA Annual Convention, Toronto, 19 March 1997; Terry Nardin, 'The Rule of Law in International Relations', paper presented at the Conference on International Norms, The Leonard Davis Institute of International Relations, Hebrew University of Jerusalem, 26–27 May 1997; Hurst Hannum, *Autonomy, Sovereignty, and Self-Determination: The Accommodation of Conflicting Rights* (Philadelphia: University of Pennsylvania Press, 1990); Friedrich Kratochwil, *Rules, Norms, and Decisions: On the Conditions of Practical and Legal Reasoning in International Relations and Domestic Affairs* (Cambridge: Cambridge University Press, 1989); Onuf, *World of Our Making*; Levi Werner, *Contemporary International Law: A Concise Introduction*, 2nd edition (Boulder, CO: Westview Press, 1991); Hans Kelson, *Law and Peace in International Relations* (Cambridge, MA: Harvard University Press, 1942); Thomas M. Franck, *The Power of Legitimacy among Nations* (Oxford: Oxford University Press, 1990); Thomas M. Franck, *Fairness in International Law and Institutions* (Oxford: Clarendon Press, 1995); Hans J. Morgenthau, *La Réalité des Normes: En Particulier des Normes du Droit International* (Paris: Libraire Felix Alcan, 1934); Robert J. Beck, 'International Law and International Relations: The Prospects for Interdisciplinary Collaboration', in Beck, Arend, Vander, *International Rules*, pp. 3–33; Harvey Starr, 'International Law and International Order', in Kegley, *Controversies in International Relations Theory*, pp. 299–315; Dorothy V. Jones, 'The Declaratory Tradition in Modern International Law', in Nardin and Mapel, *Traditions of International Ethics*, pp. 42–61; Louis Henkin, *International Law: Politics and Values* (Dordrecht: Martinus Nijhoff Publishers, 1995).

15. See Bull, *The Anarchical Society*. The norms refer to international law, moral rules, custom and established practice.

16. See Arend, 'Legal Rules and International Politics', pp. 25–6.
17. Recent studies by Constructivists have also turned to the empirical testing of their claims. See, for instance, Klotz, *Norms in International Relations*; Finnemore, *National Interests*; Richard M. Price, *The Chemical Weapons Taboo* (Ithaca, NY: Cornell University Press, 1997); Kathryn Sikkink, 'The Power of Principled Ideas: Human Rights Policies in the United States and Western Europe', in Goldstein and Keohane, *Ideas and Foreign Policy*, pp. 139–70; Amy Gurowitz, 'Mobilizing International Norms: Domestic Actors, Immigrants, and the Japanese State', *World Politics*, 51, 3 (April 1999), pp. 413–45.
18. For instance, Dorothy Jones, 'The Declaratory Tradition', ennumerates a 'code of peace', a series of agreed norms in the international system/society as follows: (1) sovereign equality of states (sovereignty); (2) territorial integrity and political independence of states; (3) equal rights and self-determination of peoples; (4) non-intervention in the internal affairs of states (non-intervention); (5) peaceful settlement of international disputes between states; (6) abstention from the threat or use of force; (7) fulfilment in good faith of international obligations; (8) cooperation with other states, including integration; (9) respect for human rights and fundamental freedoms; (10) distributive justice, including the commitment to economic development; and (11) protection of the environment.
19. See Kowert and Legro, 'Norms, Identity and Their Limits'; and Ethan A. Nadelman, 'Global Prohibition Regimes: The Evolution of Norms in International Society', *International Organization*, 44 (1990), pp. 479–526.
20. See Ann Florini, 'The Evolution of International Norms', *International Studies Quarterly*, 40, 3 (September 1996), pp. 363–89; and Stewart McLellan Patrick, 'The Evolution of International Norms – Adaptation, Learning, Socialization, and Hegemony', paper presented at the ISA Annual Meeting, Toronto, March 1997.
21. See Robert Axelrod, 'An Evolutionary Approach to Norms', *American Political Science Review*, 80, 4 (December 1986), pp. 1095–111.
22. See Katzenstein, 'Introduction: Alternative Perspectives on National Security', in Katzenstein, *The Culture of National Security*, pp. 1–32.
23. See Arend, 'Legal Rules and international Politics', p. 39.
24. Charles W. Kegley and Gregory A. Raymond, 'Normative Constraints on the Use of Force Short of War', *Journal of Peace Research*, 23, 3 (September 1986), pp. 213–27.
25. See John A. Vasquez, 'Building Peace in the Post-Cold War Era', in Manus I. Midlarsky et al. (eds), *From Rivalry to Cooperation: Russian and American Perspectives on the Post-Cold War Era* (New York: Harper and Collins, 1994), p. 213.
26. Peter Wallensteen, 'Universalism vs. Particularism: On the Limits of Major Power Order', *Journal of Peace Research*, 21 (August 1984), pp. 243–57.
27. See John A. Vasquez, 'A Territorial Explanation of War', paper presented at the Annual Meeting of the International Studies Association, Atlanta, April 1992; Vasquez, *The War Puzzle* (Cambridge: Cambridge University Press, 1993); and Vasquez, 'Building Peace in the Post-Cold War Era'.
28. See Arie M. Kacowitz, 'Latin America as an International Society: A Unique Case?', *International Politics*, 37, 2 (June 2000), pp. 143–63; Juan Carlos Puig, 'Controlling Latin American Conflicts: Current Judicial Trends and Perspectives for the Future', in Michael A. Morris and Victor Milan (eds), *Controlling Latin American Conflicts: Ten Approaches* (Boulder, CO: Westview Press, 1983), pp. 11–39; Richard H. Ebel, Raymond Taras and James D. Cochrane, *Political Culture and Foreign Policy in Latin America: Case Studies from the Circum-Caribbean* (Albany, NY: State University of New York Press, 1991).
29. Micha Bar's wonderful insight, among many others.
30. The term is suggested by Michael Doyle and I am using it here. In his own words, 'One should get about explaining (with all the tools and perspectives that fit) actual regularities in as rigorous ways as possible and then prescribe as systematically and persuasively (with transparent values) as we can. And the best of the constructivists, including Marti Finnemore and Audie Klotz, do just this, but then so do many others' (personal correspondence, 24 July 1999).

# 4  Imperialism – Predatory or Preemptive?

## EFRAIM KARSH

In analyses of the modern Middle East it has become a common-place to view regional affairs as an offshot of global power politics. Stemming from the premise that 'international rather than regional powers wielded most of the power and did most of the manipulation most of the time',[1] this system-dominant approach reduces the indigenous actors to meaningless entities which at best exercise a limited control over their own fate, and at worst are malleable objects in the hands of omnipotent great powers.

Given late-Victorian Britain's international preeminence, it was only natural for its occupation of Egypt in the summer of 1882 to be generally viewed as a quintessential feat of imperialism – a premeditated land grab by the largest empire on Earth in its ceaseless quest for world domination. 'The pretext for the British invasion was the claim that the government was in revolt against legitimate authority, and that order had broken down', wrote the British historian Albert Hourani. Yet 'the real reason was that instinct for power which states have in a period of expansion, reinforced by the spokesmen of European financial interests'.[2]

However intriguing, this standard interpretation is fundamentally misconceived. Far from being an act of imperial aggrandizement, the British invasion of Egypt affords a vivid illustration of the limits of great-power control over regional dynamics. Unaware of the brewing Egyptian crisis until it exploded in their faces, policy-makers in London found themselves sliding a slippery slope that had escaped their timely notice without a preconceived idea of how to arrest this slide. It was only after Egypt's imperial master, the Ottoman sultan, Abdul Hamid II, and his subordinate ruler of Egypt (*khedive*), Tawfiq Pasha, had miserably failed to put their house in order, and after cooperation with France had proved stillborn, that the British cabinet reluctantly took the plunge. At the end of June 1882 Britain declined an Ottoman plea to take over Egypt;[3] two months later she had been sufficiently alarmed to do precisely that, only this time without the sultan's formal approval.

The origins of the Egyptian imbroglio can be traced back to the rule of Ismail Pasha (1863–79), Muhammad Ali's grandson, whose tireless efforts to transform Egypt into a regional empire drove the country to financial ruin and internal turmoil, implicating it in the tangled web of great-power interests, fears and greed.[4] Ismail's dismissal by Abdul Hamid in June 1879 and his succession by his son, Tawfiq Pasha, brought no panacea, as the father's unsavoury bequest was too heavy for his young, lacklustre son to shoulder. The treasury was empty, the people disgruntled and the military rebellious. Anti-Western sentiments, together with pan-Islamic agitation, turned popular opinion against the international financial control and the landed Turco-Circassian aristocracy.

The military was at the cutting edge of this public discontent. Even during Ismail's reign Egyptian officers had grumbled over the privileged status of the Turco-Circassian military élite. When Tawfiq appointed a Circassian general, Osman Rifqi, as the minister of war and charged him with restructuring the armed forces, all repressed anger burst out. In January 1881 a group of officers handed the *khedive* a petition criticizing Rifqi's policy and demanding his dismissal. Their leaders were arrested and put on trial the following month but, as they were being court-martialled, their troops raided the building and secured their release. The *khedive* was terrified. He fired Rifqi and appointed one of the mutineers, Colonel Mahmud Sami al-Barudi (himself a Circassian), the minister of war.

But the moving spirit behind the officers, and the real winner of their defiant stand, was Ahmad Urabi Pasha (1841–1911). The son of a village sheikh, he was taken for military service at the age of 14, rising meteorically to reach the rank of lieutenant-colonel by 1860. When his promotion ground to a halt owing to Ismail's cultivation of the Turco-Circassian élite, Urabi joined the widening club of frustrated officers. Though poorly educated and of less than brilliant military talents, he had an imposing figure and peasant authenticity that made him *primus inter pares* among his fellow officers. Now that Tawfiq's arm had been publicly twisted, Urabi was rapidly establishing himself as a popular hero, the leader of a widespread coalition comprising provincial notables and chamber deputies alongside the officers.

Intoxicated by his newly gained prowess and fearing a backlash by the *khedive*, who seemed to be recuperating from the February débâcle, Urabi brought things to a head. On 9 September 1881, shortly after Barudi had been replaced by a member of the royal family, Urabi handed the new minister of war a strong message. 'I, together with the officers and men, have ascertained that an order has been issued by your Excellency to the third Regiment of Infantry to proceed to Alexandria', he wrote.

> And inasmuch as such an order is intended to disperse the military power with a view of revenge upon us, and as we cannot deliver up ourselves to death, we hereby give notice to your Excellency that all the regiments will assemble today at 9 o'clock, Arabic time, in the Abdin Square for deciding this question... No regiment will march in obedience to the orders given by your Excellency until ample security be given for the lives and interests of ourselves and our relatives.[5]

Urabi made good on his promise. Appearing in front of the royal palace, sword in hand, at the head of a large throng of troops, he presented Tawfiq with three demands: to dismiss the cabinet, reactivate the chamber of deputies, and restore the army to the authorized limit of 18,000. After some haggling through the British consul in Alexandria, Sir Charles Cookson, who stood in for Consul-General Sir Edward Malet, who was on leave in London, the *khedive* gave in. The cabinet was disbanded and the former prime minister, Sharif Pasha, dismissed by Tawfiq two years earlier, formed a new cabinet, with Barudi reinstated as the minister of war. The chamber of deputies, suspended since Tawfiq's accession, was to resume its activities at the end of December 1881. The officers relaxed; the threat of khedival reprisal had been removed. It was their turn to call the shots.

The confrontation in Cairo caused some concern in London but no undue alarm. The liberal leader, William Ewart Gladstone, who in April 1880 had succeeded his lifelong rival, Benjamin Disraeli, as Britain's prime minister, was scarcely aware of the Egyptian imbroglio, having divested his energies in the resolution of a Boer uprising in the Transvaal and the pacification of Irish restiveness. When his foreign secretary, Lord Granville, informed him of the events in Egypt, Gladstone hoped the episode would resolve itself without external interference. Should the worst come to the worst and extraneous force be required, the Ottoman Empire, in its capacity as Egypt's suzerain, was the obvious candidate. In any event, no British or French intervention should be contemplated 'unless ships be needful for *bona fide* protection of subjects'. The moment he heard Granville's reassurance that 'there seems to be a lull in Egyptian affairs, and I do not think it impossible that it may last', the prime minister breathed a sigh of relief. Meanwhile Edward Malet visited Istanbul on his way back to Egypt and tried to convince the sultan to reassert his authority over Egypt in case of further deterioration.[6]

Gladstone's hopes for a quick diffusion of the Egyptian crisis were shared by his French counterpart, Jules Ferry, who feared that France's tenuous grip over Tunis, occupied in April 1881, could be further weakened by the spread of nationalist fervour. But in November 1881 the French premiership passed to Léon Gambetta, perhaps the most flamboyant and unpredictable of French politicians, for whom imperialism was the key to the restoration of French greatness. He viewed the occupation of Tunis as an important milestone on this path, and rejected Ottoman intervention in Egypt lest the precedent be repeated in Tunis. If Egypt were to fall again under the sway of an imperial power, this power should be France, not Turkey or Britain.

As the scheduled reopening of the Egyptian chamber of deputies approached amid rumours that the officers were seeking to topple Prime Minister Sharif, the gap between Gambetta and Gladstone gradually narrowed. The former advocated a joint action to save the *khedive*, the latter a careful balancing act short of physical intervention. Gambetta insisted on keeping the sultan out of the picture, whereas Gladstone insisted on his active involvement. The outcome of these conflicting preferences was the Anglo-French note of 8 January 1882, expressing support for Tawfiq and implying the possibility of a joint action on his behalf.

This was a high-risk bluff. Intervention was the last thing on Gladstone's mind. As a sworn anti-imperialist he was bent on reducing Britain's overseas commitments, not increasing them. Moreover, he had no intention of allowing the Egyptian irritant to stand in the way of Britain's real problem: Ireland. Restiveness on the island was rife, the Irish Land Act prepared by Gladstone fractured his cabinet, and the prime minister's thoughts could not be further removed from Egypt. His sole concern in the Egyptian crisis was the maintenance of stability, and he hoped that the joint note would settle the problem without actual intervention; at the very least, it would preempt a unilateral French action without damaging Anglo-French relations. Personally he harboured no hostility towards Urabi and his fellow nationalists. On the contrary, as a self-styled champion of small nationalities, Gladstone was sympathetic to their cause, and deemed their demand for greater control over Egypt's finances quite reasonable. 'I am not by any means pained, but I am much surprised at this rapid development of a national sentiment and party in Egypt', he wrote to Foreign Secretary Granville.

> The very ideas of such a sentiment and the Egyptian people seemed quite incompatible. How it has come up I do not know: most of all is the case strange if the standing army be the nest that has reared it...'Egypt for the Egyptians' is the sentiment to which I should wish to give scope: and could it prevail, it would[,] I think[,] be the best, the only good solution of the 'Egyptian Question'.[7]

The prime minister was by no means the only British official to sympathize with the nascent Egyptian nationalism. So did his Egyptian envoy, Edward Malet, and even Auckland Colvin, a member of the Anglo-French Dual Control of the Egyptian debt and an arch-proponent of intervention. 'The liberal movement now going on, should, I think, in no wise be discouraged', he wrote. 'It is essentially the growth of the popular spirit, and is directed for the good of the country, and it would be most impolitic to thwart it.'[8] This, however, was not how the Anglo-French note looked in Cairo. Rather than stabilize the situation, it set in motion a chain of events that would culminate in Britain's immersion in Egyptian affairs in ways undesired by Gladstone.

Since his appointment as prime minister in September 1881, Sharif had been trying to appease the *khedive*, on whom he had been imposed, the Urabist officers, who had instated him, the chamber of deputies, which had pushed for greater powers, and the anxious Europeans. As the officers and the chamber closed ranks in an attempt to tighten their control over the national finances at the expense of the European controllers, Sharif found himself increasingly cornered. Following the great-power note, he was painted as protector of foreign interests in Egypt. On 2 February he tendered his resignation. Barudi became prime minister; Urabi was promoted to the rank of major-general and made minister of war.

From here the situation snowballed. Comfortably calling the shots from his new office, Urabi pressured Barudi to dismiss the European members of the cabinet and bring the chamber under his control. To consolidate his own power base, he embarked on a wholesale promotion of officers of Egyptian origin. This drove the Turco-Circassian military élite into a rearguard action. Some left the country under protest, others allegedly conspired to assassinate Urabi and his comrades. Whether or not this threat was real, Urabi took no chances; he spent his nights in the well-protected Abdin barracks, and his mother confided to a British friend that she was keeping her son's drinking water under lock and key to prevent him from being poisoned. In a thorough purge of political opponents, some 40 officers, including the former minister of war, Osman Rifqi, were stripped of their ranks and privileges and exiled to the Sudan. When the *khedive* commuted the sentences, Urabi refused to comply and pushed Barudi to convene the chamber of deputies, which had already adjourned for the year, to gain its support. Tawfiq condemned the move and Barudi resigned on 15 May. Though left without a prime minister, Urabi and the rest of the ministers refused to resign. Rumours of plots and counter-plots spread through the capital.

In their eagerness to resolve the situation without committing themselves to Egypt's occupation, England and France took yet another high risk. On 19 May, an Anglo-French naval squadron arrived off Alexandria in a show of support for the *khedive*. Six days later the president of the chamber was handed an ultimatum demanding the dismissal of the cabinet, the temporary exile of Urabi and the retirement of some of his closest associates into the interior of Egypt.

As in January 1882, the Anglo-French action backfired. The Egyptian cabinet resigned in protest and Tawfiq was delighted to accept their move. This, nevertheless, brought him under harsh nationalist criticism and he backed down in fear. On 27 May, Urabi was reinstated as minister of war and the *khedive* retreated to Alexandria, closer to the great-power gunboats. Westerners fled Egypt by the thousands. Disaster was in the air.

This came on 11–12 June in the form of ferocious anti-Christian riots in Alexandria, in which some 50 Europeans and 250 Egyptians were killed. According to one account, the riots were incited by Tawfiq in an attempt to discredit Urabi and the army; another account put the blame on Urabi, whose security forces did little to contain the raging mob. The truth, however, is that the arrival of the naval squadron off Alexandria had unleashed widespread anti-Western sentiments that had been brewing in Egypt since Ismail's days. Urabi might well have been fighting for his political survival, but his actions had generated a huge nationalistic wave; initially he might not have been anti-Western, but the Anglo-French muscle-flexing had made the temptation of an extremist stance irresistible. Urabi's open defiance and his immediate reinstatement by the *khedive* were taken by Egyptians as a sign of their imminent deliverance from foreign subjugation. To them Urabi was not only a national hero who would restore 'Egypt for the Egyptians' but also *al-Wahid*, the only one in living memory who dared rise against the ruling élites and foreign powers alike.[9]

The Alexandria riots caused uproar in London. There was widespread indignation at the killing of European subjects and exasperation with members of the government for allowing themselves to be humiliated by a local leader. Yet Gladstone held his ground against an increasingly militant cabinet, and his restraint received an unexpected boost from Prime Minister Charles de Freycinet, who at the end of January 1882 had replaced Gambetta. Losing his nerve following the Alexandria riots, de Freycinet acquiesced in the British view that the reassertion of Ottoman sovereignty over Egypt might be the least of all evils. An international conference thus convened in Constantinople on 23 June to discuss the Egyptian situation, with the participation of Britain, France, Austria-Hungary, Germany, Russia and Italy. There was only one fly in the ointment: the sultan would not join them.

From his palace in Istanbul Abdul Hamid followed with horror the events that were unfolding in Egypt. Three years earlier he had removed Ismail in the hope of stabilizing the situation and restoring Ottoman control over Egypt; now the country seemed to be moving towards yet greater catastrophe. The financial situation had not improved, only attracted tighter foreign control. Egyptian nationalism had not subsided, only risen to unprecedented peaks. The presence of a strong man at the helm augured the possible

revival of the Egyptian imperial dream. Under the weak and inde-
cisive Tawfiq this was a virtual impossibility; under a powerful and
ambitious Urabi, the 'Ismail syndrome' could well recur. Repeated
pleas of innocence by the Urabists did little to quiet Abdul Hamid's
suspicion. He urged Tawfiq to crush the mutineers and, if possible,
'to give Urabi [poisoned] coffee'. When he gradually realized that
the *khedive* was not up to the job and that the officers enjoyed far
wider support than initially assumed, Abdul Hamid decided to
remain on the sidelines in the hope that mutual exhaustion would
eventually force the rival camps to request the restoration of
Ottoman authority in Egypt. When in September 1881 Tawfiq
invoked his position as the sultan's official representative in Egypt
and demanded the dispatch of 20 Ottoman battalions to his rescue,
Abdul Hamid declined; all he was willing to do was to send a five-
member commission to Egypt to investigate the situation. Having
heard the commission's opinion that events in Egypt posed no
threat to his imperial order, the sultan persevered in his policy of
inaction.

It was only the arrival of the Anglo-French naval task force in
the region that shook the sultan out of his passivity. Early in June
1882, Abdul Hamid sent a delegation to Egypt, headed by one of
his generals, Dervish Pasha, to try to bring the conflict to a swift
conclusion. Dervish was instructed to effect a reconciliation
between the *khedive* and his nemesis; if this proved impractical, he
was to disband the chamber of deputies, dismiss Urabi and send
him to Istanbul, and 'arrest one by one the authors of the troubles'.
This was, of course, an impossible task and Dervish quickly found
himself playing both ends against the middle. He simultaneously
urged Tawfiq to quash the rebels and incited the Urabists to esca-
late their struggle, showering both parties with promises of
support. To sow discord among the great powers, he pretended to
seek the advice of the German, Italian and Austro-Hungarian
consul-generals.

When the crisis defied all attempts at resolution and rose to new
heights following the Alexandria riots, the sultan panicked. On the
afternoon of Friday, 23 June 1882, a few hours after the opening of
the Constantinople conference that Abdul Hamid had failed to
attend for fear of being tainted as a 'Western lackey', Reshid Bey, the
sultan's private secretary, called on the British ambassador to
Istanbul, Lord Dufferin. His master was possessed by the greatest
fear of and hatred for France, he said, and desired to come to an

understanding with Britain about Egypt to the exclusion of France. Would Her Majesty's Government be prepared to sign a bilateral treaty whereby England would be given the exclusive control and administration of Egypt, with the sultan reserving to himself only those rights of suzerainty that he possessed at the time?

Dufferin was stunned. Up to that very moment, Abdul Hamid had been violently opposed to international intervention in the Egyptian crisis. He had denounced the Anglo-French note of January 1882 and the two countries' subsequent naval show of force. Now all of a sudden Britain was being offered possession of Egypt! The shift was simply too dramatic to be true. Perhaps the sultan was playing his habitual game of divide-and-rule in an attempt to drive a wedge between England and France? Besides, military intervention in Egypt, not to speak of its physical occupation, was still anathema to Gladstone and the majority of his ministers. Without much ado Dufferin declined the offer. 'Britain's principal aims are the maintenance of the sultan's existing rights and of the *status quo*', he said.

> We not only accept the sultan's sovereignty in Egypt as a fact, but regard it with benevolence. We have but two interests in Egypt – the freedom of the Suez Canal and such a satisfactory jurisdiction of Egyptian internal affairs as to preclude any power from finding an excuse to meddle with them.

Under these circumstances, concluded Dufferin, 'if the sultan were to hand over Egypt to us as a gift, with all Europe consenting, I doubt whether the British Government would accept such a burden and responsibility'. Reshid was evidently disheartened. He pleaded with Dufferin to convey the request promptly to his superiors, and to hand the official reply in person to the sultan. This occurred within a day. Gladstone and Granville found the idea so absurd as to dismiss it without consulting their fellow ministers. 'We wish to see the sultan's sovereignty maintained without any limitation excepting those which have been conceded by the Firmans', wrote Granville to Dufferin:

> Our wish for the present is that the Sultan should be sending troops [to] support the authority of the Khedive, free His highness from the risk of the continuance or renewal of the military pressure which has been exercised against him, and

restore the normal *status quo*. Our desire for the future is that this state of things should continue without excluding safe improvement of internal Administration, but with entire exclusion of preponderating influence of any single power.[10]

Confronted with Britain's refusal to occupy Egypt on his behalf, the sultan continued to equivocate. On 28 June, he conferred a high decoration on Urabi; a couple of days later Dervish Pasha was at loggerheads with the minister of war and it was intimated that his delegation had better leave the country. When on 6 July the international conference requested that Ottoman troops be sent to Egypt, the sultan refused, against the views of his ministers. Four days later Abdul Hamid changed his mind again: he would join the conference the following day and propose 'a satisfactory solution of the Egyptian question'.

While the Constantinople conference was progressing inconclusively, developments on the ground sucked the reluctant British cabinet into the Egyptian marsh. Like Frankenstein's monster turning against its maker, the Anglo-French squadron assumed a life of its own, in ways unforeseen by its senders. Once the squadron was in place, the question of how to protect it was raised in earnest. On 31 May, the commander of the British squadron, Admiral Beauchamp Seymour, reported that the Egyptians were raising earthworks in Alexandria and requested that three more ships be added to his force. At the sultan's demand, work on these forts was suspended on 6 June but resumed a few weeks later. On 1 July, Seymour reported that Urabi was allegedly planning to trap the allied fleet by sinking stone barges in the channel. Two days later he was instructed by the Admiralty to tell the military governor of Alexandria that 'an attempt to bar the channel will be considered an act of war' and that if work resumed on the fortifications, or further guns mounted, he would 'destroy the earthworks and silence the batteries'.

On 5 July the cabinet met to approve these demands. After a heated debate members reached a compromise whereby Seymour would issue his ultimatum but would land no forces in the Canal to destroy the fortifications, as demanded by several ministers. This Seymour did the following day, only to receive the Egyptian governor's emphatic denial of both the mounting of guns and the continuation of works on the fortifications. When Seymour reported the continued mounting of guns despite the governor's reassurance, the cabinet met again on 8 July to approve a second ultimatum to the Egyptians. By now the sultan had declined the international request for the dispatch of Ottoman forces to Egypt, while France had decided to pull its forces from the naval squadron and was assiduously working to undercut the British position by negotiating a separate deal with Urabi. Without much fanfare Seymour was authorized to reissue the ultimatum if works on the fortifications resumed. The realization that Britain was on the verge of war in Egypt, however limited that war might be, hardly sank in. There was confidence that 'the explosion of one or two shells will send all the earthworks to glory, and there will be an end for the moment of the matter'.[11]

On 9 July, Seymour reported the resumption of works on the fortifications and the mounting of two guns on Fort Silsileh. The following morning he informed the foreign consuls in Alexandria that he had just issued an ultimatum and would 'commence action twenty-four hours after, unless the forts on the isthmus and those commanding the entrance to the harbour are surrendered'.

Seymour had overstepped his authority. The cabinet had approved the destruction of the fortifications, not their capture. It had never intended involvement to include a physical occupation that could embroil Britain in a costly adventure and entail adverse international implications. The irritated Gladstone demanded to know by what authority Seymour had issued the ultimatum. Once the prime minister was told that unless the fortifications were surrendered Urabi could carry on for weeks while pretending to comply with the British demand, he accepted Seymour's logic. The admiral was promptly instructed to change the wording of the ultimatum to 'temporary surrender for the purpose of disarmament'. To the Egyptian cabinet, nevertheless, these linguistic intricacies mattered little. On 10 July they rejected the ultimatum. The following morning Alexandria came under heavy bombardment from Seymour's forces.[12]

Contrary to British expectations, the shelling failed to bring Urabi down. Instead, he called a general conscription and declared a holy war against Britain. Alexandria was put to the torch as a raging mob indulged in a spree of killing and pillaging. When the *khedive* dismissed Urabi, the latter countered with a religious ruling (*fatwa*) signed by three al-Azhar sheikhs, which deposed the *khedive* on grounds of betraying Islam by inviting foreigners to occupy Egypt.

This unexpected resilience put Gladstone in a quandary. What had been grudgingly approved as a brief and limited operation was rapidly developing into a massive undertaking, the consequences of which were difficult to predict. Yet he felt that there was no way back. The most powerful empire on earth could not afford to be publicly humiliated by the subject of a much weaker empire. The job had to be completed, preferably under a great-power mandate; however, as Gladstone told the House of Commons on 22 July, 'if every chance of obtaining cooperation is exhausted, the work will be undertaken by the single power of England'.[13]

This indeed seemed to become a distinct possibility. Fearing a unilateral British intervention, de Freycinet re-donned his activist mantle and agreed to a joint Anglo-French occupation of the canal zone. But when the proposal was put to the French Chamber of Deputies on 29 July, it was decisively defeated. Attempts to harness Italy to the protection of the canal and to convince the Constantinople conference that Britain had no desire to occupy the canal indefinitely all came to nought. This made the sultan Britain's only hope. As the official suzerain of Egypt and the caliph of the largest Muslim empire, the sultan could at the very least give the operation a much needed air of legitimacy; in the best-case scenario, his support for the suppression of Urabi could exempt Britain from the need to occupy Egypt, something which was still anathema to Gladstone. After all, if Abdul Hamid was prepared to allow Britain rule Egypt on his behalf, why should he be averse to the far less dangerous option of an Anglo-Ottoman expedition?

On 12 July, while gunfire still reverberated throughout Alexandria, Gladstone dined with the Ottoman ambassador to London, Musurus Pasha. The British action had cleared the way for the dispatch of Ottoman troops to Alexandria, he argued, and the sultan had a great opportunity at hand; the Ottoman Empire had unwittingly stumbled across 'a supreme moment, which...it was still possible to use for good; but time was precious, and this opportunity would probably be the last'. The ambassador concurred with Gladstone's assessment and expressed confidence that the sultan would agree to send the requested troops, provided that he did not act as a representative of Europe. The prime minister responded that to the best of his knowledge, the idea of the sultan being a *mandataire* had not been entertained. What was of critical importance for the mission's success, however, was that there should be a unity of purpose.[14]

The ambassador's optimism was well placed, if largely premature. Even more than Gladstone, Abdul Hamid now dreaded the adverse implications of an Urabist victory. For him it was not a question of lost prestige or a mere strategic setback; it was a matter of life and death, and he knew that Britain was the only power capable of helping him stop the chain reaction caused by Urabi's nationalist surge. But much as they needed each other, the Ottoman and British empires could not overcome mutual prejudice and distrust. At the end of July, the Ottoman delegates to the Constantinople conference informed their European counterparts of the sultan's agreement to send forces to Egypt, but insisted that foreign troops evacuate the country upon the arrival of the Ottoman forces. The British government welcomed the offer, but demanded precise details of the planned intervention – the number of troops the sultan intended to send, the date of their likely departure and their proposed disposition. As a guarantee that Ottoman forces would not join with Urabi against the *khedive*, the British insisted that the sultan 'should at once, and before the dispatch of his troops, issue a proclamation upholding Tawfiq Pasha and denouncing Urabi as a rebel'. Ottoman officials were quoted as saying that 'the only reason for sending Turkish troops to Egypt would be to drive the English away'. While this assertion might have been designed to neutralize domestic opposition to the impending intervention, it raised suspicions in London of the sultan's real intentions.

Nor did Abdul Hamid's erratic negotiating style, with its constant shift of tack in accordance with the latest advice he received from his coterie, buy him any friends in London. Particularly influential was the xenophobic Sheikh Abu al-Huda al-Sayyadi, an Arab from the province of Aleppo who arrived in Istanbul in 1878 to establish himself as Abdul Hamid's Rasputin. He worked indefatigably to prevent an agreement with 'infidel' Britain and warned the sultan of the (alleged) backlash it would cause among Muslim communities. The Ottoman representatives to the talks, Said and Assim Pashas, thus found themselves in the unenviable position of trying to make sense of the contradictory instructions given to them. On 18 August they finalized a draft convention with Lord Dufferin, only to have it thrown back at them the following day by the sultan. Even the issue of provision of donkeys and mules for the expedition became a bone of contention when the sultan suspended the delivery of these beasts of burden, purchased in Asia Minor, and arrested their drivers; nearly a week of unremitting pressure by Dufferin was required to end this bizarre episode.

The most frustrating aspect of the talks was the sultan's evasiveness over the condemnation of Urabi. On 3 September, after months of procrastination, Abdul Hamid gave his consent to the immediate issuance of the condemnation, apparently removing the last obstacle to the signing of an Anglo-Ottoman convention. But when Dufferin read the official proclamation in the morning papers three days later, his heart sank. In a blatant repudiation of the agreed draft, the sultan had changed the wording in the proclamation in some material points. Enraged at 'such an inconceivable act of bad faith', Dufferin refused to sign the convention or to accept the Porte's apologies. It was only on 15 September, after another round of futile negotiations, that Abdul Hamid decided to bring matters to a conclusion. He invited Dufferin to his palace, and for 11 hours haggled with the ambassador over the amendments he wished to introduce in the convention and the proclamation.

At 1.15 am, Dufferin's young secretary and brother-in-law, Arthur Nicolson, who waited with him for the sultan's reply, observed 'the sinister figure of the sultan's astrologer [Abu al-Huda] creeping across the anteroom toward his master's room'. Half an hour later Said and Assim returned to their British interlocutors: 'His Majesty was unable to approve the compromise agreed to and further discussions would be required'.

It was nearly three o'clock when the distraught Dufferin arrived at the embassy. There, to his surprise, he was handed a ciphered telegram from Granville stating that a British force under the command of Sir Garnet Wolseley had routed Urabi's army in Tal al-Kabir, some 60 miles from Cairo, and that in view of this victory 'Her Majesty's Government contemplated shortly commencing the withdrawal of the British troops from Egypt, and presumed that, the emergency having passed, the sultan would not now consider it necessary to send troops'. Three days later, on 18 September, Dufferin was instructed to inform the sultan, 'in the most courteous terms', that Britain was dropping the negotiations of the military convention.[15] The sultan had lost yet another golden opportunity to reassert his suzerainty over Egypt.

It was an ironical twist of history that one of Britain's staunchest anti-imperialist prime ministers managed to accomplish what his avowedly imperialist precursor had carefully avoided: entangling his country in the largest and most enduring imperial acquisition in the Middle East. Indeed, while portraying the Egyptian venture as an undesirable burden passed on to him by Disraeli, Gladstone recognized the irony in the situation. On 10 August 1882 he had stated that an indefinite occupation of Egypt would be 'at variance with all the principles and views of Her Majesty's Government, and the pledges they have given to Europe, and with the views, I may say, of Europe itself'.[16] Now that Egypt had inadvertently come under British occupation, it became a hot potato that had to be disposed of before it scorched the prime minister's palms. As early as 14 September, a day after Urabi's crushing defeat, Gladstone outlined his ideas for an Egyptian settlement. British forces were to be withdrawn as soon as possible and Egypt set on the road to self-rule. Egyptian military and police forces were to be reorganized, self-governing institutions developed, and privileges enjoyed by the Europeans, such as exemption from taxation, terminated. The sultan's suzerainty over Egypt would be retained, albeit on a more restricted basis: he would still receive tribute, but he would not nominate the Egyptian ruler or command the service of Egyptian troops. The conduct of the Suez Canal company was to be reviewed, and the possible neutralization of the Canal discussed.

Dufferin was instructed to inform the sultan that 'Her Majesty's Government contemplated shortly commencing the withdrawal of the British troops from Egypt'. In a circular to the great powers on 3 January 1883, Granville promised that Britain would withdraw from Egypt 'as soon as the state of the country, and the organization of proper means for the maintenance of the Khedive's authority, will admit of it'. This promise was to be repeated 66 times between 1882 and 1922, when Egypt became an independent state.[17] What had begun as a brief and decisive military action in 1882 had turned into a long occupation that was to have a profound impact on the making of the modern Middle East.

## NOTES

1. Avi Shlaim, *War and Peace in the Middle East*, (New York, 1994), p. 5.
2. Albert Hourani, *A History of the Arab Peoples* (London, 1991), p. 283. For variants of this received wisdom see, for example, Ronald Robinson and John Gallagher, with Alice Denny, *Africa and the Victorians: The Official Mind of Imperialism* (London, 1981, second edition), p. 159; Juan R. I. Cole, *Colonialism and Revolution in the Middle East: Social and Cultural Origins of Egypt's Urabi Movement* (Princeton, 1993).

3.  See below pp. 68–70.
4.  For further discussion of this point see Efraim Karsh and Inari Karsh, *Empires of the Sand: the Struggle for Mastery in the Middle East 1789–1923* (Cambridge, MA, 1999), Chapter 4.
5.  Public Record Office (PRO), Letter by Urabi to the Egyptian Minister of War, 9 September 1881, CAB 37/6, No. 24, Inclosure 6. On the reasons for Urabi's show of force see also Malet to Granville, 23 September 1881, CAB, 37/6, No. 24; Ahmad Urabi, *Kashf al-Sitar an Sirr al-Israr*, Cairo, n.d., p. 236.
6.  Gladstone to Granville, 12, 13, 16 September 1881, PRO 30-29/124. See also Granville to Gladstone, 14 September 1881, Add. Ms. 44173, fo. 151, *British Library*; Malet to Granville, 21 September 1881, FO 78/3324, No. 246.
7.  Gladstone to Granville, 4, 12 January 1882, PRO, 30-29/160; 22 January 1882, PRO, 30-29/125.
8.  Memorandum by Colvin, 12 December 1991, CAB 37/7, No. 4.
9.  Abd al-Rahman al-Rafi'i, *al-Thawrah al-Urabiyyah wa-l-Ihtilal al-Inglizi*, 2nd edition (Cairo, 1937).
10. See Dufferin to Granville, 24 June 1882, FO 78/3397, No. 168; Granville to Dufferin, 25 June 1882, FO 78/3395, No. 302; Dudley W. R. Bahlman (ed.), *The Diary of Sir Edward Walter Hamilton, 1880–1885* (Oxford, 1972), Vol. I, pp. 208, 212, 297 (hereinafter *Hamilton Diary*).
11. Northbrook to Seymour, 3 July 1882, ADM 116/33; Seymour to Admiralty, 8 July 1882, ADM, 116/34; Admiralty to Seymour, 8 July 1882, ADM, 116/34; Lyons to Granville, 5, 6 July 1882, FO 27/2574; Granville's draft to cabinet, 8 July 1882, FO 27/2753, PRO 30-29/143.
12. Gladstone to Granville, 9 July 1882, PRO, 30-29/126; Granville to Gladstone, 9 July 1882, Add. MS. 44174, fo. 160.
13. John Morley, *The Life of William Ewart Gladstone* (London, 1903), Vol. III, p. 82.
14. Gladstone to Granville, 13 July 1882, PRO 30-29/126; *Hamilton Diary*, Vol. I, p. 306.
15. Granville's dispatch to Dufferin, CAB 37/9, p. 15.
16. *Hamilton Diary*, Vol. I, p. 340.
17. A. J. P. Taylor, *The Struggle for Mastery in Europe, 1848–1918* (New York, 1971 edition), p. 90.

# 5 New Patterns of Military Intervention

## GIL MEROM

### INTRODUCTION

The intervention of states in conflicts and the internal affairs of other states has long been part of international relations. The recent decade, however, has seen how abrupt systemic changes coupled with other long-term developments have altered the foundations of the patterns of international intervention. Most notably, the USSR collapsed and the bipolar international system became unipolar under American hegemony. As a byproduct of these monumental changes a large number of ethnic and national communities have begun to demand self-determination, and new and mostly under-developed states have been created. At the same time, two major visions of the Western world have come closer to being realized. The liberal-democratic order has become more attractive and pervasive, and the world economy has become ever more inte-grated into a single capitalist free market.[1] The combination of liberal-democratic order and capitalist economy has produced the most powerful states of the current world order. But it has also produced international non-governmental organizations (NGOs) and domestic forces that support universal human rights, often in conflict with inherent state preferences. Furthermore, it has created great restructuring pressures within underdeveloped states which exacerbate ethnic and other domestic conflicts.

Some two decades ago scholars had already concluded that the development of the world economy in particular 'made [interven-tion] endemic; in a way that it was not before, intervention has become part of the very structure of the international system'.[2] Other scholars believe that since the self-help principle still reigns supreme in international relations 'there does not appear to be any reason to believe that the future [of military intervention] will be fundamentally different from the past'.[3]

Which of these views is correct, or can they perhaps be reconciled? Who is likely to intervene, and to what end? And what patterns of intervention seem to emerge at the dawn of the new century? This essay addresses these questions. It starts with the assumption that intervention decisions are the product of a relatively rational assessment of goals, risks, costs and benefits.[4] More specifically, this essay seeks to uncover how international and domestic changes create new constraints and incentives for military intervention, and how they shape its patterns.

At the risk of omitting important variables and events, I focus on three main variables, at different levels of analysis: the end of bipolarity, the effect of the fundamental position of the state on decisions to intervene with force, and the role of Western societies and NGOs. In a nutshell, I argue that the interaction of these variables explains the following phenomena: the geographical distribution of intervention; the increased 'demand' for humanitarian intervention; the hesitation of the West to intervene and the preference of Western states for multilateral initiative and 'soft' modes of intervention (other than military power); and the delayed and often absent effective international reaction to acute humanitarian problems.

INTERVENTION: OBJECTIVES AND MOTIVATION

Intervention can be defined in several ways, two of which are the most relevant for this discussion. First, intervention can be defined in a functional way as either domestically or internationally oriented. Domestic intervention concerns the manipulation of the internal affairs of states in order to establish, change or uphold a particular regime, government or policy.[5] Internationally oriented intervention consists of the use of military power and/or other means to decide the outcomes of conflict between third parties. Some cases of intervention match these 'ideal-type' definitions. The intervention of the Clinton administration in Haiti (1994) and of other administrations in Chile (1950s–70s) are clear cases of domestic intervention. Soviet and American support of clients in the Middle East during the Cold War are relatively clear cases of international intervention. Other cases such as the American intervention in Vietnam involved components of both definitions.

Second, intervention can be defined on a normative axis as either expediential or altruistic. Expediential intervention is motivated by international rivalry and the pursuit of the national interest (conventionally defined), and is associated with the realist school of international relations.[6] Altruistic intervention is motivated by some idealist vision of a collective interest and is associated with the liberal or idealistic school of international relations.[7]

According to realism, states intervene in other states' domestic affairs and international conflicts when their self-interest in preserving their relative power or security so dictates. Thus, intervention is deemed desirable by realists when states need, for example, to thwart a threat, support a friendly regime or ally, destabilize an adversary regime, protect the supply of vital resources and prevent an unfavorable policy or policy change. At the same time, realists believe that states should not, and usually do not, intervene on behalf of universal moral principles, humanitarian or other.

Idealist liberalism holds diametrically opposed opinions to those of realism in matters that concern states' obligations.[8] It considers the state to be a moral agent of universal ethics and consequently assigns to it the duty to intervene on moral grounds. According to idealist liberalism, states should intervene whenever human rights are severely abused, as often happens when states collapse, dominant ethnic groups become exclusionary, minority groups are persecuted for their beliefs, and so on. Presumably, the magnitude and severity of the abuse dictate the extent of intervention. Limited abuse calls for the application of measured pressure, whereas massive and gross violation of human rights may call for the destruction of a regime and the prosecution of its leaders and operatives for crimes against humanity. Much like in realism, but for different reasons, altruistic intervention can target both the domestic and international scenes.

## INTERVENTION IN THE BIPOLAR SYSTEM: THE REALIST RULES OF THE GAME

The international bipolar system of the Cold War was characterized by a rough parity between two antagonistic blocs that were each led by a superpower. The superpowers represented opposing ideologies, but their rivalry made them rather like units as far as foreign policy in general and intervention in particular were concerned.[9]

In the bipolar world, intervention was largely expedient; it assumed *geopolitical* dimensions, and it matched well the postulates of realism.[10] The superpowers considered other states pieces in a worldwide game that was played in three zones. Two exclusive zones of influence were dominated, each by a superpower. The third zone included the rest of the world. Most states within the immediate perimeter of each superpower, and Western Europe and Japan in the case of the United States, belonged to one of the two zones of exclusive influence. These states were close allies. A few states, such as South Korea and Cuba, were perceived as outposts deep within the enemy's perimeter. All other states, a maze of states of different 'values' – clients, non-aligned and hostile (that is, clients of the antagonistic superpower) – were essentially in no-man's land.

Intervention in the bipolar world was influenced by three main factors: the competition of the superpowers, their concerns with prestige and credibility, and their fear of a confrontation that might end in a catastrophic nuclear war.[11] Within their own spheres of influence the superpowers intervened extensively and continuously. They usually intervened domestically, but their objectives were also international. Each superpower tried to shape the political order and social structure of aligned states in its own image. Each also sought to assure the loyalty of allies and was ready to defend them for the sake of its own national security. Indeed, Soviet forces in Eastern Europe intended to deter the international capitalist enemy, but they also protected communist regimes from domestic upheavals. Similarly, the US was engaged in Western Europe not only in order to deter the Warsaw Pact, but also to ensure that local communist parties would not bring down the capitalist order, just as they had been prevented from doing so in Latin America.[12]

Intervention by each superpower within its own exclusive sphere of influence was perceived as safe. Both the US and the USSR felt that they could intervene in their own zones with impunity and without significant opposition. Still, they tried to downplay the magnitude of such intervention because they wanted to keep their allies from feeling excessively threatened by them, prevent raising international doubts about their leadership and their legitimacy as leaders, and avoid supplying their antagonist with propagandistic ammunition. Accordingly, much of the intervention was prophylactic, subtle and covert, relying on economic means, intelligence agencies and the deterrent presence of the forces of the superpowers. The United States helped rebuild West European states and Japan, but also tied them and Latin American states to its own economy, and funnelled money to centre parties and critical social sectors within these countries. Occasionally, the Americans also ensured their control through the buying and bullying of politicians, or as Thomas Mann, Johnson's top adviser on Latin America, once explained: 'I know my Latinos... They understand only two things – a buck in the pocket and a kick in the ass.'[13] The USSR did much the same thing in respect of its allies and constituencies across the eastern lines of Central Europe and in the Far East.[14]

Of course, when allies seemed to get out of control, subtle methods and refined means of intervention were abandoned in favour of swift and brutal action. The Soviets used military force in East Germany (1953), Hungary (1956), Czechoslovakia (1968) and Afghanistan (1979–89), and imposed severe economic sanctions on Yugoslavia (1954) and Albania (1961). And the Americans used military power (often by proxies) in Guatemala (1954), Cuba (1961), the Dominican Republic (1965), Chile (1973), Nicaragua (1980s) and Grenada (1983), and coercive economic power regularly, against both foes and friends, as the UK, France, Cuba, Chile and many other states learned.[15]

Intervention in the antagonist's exclusive sphere of influence was far less likely and less massive than within one's own sphere. By definition, such intervention was subversive and covert. Open challenge within the adversary's sphere was avoided. It was perceived as carrying the risk of global conflagration and undercutting one's own claim for zonal exclusivity. Indeed, while 'in-bloc' challengers were encouraged to revolt by the rival of their master, they were pretty much left to fend for themselves once the latter decided to take action.

In the non-aligned zone that comprised the rest of the world, states were approached on the basis of their relative value.[16] States in regions that were deemed very valuable attracted more attention and intervention than states in regions that were considered marginal. Thus, both superpowers developed great interest in the oil-rich Middle East and let no other power act without their consent (as their response to the joint British–French–Israeli attack on Egypt in 1956 suggests), but left much of Africa to a second-class power such as France. The favourite methods of intervention in the non-aligned world included limited economic support, technical assistance, arms' supply and military instruction. When the application of power seemed necessary, however, the preferred methods changed to include covert operations and the use of proxies for 'liberation', 'insurgency' and 'counter-insurgency'. The superpowers displayed or used their own military power only in situations that were perceived as critically affecting their credibility. In fact, for whatever reason, the US seems to have been more inclined to do so, as its interventions in Korea (1950) and Vietnam (1964) indicate.

Finally, intervention in the bipolar world precluded normative considerations even when ideologically close constituencies in client countries were concerned. Indeed, the superpowers did not hesitate to intervene against key principles of international law, and each supported regimes whose governments and conduct were in clear violation of its own professed values. The Soviets ignored the persecution of communist parties in Arab countries, and the United States supported Latin American and Asian dictators who thrived on the abuse of liberal constituencies and human rights.

## THE INTERNATIONAL FOUNDATIONS OF INTERVENTION IN THE POST-BIPOLAR WORLD

While patterns of intervention during the Cold War were compatible with system-level realist analysis, the situation has since changed. Systemic power-based analysis alone can no longer explain patterns of intervention. Nevertheless, systemic characteristics and realist logic are still relevant, albeit in a more complex way.

In the absence of systemic competition, the most important systemic characteristic that influences intervention is the division of the world into two zones that differ in terms of their units' attributes and intra-zonal relationship. One zone, the 'zone of peace', includes the economically developed countries that are governed democratically. The other zone, the 'zone of turmoil' or 'zone of conflict', includes states that are mostly less developed and ruled in non-democratic ways.[17]

In the zone of peace international sovereignty and boundaries are uncontested, domestic mechanisms for minority expression and representation are in place, and conflict resolution norms and means within and between states are strong and in relative

abundance. While national sovereignty is respected, it is not excessively imposed. Finally, the actors in this zone have adopted
international institutions and norms that preclude the rise of
conflicts that may eventually call for military intervention.[18]

In the zone of conflict, borders are often disputed and national
identities are not contained within single states. Ethnic and
national minorities are not fully assimilated nor do they have
adequate representation or ways to express their grievances and
solicit considerate response. Economic conditions exacerbate
social and ethnic tensions. Norms and means of conflict resolution
within and between states are relatively weak, and leaders exploit
misery and prejudice in order to seize and maintain power.[19] As
events in the Caucasus and the Balkans keep reminding us, the
amount of internal and international conflict and the scope of
humanitarian problems in this zone are high, and abuse of human
rights is endemic.[20]

The second most important characteristic of the current international system is the rise of a humanitarian agenda, most notably in
the West – that is, in the core of the zone of peace.[21] This agenda is
essentially altruistic and interventionist, and it has become salient –
as the 1975 Helsinki Agreement and 1993 World Conference on
Human Rights in Vienna suggest (although both produced
watered-down declarations) – because of three key developments.
First, it became more central in politics because society consistently
increased its role in state affairs, including foreign policy.[22] Second,
it picked up force owing to the rise of the media- and human rights-
related NGOs, such as Amnesty International, Médécins Sans
Frontières, Oxfam, CNN, the Red Cross, Human Rights Watch,
which perceive themselves as guardians of international ethics.[23]
The media and these NGOs may be no match for the state,[24] but
they have access and often strong standing in international and
national market-places of ideas, where they can create an international and domestic climate that supports intervention.[25] Finally, the
end of bipolarity vacated 'space' for the humanitarian agenda that
had been building up for over a century, but remained relatively
inconsequential as long as Europe and the West were dominated by
traditional national security considerations, continental rivalries,
competition and war.[26]

In a way, the formal security position of the European Community
(EC) as of the early 1990s (and of the European Union as of January
1993) reflects the culmination of these three developments. In the

June 1992 Petersberg Declaration, for example, the members of the EC announced that their security objectives included involvement in humanitarian and rescue tasks, peacekeeping and 'tasks of combat forces in crisis management'.[27]

## THE STATE, INTERVENTION AND ABSTENTION THEREOF

Irrespective of a general theory and practice of intervention, the facts are that states remain the key agents capable of intrusive intervention, and the only agents capable of supplying the ultimate means of intervention: military force. It is therefore reasonable to begin the sub-systemic discussion of intervention with a review of the institutional foundations of the state's position on intervention.

The first point to be made about states is that while they are ready to intervene for their own expedient reasons, they are inherently opposed to intervention on behalf of universal and altruistic issues.[28] In fact, there is a good reason for this preference. Essentially, the state is an institution that was designed to serve a limited collective, be it a small faction, a single class, a coalition of social forces or a national community at large.[29] This institutional arrangement did not evolve, nor does it exist, for the benefit of collectives outside its boundaries, unless these are related to the group it serves. Thus also, when expedient and altruistic issues collide, the institutional etatist reflex is to prefer the former. This preference is strong enough for simple greed (in the form of trade revenues) to prevent states from applying even the mildest forms of intervention in support of altruistic purposes.[30] In fact, even when states claim to intervene on behalf of human rights their motivation should be suspect. The point is that leaders often couch their state's actions in altruistic rhetoric when they intervene for utilitarian purposes, or they intervene (grudgingly) in humanitarian problems only because domestic and international pressures make inaction too costly. Most certainly, the overall record of states' abstention from intervention in matters that concern others strongly suggests that altruism is not all that prevalent a form of state-behaviour.

Second, states hesitate to intervene in the internal affairs of other states in cases that do not concern their own national security, because intervention is inimical to the concept of sovereignty. In other words, being actors that calculate consequences rather than only outcomes, states fear that intervention in other states' domestic affairs may undermine their claim to the sanctity of their own sovereignty.[31] The international response to the admittedly expedient, but nevertheless desirable, Vietnamese invasion of Kampuchea (1979) seems to be a good example. Although this invasion put an end to Pol Pot's criminal regime and stopped one of the worst mass-murder campaigns in this century, not a single state supported the right of humanitarian intervention.[32] Rather, many states, including the US, the UK, Norway, Australia, New Zealand and France, considered the Vietnamese intervention illegal. In fact, later in November 1979, the General Assembly of the UN called for the immediate withdrawal of 'all foreign forces' from Kampuchea, although – if carried out – it all but assured that the poor people of Kampuchea would have been victims of another cycle of Khmer Rouge violence.

Third, military intervention lost much appeal after it proved to be entangling and risky in some cases. Even the most powerful states, the United States in Vietnam and the Soviet Union in Afghanistan, found out that in a certain context military intervention might demand more considerable investment than assumed, involve politically crippling losses, and end up with negative results.[33] Secretary of Defence William Perry succinctly summed up the lesson of such interventions, after the success of the coalition in the 1991 Gulf War. 'No one should be deluded', Perry warned, 'into believing that the military capability that can easily defeat an army with 4,000 tanks in a desert is going to be the decisive factor in a jungle or urban guerrilla war.'[34]

Fourth, intervention may entail domestic costs and risks that the state may be unhappy to accept. The point is that once states assume responsibility for the fate of other communities, they may discover that they have to cash cheques they never intended to issue. Thus, when intervention ends in failure, states may find themselves having to accept the immigration of ethnic communities that do not easily assimilate, increase socio-economic tensions and place the government in a vulnerable political position. In fact, even when the objectives of intervention are achieved, states may find out, as happened in Iraq, that they need to take further action and risks in order to address humanitarian or other problems that were created in the wake of their intervention.[35]

The above abstract consideration of inherent state tendencies sheds some light on the role of institutional forces in shaping patterns of intervention. Yet, it needs to be complemented by a reference to the relationship between relative power and intervention. The point is that the amount of power states possess decides the scope and range of their international objectives and commitments, and whether it makes sense for them to intervene (in terms of cost and the prospects of success). On average, small states display modest international ambitions and participation, whereas great powers seek to influence the world order and are much more active in international politics.[36] Given these considerations, one must consider the specific position of the most powerful state/s of the time regarding intervention, which in our case is the United States.

Presumably the best way to learn about the position of the United States is by reviewing its overall record of military intervention and abstention therefrom since the end of the Cold War. This, however, proves to be a confusing exercise. The record suggests that the United States successfully led interventions or unilaterally intervened, by displaying or using military power, in several cases (Panama 1989, Kuwait 1990–91, Haiti 1994, Bosnia 1995 and Kosovo 1999) and failed in at least one case (Somalia 1992).[37] At least one of the successful interventions was largely grounded in national security considerations (Kuwait), while another was launched for internal non-altruistic political reasons (Panama). Moreover, two of these interventions were executed under particularly convenient strategic conditions and against very weak adversaries which were strategically isolated in the American backyard (Panama and Haiti). Of equal if not greater significance, the United States (and other Western states) observed rather passively how massive human rights abuse occurred in the Balkans (1992; Srebrenica 1995), Africa (including in Rwanda 1994), Tibet, the republics of the former Soviet Union (the Caucasus) and elsewhere.[38] In short, the record of American military intervention is too limited and fuzzy to allow clear-cut conclusions. The formulations of key American policy-makers, however, are quite revealing. In 1986, Reagan's Secretary of Defense, Caspar Weinberger, expressed his views concerning the conditions that justified American military intervention in foreign affairs. According to Weinberger intervention could be justified only when vital American interests were involved; the size of the force assured victory; clear military and political objectives were drawn; the means–ends ratio was constantly reassessed and adjusted; domestic (and Congressional) support was assured; and intervention was the last resort.[39] Two presidential terms later (in January 1993) President George Bush formulated the conditions for American military intervention in a rather similar spirit:

> Using military force makes sense as a policy where the stakes warrant, where and when force can be effective, where no other policies are likely to prove effective, where its application can be limited in scope and time, and where the potential benefits justify the potential costs and sacrifice.[40]

Taken together with the record of American interventions, these declarations suggest that in spite of a professed mystical sense of mission, the United States is a rather regular state as far as international intervention is concerned. While human rights issues occasionally reign supreme in the rhetoric of American leaders and opinion-makers, expedient national security impulses and domestic political considerations continue to guide the overall American attitude towards intervention.[41]

## WESTERN SOCIETIES, HUMANITARIAN INTERVENTION AND THE STATE

Unlike the abrupt systemic change from bipolarity to unipolarity, the change of the relations between state and society influenced foreign affairs long after it started and in an inconsistent manner. While international and domestic relations in Western states have become intimately related as they have evolved for over two centuries, for a long time their conversion has worked largely in favour of the statist rather than the altruistic agenda.[42]

The situation at present is different. Western societies find themselves at odds with the state in matters that concern intervention for three reasons. First, Western societies have become increasingly sensitive to the humanitarian plight of other people as well as to their rights in times of war.[43] This sensitivity greatly increased after the revelations about the German conduct, particularly against the Jews, during the Second World War, and has further increased with the rise and spread of electronic media in general and visual means of communication in particular.[44] Second, Western societies have become more sensitive to their own casualties and therefore less patient with the use of their armed forces as fatalities accumulate. The uninterrupted assault of Serb forces on Srebrenica could take place, writes Geoffrey Robertson, 'because of the Mogadishu factor: states intervening from humanitarian motives refused to risk the lives of their own soldiers to make the intervention effective'.[45] Third, increasingly sensitive to the human suffering of others, Western societies have become uncomfortable at the cost intervention exacts from the population of target countries, even when this population supports the regime whose policies have brought about the intervention.

These foundations of the position of Western societies towards intervention impose conflicting demands on the state. While the elevated sensitivity to human suffering prompts societies to expect their states to intervene, including with military force, it also raises expectations for effective results with minimum casualties for both the intervening force and the population of the perpetrators of abuse. Now, while each of these expectations, and even their majority, can be fulfilled, it is extremely unlikely that all will be properly addressed. Thus, while Western states may have found in the combination of air power, precise guided munitions and professional armies the means to effectively use power while keeping down their own rate of casualties, they still inflict significant harm on the populations of the perpetrators of human rights abuse.[46] In other words, the political effectiveness of the efficient and effective use of force is undercut for operational and practical reasons. First, as has been repeatedly shown in Iraq, Kosovo and Israeli raids in Lebanon, the central means of armed intervention – air power – cannot yet preclude the inadvertent destruction of civil targets and the loss of innocent lives. Second, civil damage is inflicted intentionally because intervening forces assume that pressure on their adversary's civil population will either force a culprit regime to comply with their demands or initiate its collapse.[47] Now, irrespective of how compelling the logic of this sort of social manipulation of politics is, the military actions that it necessitates are certain to produce misery that does not present itself well in the Western media. In short, decisions on military intervention make Western states walk a tight-rope. While the military policy of intervening forces is aimed at building social pressure within target countries, it can also easily create such pressure in their own home societies, albeit against intervention.

Having stated the inconsistent effect Western societies have on the calculus and application of intervention, it is still important to point out that today Western states find themselves forced to respond to international humanitarian problems and public

demands for action, more than ever before.[48] Indeed, recent cases of
military intervention for humanitarian purposes – that is, discrepancies between institutional inclinations and behaviour – indicate
that Western societies and NGOs occasionally manage to move
liberal democracies towards intervention.[49]

## THE NEW UTILITY FUNCTION OF INTERVENTION AND THE DRIVE FOR MULTILATERAL INITIATIVES

All in all, then, societal demands regarding humanitarian strife
create pressure for action within Western countries, but they do not
provide solid political foundations for military intervention.[50] If
anything, the conflicting demands and expectations of the public
complicate further the intervention-calculus that already includes
inherent aversions to paying for altruism and accepting the risks
that are associated with both launching and aborting military intervention. Consequently, Western states display little political will to
intervene.[51] Gow's description of the European response to the
events that followed the breakdown of Yugoslavia succinctly
captures this state of affairs:

> From an early stage … politicians in virtually every significant
> country had decided that the situation was practically and
> politically uncertain, unclear, complex, too danger-ridden and
> potentially costly [which] meant that armed intervention was
> always highly unlikely… The political worries of Western
> politicians concerned popular opinion and the need to win
> votes at the next election… The fear that it could be another
> Northern Ireland, Dien Bien Phu or broader Vietnam
> weighted heavily on the minds of politicians wanting to avoid
> similar problems.[52]

What then are Western states to do when their two-level game[53]
function of intervention is likely to produce negative utilities on
both the international and domestic levels?[54] The empirical answer
seems evident: they will resort to multilateralism because presumably it has the advantages of sharing both the burden and the risk.
Whereas acting alone is laden with risk and potentially costly,
acting collectively increases the political legitimacy of action,
reduces the absolute investment of each participant and increases

the absolute (aggregate) power of the intervening force. Moreover, while acting together improves the chances of success, it also lowers the costs in case of failure for each participant.[55] Yet, there is more to the preference of multilateralism than can be seen in a first blush.

Multilateral intervention is in all but name a collective action that involves a common-good problem. In short, multilateralism is likely to reduce the prospects of action, involve free-riding, and shape the nature of the intervention according to the lowest possible denominator (if indeed the parties do manage to reach a decision to intervene). But then, what is the point of acting multi-laterally if it is likely to prove a futile exercise? The answer, I would argue, is its futility, but this needs a brief explanation.

Let us reiterate that while every state wishes the humanitarian problem to be solved or to disappear, none is eager to commit its own forces for intervention (both because of domestic considerations).[56] This contradiction cannot be solved individually, but it can be addressed in a multilateral setting. On the one hand, the call for a collective action conveys a desire to act, yet on the other it almost promises paralysis. Indeed, as Richard Falk notes, 'when the Security Council wanted to send 5,500 soldiers to Rwanda...all 19 governments that had previously pledged a total of 31,000 troops for peace keeping missions refused to take part on this occasion'.[57] In fact, this is occasionally the case even after forces have been committed. In January 1994 (shortly before resigning), the French commander of the UN force in Bosnia-Herzegovina, Lieutenant-General Briquemont, complained that there was a 'fantastic gap between the resolutions of the Security Council, the will to execute these resolutions, and the means available to commanders in the field'.[58]

To sum up, calls for collective action originate in each state's desire to alleviate domestic pressures by transferring the problem to the international level. However, turning intervention into a collective action increases the chances of reaching a dead-end or weak intervention decisions. These are presumed drawbacks but, seen from the state's perspective, they are advantages. Promising to be infertile or deficient, multilateral action provides Western states with an opportunity to cater to public demands and ride high moral grounds, but risk little that cost will be associated with their initiative.[59] In a way, the endorsement of multilateral action can be seen as the international equivalent of some *ad hoc* committees at home. It promises a much desired foot-dragging and watered-down intervention decisions.

CONCLUSION

What are we to conclude about current patterns of intervention from the attributes of the international system, inherent state inclinations, the military supremacy of the West, the power of domestic forces in liberal democracies and the reaction of Western states to all of these?

The first conclusion is that the foundations of interventions have changed. The bipolar structure and the competition of the superpowers no longer define the context of international intervention. Rather, the most important systemic attribute in the context of intervention is the bifurcation of the world into two zones, along regime-type and economic-development lines.

Second, this division makes the nature of the units in each zone the key factor that decides the patterns of intervention within each zone as well as between them. In significant parts of the less developed and non-democratic zone heterogeneous populations live in poorly organized states. Latent internal and international disputes that were previously contained by the superpowers now surface. Finally, the nature of the parties involved in conflicts in this zone and the lack of a tradition and means of peaceful conflict-resolution almost guarantee the following two outcomes:

(1) intra-zonal interventions that are sparked by national challenges, historical rivalries and fears for the integrity of states; and

(2) the creation of acute humanitarian problems that involve forced migration, attacks on civil populations, ethnic cleansing, starvation and other terrible forms of human rights abuse.

In short, in the non-democratic zone the dominant patterns of intervention include intra-zonal intervention that conforms with the most basic tenets of the realist paradigm, and a 'need' for international humanitarian intervention that conforms with the noblest aspects of the liberal idealism.

In the zone of peace the patterns of intervention will be radically different. By and large the liberal democratic states have resolved their internal and external conflicts, and they have the means to resolve further conflict peacefully. Therefore, no military intervention is expected in this zone, nor a rise of humanitarian problems that call for such intervention. At the same time, the advanced and wealthy states of the West remain those best capable of intervening militarily in connection with humanitarian problems.

The patterns of intervention at the dawn of the twenty-first century reflect, then, a great asymmetry that originates in the distribution of power along regime-type and economic-development fault lines. Whereas one zone produces most conflicts and the bulk of humanitarian problems that call for intervention, the other precludes military intervention, yet its states are most capable of intervening from afar. What are the emerging patterns of cross-zonal intervention in this asymmetric situation? Would the 'demand' for intervention in one zone be met by 'supply' from the other?

Unfortunately, the third conclusion is that 'demand' will not be met by adequate 'supply', at least not in the near future. Cross-zonal intervention is likely to remain limited because the pulling-apart effects of Western societies and states render the utility function of altruistic intervention negative. That, of course, does not mean that international reality is fully predetermined. Events that deviate from dominant patterns of international behaviour – inter-zonal intervention included – do occasionally occur. In fact, the chances of altruistic Western military intervention have somewhat increased with the ascent of the humanitarian agenda, the rise of constituencies that are concerned with it, and the growth of NGOs that act as guardians of international morality. But such interventions will remain in the near future sporadic, selective and limited. Moreover, they will follow a rather predictable pattern.

The fourth conclusion therefore is that Western states will continue to prefer softer methods of intervention, including economic sanctions and financial pressure,[60] and that consequently humanitarian problems will in some cases get worse. It is not that soft methods are a priori futile, but rather that their desired effects are produced only under specific conditions. When target countries or societies do not have the political structure or socio-economic level of development that provide an effective conveyer belt that helps translate international deprivation into policy change, soft methods are doomed. Similarly, they are doomed when the leaders who defy international standards of acceptable behaviour control a strong, repressive mechanism and assess the situation as involving critical domestic or national-security issues. Thus, while Indonesia has succumbed to international pressure in the case of East Timor, other states, regimes, groups and warlords – in Iraq, former communist Yugoslavia, Rwanda and elsewhere – have proved immune to all but military coercion, willing to let their societies pay the diplomatic and economic price of their own defiance. In short, the transferring of the problem by individual Western states to the international level of joint economic and diplomatic pressures can be effectively matched by the transferring of the consequences of the latter to the popular level of culprit regimes. Moreover, softer methods of intervention are most likely to fail precisely where the abuse of human rights is expected to be the worst, because the state is either too 'strong' or too 'weak'.

In some cases, then, international military intervention is the only possible remedy. But will it take place and solve the humanitarian problem that evoked it? The fifth conclusion is that at least in a few cases, the brazen abuse of human rights by parties that seem sufficiently weak will evoke military intervention. However, the sixth conclusion is that such intervention will have to follow a Western debate over the proper response and multilateral action. We are thus likely to first observe a further deterioration of humanitarian conditions and only then, most likely after a long delay, a real possibility of military intervention. In the final analysis, then, the future of altruistic military intervention will depend on the actor that can resolve the international common-good problem of intervention. In that respect, the seventh conclusion is that excessive optimism is misplaced. The fundamental political calculations in the United States remain concerned with the domestic risks and costs that are associated with initiating and aborting intervention. These calculations minimize the number, objectives and scope of intervention.[61] Indeed, American leaders have consistently been careful not to adopt any sweeping interventionist mission, while strategists and intellectuals who debate America's global role following the Cold War call for restraint and even a measure of disengagement from global politics.[62]

The final conclusion then is disheartening. The world will continue to display international asymmetry, inequality and injustice. Organized political violence will continue to plague certain regions of the non-democratic zone. This violence will not be resolved, but in certain cases it will be brought to levels that can be tolerated in the West. No major actor, or any combination of actors, is likely to accept a long-term commitment to an altruistic moral agenda of the sort great powers were ready to undertake for the sake of their national security and credibility during the Cold War.[63]

In the long run, the variables that push states away from the traditional institutional agenda may be joined by a technology that can address public expectations for both effective and selective action, thereby resolving the intervention dilemma in favour of action. Then, the international approach to humanitarian intervention may be thoroughly reconstructed in a way that is much more compatible with idealist liberalism. But, as noted, this is unlikely to be seen in the near future.

## NOTES

1. Samuel P. Huntington, *The Third Wave: Democratization in the Late Twentieth Century* (Norman, OK: University of Oklahoma Press, 1991); and Martin Shaw, 'Global Voices: Civil Society and the Media in Global Crises', in Tim Dunne and Nicholas J. Wheeler (eds), *Human Rights in Global Politics* (Cambridge: Cambridge University Press, 1999), pp. 215–16.
2. Hedley Bull, 'Intervention in the Third World', in Bull (ed.), *Intervention in World Politics* (Oxford: Clarendon Press, 1984), p. 153.
3. Ariel E. Levite, Bruce W. Jentleson and Larry Berman (eds), *Foreign Military Intervention* (New York: Columbia UP, 1992), p. 320. See also the discussion, pp. 319–23.
4. For a sociocognitive (as opposed to rational) argument about decisions on military intervention see Yaacov Y. I. Vertzberger, *Risk Taking and Decisionmaking: Foreign Military Intervention Decisions* (Stanford: Stanford University Press, 1998).
5. For definitions and discussions of the concept of intervention see Vertzberger, *Risk Taking*, pp. 114–16; Thomas G. Otte, 'On Intervention: Some Introductory Remarks', in Andrew M. Dorman and Thomas G. Otte, *Military Intervention* (Aldershot: Dartmouth Publishing, 1995), pp. 3–15; Bull, *Intervention in World Politics*, p. 1; Stanley Hoffmann, 'The Problem of Intervention', in ibid., p. 10; Philip Windsor, 'Superpower Intervention', in ibid. p. 50; Levite *et al.*, *Foreign Military Intervention*, pp. 3–11; and Richard Little, *Intervention: External Involvement in Civil Wars* (London: Martin Robertson, 1975), pp. 1–11.
6. See Hans J. Morgenthau, *Politics Among Nations* (New York: Knopf, 1967); Michael J. Smith, *Realist Thought from Weber to Kissinger* (Baton Rouge: Louisiana State University Press, 1986); Stephen D. Krasner, *Defending the National Interest: Raw Materials Investments and U.S. Foreign Policy* (Princeton: Princeton University Press, 1978); Robert Gilpin, *War and Change in International Politics* (Cambridge: Cambridge University Press, 1981); and Kenneth Waltz, *Theory of International Politics* (Reading, MA: Addison-Wesley, 1979).
7. See Rhoda E. Howard and Jack Donnelly, 'Liberalism and Human Rights: A Necessary Connection', in Micheline R. Ishay, *The Human Rights Reader* (New York: Routledge, 1997), pp. 268–77; Nicholas J. Wheeler and Justin Morris, 'Humanitarian Intervention and State Practice at the End of the Cold War', in Rick Fawn and Jeremy Larkins (eds), *International Society after the Cold War* (London: Macmillan, 1996), pp. 140–1; Andrew Moravcsik, 'Explaining International Human Rights Regimes: Liberal Theory and Western Europe', *European Journal of International Relations*, 1, 2 (1995), pp. 157–89, and 'Taking Preferences Seriously: A Liberal Theory of International Politics', *International Organization*, 51, 4 (1997), 513–53; Michael Freeman, 'Human Rights: Asia and the West', in James T. H. Tang (ed.), *Human Rights and International Relations in the Asia–Pacific Region* (New York: Pinter, 1995), pp. 18–23; and Nicholas J. Wheeler, 'Agency, Humanitarianism and Intervention', *International Political Science Review*, 18, 1 (1997), pp. 9–26.
8. For an interesting effort to strike a balance between realist and liberal imperatives see

Ernst B. Hass, 'Human Rights: To Act or Not to Act?', in Kenneth A. Oye, Donald Rothchild, Robert J. Lieber (eds), *Eagle Entangled: U.S. Foreign Policy in a Complex World* (New York: Longman, 1979), pp. 167–96.

9. For a rationale for similarity in the behaviour of states see Waltz's discussion of socialization in *Theory of International Politics*, pp. 74–6, 97.

10. See Hoffmann, 'The Problem of Intervention', pp. 18–20.

11. See also Henry Kissinger's discussion in *American Foreign Policy* (New York: Norton, 1969), p. 56; Christopher Layne, 'From Preponderance to Offshore Balancing', *International Security*, 22, 1 (1997), pp. 102–3; Robert J. McMahon, 'Credibility and World Power: Exploring the Psychological Dimension in Postwar American Diplomacy', *Diplomatic History*, 15, 4 (autumn 1991), pp. 455–7; Charles A. Kupchan, 'Getting In: The Initial Stage of Military Intervention', in Levite *et al.*, *Foreign Military Intervention*, p. 248; and Vertzberger, *Risk Taking*, pp. 147–8.

12. See, for example, John Ranelagh, *The Agency: The Rise and Decline of the CIA* (London: Weidenfeld & Nicolson, 1986), pp. 216, 248, 260–9, 274–6.

13. Quoted in Walter Lafeber, *The American Age* (New York: W. W. Norton, 1989), p. 575. On US interventions of all sorts see Andrew M. Scott, *The Revolution in Statecraft: Intervention in an Age of Interdependence* (Durham, NC: Duke University Press, 1982), pp. 68–112; and Ranelagh, *The Agency*.

14. See also Scott, *The Revolution in Statecraft*, pp. 177–97.

15. See Gary Clyde Hufbauer and Jeffrey J. Schott, *Economic Sanctions Reconsidered: History and Current Policy* (Washington: Institute for International Economics, distributed by MIT Press, 1985).

16. See Michael Desch, 'The Keys that Lock up the World', *International Security*, 14, 1 (1989), pp. 97–100.

17. James M. Goldgeier and Michael McFaul, 'A Tale of Two Worlds: Core and Periphery in the Post-Cold War Era', *International Organization*, 46, 2 (1992), pp. 467–91. See also Max Singer and Aaron Wildavsky, *The Real World Order: Zones of Peace/Zones of Order* (New York: Chatham House, 1993).

18. See Paul Hirst, 'Security Challenges in Post-Communist Europe', in Lawrence Freedman (ed.), *Military Intervention in European Conflicts* (Oxford: Blackwell, 1994), pp. 177–8

19. See Michael E. Brown, 'The Causes and Regional Dimensions of Internal Conflict', in Michael E. Brown (ed.), *The International Dimensions of Internal Conflict* (Cambridge, MA: MIT Press, 1996), pp. 571–601.

20. See Richard Falk, *Human Rights and State Sovereignty* (New York: Holmes and Meier, 1981), pp. 63–5. On the relations between non-democratic regimes and domestic violence see Rudolph J. Rummel, *Death by Government* (New Brunswick, NJ: Transactions Publishers, 1994), pp. 1–3. Indeed, Charles Humana found that the states that scored the lowest human rights rating were all non-democratic. See *World Human Rights Guide* (New York: Oxford University Press, 1992), p. xi.

21. On the rise of the humanitarian agenda see Geoffrey Robertson, *Crimes against Humanity* (London: Allen Lane/Penguin Press, 1999); Richard S. Hartigan, *The Forgotten Victim: A History of the Civilian* (Chicago: Precedent Publishing, 1982); Geoffrey Best, *Humanity in Warfare* (London: Methuen, 1983), Michael Howard (ed.), *Restraints on War* (Oxford: Oxford University Press, 1979); Donald A. Wells, *War Crimes and Laws of War* (NY: University Press of America, 1984); Rein Müllerson, *Human Rights Diplomacy* (London: Routledge, 1997), pp. 73–101; R. J. Vincent, *Human Rights and International Relations* (Cambridge: Cambridge University Press, 1986), pp. 17–36; Paul Gordon Lauren, *The Evolution of Human Rights* (Philadelphia: University of Philadelphia Press, 1998); and Gil Merom, *Blood and Conscience* (unpublished manuscript), pp. 74–7.

22. Edward L. Morse, 'The Transformation of Foreign Policies: Modernization, Interdependence, and Externalization', *World Politics*, 22, 3 (1970), pp. 371–92.

23. See Rachel Brett, 'The Role and Limits of Human Rights NGOs at the United Nations', in David Beetham (ed.), *Politics and Human Rights* (Oxford: Blackwell, 1995), pp. 96–110; and Thomas G. Weiss, 'Nongovernmental Organizations and Internal Conflict', in Brown, *The International Dimensions of Internal Conflict*, pp. 435–59. For a general book on human rights-related NGOs see Henry J. Steiner,

*Diverse Partners: Non-Governmental Organizations in the Human Rights Movement* (Cambridge, MA: Harvard College, 1991).

24. On the weakness of NGOs *vis-à-vis* states see Brett, 'The Role and Limits of Human Rights NGOs', pp. 104–6, 110.

25. See Moravcsik, 'Explaining International Human Rights Regimes', p. 184. It is worthwhile to note that Charles Humana's sources for the *World Human Rights Guide* were mostly from among NGOs and the media. See also James Gow, 'Nervous Bunnies – The International Community and the Yugoslav War of Dissolution', in Freedman, *Military Intervention in European Conflicts*, p. 19; David P. Forsythe's discussion of the partial influence of the 'CNN factor' in 'Human Rights and US Foreign Policy: Two Levels, Two Worlds', in David Beetham (ed.), *Politics and Human Rights* (Oxford: Blackwell, 1995), p. 126; and Steven L. Burg and Paul S. Shoup, *The War in Bosnia-Herzegovina: Ethnic Conflict and International Intervention* (Armonk, NY: M. E. Sharpe, 1999), p. 164.

26. See also Müllerson, *Human Rights Diplomacy*, p. 180; James Mayall, 'Introduction', in Mayall (ed.), *The New Interventionism 1991–1994* (Cambridge: Cambridge University Press, 1996), pp. 5–6; and Jan Nederveen Pieterse, 'Sociology of Humanitarian Intervention: Bosnia, Rwanda and Somalia Compared', *International Political Science Review*, 18, 1 (1997), p. 72.

27. Jolyon Howorth, 'The Debate in France over Military Intervention in Europe', in Freedman, *Military Intervention in European Conflicts*, p. 122.

28. On the causes of non-intervention see Little, *Intervention*, pp. 23–8, 30–2.

29. Wheeler and Morris, 'Humanitarian Intervention and State Practice', pp. 138–9.

30. See Müllerson, *Human Rights Diplomacy*, p. 134.

31. See also Wheeler and Morris, 'Humanitarian Intervention and State Practice', p. 143.

32. Michael Akehurst, 'Humanitarian Intervention', in Bull, *Intervention in World Politics*, pp. 97–8.

33. See also Richard Connaughton, *Military Intervention in the 1990s* (New York: Routledge, 1992), pp. 29, 42; and Barry M. Blechman and Tamara Cofman Wittes, 'Defining Moment: The Threat and Use of Force in American Foreign Policy', *Political Science Quarterly*, 114, 1 (1999), p. 27.

34. Quoted in Levite *et al.*, *Foreign Military Intervention*, p. 308.

35. See Shaw, 'Global Voices', p. 229.

36. France is a good example. Intervention has been a cornerstone of its foreign policy as a great power and, as its leaders never fully abandoned the dream of grandeur, it continues to intervene where it can, most notably in the African continent. See Dominique Moïsi, 'Intervention in French Foreign Policy', in Bull, *Intervention in World Politics*, pp. 67–77.

37. See also the assessment of Blechman and Cofman Wittes in 'Defining Moment', p. 26.

38. See also Shaw, 'Global Voices', p. 220.

39. Quoted in Thomas Halverson, 'Disengagement by Stealth: The Emerging Gap between America's Rhetoric and the Reality of Future European Conflicts', in Freedman, *Military Intervention in European Conflicts*, p. 83.

40. Ibid., p. 76.

41. See also Forsythe, 'Human Rights and US Foreign Policy', pp. 111–30, and 'Human Rights in US Foreign Policy: Retrospect and Prospect', *Political Science Quarterly*, 105, 3 (1990), pp. 435–54; and Ivo H. Daalder, 'The United States and Military Intervention in Internal Conflict', in Brown, *The International Dimensions of Internal Conflict*, pp. 461–88. Even President Carter, who claimed that commitment to human rights was 'a fundamental tenet of [America's] foreign policy', hastened to add that 'this does not mean we can conduct our foreign policy by rigid moral maxims. We live in a world that is imperfect, and which will always be imperfect.' Quoted from a May 1977 presentation in Notre Dame, in Falk, *Human Rights and State Sovereignty*, p. 22.

42. Gil Merom, 'Blood and Conscience' (unpublished manuscript), pp. 60–106.

43. On the Western nature of current human rights ideas see James T. H. Tang, 'Human Rights in the Asia–Pacific Region: Competing Perspectives, International Discord, and the Way Ahead', in Tang, *Human Rights and International Relations in the Asia–Pacific Region*, pp. 1–6; Freeman, 'Human Rights: Asia and the West', pp. 13–17; and Müllerson, *Human Rights Diplomacy*, pp. 73–101.

44. Shaw, 'Global Voices', p. 229. For an argument about the role of globalization, the making of transnational civil society and the revolution in communications, see Mary Kaldor, 'Transnational Civil Society', in Dunne and Wheeler, *Human Rights in Global Politics*, pp. 195–213, and in particular pp. 207–9.

45. Robertson, *Crimes against Humanity*, p. 71. On low tolerance for casualties and its effects see also Blechman and Cofman Wittes, in 'Defining Moment', pp. 27–8; and Gil Merom, 'Democracy, War and Peace: The Third Dimension' (unpublished manuscript). In August 1992 Deputy Secretary of State Lawrence Eagleburger cooled down calls for military action in Bosnia by raising the spectre of 'another Lebanon or Vietnam', quoted in Burg and Shoup, *The War in Bosnia-Herzegovina*, p. 210.

46. Robertson, *Crimes against Humanity*, p. 65. See, for example, the report by *Human Rights Watch* on the use of cluster bombs in Kosovo: 'Ticking Time Bombs', in *www.hrw.org/hrw/reports/1999/nato2*; 'Pentagon Report Whitewashes Civilian Deaths in Yugoslavia', in *www.hrw.org/hrw/press/2000/02/nato208*; and 'Civilian Deaths in the NATO Air Campaign', in *www.hrw.org/reports/2000/nato/Natbm200.htm#P39_994*.

47. The choice of civil targets in NATO's recent intervention in Kosovo, as revealed in a June interview by General Wesley Clark to the BBC, is a good example. See Phillip Knightley, 'Fighting Dirty', *Guardian*, 20 March 2000.

48. For example, in 1994 the Clinton administration instructed officials to avoid depicting the events in Rwanda as genocide because it feared that this would encourage public pressure to take action. See Richard Falk, 'The Challenge of Genocide and Genocidal Politics in an Era of Globalization', in Dunne and Wheeler, *Human Rights in Global Politics*, p. 185.

49. Scott, *The Revolution in Statecraft*, p. 11; Shaw, 'Global Voices', pp. 219–20, 228; and Wheeler and Morris, 'Humanitarian Intervention and State Practice', p. 161.

50. See also Wheeler, 'Agency, Humanitarianism and Intervention', p. 13; and Mayall, 'Introduction', p. 22.

51. This is also the opinion of the former secretary of NATO, General Manfred Werner. See Gow, 'Nervous Bunnies', p. 30. See also Jane M. O. Sharp, 'Appeasement, Intervention and the Future of Europe', in Freedman, *Military Intervention in European Conflicts*, pp. 49–50.

52. Gow, 'Nervous Bunnies', p. 31. See also ibid., p. 14.

53. Robert Putnam, 'Diplomacy and Domestic Politics: The Logic of Two-Level Games', *International Organization*, 42, 3 (1988), pp. 427–60.

54. For the components of a utility function of intervention in all but name, see Müllerson, *Human Rights Diplomacy*, p. 165.

55. See also Vertzberger, *Risk Taking*, pp. 149–50.

56. See, for example, Ivo H. Daalder on the policy of the great powers in the crises that followed the disintegration of Yugoslavia in 'Fear and Loathing in the Former Yugoslavia', in Brown, *The International Dimensions of Internal Conflict*, pp. 59–61.

57. Falk, 'The Challenge of Genocide', p. 185.

58. Quoted in Mayall, 'Introduction', p. 16. See also ibid., p. 21.

59. In this respect, the debate within France over the deteriorating situation in Bosnia is a good example. Leading French intellectuals supported decisive intervention for moral reasons, a number of politicians followed suit, the media provided a sympathetic arena for the debate, but the authorities exercised great caution, agreeing to intervene only in a multilateral setting and under the umbrella of the UN. See Howorth, 'The Debate in France', pp. 111–21.

60. Bull, 'Intervention in the Third World', pp. 150–1. Indeed, even in the case of the Iraqi destruction of Kuwait, many European states (which had a direct national stake in the structure of the oil market) preferred non-military measures. See Connaughton, *Military Intervention in the 1990s*, p. 114.

61. See also Vertzberger, *Risk Taking*, p. 149.

62. See Barry Posen and Andrew L. Ross, 'Competing Visions for U.S. Grand Strategy', *International Security*, 21, 3 (1996/97), pp. 5–53; Eugene Gholtz, Daryl G. Press and Harvey M. Sapolsky, in 'Come Home, America', *International Security*, 21, 4 (1997), pp. 5–48; and Layne, 'From Preponderance to Offshore Balancing', pp. 86–124.

63. See also Mayall, 'Introduction', pp. 1–2.

# 6 Proximate Policy-makers

## AHARON KLIEMAN

This essay addresses international state behaviour and foreign policy decision-making at the level of domestic bureaucratic politics, but does not follow the dominant institutionalist approach, with its structural perspective of organizations-as-actors engaged in constant interagency tasking, coordination, competition, bargaining, accommodation and compromise. Rather, a basic distinction is made at the very outset between officialdom and officials, between bureaus, bureaucracy and governmental machinery, on the one hand, and the solitary bureaucrat.

Just as ministers at the pinnacle of governmental hierarchies have a persona of their own and stand apart from the corporate ministries they head, so, too, for analytical purposes, do individual bureaucrats warrant being differentiated from the collective, impersonal bureaucracies they serve. Singled out for closer consideration here is a singular type of bureaucrat, the Proximate Policy-maker.[1]

By 'proximate policy-maker' the reference is to a select category of middle-level officials – senior civil servants and key advisers – situated at the highest echelon of bureaucracy. While media reporting on behind-the-scenes policy-making and diplomatic histories on interstate relations invariably leave these seemingly marginal and admittedly secondary bureaucratic actors nameless and faceless, they are in fact the unsung heroes, or rogues, of foreign affairs.[2]

In practice, they manage to exercise an inordinate amount of influence on policy formulation through their timely and often telling interventions as decision-making processes wend their way from pre-decision to implementation. And on both types of decision-making: routine, incremental matters, but no less so in 'watershed policy episodes' of a 'sufficiently consequential, controversial, or precedent-setting' nature.[3]

These assertive bureaucratic players are identifiable through a set of distinguishing characteristics, starting with *anonymity*, since this particular class of administrator tends to be reclusive and self-effacing. That he or she remains safely removed from the public eye and cosseted deep within the recesses of depersonalized government machinery stands in sharp contradistinction to their actual behind-the-scenes prominence. A serious problem, however, in researching the subject is precisely this lack of corroborating documentation. Only much later, and long after the fact, does the true significance of Proximates usually come to light, with the aid of declassified state papers and internal ministerial files.

What best explains this disproportionate influence is, in a word, *proximity*. Our subject, the proximate policy-maker, has the exquisite good fortune of being strategically located within the policy-making apparatus, close to, yet not formally inside the nuclear circle of power. *Positioning* in effect is what separates such intermediate actors from authoritative, so-called 'high policy élites', on the one hand, and lower-echelon support staff, on the other. Positioning is what provides *access*. Worth emphasizing, however, is that positioning by itself presents only the opportunities for personally making a mark on decision-making outputs.

In addition to being well placed and well connected, to truly qualify as Proximates such individuals have to be both *enterprising* and *energetic*. I would also venture that there has to be something manipulative about them, whether in their character and personality, or in their professionalism, meaning in how they approach bureaucratic life and the rules of organizational behaviour.

Likewise, they must be exceptionally *motivated*, and *committed*, to their own career, certainly but, perhaps even more, to a given policy course or option they are prepared not only to advocate but forcefully to promote. In the absence of this will to determinedly and effectively seize potential openings, in combination with the above other attributes, the vast majority of other bureaucrats automatically disqualify themselves as *proximate* contributors in the second sense of meaningfully impacting on decisions as *auxiliaries* to the *actual* takers of decisions.

PUTTING THE PERSONAL BACK INTO BUREAUCRATIC POLITICS

David Vital was among the first generation of researchers during the 1960s to break new ground in the deeper understanding of international politics by going beyond interstate relations and describing the domestic political dynamics and internal procedures involved in the conduct of foreign policy. In their 1962 book, Snyder, Bruck and Sapin were the first to put forward a systematic decision-making approach built on the conception of 'The State as Actor in a Situation'. Their pioneering work offers an impressive theoretical framework and itemized list of decisional variables combined with a case study of American policy-making by the Truman administration during the Korean War crisis.[4]

Joseph Frankel followed with his 1963 study, *The Making of Foreign Policy*, in which he acknowledged something called 'bureaucratic power', simply because leaders are compelled to delegate authority to subordinates who are, however, 'sufficiently unimportant, docile and subservient'.[5] But instead of representing this as a universal phenomenon, Frankel restricted the sway of bureaucrats to modern totalitarian states, arguing that 'even docile and near-anonymous bureaucrats can become extremely powerful when habitually wielding the power of decision. This is particularly true about all dictatorships.'[6] Whereas, it is long since clear that any overburdened leader, irrespective of regime type, is going to be dependent on a narrow, close circle of advisers.

Vital took the discussion of bureaucracy another step further in his first published book, *The Making of British Foreign Policy*, in 1968. In a chapter on 'The Machinery' an important distinction was made between 'junior' and 'senior' officials. The former are referred to as 'subordinates', who tend to congregate at 'the lower reaches of the official hierarchy' and ordinarily play 'no more than a contributory role in the course of the process'; whereas the latter includes what I have chosen to call the 'artful bureaucrat', having in Vital's words 'the authority or, more rarely the courage to take major decisions without reference to higher authority'.[7] Showing a heightened appreciation for the influence of civil servants in general, in a later passage he speaks of an uneven balance between ministers and officials actually favouring the latter, given that 'Generally it is the officials' responsibility for defining issues, envisaging consequences and proposing policy that is crucial'.[8]

Nevertheless, the real breakthrough in the analysis of bureaucratic politics had to await Graham Allison's 1969 *American Political Science Review* milestone essay and expanded 1971 *Essence of Decision* book-length comparison of three alternative explanatory paradigms for state behaviour: Rational Actor, Organizational

Process, Governmental Politics. His Model II treats governments as 'a conglomerate of semi-feudal, loosely allied organizations' and perceiving problems through 'organizational sensors', thus fostering the impression that 'the office – not its occupant – determines how players behave'.[9] Model III goes still further in demolishing the image of states as indistinct black boxes by highlighting 'differences in roles, responsibilities, perceptions, and priorities among players focusing on slightly different faces of a complex issue'.[10]

Recalling one of Allison's more frequently quoted aphorisms, 'each person comes to his position with baggage in tow',[11] his principal contribution for our purposes lies in stressing two facts of bureaucratic politics. First, that 'The "leaders" who sit on top of organizations are not a monolithic group; rather, each individual in this group is, in his own right, a player in a central, competitive game'.[12] Second, the importance of 'How each man manages to stand the heat in *his* kitchen, each player's basic operating style, and the complementarity or contradiction among personalities and styles in the inner circles are irreducible pieces of the policy blend'.[13]

My problem with this is threefold. Allison and others either fail to define 'leaders' or restrict them to those at the presidential, ministerial or cabinet-secretary level who do indeed sit 'on top of organizations' and in the 'inner', innermost circles. To be sure, the subsequent post-Allison literature on foreign policy decision-making does show respect for the heightened role and power of permanent civil servants and senior advisers.[14] Such references, however, are often restricted on average to a single parsimonious sentence or a general comment, without any in-depth analysis or specific case histories.

Second, even long after Allison's Model III, greater weight continues to be assigned to formal and complex organizations, structures, institutions and processes than to the role of individuals and personality factors.[15] Cognitive studies like those authored by Robert Jervis, Fred Greenstein, Ole Holsti, Alexander George and several others go a long way towards compensating for this dominant institutional–procedural bias. Nevertheless, as a rule, bureaucrats are still (a) conveniently lumped together and then (b) cast in negative, unflattering terms: as 'paper pushers' suffering from a lack of imagination and narrow tunnel vision, pettiness, red tape, inertia and the like.[16]

In short, too easily overlooked in this preoccupation with 'Chiefs' (again, Allison's term) are a few 'Indians' – the Proximates – who happen to be the real masters of 'pulling and hauling'. So that as recently as 1997 Alexander George was still arguing the imperative for foreign-policy analysts 'to attend to the diversity of types of relationships that may develop between executives, advisers, and other autonomous political actors'.[17] Taking our cue from him, we proceed by pinpointing Proximate policy-makers more precisely within the bureaucratic hierarchy.

## POSITIONING THE PROXIMATES

Views of the foreign policy establishment still essentially favour the traditional two-tiered pyramid comprising a thin upper stratum – a handful of privileged office-holders, the authoritative decision-makers and hence alone worthy of serious attention; and officialdom, meaning basically all other employees and staffers:

Decision-makers

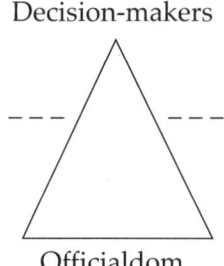

Officialdom

Accordingly, bureaucracy and bureaucrats are imagined as inhabiting an impenetrable lower labyrinth of rather nondescript departments, agencies and offices peopled by similarly grey officials – 'underlings' really – dutifully performing clearly assigned roles according to prescribed standard operating procedures.

This bifurcation – Vital's 'those who are at the top' juxtaposed against 'those at its base'[18] – is amply reflected in the literature. Take, for example, former US Secretary of State Henry Kissinger's own depiction of how President Richard Nixon regarded him as 'a mere staff assistant, a kind of puppet pulled by strings in the hands of the master manipulator'.[19] While Kissinger was too high up on the government totem pole to qualify as an auxiliary player or Proximate, and far too prominent a public and media figure, nonetheless he serves nicely to reopen the fundamental question in foreign policy-making of who really is the master manipulator and who the puppet. Better still, the superior–subordinate conventional model is mirrored in the terminology of bureaucratic politics. Culled from scholarly writings in the field, the list features such accepted contrasts as:

| Leaders | Followers |
|---|---|
| Superiors | Subordinates |
| Seniors | Juniors |
| Chiefs | Indians |
| Ministers | Mandarins |
| Politicians | Officials, bureaucrats, technocrats |
| High policy élites | Technical élites |
| Executives | Executors |
| Commanders | Staffers |
| Principals | Supporting actors |
| Insiders | Outsiders |

Alternative models at best depict bureaucracy as two concentric circles, or 'loops', with officials dividing into an 'inner and outer' circle: those inside the loop and those excluded from it.

Either way, the strong impression is of delineated boundaries and a clear administrative chain of command. Interestingly, bureaucracy's defenders inadvertently conspire in preserving this basic compartmentalization even while turning the tables by unfavourably matching 'Pols' against 'Pros', the dilettantes and the generalists against the experts and the specialists.

Inserting middle-echelon Proximates between the so-called Principals, and, only then, the broader base of technocrats – Cubicle-rank Employees – serves a number of useful purposes. It underscores organizational complexity by drawing further, necessary distinctions between multiple levels of government, thereby producing, at a minimum, a triple-layered pyramid:[20]

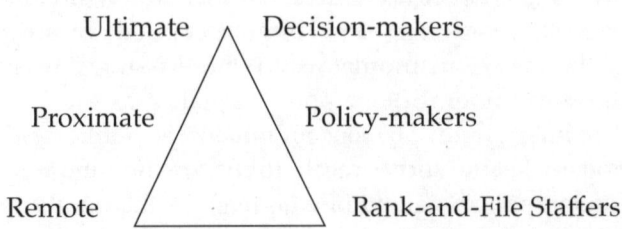

Ultimate     Decision-makers

Proximate     Policy-makers

Remote     Rank-and-File Staffers

Deploying them in this way also demolishes the above false dichotomies by blurring the lines of Bosses *versus* Subalterns, for the simple reason that Proximates are both 'followers' and 'leaders' at one and the same time, giving as well as taking orders.[21]

Hence, in straddling the line, Proximates appreciate perhaps more than anyone else that the art of bureaucracy lies in gauging the limits of what is permissible and what is impermissible behaviour. This privilege, alternatively this onus, qualifies such people in Holden's apt turn-of-phrase as 'administrative politicians'.[22] Indeed, their particular dilemma is knowing precisely when and where to draw the thin line in bureaucratic politics between obedience and disobedience that is tantamount to insubordination.

Furthermore, Proximates restore people – especially the individual bureaucrat – to bureaucracy. As Kissinger wrote in 1966, one of the original aims in creating bureaucracy might very well be 'to liberate decision-making from the accident of personalities'.[23] But as bureaucratic Proximates readily confirm, this is, of course, a total impossibility. Personality, and not only organization, matters,[24] at the highest, that is, political, level but also throughout the organizational chain of command.

Not least, insisting upon this three-tiered figure gives positioning in a hierarchical or pyramidal apparatus and Proximates in particular their full due. Removing the cloak of bureaucratic invisibility from officials and counsellors operating just below the highest levels of government and yet having a direct *entrée* to them teaches another important lesson. Namely, that there is a useful distinction to be made between formal authority and informal power, which is what Proximates represent as well as wield. This last point is illustrated by former Israeli prime minister Shimon Peres in reminiscing about the beginning of his long public career in 1948 as a junior official in the ministry of defence. He relates:

> During the War of Liberation they wanted to give me the rank of a high officer and I refused because even without the rank I had the highest rank. There was nobody above me. I could move around and do whatever I wanted. I established informal authority. I didn't need rank. I thought it would limit me.[25]

Public recognition and public prominence are one thing. Effectiveness is another.

## MIDDLE EAST MASTERS

To be sure, independent research conducted in the United States, France and a dozen (if not more) other countries is bound to yield documentary proof of the existence of Proximate Policy-makers and of their true behind-the-scenes influence. Shimon Peres aside, Israel alone offers any number of examples. Thus, I am confident, for instance, that future historians of the 1993 Oslo initiative towards the Palestinians will confirm how, even though vastly outshadowed in the limelight of public and international attention by Nobel Peace Prize-winners Prime Minister Yitzhak Rabin and Foreign Minister Peres, it is Deputy Foreign Minister Dr Yossi Beilin who was the true Proximate architect.

Let me draw, however, upon two concrete examples from my own experience in analysing the role of great powers in the Middle East, and, more specifically, England's declining imperial fortunes during the inter-war period at two specific points in time.

In the first instance, history notes that in December 1921 Great Britain decided to renew Amir Abdullah's status as tribal law enforcement officer east of the Jordan River after an unimpressive six-month initial trial period.[26] In the second instance, the annals of Palestine affairs chronicle how in July 1937 the Chamberlain government initially adopted a policy of partitioning Palestine as the only alternative to Arab–Jewish nationalist bloodshed, only to retract its endorsement shortly thereafter.[27]

Both episodes involved specific policy decisions of far-reaching consequence for Britain, for regional affairs and for the Palestine struggle. In the earlier of the two decisional crossroads, electing to reconfirm Abdullah's presence as titular ruler rather than dispensing with his services initiated a process that would eventually climax in the independent Hashemite Kingdom of Jordan, alter the inter-Arab balance of power and insert a third, complicating factor in the Palestine equation. Whereas in the later Palestine policy contretemps Britain's failure to implement its own partition plan in 1937 would be remembered as delaying for a full decade the inevitable painful disengagement from an untenable situation of being caught in the crossfire between militant Arab and Jewish nationalism. So, too, is it remembered as the first real 'missed opportunity' for peaceful dispute resolution in the Holy Land which, had it been seized, might have averted the long and bloody stalemate long since known as the Arab–Israel conflict.

From our standpoint the most influential figure behind the Abdullah decision is none other than the famous T. E. Lawrence ('Lawrence of Arabia'), serving at the time as political adviser to the newly established Middle East Department of the Colonial Office. It was at his strong personal recommendation that the Transjordan decision was taken. In contrast, the decisive individual behind the partition policy reversal had no name recognition whatsoever: George Rendel, veteran head of the Foreign Office's Eastern Department.

This same Rendel, in his memoirs, would later advise future generations of civil servants:

> if you really want to bury and conceal a document so effectively as to defeat the most acute historical detective of the future there is no safer way of doing so than to include it in the mountainous archives of a Governmental Department.[28]

But to little avail, since his major personal impact, like that of Lawrence before him, is amply documented through close content analysis of internal papers and departmental minutes long buried and concealed but now retrieved from British state archives in London courtesy of the Public Record Office. These unimpeachable records confirm both men as Proximate Policy-makers *par excellence*.

The similarities between these two officials are important for what they tell us about Proximate bureaucrats acting in administrative settings:

- Lawrence and Rendel each meet Allison's criterion of 'an official with operational responsibilities': Lawrence for putting Britain's new postwar Arab house in order, Rendel for overseeing Britain's Middle East regional strategy;
- both qualify as key aides and policy consultants. Both were the driving force behind measures adopted in London within the policy establishment;
- each enjoyed the highest respect and personal trust of his ultimate superior: Colonial Secretary Winston Churchill and Foreign Secretary Anthony Eden.

In fact, both ministers depended heavily on their counsellors. On this point Kissinger is closer to the mark in describing how 'The ultimate decision often depends less on knowledge than on the ability to brief the top administrator – to present the facts in such a way that they can be absorbed rapidly'.[29] His comment applies in full to Lawrence and Rendel in their close working relationships.

- Their reliance in turn meant that, like Lawrence, Rendel was in effect acting with the authority of an agent deputized to represent his minister and ministry, and, just as important, was perceived to be doing so by other bureaucrats. This, parenthetically, gives yet another definitional twist: Proximates as proxies;
- in practice, though, these two very different individuals clearly had a mind of their own regarding Middle East policy, its ends and appropriate means, and then dared to act on their own in advancing these views;
- consequently, both advisers ended up exercising considerable influence over the thinking and public stand of their superiors:[30] Churchill in supporting Abdullah's candidacy before parliament, Eden in his cabinet opposition to partitioning Palestine.

Yet what really stands out about both men is their marked diffidence. While it is possibly quite natural for Rendel, the quintessential grey bureaucrat, this false modesty is especially striking in Lawrence's case given the media image of the desert warrior he so assiduously cultivated. Rather than claiming any credit for their decisive role in these two chapters of British diplomacy, Lawrence and Rendel each opted for playing down his part, insisting he had been nothing more than a fringe player on the margins of policy-making.

In a final shared trait, Lawrence and Rendel were bureaucratic winners, each in their time. Each got his way. At Lawrence's insistence, Abdullah was enthroned with British backing; in the second, later episode government support was withdrawn from the policy initiative aimed at an early conflict-averting territorial compromise in British-mandated Palestine.

Their immediate objective achieved – promoting Arab nationalism by stabilizing Transjordan; safeguarding Arab friendship by defeating the scheme of Zionist statehood – both Proximates bowed out of bureaucratic life soon thereafter, Lawrence to join the Royal Air Force, Rendel in return for an ambassadorship to Bulgaria. For all these reasons our two Proximates emerge with high marks from the documents as singularly effective 'administrative politicians'.

On the other hand, important as these likenesses may be for understanding proximacy, so, too, are the main dissimilarities between Lawrence the nonconformist and Rendel the conformist meaningful. These two men actually differ quite widely when it comes to their background and career patterns, status, operational base, role and objective.

Both men may be bureaucrats and Proximates by our definition, yet political adviser T. E. Lawrence was the quintessential 'outsider', whereas Middle Eastern Department head George Rendel represents the more conventional Prioximate 'insider' – a professional's professional.

- Lawrence was Churchill's political appointee, called away from private seclusion at Oxford and recruited into government service for his first-hand knowledge of the Arab region, while Eden 'inherited' Rendel as a 'careerist official' and permanent fixture at the Foreign Office.[31]
- As such, Lawrence was regarded circumspectly by colleagues in Whitehall as a novice and something of a maverick, an undisciplined outsider 'parachuted' into their midst, indifferent to office procedures and best kept at arm's length. Rendel, by contrast, was a permanent civil servant and respected departmental head, a seasoned veteran of the bureaucratic wars who knew how to draw considerable strength and support from foreign ministry staff members by working according to the book and through official channels.
- Consistent with their contrasting backgrounds and styles, the one employed tactics aimed at bypassing the existing power structures, the other at exploiting them.[32]

If Churchill's Lawrence is the bureaucratic world's Mover then Eden's Rendel is the Groover.

- The former official was principally a field man – a sort of free agent and roving ambassador shuttling around Arabia. Although, all told, he probably spent more time away from the office than he did at the Colonial Office, Lawrence's urgent cables to Churchill's personal attention and occasional reports from Amman and Jerusalem had a decisive impact on the deliberations in London. The latter official, Rendel, was a classic desk man whose effectiveness lay not only in directing cable traffic, in writing and circulating a steady stream of anti-partition memoranda, but in orchestrating an interdepartmental coalition formed among like-minded associates in Whitehall.
- Similarly do they vary in their respective office roles: Lawrence,

the determined policy proponent (on behalf of permanently seating Abdullah), Rendel, the implacable policy opponent (arguing against offending Arab sensitivities were Britain to proceed with plans for dividing Palestine).

Accordingly, Lawrence represents the Proximate as policy Initiator, while Rendel epitomizes the Proximate as policy Impeder.

In the last analysis, however, what counts most is that when studied together, above and beyond their idiosyncratic differences, these two officials highlight what can happen when Proximate 'indians' aspire to be, and actually succeed in becoming, 'chiefs' for at least a single decisional moment.

T. E. Lawrence and George Rendel, each in his own way, thus confirm the subtle bureaucratic power of Proximate Policy-makers: the kind of power and indirect influence[33] potentially available to otherwise 'subordinate' officials if only they are astute enough to assert it in either of two alternative guises.

Lawrence, to my mind, falls within the category of those forward players who are bent on breaking policy deadlocks and inaction, on dislodging the status quo and on 'scoring' a particular goal, whereas the spoiler role fits Rendel perfectly. He saw himself as essentially a goalkeeper responsible for blocking ill-advised policy departures potentially inimical to the national interest as defined or, better still, as he prioritized them for the actual decision-makers.

Neither official, however, could accept policy drift, so that in a sense both individuals were at one and the same time opponents of indecision and proponents of a point of view – theirs. Lawrence was keen on England pursuing its imperial interests in the Middle East through support for moderate, dependent Arab leaders like Abdullah and his family. Sixteen years later Rendel felt strongly the imperative for Britain's crafting a Palestine policy more amenable to King Ibn Saud and the other Arab monarchs, including Abdullah, lest they align themselves with Mussolini and Hitler's Germany.


### THE ARTFUL BUREAUCRAT

Moving from the particular to the general, what we confront here are merely two examples from many of the Proximate's potential for escaping the mould of dutiful policy facilitator and becoming a policy advocate or, at times, a one-man resistance front. Thus, when viewed sympathetically, Proximates can be a positive factor in helping to counteract the bureaucratic tendency towards, for instance, what Janis diagnoses as groupthink[34] by challenging any given consensus and going against conventional wisdom. This healthy role in serving not only as a brake on mistaken policies, even non-decisions, but in accepting to be the catalyst for innovative, possibly even breakthrough, decisions ought to be respected.

But then again, when reinterpreted negatively these bureaucratic interventions by Proximates or would-be Proximates may just as easily end up by being denounced as contrarian and dysfunctional in nature, like, for instance, 'stepping out of line' and bordering on insubordination – charges actually levelled against Rendel by establishment rivals. The very same actors and interventions are then characterized by critics as an unacceptable form of subversive 'rogue operation', one that because of questioning existing decisions encourages policy disarray, or by countermanding and slowing down the execution of a given course of action leads to policy attrition.[35] Either of which clearly frustrates bold foreign-policy departures.

This inevitably leads us to the judgmental question of when exertions by Proximates are praiseworthy, and when objectionable. The answer is that no hard-and-fast rule exists. Rather, any one of three gauges can be applied. *Context-dependency* means acceptable or unacceptable bureaucratic behaviour relative to such variables as the specific policy setting or a particular country's bureaucratic culture, with its own tolerable levels or definitions of permissible/impermissible practices. *Hindsight* and *effectiveness*, are, I suppose, based upon awaiting the ultimate policy consequences of a Proximate Policy-maker's intervention, whether legitimate or not. The *means* test is based on first sourcing where it is that the Proximate's influence derives from, and then assessing how this influence is wielded.

Since the two former yardsticks are altogether case-dependent, it is really only this last means test which is conceptually relevant, and promising for a theory of proximate policy-making. What follows, therefore, are some preliminary hypotheses and a number of potential future research directions.

First, proximate policy-making is inversely proportional to organizational complexity. The inability of high-ranking leaders to monitor the activities of all those officials and offices over which they have nominal authority gives our Proximates considerably freer reign than usually assumed,[36] as well as bureaucratic cover for their quiet backstage activity.

Second, the situational variable would seem to be of lesser importance. Crisis or non-crisis, a policy impasse or a fluid policy situation – each in its own way makes Proximates the principal beneficiaries. An acute crisis works much like an impasse, because of decision-makers' heightening reliance on the smallest intimate circle of wizened advisers and reputed experts in closest proximity to them. Routine, non-crisis matters will generally be conducive to devolutions of authority and responsibility, leaving seconds in command, while fluid situations of great hesitancy and uncertainty create policy vacuums providing assertive bureaucrats with the opening needed to advance their unequivocal point of view. In short, Allison's law for senior executives – 'He who hesitates loses his chance to play at that point and he who is uncertain about his recommendation is overpowered by others who are sure' – extends to the tier of officials we are dealing with in this chapter.[37]

Third, working relations inside foreign policy establishments emphatically do not conform to the outdated bureaucratic theory of superiority–servility. Interrelationships between Proximates and their immediate superiors feature far greater complexity deriving from a pattern of in-built dualism resting on mutual respect–disrespect and mutual dependency, in the sense that each party is forced to rely on the other at various times for crucial support.[38] This mixed relationship of dependency–interdependence deserves closer study by bureaucratic analysts.

It is of course true that political élites are anything but defenceless. They certainly have sanctions at their disposal for curbing any bureaucratic zealot whose conviction, enthusiasm or dissent leads to trespassing territory and authority already staked out by the highest decision-makers themselves. This said, however, Proximate Policy-makers are anything but mere technicians or technocrats. They, too, possess resources of their own, as well as ways of bringing them to bear in the competitive interrelationship.

Fourth, Proximates know how to make their presence felt. As a rule, such officials have surprisingly wide latitude in pressing beyond the outermost limits of their spheres of competence and authority. Much derives from their ubiquity, since they appear in nearly all phases of policy-making, and in most functions. Building upon the typology offered by Allison and Szanton,[39] Proximates tend to have a direct hand in:

- developing coherent conceptions of the national interest;
- scanning for problems and providing situation analyses;
- collecting information;
- defining issues that require a decision;
- developing assessments and alternative courses of action;
- analyzing each option's relative benefits and costs;
- submitting a personal recommendation.

Then, assuming a decision has been reached by those higher-up:

- seeing to its implementation;
- coordinating departmental efforts at policy execution;
- assessing the results;
- making sure that standing policies are revised accordingly.

More often than not such expert counsel and input are duly heeded at the top. Yet, even in instances when their best advice has been overridden, Proximates may still affect the course of policy through an additional repertoire of evasive tactics.[40]


## MUDDLING THROUGH

Before ending, here are two quotations from the recollections of one other Proximate Policy-maker which provide us with a vivid illustration of the degree to which people operating below the highest levels of government regularly exert tremendous influence on decisions affecting hundreds of millions or even billions of dollars.

In 1987, Dr Dov Zakheim was on the US negotiating team that eventually succeeded in forcing Israel to cancel its vaunted Lavi jet-fighter project. In his later telling of the Lavi story Zakheim makes the following admission, rather rare for Proximates in its candour:

> On [Undersecretary of Defense Fred] Iklé's instructions, I ordered a full-dress Lavi briefing for [Secretary of Defense Caspar] Weinberger on Monday, May 5, in anticipation of his scheduled meeting with [Israeli Prime Minister Yitzhak] Rabin the following day. Despite all the publicity surrounding the Lavi controversy, Weinberger had never been fully briefed on the matter. Instead, he issued his instructions on the basis of initialing one-page decision memos, effectively leaving Iklé, and by extension me, to manage the American effort to kill the program.[41]

This is followed by a pensive glimpse into the private world of the Proximates:

> It is important to recognize that life is hardly a bed of roses for the subcabinet political appointees who daily grease the wheels of government. Burdened with long stressful hours, rewarded with relatively low pay for jobs of significant responsibility, absent from the daily activities ... that make life bearable and family meaningful, the under, assistant, deputy under, and deputy assistant secretaries that populate the capital require other outlets for job satisfaction.[42]

Surely one outlet has to be the gratification that comes with being in such close and intimate proximity to real power in national and international affairs – what Kissinger, in moving from a student to a player of bureaucratic politics, once described as a potent aphrodisiac.

In introducing second-tier decision-makers as a subject worthy of further study and refinement by students of foreign policy-making, I recall somewhere a sign reading 'We do not lead, but we enable' that is singularly appropriate in establishing our central hypothesis. In the domestic handling of foreign and diplomatic affairs, Proximates possess far more leverage than they are usually given credit for at the time. What is now called for is a series of additional documented country and case studies, including Israel's extensive diplomatic records, which are especially promising on bureaucratic politics. It is time to centre more of our attention on the role of Proximates.

## NOTES

1. Apparently the first to introduce the term was David Kozak in D. Kozak and M. Keagle (eds), *Bureaucratic Politics and National Security: Theory and Practice* (Boulder/London: Lynne Rienner, 1988), where he discusses 'indigenous power structures' comprising 'specialists representing different organizations' and 'actors within each of the programmatic areas of government' who 'as bureaucrats attempt to defend their interests, influence events, and court favor' (Chapter 1, 'The Bureaucratic Politics Approach: The Evolution of the Paradigm', p. 9). Kozak leaves it at that, however, without really defining or further refining his notion of 'proximate policy-makers'. Nor does he account for what makes them any different from other administrators down the line who strive no less to 'defend their interests, influence events, and court favor'.
2. Stephen Krasner, 'Are Bureaucracies Important? Or Allison Wonderland', *Foreign Policy*, 7 (summer 1972), p. 46, refers to 'faceless bureaucrats'.

3. Paul 't Hart, Eric K. Stern, Bengt Sundelius (eds), *Beyond Groupthink* (Ann Arbor: University of Michigan Press, 1997), p. 8.
4. Richard C. Snyder, H. W. Bruck, Burton Sapin, *Foreign Policy Decision-Making* (New York: The Free Press of Glencoe, 1962). To be sure, Max Weber's 'Essay on Bureaucracy' remains the classic statement on the way in which bureaucrats draw power from the expertise they bring to policy-making.
5. Joseph Frankel, *The Making of Foreign Policy* (London: Oxford University Press, 1963), p. 31. Another book immediately preceding Frankel's which had a strong impact in the United States on views of how the internal political process actually works was Richard Neustadt's *Presidential Power: The Politics of Leadership* (New York: John Wiley & Sons, 1960).
6. Frankel, *The Making of Foreign Policy*, p. 32.
7. David Vital, *The Making of British Foreign Policy* (London: George Allen & Unwin, 1968), pp. 44, 45.
8. Ibid., p. 92.
9. Graham T. Allison, *Essence of Decision: Explaining the Cuban Missile Crisis* (Boston: Little, Brown and Company, 1971), pp. 67, 121.
10. Ibid., p. 153.
11. Ibid., p. 166.
12. Ibid., p. 144.
13. Ibid., p. 166. Returning to the theme in a later book, he emphasizes (a) the structure of government and (b) processes but also (c) those people 'whose energies, skills, and values more nearly than any other factor determine whether government works', Graham Allison and Peter Szanton, *Remaking Foreign Policy: The Organizational Connection* (New York: Basic Books, 1976), Chapter 1, 'The Argument: Organization Matters', p. 14.
14. See, for example, Morton H. Halperin, *Bureaucratic Politics and Foreign Policy* (Washington, DC: Brookings Institution, 1974); Dan Caldwell, 'Bureaucratic Foreign Policy-Making', *American Behavioural Scientist*, 21, 1 (September/October 1977), pp. 87–110.
15. A step forward is the attention drawn to 'bureaucratic minorities', to 'subordinates and less powerful departments', by Juliet Kaarbo, 'Power Politics in Foreign Policy: The Influence of Bureaucratic Minorities', *European Journal of International Relations*, 4, 1 (1998), pp. 67–97.
16. Typical of the disparaging image is the colourful one James David Barber offers. Defining bureaucrats as 'Just people propping each other up with paper', he traces 'the bureaucracy's tired blood problem' as follows: 'give a man a pencil and a desk and he is going to do something. Pretty soon you'll need another man to coordinate him. A committee might help. A liaison person. An executive director. A press office and a grievance office and a legal office and so on. The list of people who have, in effect, veto power over the vigorous pursuit of policy stretches down the page, and the odds of policy survival drop off.' See James David Barber, *Politics by Humans: Research on American Leadership* (Durham and London: Duke University Press, 1988), p. 22.
17. Alexander L. George, 'From Groupthink to Contextual Analysis of Policy-making Groups', in 't Hart, Stern and Sundelius, *Beyond Groupthink*, p. 50. In assessing the state of the art in his 1992 essay on 'The Organizational Process and Bureaucratic Politics Paradigms: Retrospect and Prospect', David A. Welch notes (p. 125): 'Again, it is difficult to assess the extent to which a player's influence in a decision-making process flows from his or her bureaucratic position since no serious attempt has been made to gauge it', *International Security*, 17, 2 (autumn, 1992), pp. 112–32.
18. Vital, *The Making of British Foreign Policy*, p. 47. Writing several years later, Michael Brecher sought to draw his own two-fold distinction: first, between the 'High Policy Elite' and other grade officials, 'The Technical Elite'; and the latter subdivided into the 'FSTE' (Foreign Service Technical Elite) and the 'PTE' (Parallel Technical Elite), *The Foreign Policy System of Israel: Setting, Images, Process* (New Haven: Yale University Press, 1972), p. 477.
19. Henry Kissinger, *Years of Upheaval* (New York: Simon & Schuster, 1999), p. 47.
20. Dov S. Zakheim refers to civilian–military steering groups nominally at the

'two-star' level of major-generals or their civilian equivalents as 'tertiary officials'. Only later does he define them as 'people operating at below the highest levels of government', but this leaves unclear who are the inferred secondary officials, *Flight of the Lavi* (Washington and London: Brassey's, 1996), pp. 49, 255.

21. In their book *Conflict Among Nations* (Princeton: Princeton University Press, 1977), Glenn H. Snyder and Paul Diesing divide government officials into two basic types – 'the central decision maker' and 'the ordinary department member' – but then add a third group, 'the in-and-outers', pp. 352–3.

22. Matthew Holden, Jr, 'Imperialism in Bureaucracy', in Francis E. Rourke (ed.), *Bureaucratic Power in National Policy Making*, 4th edition (Boston: Little, Brown and Company, 1986), p. 29.

23. Henry Kissinger in his early essay, 'Conditions of World Order', *Daedalus*, XCV (spring 1966), pp. 503–29, reprinted as 'Domestic Structure and Foreign Policy', in James N. Rosenau (ed.), *International Politics and Foreign Policy* (New York: The Free Press, 1969), p. 266. Kissinger's emphasis throughout is oriented towards formal governmental machinery, reflected in his repeated usage of terms like 'institutionalization', 'bureaucratic mechanisms' and 'administrative structure'.

24. Taking direct issue with the 'accident of personality' thesis, David Welch, for example, counters with a quote from no less than Allison himself, whereby 'The hard core of the bureaucratic politics mix is personality', 'The Organizational Process and Bureaucratic Politics Paradigms: Retrospect and Prospect', *International Security*, 17, 2 (autumn 1992), p. 122.

25. Shimon Peres, as told to Robert Littell, in Shimon Peres and Robert Littell, *For the Future of Israel* (Baltimore and London: Johns Hopkins University Press, 1998), p. 54. Later in his recollection (p. 126) Peres adds: 'I started to work with generals when I was twenty-eight or twenty-nine, and I was already running the show then'.

26. The episode is described in greater detail in Aaron S. Klieman, *Foundations of British Policy in the Arab World: The Cairo Conference of 1921* (Baltimore: Johns Hopkins Press, 1970) and in 'T. E. Lawrence as Bureaucrat', in Stephen Tabachnik (ed.), *The T. E. Lawrence Puzzle* (Athens, GA: University of Georgia Press, 1984), pp. 243–68.

27. For a fuller study of the abortive partition initiative, see the author's 'Bureaucratic Politics at Whitehall Toward the Partition of Palestine', in Uriel Dann (ed.), *The Great Powers and the Middle East* (New York: Holmes & Meier, 1988), pp. 128–53.

28. Sir George Rendel, *The Sword and the Olive* (London: George Murray, 1957), p. 50.

29. Kissinger, 'Domestic Structure and Foreign Policy', p. 265.

30. I find Robert J. Strong's claim needlessly excessive in *Bureaucracy and Statesmanship: Henry Kissinger and the Making of American Foreign Policy* (Lanham: University Press of America, 1986) that leaders 'become the prisoners of their advisers' (p. 44). Nor is this a minor semantic difference. Portraying the relationship as a two-way street in the sense of reciprocal dependency, or interdependency, is in itself a contribution to a better understanding of internal bureaucratic politics.

31. The term is Lawrence Freedman's in his article 'Logic, Politics and Foreign Policy Processes: A Critique of the Bureaucratic Politics Model', *International Affairs*, 52, 3 (July 1976), p. 438.

32. Looking back over his career, Rendel later wrote: 'Heads of Departments were left a wider measure of discretion than they are today – or perhaps I was particularly fortunate in this respect – and, provided I did nothing which might run counter to Government policy, and was careful to secure official approval for any major decisions, I was free to take a great deal of personal initiative' (p. 82). Conveniently unmentioned is his activist role in fighting partition, which did in fact run counter to the official July 1937 government policy of moving forward with the Palestine Royal Commission plan for dividing Palestine.

33. Juliet Kaarbo points to the need to distinguish power from influence in her article 'Power Politics in Foreign Policy: The Influence of Bureaucratic Minorities'.

34. Irving L. Janis, *Victims of Groupthink* (Boston: Houghton Mifflin, 1972). Emphasizing social and group dynamics, Janis warns of excessive solidarity when officials or agencies unquestioningly march in lockstep. Alexander George, in his work, has called for policy establishments to hedge against fiascoes by encouraging what he terms 'multiple advocacy'. See his article, 'The Case for Multiple Advocacy in

Making Foreign Policy', *American Political Science Review*, 66 (September 1972), pp. 751–85.

35. Harvey Robbins does a nice job in showing both the positive and negative side of what he calls 'turfism'. His observations, while pitched at the level of interdepartmental struggles, seem equally applicable to Proximate Policy-makers. He notes that just as 'intramural' jockeying for attention and rewards can be an 'invigorating tonic', to the same or even greater extent 'squabbling in the trenches' can have 'a stifling effect on initiative' when 'The parts of the body move in spastic, herky-jerky movements, unable to coordinate'. See *Turf Wars: Moving from Competition to Collaboration* (Glenview, IL: Scott, Foresman, 1990), especially pp. 3, 6–9.

36. One wonders whether Henry Kissinger's later personal exposure to bureaucratic politics in the White House as head of the National Security Council and then at the State Department would have led him to reconsider his earlier statement that 'The more elaborate the administrative structure, the less relevant an individual's view becomes', 'Domestic Structure and Foreign Policy', p. 266.

37. Allison, *Essence of Decision*, p. 171.

38. In making the point that leaders are constantly on their guard against encroachment or sabotage from overzealous bureaucrats, Morton Halperin quotes President Harry Truman: 'The difficulty with many career officials in the government is that they regard themselves as the men who really make policy and run the government. They look upon the elected officials as just temporary occupants...Too often career men seek to impose their own views instead of carrying out the established policy of the administration', *Bureaucratic Politics and Foreign Policy*, p. 245.

39. Allison and Szanton, *Remaking Foreign Policy*, p. 21.

40. Halperin is very good on this point, citing how 'officials find ways to overlook, twist or resist orders' through such techniques as simply 'forgetting' to carry out directives, or by citing 'overriding circumstances', p. 250. Kaarbo supplements the stratagems in similarly showing how bureaucratic minorities can win through skill, will and successful strategies like manipulating decision-making procedures and exerting 'expert power' by building up a line of credibility as reputable and reasonable players, and by using expertise as a source of bargaining advantage, pp. 77–82.

41. Zablein, *Flight of the Lavi*, p. 99. In a later admission (p. 255), Zakheim confides: 'Although the Israelis inaccurately cast me as the evil spirit behind the attack on the Lavi, they were correct in their assessment that, despite my relatively low rank as a fourth-level administration official, I exerted influence on the fate of the program'.

42. Ibid., p. 111.

# PART TWO

## Israeli Foreign Relations

# 7  The Palestinian Issue: Changing Israeli Perspectives

## ITAMAR RABINOVICH

In October 1975, Harold (Hal) Saunders, a senior American diplomat and one of the US government's better-known Middle East experts, testified before a subcommittee of the House of Representatives' Committee on International Affairs. The subcommittee, chaired by Congressman Lee Hamilton, held hearings on the Palestinian problem (a significant fact in itself) and invited Saunders to formally present the Ford administration's views in this matter. Saunders's testimony and the written statement he deposited with the subcommittee are best remembered primarily because of one sentence – his reference to the Palestinian issue as the 'core of the [Israeli–Arab] problem'. Saunders did not elaborate on it at the time, but his observation would come to have far-reaching implications. For if the Palestinian issue was indeed becoming the crux of the entire complex Middle East regional dispute, then all efforts at conflict resolution which failed to address the Palestinian dimension were fated to have – at best – only a partial, limited and perhaps momentary effect.[1]

This caveat resonated first and foremost in the context of the efforts conducted by Saunders's boss, Henry Kissinger, who led the post-1973 Israeli–Arab peace process under a strategy of step-by-step diplomacy. Accordingly, the American Secretary of State proceeded to construct a series of partial or interim bilateral Arab–Israeli agreements precisely because he felt the parties were unready as yet for a comprehensive settlement – and this largely because of the difficulties inherent in any attempt to address, let alone resolve, the Palestinian issue.

Israeli officials and other observers at the time pondered long and hard over the significance of the Saunders testimony. Was it a manifestation of the determination of the State Department 'Arabists' in promoting their particular professional and personal convictions in the face of their superiors' policies? Or were the latter losing faith in the viability of their 'step-by-step' policy?

Israeli policy-makers and officials were worried by this development for more than one reason. In immediate terms, they were concerned with the prospect, slim though it might be, of a radical change in US bedrock policy. On a deeper level, they perceived a severe challenge to a major tenet of Israel's official orthodoxy: its diplomatic doctrine that the Arab–Israeli conflict was essentially a conflict between Israel and the Arab states and that its core was not the Palestinian problem but the Arab nationalist refusal to accept Zionism and the State of Israel.

The evolution of this thinking and its adoption by successive Israeli governments as a semi-official doctrine is in itself a most curious turn of events. After all, it was well remembered and not at all denied in Israel that the full-fledged Arab–Israeli conflict, as it became known after 1948, originated in a Zionist–Palestinian Arab (or Jewish–Arab as it was commonly known) conflict in and over Palestine. Consequently, Zionist policy and diplomacy were always of two minds with respect to the larger Arab world's involvement in this conflict. On several occasions, Zionist leaders felt that broader Arab involvement could facilitate an accommodation by expanding the arena and the agenda. It should, after all, be easier to obtain a concession over Palestine from an Arab entity concerned with larger territorial aspirations and a larger set of issues than from a Palestinian Arab leadership narrowly focused primarily and intensely on this small territory. But at other times, the Zionist leadership felt that the involvement of the larger Arab world would only serve to add wider participation and deeper resources to the struggle against Zionism.[2]

Ultimately, whatever Zionist leaders thought and did in this matter was of little consequence. British policies, the Palestinian Arab leadership's pressure and, above all, the combined lethal mix of political interests, ideology and emotional commitment drove the newly independent Arab states into greater involvement, and ultimately to military intervention in May 1948.

Their invasion of Palestine, subsequent defeat and the consequent disintegration, fragmentation and dispersal of the Palestinian Arab community transformed the original Zionist–Palestinian Arab conflict in and over Palestine into the larger Arab–Israeli conflict. Initially, the leadership of the young Israeli state consciously endorsed this shift. After all, under David Ben-Gurion it had accepted: (a) the 1947 UN partition resolution; (b) the notion of a Palestinian Arab state alongside with the State of Israel; and (c) the awkward delineation of its own prospective territory and borders. But the Arab rejection of the partition plan and effort to quash the young Israeli state, combined with the latter's own success in a war for survival, altered Israel's central perspective. Was it not the case that aggressors should be penalized and victors rewarded? Israel now sought to preserve the territorial and demographic status quo. Under Ben-Gurion's direction it also preferred to seek political settlements with the Arab states and not with the Palestinians. Negotiations were conducted in the war's aftermath with Jordan, Syria and Egypt, but not with Palestinian spokesmen and representatives who belatedly wanted or might have wanted to negotiate with Israel. It is also true that these individuals did not necessarily represent a large and powerful segment of Palestinian opinion. But above all there was a clear preference on Israel's side for dealing with the Palestinian issue through an Arab state like Jordan. If King Abdullah had annexed the West Bank and had given Jordanian citizenship to the Palestinians, if he was also eager to incorporate the Gaza Strip and to present himself as the custodian of the Palestinian issue, why not go along with him? Indeed, the advantages of this option were quite enticing from Israel's point of view. Jordan, a state based in historic Palestine and in control of the West Bank and part of Jerusalem, would annex the Gaza Strip and would provide the Palestinians with a surrogate state.

To achieve this, Ben-Gurion was willing to go so far as to agree to cede a narrow corridor linking the West Bank and the Gaza Strip as part of an Israeli–Jordanian agreement. Although duly negotiated and initialled, the agreement was never signed. When it came to the moment of truth, Abdullah realized that he did not have the power to carry such an agreement through his own domestic political system. Ironically, the very incorporation of the Palestinian population, which provided substance to his claim to represent the Palestinian cause, also denied him the power to implement an agreement with Israel that was predicated on this assumption.[3]

Thereafter, and for the balance of the 1950s, the Palestinian component of the Arab–Israeli conflict was entirely overshadowed by the conflict's other dimensions: bilateral disputes with the neighbouring Arab states, radical pan-Arabism's hostility to Israel, grafting of the Cold War on the regional conflict. The Palestinian issue was perceived primarily as a refugee problem. Many Palestinians were carried away by the radical pan-Arab nationalism of the Nasserists and of the Ba'athist movement, both highlighting immediate Arab unity. Their particular problem would be resolved when Arab nationalism carried the day.

Only in the early 1960s was the notion of a distinct Palestinian entity and its role as Israel's rival and antithesis revived. This process derived both from internal developments among the Palestinians and from the rivalry between various Arab states – Iraq versus Egypt, Egypt and Syria versus Jordan. By the mid-1960s, several authentic Palestinian movements and the PLO (originally a creation of the Arab states led by Egypt) began to play an increasingly important role in Arab and Arab–Israeli politics. The Palestinian National Charter originally drafted in 1964 and amended in 1968 represented the single most important Palestinian attempt to present Arab Palestine as Israel's counterpart and nemesis – the state that was negated by Israel's creation and destined to replace Israel when the Arabs finally win.[4]

Ironically, it was during the very same period of Palestinian nationalist revival that the Six Day War broke out (primarily as a conflict between Israel and the Arab states), ending in Israel's obtaining control of the whole of Palestine west of the Jordan and of a significant body of Palestinians.

From our present perspective it is clear that the Six Day War created the basis for the Israeli–Arab peace process. The peace since made between Israel and two Arab neighbours (Egypt and Jordan) – and nearly made with a third (Syria) – has been predicated on the notion of 'territory for peace' – the return of land captured by Israel in 1967 in exchange for recognition by the Arabs of Israel and of its legitimacy. In the unfolding Israeli–Palestinian peace process, the notion of a 'two-state solution' has played an equivalent role to the 'land for peace' idea.

To some policy-makers, observers and analysts, the prospect of seeking a resolution of the Arab–Israeli conflict on that basis was already clearly visible in June 1967. But in any event, all the indirectly and directly concerned parties to the conflict needed time to accept the notion of a genuine compromise. A real peace process (as distinct from the diplomatic aftermath of the Six Day War) began only later, in the wake of the 1973 October War.

Israel's strategy in this peace process continued to rely on a clear preference for dealing with the Palestinian issue through the Arab states, and more specifically under the aegis of Jordan and King Hussein. Conceivably, Israel could take the initiative in seeking the formation of a Palestinian entity in the West Bank and the Gaza Strip, thus offering a reasonable accommodation with Palestinian nationalism. But this option was not considered seriously for several reasons. The PLO was becoming the recognized, authoritative spokesman for Palestinian nationalism. The organization was still far from resigning itself to the notion of a compromise and was seen as a diabolical archenemy by an overwhelming majority of Israeli opinion. In Israel itself, the victory of June 1967 unleashed a wave of messianic nationalism as well as a secular Greater Israel movement that were both focused on the West Bank. Less clearly articulated but hardly less important was the lingering sense that unlike Israel's relationship with the neighbouring Arab states, the Israeli–Palestinian conflict was a zero-sum game, whereby a Palestinian state by definition, and of necessity, would have an adverse effect on Israel.

The flip side of this Israeli outlook was the age-old perception of Jordan as Israel's natural partner in addressing, if not resolving, the Palestinian issue. The Labour Party's Allon Plan and the notion of a Jordanian–Palestinian federation were two important manifestations of this trend. In a very different vein, some of Israel's right-wing leaders conceived of a different role for Jordan in resolving Israel's Palestinian dilemma by claiming that 'Jordan was Palestine'.[5]

In the mid-1970s the notion of 'the Jordanian option' sustained two major setbacks. In the spring of that year, Henry Kissinger came up with the idea that the first round of interim agreements (signed by Israel with Egypt and Syria in 1974) should be followed by a second round in which Jordan rather than Syria would be Egypt's Arab partner. Kissinger argued that such a move would have a dual advantage – sparing everyone the need to go through yet another arduous negotiation with Hafez al-Assad, and promoting Jordan's case as Israel's moderate partner in resolving the Palestinian problem. In more concrete terms, he wanted Israel to withdraw from the area of Jericho and, as a first step, to accept Jordan's return to that area. Yitzhak Rabin had just begun his first term as Israel's prime minister, however, and he and his coalition government were not ready for such a bold move.

Jordan's claim to the West Bank was dealt a second blow a few months later when the October 1974 Arab summit meeting in Rabat formally affirmed the right of the Palestinian people to set up an independent national authority under the leadership of the Palestine Liberation Organization, in its capacity as the sole legitimate representative of the Palestinian people and the claimant of any liberated Palestinian land.[6]

Kissinger's immediate policy dilemma was resolved by persuading Egypt 'to go it alone' and to conclude the September 1975 interim agreement over the Sinai without a second Arab partner. But the fundamental debate over the comparative importance of the Palestinian dimension of the Arab–Israeli conflict (and now peace process) continued. Israel maintained its policy of dealing with the Arab states (specifically Egypt), while the PLO, through diplomacy, terrorism and other forms of opposition to Israel, continued to build its own independent power base. It was against this background that Harold Saunders gave his testimony in October 1975, just a few weeks after the signing of the Egyptian–Israeli interim agreement.

In effect it took Israel 17 years to change its own view of the Palestinian issue, its place and role both in the Arab–Israeli conflict and in the Middle East peace process. This period can be reviewed through four principal phases.

## THE CAMP DAVID ACCORDS

Jimmy Carter's victory over Gerald Ford in the November 1976 presidential elections spelt the end of Kissinger's Middle Eastern diplomacy. The new president brought with him a set of personal convictions and a new foreign policy team that chose the Arab–Israeli arena as an early locus for the conduct of the new administration's policies. These changes had a profound impact on Israeli–Arab relations. The Carter White House began by pursuing two ambitious objectives: to produce a comprehensive settlement, and to put the Palestinian issue and its resolution at the very centre of its efforts. Ironically, the immediate effect of Washington's revised policies and priorities was to accelerate the process of Israeli–Egyptian reconciliation, and to help bring about the first bilateral peace treaty between Israel and a major Arab protagonist.

This turn of events forced Israel, under the leadership of

Menachem Begin, to rethink its traditional, indeed entrenched position on the Palestinian issue. As Begin himself saw it, Sadat was essentially ready for a separate deal with Israel. To be sure, he, Sadat, insisted on a high price – the return of the whole of the Sinai, to the last inch – but was willing at the end of the day to offer full peace and a satisfactory security regime. There was less clarity, though, with regard to the Egyptian stand on the Palestinian issue. In his Knesset speech as well as on other occasions Sadat reiterated the standard Arab line. He presented himself as the bold visionary who paved the way for the other Arabs. If they followed his lead, all the territories lost in 1967 would be regained. But he was also willing to complete his peacemaking with Israel without waiting for the others. In the Isma'iliyya meeting with Begin, he was willing to move ahead as long as Israel agreed in principle and however vaguely to recognize the rights of the Palestinians.

For Begin, a great believer in the power of abstract ideas and legal principles, this seemed too risky. Instead, in order to satisfy Washington's and Cairo's insistence that the Palestinian issue be addressed as part of the Israeli–Egyptian settlement, he devised his 26-point autonomy plan. While Begin's concept of Palestinian autonomy was very limited, at the subsequent 1978 Camp David summit, under pressure from both Carter and Sadat, he was forced to expand the notion of autonomy and to include recognition of Palestinian rights in the text of the agreement.

All three parties left Camp David, however, with markedly different interpretations. Understandably so, because sensitive matters of state were left highly ambiguous and open-ended. Thus, in Begin's view of things, he had obtained full peace with Egypt while only agreeing to limited Palestinian autonomy, and only for an interim period. His American and Egyptian partners, on the other hand, saw things rather differently. In their versions the foundations of Palestinian statehood had been laid at Camp David. The building blocks were there; if only the Palestinians would know how to play their hand, statehood would be guaranteed.

These contradictory interpretations go a long way towards explaining both the collapse of the follow-up autonomy negotiations and Begin's decision to launch the 1982 war in Lebanon. By the end of 1981 Begin understood that his gamble had failed. He had given back the whole of the Sinai to Egypt and had obtained a very significant peace treaty with the senior Arab state; yet it was also becoming patently clear that he had failed to circumvent or put

aside the Palestinian issue. The conflict with the PLO and the struggle against Palestinian nationalism proceeded with full force in
Lebanon, in the West Bank and elsewhere. Against this background,
any expectation of a radical solution to Israel's Palestinian challenge could only be dismissed as a false prospect.[7]

## THE 1980s

Hence, the broader Arab–Israeli peace process was suspended for
the rest of the decade. Israel's peace with Egypt survived but
remained controversial, beleaguered and cold. Moreover, Egypt's
departure telescoped the Arab–Israeli conflict, refocusing it on
Syria, but also in the direction of the Palestinians. Put differently,
the Israeli–Palestinian conflict continued to unfold dialectically. The
PLO may have lost its important base in Lebanon but the *intifada*
which erupted spontaneously in December 1987 dramatically
helped to revive its shrinking fortunes. The United States opened a
dialogue with the PLO; and in Israel itself the sense that the
comparatively painless occupation of the West Bank and Gaza
could continue indefinitely was shattered.

At decade's end the needle shifted yet again – Saddam's challenge presented a powerful Arab state as the more severe threat to
Israel, while the PLO's mistaken gamble on Saddam left it, at the
end of the Gulf War, weak and discredited. This low ebb was clearly
reflected in the diminished role and status offered the organization
at the Madrid peace conference under a Jordanian umbrella.[8]

## FROM MADRID TO OSLO

The Madrid conference of October 1991 and the ensuing Madrid
process which it set in motion have represented the most ambitious
and sustained effort yet to resolve the Arab–Israeli conflict. Fuelled
by the end of the Cold War and by the Gulf War, the Madrid
formula rested on two sets of parallel tracks. The first attempted to
address both the Israeli–Palestinian conflict and Israel's bilateral
conflicts with the respective Arab states (Syria, Jordan and Lebanon
most immediately) at one and the same time. The other, second
thrust was the construction of a multilateral track composed of five
working groups, dealing with the issues of water, refugees,

environment, arms control and regional security, and economic development.

From a Palestinian perspective, the Madrid formula was a mixed bag of setbacks and achievements. On the plus side, the Palestinians were represented in the Madrid conference and in the ensuing negotiations – but not as a self-standing delegation, and not by the PLO. A delegation representing the residents of the West Bank and the Gaza Strip was included in the process under the umbrella of a Jordanian–Palestinian delegation. Similarly, on the multilateral track, Israel was indeed expected to raise the issue of Jewish refugees from Arab countries in the deliberations of the working group on refugees, but clearly it was primarily designed to deal with the Palestinian refugees. And so, in sum, the shadow of that issue and of the Palestinian insistence on 'the right of return' hovered over a process in which the Palestinians, nonetheless, were relegated to junior or marginal status.[9]

In any event, much of potential significance did not happen in the negotiations that began in the immediate aftermath of the Madrid conference. In fact, by the spring of 1992, in anticipation of the Israeli general election, the entire Madrid process format came to a grinding halt.

Yitzhak Rabin began his second tenure as Israel's prime minister determined to put new life into this moribund Madrid process. Rabin, to say the least, was not particularly enamoured of the process as such. He did not believe in seeking comprehensive peace in one fell swoop, and much preferred incremental progress through bilateral negotiations with individual partners. Yet he also believed in (and eventually demonstrated) his ability to insert his own priorities into the Madrid formula.

Rabin conducted his election campaign on the assumption that peace with Syria was not feasible, and that Hafez al-Assad would not be ready to offer a peace package to meet his and Israel's own criteria. But he did expect, on the basis of his own experience in the late 1980s, that an interim agreement with the Palestinians could be obtained – an understanding that would offer autonomy to the Palestinians and a measure of separation to both sides and might therefore postpone resolution of the underlying issues to a future, unspecified date.

Instead, upon assuming power, Rabin was advised by the out-going secretary of state, James Baker, that Assad was in fact willing to sign a full-fledged peace treaty with Israel and that the Bush administration was prepared to invest a major effort to help obtain such a breakthrough accord. As a result the new prime minister revised his priorities and modified his peace strategy accordingly. He thus proceeded in the summer of 1992 to launch a two-pronged effort on both the Syrian and the Palestinian tracks. Although it was not explicitly stated as such, on the assumption that Rabin's government could muster public support domestically for one major deal, a competition of sorts was encouraged between the Syrian and Palestinian tracks.

During the following year two facts transpired. First, the Washington talks failed to produce a meaningful Israeli–Syrian give-and-take. It is true that some important beginnings were made in Washington but President Assad insisted on obtaining an Israeli commitment to full withdrawal from the Golan Heights as a precondition and he was not prepared to enter into any meaningful discussion on the terms of the peace he was willing to offer in return for such a full withdrawal by Israel. For both reasons Assad's approach was entirely unacceptable to Rabin. The result was a complete stalemate. Second, Rabin was no more successful in moving forward his idea of an interim agreement with the Palestinians. According to the Madrid ground rules the Palestinian delegation to the Washington talks was made up of individuals representing the population of the West Bank and the Gaza Strip whereas, in fact, the delegate members took their marching orders and detailed instructions directly from the PLO leadership in Tunis. Consequently, Yasser Arafat was totally successful in blocking any agreement which conspicuously failed to assign a formal role to the PLO or did not firmly link the interim agreement then under discussion in Washington to a final-status agreement.[10]

Against this backdrop, Rabin endorsed a secret channel with the PLO started by Foreign Minister Shimon Peres and his deputy Yossi Beilin. Conducted alongside the Washington talks, the Oslo channel produced by July 1993 the draft of an interim agreement for a five-year period. Consistent with Arafat's two minimal conditions, and in contrast to the formal Washington proceedings, the Oslo declaration of principles was negotiated with the PLO and was firmly linked to a final-status negotiation.[11]

Before authorizing this draft, though, Rabin made one more attempt at establishing whether a deal with Syria could still be made. In August 1993, he asked the new American secretary of state, Warren Christopher, to employ the 'hypothetical question' technique in order to find out whether, in return for full withdrawal from the Golan, Assad would be willing to sign a peace agreement modelled on the Israeli–Egyptian peace treaty of 1979. Rabin led Assad to understand that in the event of a positive Syrian response, he would offer the Palestinians a more modest agreement predicated on autonomy in Gaza.

In the event, Rabin was disappointed by Assad's response and chose to go ahead with the Oslo accord. This was a major turning-point in the history of both the Arab–Israeli conflict and the peace process because it established a framework for resolving the Palestinian dimension of the dispute while bringing about mutual recognition between Israel and Palestinian nationalism as embodied in the PLO. It also predicated that the next phase of the peace process should take place on the Israeli–Palestinian rather than Israeli–Syrian (and Lebanese) track.

Emotionally and conceptually, the Oslo gambit and the Washington signing ceremony represent a radical break with long-standing traditions and dogmas in Israeli policy. So much so that Rabin himself was assassinated by a person acting on his own but who, at the same time, reflected a significant body of opinion on the right wing of the Israeli political spectrum which castigated Rabin's policies as nothing short of an act of treason.

One measure of the revolutionary change in Israel's outlook in the aftermath of the Oslo accords is the comparatively recent adoption of a fresh perspective on the question known traditionally as 'the core of the conflict'. Now that Israel and Palestinian nationalism have legally and formally recognized each other and have established both political frameworks and diplomatic processes for working out a historic compromise, it encourages Israel to argue that the rest of the Arab world by right and by logic ought to emulate the Palestinians and follow suit in reconciling themselves to the Jewish state's existence and legitimacy.

Again, returning to the diplomatic front with Syria, obviously no truly comprehensive peace can be envisaged without an Israeli–Syrian agreement. Ostensibly, a great deal of progress could still be made in this direction precisely on the strength of the Oslo accords, as well as the subsequent autonomous Palestinian government instituted in a large part of the West Bank and the Gaza Strip.

One typical manifestation of the change in Israel's official view and presentation of this issue is the June 2000 newspaper article by David Dadon, director of the Maghreb, Syria and Lebanon department in the foreign ministry. Writing under the title 'On the Road to a Reconciliation with Algeria' Dadon, who served as Israel's diplomatic representative in Morocco, argues:

> another consideration, which applies to Morocco, Mauritania and Tunisia and possibly also to Algeria, is the will to recipro- cate for Israel's willingness to recognize the PLO and to solve the Palestinian problem. It should be emphasized that for the North African states the Palestinian track is different from the Syrian one. The Israel–Syria clash is a dispute between two sovereign states. When an agreement is signed between the two, no euphoria can be expected among the states of North Africa that would lead to an upgrading of relations. But the Palestinian problem is perceived by them as the core of the conflict between Israel and the Arab nation, and only rectifi- cation of the injustice inflicted on the Palestinian people by the establishment of the Jewish state could lead to acceptance of the [Jewish] state and to reconciliation between the peoples.[12]

## THE CRISIS OF THE PEACE PROCESS AND ITS AFTERMATH

Negotiations between Israel and the Syrians were suspended in June 1995, leaving the Middle East peace process to proceed along a dual track: formal, ongoing Israeli–Palestinian reconciliation together with the larger process of broader regional Israeli–Arab normalization. Nevertheless, to all intents and purposes the peace process initiated and conducted by Yitzhak Rabin's government reached its zenith in the autumn of 1995. In September of that year a second Israeli–Palestinian agreement was signed regarding further implementation of the Oslo accords in the West Bank. Then, in October, the second Middle Eastern economic conference was held in Amman – yet another landmark in Arab–Israeli normaliza- tion.

This gradual progression was effectively set back by a series of developments and the forces at work, in the region and inside Israel, most notably, Prime Minister Rabin's assassination, the wave of terrorist attacks by Palestinian opponents of the peace process, the fighting in South Lebanon and Benjamin Netanyahu's victory over Shimon Peres in the Israeli general elections of 1996. In the light of these reverses and developments it is more than a mere item of curiosity that during his brief tenure as Rabin's successor Shimon Peres, architect of the Oslo accords, chose to shift the primary focus of Israel's policies back to the Syrian track rather than maintaining, or accelerating, momentum on the Palestinian track. For, in November 1995, Peres opted to launch a bold effort to reach a full and comprehensive solution to the Arab–Israeli conflict within a matter of months.

What predicated and informed this strategy was the two-fold assumption that, in the first instance, an Israeli-Syrian deal could be successfully, and fairly swiftly, negotiated and that, in the second instance, Syria could then exercise its not inconsiderable prestige and influence in bringing most of the Gulf countries and the North African states to a signing event in Washington – all this, even in the absence of a final Israeli–Palestinian agreement. This option was chosen by Peres in preference to a quest for a final-status agreement with the Palestinians. An accord with Damascus might then serve as the cutting edge of a successful peace strategy to be confidently submitted to the Israeli public in the general elections scheduled for October 1996.

In retrospect, it is impossible to speculate on what were the prospects for a final-status negotiation with the Palestinians in early 1996 as compared with, or opposed to, a negotiation with Syria which, as we know, failed and, according to some commentators, was doomed to fail. Whatever else, this failure of the ambitious Peres strategy, exacerbated by the ruinous terrorist campaign of February–March 1996 in Jerusalem and Tel Aviv and the abortive 'Grapes of Wrath' military operation undertaken by Israel in Southern Lebanon in April 1996, provides the backdrop to Benjamin Netanyahu's electoral victory.

Before entering office, Netanyahu's original outlook on Israel's relationship with the Arab world, as reflected in his 1993 book *A Place Among the Nations* and in the earlier phases of his career, was conducive neither to the quest for a comprehensive settlement nor to assigning the Palestinian issue pride of position in his government's policies. Nevertheless, during the election campaign and in his first year in power Netanyahu was forced to endorse the Oslo accords as well as some of the ideas and policies they entailed. However, even these powerful objective constraints were effectively countered by three opposing forces: the policies the Likud nationalist government grudgingly pursued; Netanyahu's personal reservations about the wisdom of the course dictated by his two predecessors, Rabin and Peres; and the limitations imposed by the composition of the governing coalition. Factually, Netanyahu may have advanced the historic course of reconciling Israel to Palestinian nationalism by first signing, as Israel's prime minister and as leader of the country's right-wing, a specific agreement with regard to the city of Hebron and subsequently the larger Wye Agreement, but in both instances acquiescence was reluctant, implementation only partial.[13]

As documentary historians we may still lack definitive information on Netanyahu's dealings with Syria. But what we do know is that negotiations were conducted on his behalf by the American Jewish businessman Ronald Lauder in the autumn of 1998, and that the latter conveyed, according to his own testimony, readiness for full withdrawal from the Golan in the framework of an Israeli–Syrian peace. On the assumption that the Lauder episode represents a genuine effort by Netanyahu to reach an accommodation with Syria, it should also be viewed as yet another attempt to promote Israel's relationship with the Arab states as the principal track of the peace process and to de-emphasize the importance of the Palestinians and the Palestinian issue as the 'core' and 'key' to resolving the protracted Middle East dispute.

It is against this longer, 50-year background and evolutionary process that Ehud Barak came to power in 1999 with an ambitious plan to seek the ultimate, elusive comprehensive settlement. According to his own statements, he wanted to reach agreements on both the Syrian and the Palestinian track at one and the same time. He also had a clear sequence in mind: an agreement with Assad's Syria then a final-status agreement with the Palestinians. This choice rested on two principal considerations: that it would be comparatively less complicated and thus easier to reach an understanding with Syria in a matter of months, and that once reached, the Syrian agreement would improve Israel's posture and bargaining leverage *vis-à-vis* the Palestinians.

From our later perspective, it is clear that this ambitious design failed to clear its first phase. Almost the whole of Barak's first year in power was devoted to what proved to be abortive negotiations with Syria. With the collapse of that failure, Assad's death and complete withdrawal from South Lebanon, Israel under Barak proceeded to refocus policy and peace efforts towards reaching the final-status agreement with the Palestinians envisaged in the original Oslo accords.

The extreme complexities and uncertainties of that Palestinian negotiating track, exemplified by Camp David II in July 2000, work to restrain Israeli pronouncements regarding its deeper significance. If successful, Israel is likely to argue that the finality of the agreement and a Palestinian proclamation to that effect do represent the end of the conflict and that the lingering conflict with Syria is but a conventional bilateral, interstate territorial dispute that should, and will, be sorted out in due time. Alternatively, failure to reach full reconciliation and normalization with the Palestinians, whether marked by recurrent crises or by a long-term interim agreement, are equally likely to generate a tendency to play down once again the centrality of the Palestinian issue and the linkage between progress on the Palestinian track and Israel's overall relationship with the collective Arab states.

## NOTES

1. For Saunders's own perspective, see his book *The Other Walls* (Princeton, NJ, 1991).
2. Itamar Rabinovich, *Waging Peace* (New York, 1999) and 'Zionism and the Arab World', in S. J. Zipperstein and E. S. Frerichs (eds), *Zionism, Liberalism and the Future of the Jewish State* (Providence, RI, 2000), pp. 47–76.
3. Itamar Rabinovich, *The Road Not Taken* (New York and Oxford, 1991), pp. 111–67.
4. Yehoshifat Harkavi, *The Palestinians from Quiesence to Awakening* (in Hebrew) (Jerusalem, 1979).
5. Dan Schueftan, *The Jordanian Option* (in Hebrew) (Tel Aviv, 1986).
6. Walter Laqueur and Barry Rubin (eds), *The Israel–Arab Reader* (New York, 1984), p. 518.
7. William B. Quandt, *The Peace Process* (Washington, DC and Berkeley, CA, 1993).
8. Asher Susser, 'Jordan, the Intifada and the Palestinians – The Breaking Off', in A. Susser and G. Gilbar, *At the Core of the Conflict: The Intifada* (Tel Aviv, 1992), pp. 128–48.
9. Eytan Ben-Zur, *The Road to Peace Goes through Madrid* (in Hebrew) (Tel Aviv, 1997).
10. Itamar Rabinovich, *The Brink of Peace* (Princeton, 1998), pp. 85–119; and Itamar Rabinovich, *Waging Peace*, pp. 44–61.
11. Uri Savir, *The Process: 1100 Days that Changed the Middle East* (New York, 1998).
12. *Ha'aretz*, 13 June 2000.
13. Itamar Rabinovich, *Waging Peace*, pp. 83–127.

# 8 Israeli Intervention in Intra-Arab Affairs

## ZEEV MAOZ

### INTRODUCTION[1]

Immediately following the country's inception, Israel's leaders felt that Israelis were living in a double state of siege. First and foremost, the surrounding Arab states were violently hostile to the very idea of an independent Jewish state, as amply documented by their diplomatic resistance to the 1947 UN partition resolution, support for the Palestinian struggle against the resolution's implementation and invasion of Palestine on 14 May 1948.

Second, the Israeli leadership also felt relatively isolated on the global scene. While both the US and the Soviet Union immediately recognized the State of Israel, they had been unable to prevent the Arab invasion. The US also avoided any kind of direct military or economic support to the Jewish state. While allowing the Israelis to purchase weapons from Czechoslovakia, the Soviet Union was not overly active in providing either political or military support to the newly founded state. Finally, by 1950, a tripartite (American–British–French) declaration imposed an embargo on weapon sales to the Middle East, the principal victim of which was Israel. Against this background, and the failure to convert the 1949 armistice agreements that terminated the War of Independence into a series of peace treaties, key members of the Israeli leadership began to brace themselves for a protracted conflict with the Arab states.

The notion of a protracted conflict was less than popular in the wake of the 1948–49 war. Even less popular was the notion that this conflict would probably involve additional rounds of all-out war, thus requiring Israelis to make major sacrifices. Yet the political–military leadership, whose ideas were embodied in the basic convictions of Ben-Gurion regarding the nature of the Arab–Israeli conflict, assumed that if Israel were to survive this protracted conflict, it had to become both tenacious and inventive. Given the basic geographic, demographic and military asymmetries this conflict entailed, Israel had to devise original stratagems for surviving.[2]

One of these devices involved attempts at intervening in the domestic affairs of Arab states and the Palestinians. These efforts were carried out after the end of the War of Independence, and have been pursued to the present. Some of these interventions were of an ad hoc nature motivated by a desire to capitalize on opportunities that seemed to present themselves or to deal with what seemed imminent threats. Other interventions were long-term and systematic in nature.

While many of these episodes of direct or indirect interventions are documented in the writings of scholars and practitioners, there is a need for an analytic and comparative evaluation of this policy, as well as an assessment of the effectiveness and ramifications of the policy for Israel's security and foreign policy. Accordingly, this study seeks to examine the following issues:

1.  What were the objectives of these policies of intervention?

2.  How were they carried out? Specifically, to what extent were they subject to any kind of public or legislative scrutiny?

3.  To what extent did they accomplish the stated (or implicit) objectives?

4.  What were their short- and long-term implications for Israel's national security and diplomacy?

5.  Can we derive any systematic lessons from this tradition of intervention in the domestic affairs of rival states?

This study examines several operations and policies involving both direct and indirect intervention in intra-Arab affairs. Most – but not all – such operations were covert at the time, but all of them leaked out at one point or another.

Before discussing these episodes, it is instructive to define the key term of this study. Intervention in internal affairs of a foreign actor is a deliberate (overt or covert) use of intelligence, military, political or economic means aimed at affecting the policies and/or government of a foreign (-state or -substate) actor by aligning with, or manipulating groups within, that actor's internal environment.

This type of process is distinguished from military or political intervention in that it does not directly involve intergovernmental interaction. Rather, the government of one state – typically through its political or military services and intelligence agencies – operates within the other actor's social and political system in a manner intended to influence the makeup or policy of the other actor.[3] Intervention, as Jentelson and Levite[4] point out, differs from direct use of military force in two dimensions. First, in that the central objective concerns the opponent's authority structure as opposed to principal territorial objectives in warfare. Second, intervention entails a combination of political and military (or para-military) strategies, with emphasis on the former. In contrast to other studies that combine direct military intervention with indirect intervention, I focus on the latter, expanding the focus of intervention from the strictly military manipulation of actors in the target's internal setting to a broader range of manipulations. This expansion examines economic aid and technical advice, as well as seemingly humanitarian support (for example, medical) to groups within the target's domestic setting. Direct military intervention, in many cases, is an outgrowth of indirect intervention. Military intervention may become necessary when the covert or indirect forms of intervention either fail or drag the intervener deeper into the mess formed by the less direct forms of intervention.

The Israeli policy of intervention is examined here through a comparative study of several incidents. Table 1 provides the list of these incidents and their characteristics.[5]

TABLE 1: EPISODES OF ISRAELI INTERVENTION IN INTRA-ARAB AFFAIRS

| Year(s) | Nature of Episode | Consequences | Comments |
|---------|-------------------|--------------|----------|
| 1954 | Activation of an Israeli spy ring in sabotage operations in Egypt designed to prevent the planned British evacuation of the Suez Canal | The spy ring was caught by Egyptian police, British plans for withdrawal from the Canal not altered | |
| 1955–65 | Covert support to the Sudanese and Kurd rebellions | No noticeable effect on the outcome, eventual failure of the whole rebellion | |
| 1965–67 | Covert support to the North Yemenis in the Yemen civil war | War ends in a stalemate and political settlement | |

| Year(s) | Nature of Episode | Consequences | Comments |
|---------|-------------------|--------------|----------|
| 1976 | Municipal elections in the West Bank major cities, designed to defeat pro-PLO leaders and to maintain support for pro-Jordan cliques | Sweeping victories of pro-PLO leaders in most West Bank large cities | |
| 1975–2000 | Alliance with the Christian phalange in Lebanon designed to balance, and later to expel the PLO and the Syrians from Lebanon | Israel drawn by Christians into invasion of Lebanon, formation of Hizballah, withdrawal, security zone, decision on unilateral withdrawal | |
| 1981–87 | Formation of 'village leagues' in the West Bank; support of religious Muslim institutions and activities designed to counterbalance the PLO influence in the WB | Failure, emergence of Hamas, radicalization of Palestinian politics and rise of anti-Israeli and anti-peace forces | |

This study explores these incidents in terms of the issues raised by the questions. Each incident is discussed in terms of the reasoning underlying the Israeli policy of intervention and the choice of a particular strategy. The impact of Israel's policy on the eventual outcome of this process is examined, and implications are derived. Following the discussion of each incident, I provide a comparative evaluation of these policies, and discuss the implications of the Israeli interventionist approach.

The analysis of each of these episodes of intervention is not intended to be a comprehensive historical account. Rather, my aim is to explore the underlying rationale of the decision to intervene and to relate the process of intervention to its outcome. This would enable us to assess in a comparative fashion the advantages and liabilities of these interventions.

Since the aim of this study is to evaluate the policy of intervention in the domestic affairs of Arab states, understanding why Israel engaged in these processes provides us with only part of the puzzle. The question is whether, in the long run, Israel has learned something from its past adventures. For that purpose, we need to consider not only how the participants understood things at the time but also to understand whether Israel could have acted differently. We must also consider whether the results matched the short-term and long-range goals of Israel's national security.

## THE 'MISHAP': ISRAEL'S INTERVENTION IN EGYPTIAN POLITICS[6]

On 23 July 1952, a group of mid-level officers in the Egyptian armed forces staged a coup, overthrowing the constitutional monarch, King Farouq. This relatively bloodless coup, which turned out to be a 'revolution from above',[7] brought to power a seemingly radical junta that adopted a revolutionary, pan-Arab, anti-Israeli rhetoric. Many of these officers were known for their anti-British attitudes, and some had spent time in jail during the Second World War due to contacts with the approaching Nazi forces.

Topping this new regime's agenda was negotiating an agreement that would terminate British military control of the Suez Canal. These negotiations were seen by some elements in the Israeli security establishment as posing several major threats to Israel. In particular:

1. Removal of the British military buffer zone between Israel and Egypt;

2. Significant improvement of Egyptian military potential;

3. American military assistance to Egypt; and

4. Removal of the main obstacle to the Arab countries' joining in a regional defence pact.[8]

For these reasons, the conclusion of the Anglo-Egyptian negotiations was seen as a threat by the military and the foreign-policy establishment in Israel. The latter community – represented by the prime minister and foreign minister Moshe Sharett – viewed this as a problem calling for political and diplomatic assurances to compensate Israel for the deterioration in its regional position.[9] Sharett did not view Britain's prospective withdrawal as posing a clear and present military danger, in contrast to the prevailing perception within the security establishment.[10]

The difference of threat perceptions between the foreign and defence establishment was an indicator of a broader conflict of conceptions regarding the Arab–Israeli conflict as a whole. On the one hand, a moderate coalition, represented by various people in the foreign ministry and led by Moshe Sharett, believed that a political resolution of the conflict was possible, and that Israel had to exhaust diplomacy before it turned to the use of force.[11] On the other hand, a hard-line group, located principally at the defence ministry and the IDF, believed that developments in the Arab world were increasingly threatening, and that time was not in Israel's favour. Thus, Israel had to establish a resolute stand *vis-à-vis* the Arab world, and the use of force against Arab terrorists and those Arab states harbouring them was a necessary element in Israel's security.[12]

Along with the perceived threats associated with an imminent Anglo-Egyptian agreement, a set of opportunities also presented themselves. Intelligence information leaked to the Israelis told of a planning process in the British army to occupy Cairo by force – under the pretext of protecting British nationals – if attacks on British forces intensified. This concern with growing anti-British activities in Egypt was seen in Israel as a ray of hope. If the British grew sufficiently frustrated with the chaos along the Suez Canal and in the Cairo area, they might take military steps, thereby halting or indefinitely delaying the evacuation of the Canal zone.[13]

The threat of an escalation in Anglo-Egyptian relations during the first half of 1954 was sufficient to quell anti-British activities in Egypt, facilitating renewal of the Anglo-Egyptian negotiations. On 27 July 1954 an Anglo-Egyptian agreement on the transfer of the Canal zone to Egypt was initialled.

Preparations for activating the intelligence group in Egypt began in March 1954, and the actual operational order was given in early July. The first operation of the spy ring – the planting of bombs in the central post office in Alexandria – was conducted on 2 July, and the last operation – which brought about the exposure of the ring – was conducted in July. By early August the entire ring was exposed and arrested by the Egyptian police.[14]

The implications for Israeli–Egyptian relations were grave. Since 1953, secret negotiations through various channels had been conducted between Israel and the new regime in Egypt. The 'mishap' created a break in these negotiations. When the negotiations resumed in October 1954, the Israeli side added a new concern: trying to dissuade the Egyptians from issuing death sentences to members of the spy ring. Most importantly, however, this affair may have increased Egyptian suspicion of Israel's intentions and sincerity.

To this day, the decision to activate Unit 131 – the Israeli spy ring in Egypt – in a series of sabotage operations designed to slow down or prevent the Anglo-Egyptian alliance is fraught with controversy. The jury is still out on the question of whether the minister of defence, Pinhas Lavon, approved this order, or whether it was a strictly rogue operation initiated by the Director of Military Intelligence (DMI), Colonel Benjamin Givli.[15]

The DMI was not alone in his assessment of the threats the Anglo-Egyptian agreement posed to Israel, although he may have been alone in assuming that a series of terrorist operations by an Israeli spy ring could possibly reverse the course of political events in Egypt. Yet despite the abysmal failure of this operation and despite its grave implications, it did set a precedent for other covert interventions in intra-Arab affairs.

## INTERVENTIONS IN SUDAN AND KURDISTAN[16]

These cases are a part of a broader conception of cooperation with elements in the Middle East providing some sort of regional balance against the anti-Israeli Arab world. As Black and Morris wrote:

> The method was to break through [Israel's] regional isolation by forging links on the edges of the Middle East with non-Arab regimes that were deeply concerned, for their own reasons, by the spread of Nasserism and Communism.[17]

In the words of Isser Harel, the all-powerful head of the civilian intelligence services (Mossad and Shin Bet) at the time, 'my aim was to build a dam against the Nasserist–Soviet flood'.[18]

The Sinai war of October–November 1956 had paradoxical implications for Israel's foreign and security policy. Nasser was able to convert his military defeat into inter-Arab political capital. He emerged as a regional hero who had confronted an imperialist coalition including Israel, France and the United Kingdom, and emerged politically victorious. The wave of Nasserism that seemed to have swept the Middle East evoked grave concerns in Israel. The spread of radical pan-Arab fervour into other Middle Eastern states was fuelled also by a growing degree of subversive activity by pro-Nasserist elements in Jordan, Syria, Lebanon and Iraq.[19] The Israeli political response to this trend, the outer-tier policy, consisted of several projects of cooperation with the ruling élites in peripheral non-Arab states, principally Turkey, Iran and Ethiopia. However, since these efforts entailed intergovernmental relations and were conducted quite overtly, they are not examined in this study.

The efforts in Sudan and Kurdistan were based on a variation on the general periphery strategy theme. The plan in these cases was to support opposition groups, thereby weakening and sabotaging the ruling regimes in peripheral countries. It is interesting to note that little evidence exists of active projects aimed at subverting the governments of the surrounding Arab states.[20]

### Sudan

The underlying rationale of the Sudanese and Kurdish interventions was the simple concept of 'the enemy of my enemy is my friend'. Neither Iraq nor Sudan constituted a clear and present danger to Israel's security. Yet these states' support of the Egyptian-led anti-Israeli front was sufficient to induce Israeli leaders to support domestic opposition in these states in the hope that this would serve Israel's interests.

The south Sudanese rebellion against the government was an ethnic and religious clash between the Muslim north and the black, mostly Christian, south. The socialist government in Sudan adopted highly oppressive policies *vis-à-vis* the southern regions. This oppression peaked with the expulsion of the Christian missionaries in 1963–64. Various political groups in the south formed a para-military guerrilla movement, named Anya Nya, which led the military struggle against the central government in Khartoum.[21]

There is little direct evidence on the scope, extent and duration of the Israeli support given to the Anya Nya rebels in southern Sudan. However, it appears that the rebels received both weapons and direct training by Israeli experts. This support was clandestine and highly restricted. It is also not clear to what extent the Israeli political leadership was in the loop of this particular operation. Because of the limited nature of this operation, it had little effect on the Sudanese civil war. This war lasted ten years, until the central government and the rebels in Sudan reached some sort of accommodation in 1972, granting the southern region a substantial degree of autonomy.[22] At any rate, the intervention in Sudan had little or no impact on the outcome; it was too small and too limited to have any effect on the rebels' capacity or their combat-effectiveness. Fortunately for Israel, the military aid was largely uncovered by the Sudanese government, probably owing to the decision of the Khartoum government not to make an issue of it.

## Kurdistan

The Kurdish struggle for autonomy from various occupiers is centuries-old. However, its more recent incarnation centred on a struggle against the Iraqi state. The leader of this struggle was Mullah Mustafa Barazani, who began a series of guerrilla campaigns in 1942.[23] This struggle lasted for almost two decades and was inconclusive. Fighting from mountainous bases in Kurdistan, the Kurds managed to survive several direct and indirect (subversive) attempts by various Iraqi regimes to crush the rebellion, but they were not sufficiently strong to convert this staying power into a political decision.

Among the principal difficulties that the Kurds confronted, none was more frustrating than the quest for outside allies. Barazani explored various avenues for securing practical support for the Kurdish struggle, going to Iran and Turkey and later to the superpowers. The Shah of Iran agreed to provide shelter to Barazani and his people, but no more than that. Barazani's efforts to receive support from the United States proved futile, but his approach to the Soviet Union was more successful. After a long walk through Iran and Turkey – reminiscent of the Chinese long journey of 1927 – Barazani and his people reached the Soviet Union, where they stayed and received shelter and training over a period of 11 years (1947–58).

Following the 1958 *coup d'état* in Iraq, Barazani decided to return to Iraq. A major trigger of this decision was a pledge from Abd Al-Kader Qassem, the coup's leader, to recognize Kurdish autonomy.[24] In practice, however, the Iraqis engaged in a concentrated 'divide-and-rule' strategy aimed at splitting the Kurdish national movement. In addition, actions against Kurdish newspapers and Kurdish activists indicated to Barazani that the Iraqis had never intended to allow the Kurds to acquire autonomy.[25]

In late 1959, a number of Kurdish guerrilla units in the mountains of Kurdistan began a series of raids against Iraqi military targets. By 1961, the Kurdish activities intensified considerably, amounting to a *de facto* guerrilla war. By 1962, the Kurds had an army of 15–20,000 fighters equipped with light weapons and short-range artillery.[26] Despite this guerrilla activity, the Kurds encountered major difficulties in acquiring weapons and ammunition. They lacked professional training and medical supplies.

Following the 1963 coup led by Abd al-Salam Arif, an effort was made to initiate talks leading towards an Iraqi–Kurdish agreement. However, it soon became evident to the Kurdish negotiator, Talabani, that the Iraqis had no intention of accepting the Kurdish notion of autonomy. At that point, the Kurdish rebellion reached full speed, as the Kurds began to develop unilateral state-like institutions.[27]

Israeli–Kurdish ties began in the late 1950s through clandestine contacts in Paris. In 1963, Badir Khan conducted a series of meetings in Israel with Ben-Gurion and other officials. The deliberations in Israel regarding the form and scope of support to the Kurds entailed various considerations. First, Israeli–Kurdish relations were seen in the context of Israeli–Iranian relations. The Iranians developed an interest in a limited but protracted Kurdish–Iraqi war.[28] Accordingly, they encouraged limited Israeli support to the Kurds so 'as to keep the flame [of rebellion] burning, but not to convert it into an uncontrollable blaze'.[29]

The first decision to provide extensive aid to the Kurds was made on 15 April 1965. The first aeroplane with Israeli weapons reached Tehran a few days later. Several considerations brought about this decision. First, this aid fitted very well into the policy of a 'dam against Nasserism and communism'. By 1965, the Iraqi regime was vehemently pro-communist and anti-Western, siding with the more radical elements in the Arab world. Second, this aid also assisted Israeli–Iranian relations. The Kurdish rebellion reduced the capacity of the Iraqi regime to embark on adventures against Iran.[30] Third, an effective guerrilla war in Kurdistan would have the effect of reducing substantially the Iraqi military capability allocated to the Arab–Israeli conflict.

Between 1965 and 1967, the Kurds received weapons ranging from small firearms and munitions to long-range and anti-tank artillery. Israeli military advisers trained the Kurds, providing both direct tactical advice and strategic planning to the Kurdish leaders. There were also several Israeli medical teams. During this period, various Israeli officials, including Meir Amit, the head of Mossad, and Rehavam Zeevi, then head of the IDF planning division, visited Barazani in Kurdistan.[31]

The expectation that the Kurds would help prevent Iraqi forces from being dispatched to the Israeli borders at times of crisis was tested during the May–June 1967 crisis. In the heat of the crisis, efforts were made to persuade Barazani to put military pressure on Iraq so as to prevent it from dispatching forces to Jordan. Meir Amit 'tried to convince Mullah Mustafa to start some sort of front against the Iraqis, to put some sort of [military] pressure on the Iraqis that would prevent them from transferring forces to the front against Israel. He [Barazani] did not say no, but in practice did very little.'[32] At the same time, Barazani resisted Iraqi demands to declare solidarity with the Arabs and even to expel the Israeli advisers.[33]

Following the 1968 coup, Saddam Hussein initiated negotiations with the Kurds. Hussein's ambitions resided in the east and south, and the enemy was Iran. An agreement with the Kurds would facilitate an Iraqi military move in the Persian Gulf. In March 1970, Hussein and Barazani signed an agreement granting the Kurds 'territorial autonomy'. However, as in previous cases, the Iraqi–Kurdish *rapprochement* was soon converted into a new anti-Kurd campaign. Indeed, another Iraqi attempt to assassinate Barazani on 29 September 1971 failed. In November 1971, the Iraqis prepared their forces for an all-out attack on the Kurdish areas.

Despite a growing rift between Iran and Iraq during 1971 and 1972 (against the background of an Iranian occupation of three islands in the Persian Gulf), the Iraqis kept the military pressure on the Kurds via sporadic aerial attacks and occasional armoured and infantry incursions. Repeated visits by key Israeli intelligence and military officers to Kurdistan and return visits by Kurdish leaders to Israel intensified this relationship. In 1972, Moshe Dayan, the Israeli defence minister, authorized the transfer to the Kurds of Soviet-made T-34 tanks and several Kurdish tank crews received training in Israel.[34]

The story of the Kurdish–Israeli dialogue before the 1967 war repeated itself in 1973. At the height of the war, Mossad and IDF representatives requested Barazani to intensify military operations so as to prevent or slow down the dispatch of Iraqi troops to the Syrian front. Barazani was sympathetic to Israeli requests, but in practice did nothing to help. Nahum Admoni, then the head of the major operational department in Mossad, noted, 'We expected that [the Kurds] would do something, however minimal, to stop any Iraqi force from leaving for the front, but they let us down'.[35]

This did not in any way affect Israeli aid to the Kurds, as these relations were not based on sympathies but on perceived interests. On the contrary, the Iraqi involvement in the Yom Kippur War as well as the seemingly growing rift between Iraq and Iran[36] intensified Israeli interest in the Kurdish rebellion. By 1974, Kurdish forces were estimated at 40,000–50,000, with additional paramilitary groups roughly the same size.[37] Short of tanks, the Kurds had ample weapons including medium- and short-range artillery. The Israeli involvement in training and operational planning mounted.

In April 1974, Saddam Hussein ordered a major Iraqi campaign against the Kurds. Coupled with an economic blockade of Kurdish areas and massive aerial bombardments, the Iraqis made considerable strides, causing floods of refugees. However, by September, the Iraqi attack was repelled. In a series of battles, planned and overseen by Israeli officers, the Kurds accomplished a major victory causing the Iraqis over 7,000 fatalities.[38]

The Iraqis managed to make some territorial strides but the price they paid was exorbitant. By the fall of 1974, however, secret Iraqi–Iranian talks resumed in Istanbul. The trigger to these talks was the military stalemate in Kurdistan. In March 1975, the Shah of Iran and Saddam Hussein reached an agreement over the Shat-al-Arab. The Iraqis made major concessions to Iran and formally accepted Iran's occupation of the three islands in the Gulf. The Iranian *quid pro quo* was relinquishing their support of the Kurdish rebellion in Iraq. This also terminated the Israeli ability to help the Kurds, as Iran was the only access route to Kurdistan for both weapons and Israeli experts. Without the Irani–Israeli umbilical cord that provided the political, military and economic lifeline to the Kurd rebellion, the rebellion collapsed. Barazani fled the country to find refuge in Tehran.

In retrospect, the record of Israeli support for, and involvement in, the Kurdish rebellion suggests a twofold failure. First, the Israelis obtained very little in return. At times of need – particularly during the May–June 1967 crisis and during the 1973 Yom Kippur War – the Kurds failed to repay the enormous debt they owed to Israel in real and tangible terms. The Kurds refused to put military pressure on Iraq in order to prevent, slow down or sabotage the dispatch of Iraqi troops to the front. At the height of the rebellion (in 1974), the Kurds forced the Iraqis to concentrate three infantry divisions and one armoured division. The Israeli advisers to Barazani estimated the Iraqi forces facing them at about 85,000 troops, 600 tanks and over 200 aeroplanes.[39] The fact that the

Kurdish rebellion was the principal motivator of Iraqi concessions to the Shah in 1975 clearly suggests that, had Barazani wanted to do so, he would have been able to hamper seriously the Iraqi involvement in the 1967 and 1973 wars.

Second, it is quite possible that the Israeli involvement in the Kurdish rebellion, which had been an open secret since the mid-1960s, had an adverse effect on the chances of the Kurds to obtain a decent deal from the Iraqi government. The Israeli involvement served to create greater Iraqi hostility to Kurdish demands. The Kurds were seen as traitors for cooperating with the Israelis. Concomitantly, the Israeli financial and military support to Barazani served to intensify Kurdish demands. This aid led the Kurds to believe that they were stronger, internally and externally, than they really were. This perception of power also generated stronger incentives of the central Iraqi government to quell the rebellion; a victory by the Kurds would be a victory for Israeli money, advisers and weapons.

Most importantly, Israel became entangled between two allies – the Iranians and Kurds – who were themselves walking a tight-rope and holding a balancing rod that was itself very slippery. As long as the rift between Iraq and Iran was open, Iran had an interest in destabilizing the Iraqi regime. However, the Kurds in Iraq were the brothers of the Iranian Kurds, who had even less rights and autonomy than the Iraqi Kurds. A success of the Kurdish rebellion in Iraq would have had major ramifications for Iran. Once the Shah decided to make peace with Iraq, the Kurds became dispensable. Israel had to decide whether to stick with its Kurdish allies or with its seemingly powerful ally – at the time its key oil supplier – in Iran. The decision was not difficult to make. The Kurds were abandoned.

## THE MUNICIPAL ELECTIONS OF 1976

The growing influence and political prestige of the PLO following the 1974 speech by Arafat in the United Nations had important implications for politics among the Palestinians in the occupied West Bank and Gaza Strip. Israeli military intelligence (AMAN) and the security service (Shin-Bet) estimated that the moderate, pro-Jordan Palestinian leaders in the West Bank and Gaza were fast losing popularity. The political strides of the PLO in the occupied territories presented a major threat to the clan structure of the 'moderate' leadership.[40]

The 1972 municipal elections maintained in power pro-Jordanian leaders in the major cities of the West Bank and Gaza.[41] The mayors of most West Bank cities were pro-Hashemite, and were interested in relatively peaceful coexistence with the Israeli military government. While there had been no official Israeli policy regarding the future of the West Bank and Gaza, the government followed a policy consistent with the basic principles of the Allon plan that envisioned the transfer of most densely populated areas in the West Bank to Jordan in the context of a peace treaty.

The pro-Jordanian municipal leadership and most officials in the West Bank accepted their pay from Jordan. This created a fundamental dependence between the West Bank leadership and Jordan, a dependence that was seen as having a moderating influence on the population.

Israeli decision-makers faced a dilemma. The Jordanian law, according to which things were run in the West Bank (and extended to Gaza which had been under Egyptian law prior to its occupation in 1967), required municipal elections every four years. Yet the growing popularity of the PLO put the heat on the local leadership. The conservative mayors were opposed to the elections, fearing that they would be defeated by 'nationalist' contenders.

The Israeli defence minister, Shimon Peres, believed that if the elections could be handled in such a way as to ensure that at least the mayors of some of the large cities would be re-elected, then this would legitimize their position considerably, thus handing a political defeat to the PLO. The estimate was that PLO supporters would not win in more than a third of the contested municipalities.[42] Even if the PLO did gain some support in this election, Peres believed that the new mayors could be 'channelled' into local management issues, which would divert them from nationalist activity.[43]

This assessment was based on several considerations. First, the basic idea of municipal elections was part of a larger Israeli programme of granting increased municipal autonomy to local leaders. This plan was designed to dilute rising nationalistic aspirations especially among younger Palestinians.[44] Second, the Israelis believed that new legislation granting voting rights to women and to people lacking any property would add a conservative element to the electorate. This new element was seen as offsetting growing support for the PLO among younger voters.[45]

Finally, in order to ensure the re-election of the conservative mayors, the Israeli military administration expelled to Lebanon some of the radical candidates who threatened the conservative leadership. Thus, on 23 March 1976 the Israelis expelled Dr Hamzi Natsha, a candidate for mayor in Hebron, and Dr Abd al-Azziz from El Bireh. 'This hasty move...that was taken while the Israeli supreme court was scheduled to review the petition of the individuals expelled, invoked a new wave of students' demonstrations [in the West Bank]...One could hypothesize that this move gave the final push for the ultimate victory of the nationalistic candidates in the municipal elections of April 1976.'[46]

The Israeli effort to manipulate Palestinian politics was carried out in the almost full knowledge of what was going on within the local population. The effort to legitimize a group of leaders through a mix of democratic and oppressive tactics and to manipulate democracy in a manner consistent with Israeli goals backfired. Not only was the heavy Israeli hand felt throughout the election campaign, in some instances – such as the expulsion of nationalistic leaders – this hand turned into a weapon directed at the one using it. The seemingly stupid, innocent, uneducated, and patriarchal Palestinian population outwitted the seemingly sophisticated, experienced and highly educated Israels.


## THE RISE OF HAMAS

The march of folly in the occupied territories entered a new phase with the rise to power of the Likud government in 1977. Labour's policy had aimed at blocking the PLO in order to leave some space for a future settlement with Jordan. In contrast, the Likud, headed by the hard-liner Menachem Begin, perceived the PLO as a bitter enemy for its own sake. The Likud did not have a clear vision of the future of the West Bank. Begin was aware that an attempt to annex it would bring about enormous international pressure on Israel. Yet he was ideologically committed to Israeli control of the West Bank, and this commitment translated into support for Jewish settlement in the area.

However, the growing Palestinian population required some sort of leadership. Begin and his new defence minister, Ezer Weizman, inherited the nationalist West Bank leadership that came to power in 1976, and had to deal with it as a democratically elected leadership. There was an urgent need to curb or slow down the

PLO's influence in the West Bank.[47] The Likud developed a two-track strategy. First, the new minister of agriculture, Ariel Sharon, pursued an aggressive settlement policy.[48] The number of Jewish settlers in the West Bank grew from less than 5,000 in 1977 to over 25,000 in 1983. At the same time, the defence ministry kept up its efforts to find a more moderate local leadership with whom it could interact. One project consisted of attempts to form alternative municipal authorities for the perceived radical mayors in the West Bank. A second project was to provide support for religious groups in the Gaza Strip to divert the frustration of the Gaza population in to welfare and religious activities rather than nationalistic ones.

The project focusing on alternative Palestinian leadership centred on the establishment of village leagues, first around the Hebron area, and later in other areas of the West Bank.[49] The formation of the village leagues took place against the background of the Israeli–Egyptian peace negotiations and the Begin autonomy plan. These developments invoked a great deal of concern among the Palestinians in the West Bank and Gaza, namely, that a deal would be imposed them against their will. The aggressive settlement policy of the new Likud government and its harsh treatment of the nationalistic mayors further fuelled this concern.

Throughout the Israeli–Egyptian peace and autonomy talks, growing tension in the occupied territories led to occasional outbreaks of civil unrest in the cities and to terrorist activity in Israel proper. The military government responded by arresting some of the local mayors (such as Bassam Shakah of Nablus in 1979) and expelling others (Kwassma of Hebron and Milhem of Halhoul). These activities backfired. Acts of terrorism intensified and meshed with a growing level of popular unrest, demonstrations and other acts of protest. The Israelis knew that at some point or another they would have to allow local Palestinian representatives to participate in the talks, but the nationalist mayors were not seen as real partners.

The idea to turn to the conservative elements in the West Bank – headed by Mohammed Doudin, a former minister of labour and welfare in the Jordanian government – originated during the first term of the Begin administration, under the auspices of defence minister Weizman. However, it was upgraded after the resignation of Moshe Dayan in October 1980 and Ezer Weizman in May 1981. From May 1980 to June 1981, as Dayan and Weizman's impact on government policy gradually diminished, Begin relied increasingly on the advice of the chief of staff, Rafael Eytan. Eytan believed in an iron-fist policy in order to crush Palestinian nationalism. This was strictly a military policy, and was not accompanied by political action on the part of the military or civilian administration in the West Bank and Gaza.[50]

Sharon's entry into the defence ministry following the 1981 elections in Israel fundamentally changed Israel's policy towards the Palestinians in general, and the PLO in particular. Sharon saw the PLO as the major threat to Israel, given that the Israeli–Egyptian treaty promised to remove Israel's major strategic enemy. In his view, the ascendance of the PLO threatened not only Israeli interests in the occupied territories, but also created a potential for escalation elsewhere. The nationalist mayors and the National Guidance Committee (NGC) that shaped Palestinian policy in the occupied territories[51] were seen as the local representatives of the PLO in the occupied territories. But, unlike Eytan, Sharon realized that attempting to crush the NGC without finding a local political alternative might backfire. Accordingly, he decided to upgrade the village league, in parallel with disbanding the NGC. First, he used Doudin's village league in the Hebron area as a model for establishing additional unions, based on Hammula leaders, in rural parts of the West Bank.[52] Simultaneously, he separated the civilian and the military administration in the occupied territories, and initiated actions, including deliberate political provocations, designed to terminate the nationalistic hold over the municipal councils in the West Bank.[53]

The aims of this policy were difficult to conceal, but reaction to it managed to unite the PLO, the local nationalist mayors and Jordan for the first time since the Rabat summit of 1974. The opposition to these policies took place at several levels. First, the heads of the newly established village leagues received repeated death threats. Several attempts were made on Doudin's life. On 17 November 1981, Youssuf Khatib, the head of the village union in the Ramallah area, was shot dead. The PLO claimed responsibility.

Second, virtually all of the Palestinian leaders in the West Bank and Gaza, as well as communications by the PLO headquarters in Lebanon, called for the boycotting of the village leagues. Jordan's prime minister, Moudar Badran, echoed this call in March 1982, threatening a death sentence on anyone who joined one of these leagues. By the time Israel invaded Lebanon in June 1982, two things happened in the West Bank. The nationalist mayors were all thrown out of office by the new civil administration, and were replaced by Israeli officers. The village leagues ceased to function, living in name only. The civilian administration, which sought to improve the standard of living of Palestinians in the West Bank, was left without Palestinian partners.

The Israeli invasion of Lebanon and the forced departure of the PLO leadership from Beirut in 1982 had two, opposing effects on the population in the occupied territories. On the one hand, the iron-first policy and the aggressive policy of settlement and land expropriations under Sharon caused substantial resentment. At the same time, the lack of a local leadership and the defeat of the PLO in Beirut caused many Palestinians, especially among the youngest and poorest (the highest concentration of whom was in the Gaza Strip), grave disappointment with the PLO. Many young Palestinians sought refuge in religious practice. This growing religious activity was seen as a positive development by the Israeli defence establishment, as it suggested a weakening of the PLO position in the occupied territories.[55]

A similar view was adopted by Jordan, which had perceived the PLO and Palestinian nationalism in the occupied territories as a threat to its status and position.[56] The logic was that if enough money were funnelled into religious and social activities, and if the younger generation turned to religious activity, there would be less appeal to nationalist activity. This concept was also based on a feeling that the PLO represented a secular force in general. Some of the member organizations of the PLO and the communist party in the West Bank were seen as having Marxist leanings. Shaliyeh[57] provides a cogent account of the growth of the Islamic movement in the Gaza Strip and especially in the West Bank.

The radical ideology of the Islamic movement was far more anti-Israeli and anti-settlement than that of the PLO. Yet it was not seen as a threat by the Israeli authorities for several reasons. First, the Islamic fundamentalists initiated relatively few terrorist activities before the outbreak of the *intifada* in 1987.[58] Second, there were objective difficulties in using oppressive measures against this movement because of the risk of being portrayed as anti-Islamic.[59] Third, for the first time since 1981, Israel found common ground for cooperation with Jordan. Given the resentment in the Arab world of the Israeli invasion of Lebanon, the emergence of a seemingly common interest with Jordan was seen as an asset. Above all, however, the Islamic movement lacked a clear organizational structure. It was seen as a loose, ill-structured organization. In contrast to other organizations in the occupied territories, which represented a major threat by virtue of their ability to convert a political decision into military or political action on the ground, the Islamic movement was not considered a significant threat.

When the *intifada* broke out in December 1987, Sheikh Ahmed Yassin brought together a number of leaders from Gaza and the West Bank and formed Hamas. Before the Israeli military and civilian administration understood what had hit them, Hamas took over the streets as well as the bulk of the anti-Israeli military activity, raising the level of public protest and military activity to suicidal terrorism, something hitherto unknown in the occupied territories. The Israelis helped to create the monster with which they have had to cope up to the present day.

Israeli attempts to manipulate Palestinian politics in the occupied territories are particularly perplexing. Presumably Israel had both the power and information to conduct a more sagacious policy. Naïvety, stupidity or ignorance cannot explain Israeli's reliance on military and economic bullying, on the one hand, and its inability to understand the social and political trends among the Palestinians, on the other. It is also difficult to find a single explanation for the municipal election of 1976, the establishment of the village leagues in 1981, and the support for the Islamic fundamentalist movement in 1981–87. However, overriding the many specific considerations that influenced each of these policies was a notion that Israel could mould the Palestinian population in the West Bank in a way that served her interests. These episodes illustrate not only the futility of these notions, but also their paradoxical implications: each of these policies helped bring about the very outcomes they sought to prevent.

## THE LEBANESE QUAGMIRE[60]

The forced expulsion of the PLO from Jordan in 1970 moved most of the PLO guerrillas to Lebanon. The volume of infiltrations to Israel from Lebanon increased markedly compared with previous years. Over the months between 1971 and October 1973, 21 Israelis – civilian and soldiers – died and 59 were wounded by infiltrations from Lebanon. Between the end of the Yom Kippur war and the end of 1975, 83 Israelis were killed and over 200 wounded by infiltrations from Lebanon (including the well-known hostage operations of Ma'alot, the Savoy Hotel in Tel Aviv, Naharia and Misgav-Am).[61]

Israel, for its part, stepped up its retaliatory policy in Lebanon, including a raid on Beirut airport and multiple raids on PLO bases and strongholds in the country. Israeli retaliatory activity culminated in the May 1973 raid on PLO and PFLP headquarters in Beirut and the assassination of key guerrilla leaders (an operation nicknamed 'the Spring of Youth'). Yet the PLO's influence in Lebanon grew to such a degree that the Lebanese government seemed to have lost its ability to curb its activity and prevent Israeli retaliatory raids. In the early 1970s and more so after 1973, the Israeli air force became increasingly involved in bombing PLO bases in various parts of Lebanon.

However, until the outbreak of the Lebanese civil war in 1974, Israeli clandestine activity in Lebanon was limited to typical intelligence-gathering work through both electronic and human means. Occasionally there were secret meetings between Israeli agents and Lebanese leaders, but there was no actual Israeli involvement in Lebanese policies. In contrast to Israel's other neighbours, Lebanon was still seen as posing a relatively low threat to Israel's security.

The outbreak of the civil war in Lebanon posed both threats and opportunities to Israel's security.[62] The collapse of the central government in Beirut meant the absence of a powerful central authority that was able and willing to curb PLO activity in Lebanon. On the other hand, depending on the outcome of the war, this could present an opportunity to reassert a strong government in a country that had gradually lost its ability to control itself. If such a new government were more pro-Israeli (or less anti-Israeli) than previous governments, this might reduce the basic security threats emanating from Israel's northern boundary.[63]

The Syrian decision to intervene in Lebanon was seen as having net benefits in terms of the Israel–PLO relationship. Indeed, for the most part the Syrian presence in the country helped reduce the extent of PLO activity from Lebanon. Between 1976 and 1978, PLO activities emanating in Lebanon declined both in number and in severity compared to the previous five years.[64] In 1978, a terrorist raid emanating from Lebanon resulted in the deaths of 38 Israelis. This provoked a major Israeli military operation in southern Lebanon (the Litani operation), which again calmed things down considerably.

Throughout this time, Israeli intelligence developed strong ties with the Christian militias, especially the Christian Phalanges led by the Gemayel family. These ties involved typical interventionist tactics: supply of weapons, tactical advice, intelligence- sharing and so forth. In southern Lebanon a Christian paramilitary force headed by Major Sa'ad Haddad developed strong ties with the Israelis.[65] The support given to the Christians during the Rabin administration (1975–77) and first Begin administration (1977–81) was limited. However, in April 1981, owing to a Christian provocation in the Mount Sanin–Zahle area, the Syrians introduced helicopters into south Lebanon in violation of the 'red lines' agreement of 1976.[66] There was a major crisis when Israel shot down two Syrian helicopters and the Syrians responded by introducing surface-to-air (SAM) missiles into Lebanon in flagrant violation of the 'red lines' agreement. Israel was on the verge of escalating the incident, by launching an aerial raid designed to destroy Syrian SAM batteries, but was prevented from doing so at the last moment.[67]

When Ariel Sharon was appointed defence minister, Israeli policy towards Lebanon in general and the Christians in particular underwent a major change. Rabin and Weizman viewed the Christians as a minority that required some help in the form of clandestine cooperation or humanitarian support. Sharon viewed them as principal players in a grand scheme. This scheme consisted of four principal goals:

1. Pushing the PLO out of Lebanon;

2. Pushing the Syrians out of Lebanon;

3. Restoring a strong central government in Lebanon headed by a Christian president;

4. Signing a peace treaty between Israel and Lebanon.[68]

In order to accomplish these goals, Sharon had to rely on the full cooperation of the Christian Phalanges. Thus, in February 1982, Sharon and Bashir Gemayel, the leader of the Phalanges, signed a treaty detailing the nature of military cooperation between Israel and the Phalanges in the course of the coming war. According to this agreement, Israeli forces would reach Beirut from the south and east, and the Christians would occupy the northern and western parts of the Lebanese capital and attack the PLO headquarters located in the city. At that point, it would be possible to call for a presidential election and have Bashir Gemayel elected president of Lebanon.

The plan worked quite well, although with some glitches, such as a prolonged siege of West Beirut and US pressure on Israel. However, no sooner was the scheme completed then it began to crumble. The assassination of Bashir Gemayel on 12 September 1982 and the subsequent bloodbath in the Sabra and Shatilla refugee camps ultimately brought about the resignation of Sharon as defence minister. Israeli forces in Lebanon encountered growing resentment from groups that had initially welcomed them, most importantly the Shi'ites in south Lebanon.

Several Lebanese groups had viewed both the PLO and the Syrians as a major problem, preventing the country's recovery from the civil war. The prospect of forcing the Palestinians and Syrians out of the country was welcomed. Thus, these groups had initially welcomed Israel's invasion of Lebanon. However, once they realized the scheme was to impose a Christian-dominated government, the threat of Christian domination was perceived as more ominous than the threat of a Syrian or PLO presence. The fact that this kind of government would rest on Israeli occupation was even more threatening. Thus, without prior coordination, an anti-Christian and anti-Israeli coalition began to form in Lebanon. This coalition served to drive Israel out of Lebanon.[69]

Towards 1984, once it became evident that the May 1983 non-aggression agreement it had signed with Lebanon was not worth the paper on which it had been printed, Israel started redeploying its troops to the south of Beirut and Sidon. In the process, it indicated clearly that, in order to ensure that the southern part of Lebanon would not become a basis for terrorism against Israel, a strong pro-Israeli element would have to be developed there. The Israelis began to establish a local militia, under the command of Christian Lebanese officers, which would take charge of law and order in that part of the country.[70] This, of course, invoked a great degree of resentment among the Shi'ite population in the south.

Hizballah was an outgrowth of Israeli policies in south Lebanon following its invasion of the country. Specifically, Israel attempted to impose a system of governance in the south which was seen as an anathema by many of the Shiite inhabitants of the area.[71] When Israel decided to withdraw from Lebanon, it left a substantial contingent of its own troops which served to mobilize elements in the Shi'ite population against it. Consequently, the bitter struggle between Israel and the Hizballah, a struggle that had not existed before Israel's invasion of Lebanon but one which rages to this very day, became a major problem for Israel. This struggle has thus far resulted in over 400 Israeli soldiers dead since 1984, and an enormous economic and political cost.

The Lebanese quagmire is perhaps an extreme example of how a low-key attempt to manipulate internal affairs in a neighbouring state can pull the intervening actor deep into an unmanageable mess, and how disastrous this interventionist policy can turn out to be. The alliance with the Christians may well have been ill-conceived from the start; not only did the Phalanges fail to fulfil their part of the bargain during the war, it was preposterous to suppose that such an alliance would bring a cure to this war-torn country. It was ludicrous to expect that it would somehow work to Israel's benefit. We now turn to a more general assessment of this practice of intervention in intra-Arab affairs.

CONCLUSION

Israeli efforts at manipulating Arab and Palestinian politics offer a saga of repeated disasters. In none of the cases discussed here is there evidence that Israel achieved goals that had been at the heart of the intervention effort. This chapter provides a series of illustrations amounting to a 'march of folly'.

A great deal of thought and human and material effort was invested in making some of these interventions work; yet had a fraction of this effort been expended on analysing our past performance, considerable damage might have been averted in subsequent efforts. Why Israel kept trying to divide the Arab world or to deepen the divisions within Arab states appears clear in the light of the 'periphery' theory developed by Ben-Gurion and adapted by his successors. Unfortunately, in the process, policy-makers never stopped to reassess the applicability of this theory to intervention in the internal affairs of neighbours. Exactly why no meaningful learning took place regarding the outcomes of these interventionist policies is a question that should be addressed in a wider context.

Most people in the defence and foreign-affairs establishment accepted Ben-Gurion's fundamental conceptions at face value. After Moshe Sharett's forced resignation in 1955, most of Ben-Gurion's assumptions were left unchallenged. Ben-Gurion's conception could at least be documented in his many writings. By contrast, his successors were less disposed to put their thoughts on paper, at least on a more strategic level.[72] In addition, within the security establishment no systematic effort was made to spell out a consistent security doctrine. Consequently, we lack a clear benchmark against which we could evaluate the policy of intervention.

On questions of peace and war, criteria for successful or disastrous policies readily suggest themselves (although in these cases too the ultimate verdict about a policy is not always universally shared by observers). However, on matters inherently less dramatic and more clandestine, judging success or failure is far more problematic, especially because institutional mechanisms that enable systematic analysis and evaluation of policies in the foreign policy and security domain are lacking.

The exception concerns cases of policy fiascoes that, by their very nature, generated public demand for inquiry. In such cases, politicians – typically against their will and better judgment – are compelled to instigate independent inquiry commissions. This was the case following the 1953 'mishap', the 1973 Yom Kippur War, the 1982 Sabra and Shatilla massacre, the 1993 massacre in Hebron, the 1995 assassination of Yitzhak Rabin and the 1997 assassination attempt of Haled Mashal in Amman. In most of these cases the inquiry commissions issued two types of recommendation – one involving specific individuals held responsible for part or all of the fiasco in point, the second a set of structural recommendations for improving the performance of the organizations involved.

The typical government reaction in such cases was to accept the commission's personal recommendations while avoiding implementation of the structural ones, or to limit implementation in such a way that it perpetuated the failed policies, practices and organizational structures. Since there is no mechanism for enforcing the reforms recommended by such inquiry panels, or for following up on the changes that have been adopted, nobody is held accountable for perpetuating ineffective institutions or defective practices. Moreover, these recommendations concern classified aspects of the operation of security organs so that even public oversight is denied.

This essay has highlighted examples that share elements in common:

1. Intervention policies were based on a fundamental assumption (the validity of which has never been established) that the weaker and more divided the Arab world in general, or the more

internally unstable a given Arab country, the better it is for Israel in terms of national security. Alternatively, a state in the Arab world or periphery can be strengthened if only the 'right' elements are brought to power – thus the notion that Israel has a major stake in the internal composition and stability of core Arab states or peripheral ones.

2. Another premise was that Israel can effectively manipulate intra-Arab politics or the domestic politics of individual states.

3. All interventions began as clandestine efforts. All were managed by various intelligence agencies, although some of them involved foreign and security organizations outside the intelligence community and avoided public scrutiny. As noted, in most cases, there was no effective parliamentary oversight of these initiatives until they emerged on the public agenda – typically after the extent of the disaster had become public knowledge.

4. There is a basic consistency in the pattern of intervention that cuts across parties in power and individuals in given positions. It is therefore incorrect to associate these operations with a particular party in power. Interventionist policies were conducted by both major parties with about the same degree of persuasion, and with the same degree of stupidity. Likewise, it is unfair to ascribe to a given individual in power greater responsibility than to another individual in the same position.

5. In most cases, there was a humanitarian motive underlying the intervention which reappears in the negotiations between Israeli decision-makers and their potential 'clients', as well as in internal communications among Israeli decision-makers or between political leaders and military/intelligence personnel. Nonetheless, the basic pattern of intervention suggests ulterior motives were always secondary to the fundamental *Realpolitik* motives enumerated in the basic premises of such policies.

6. It is important to note not only where interventions did occur, but also where they did not. Israel, for example, did not intervene in Syrian or Jordanian politics, and did not aid the Kurds against Turkey.

These points suggest three policy conclusions:

1. Schemes aimed at changing domestic balances within Arab states should be weighed extremely carefully given the abysmal record of past interventionist strategies.

2. It is important that the assumptions underlying these policies be carefully examined. This study suggests that even at the height of the Arab–Israeli conflict, the overall premise underlying the divide-and-rule approach was tenuous. It is probably more shaky as this conflict approaches its end.

3. If initiated, it is crucial to establish independent oversight by individuals and organizations that are not part of the security system and outside the network of people and institutions involved in implementing such policies. These episodes suggest that the system is extremely capable of fending off criticism even when it comes from official inquiry commissions. The most effective oversight is a public one, but, given the clandestine nature of many of these activities, it is impossible to impose a public review on such policies. Therefore, either a national security council, not involved in policy implementation, or a more effective DFAC in the Knesset (parliament), would qualify for this oversight role.

Today, the key threats to Israel's security lie with 'second-circle states' like Iran and Iraq. The nature of conflict with such states and their internal instability make interventionist policies extremely appealing. For precisely this reason, the insights derived from past experience should serve as a clear warning of what it is we need to avoid. As 50 years of foreign and security policy have come and gone, and as we approach a comprehensive settlement with our neighbours, it is all the more important to look critically at our past.

## NOTES

1. I wish to thank Avi Ben-Zvi and Aharon Klieman for their perceptive comments on a previous draft. The remaining errors are mine alone.
2. Avner Yaniv, *Politics and Strategy in Israel* (Tel Aviv: Sifriat Poalim, 1994), pp. 26–30 (in Hebrew); Israel Tal, *National Security: The Few Against the Many* (Tel Aviv: Dvir Publications, 1997), pp. 11–12.
3. There are numerous definitions of the term and each of them emphasizes different criteria for and dimensions of intervention. Space constraints preclude a more elaborate discussion of the concept. For discussions which consider the various definitional issue involved see Bruce W. Jentelson and Ariel E. Levite, 'The Analysis of Protracted Foreign Military Intervention', in Ariel E. Levite, Bruce W. Jentelson

and Larry Berman (eds), *Foreign Military Intervention: The Dynamics of Protracted Conflict* (New York: Columbia University Press, 1992), pp. 5–11; and Yaacov Y. Vertzberger, *Risk Taking and Decisionmaking: Foreign Military Intervention* (Stanford, CA: Stanford University Press, 1998), pp. 3–7.

4. Jentelson and Levite, 'Protracted Foreign Military Intervention', pp. 5–6.
5. The list is far from comprehensive. There were several other instances of intervention efforts, including an exchange of ideas of plots in Syria in 1957–58 (Moshe Maoz, *Israel and Syria: From War to Peacemaking* (Tel Aviv: Ma'ariv Publications, 1995), pp. 45–6 (in Hebrew); participation of Israeli agents in the kidnapping and assassination of the Moroccan opposition leader Mehdi Ben-Barka in 1965 (Ian Black and Benny Morris, *Israel's Secret Wars: A History of Israel's Intelligence Services* (London: Futura Publications, 1991), pp. 202–5); provision of information regarding Algerian FNL leaders to the French secret service in 1956 (ibid., pp. 172–3); and other cases. However, these were brief and relatively insignificant episodes.
6. Uri Bar-Joseph, *Intelligence Intervention in the Politics of Democratic States: The United States, Israel, and Britain* (University Park, PA: Pennsylvania State University Press, 1995), p. 149, translates the Hebrew phrase 'Esek Bish', which was the code name of this episode in the censored Israeli press at the time, as 'unfortunate affair'. I think a better translation is 'the mishap'. See Gabriel Sheffer, *Moshe Sharett: Biography of a Political Moderate* (New York: Oxford University Press, 1996), p. 750.
7. Ellen Kay Trimberger, *Revolution from Above* (New Brunswick, NJ: Transaction Books, 1978).
8. This is cited from an official estimate by the chief of military intelligence on 16 June 1954. See also Bar-Joseph, *Intelligence Intervention*, pp. 149–50.
9. Sheffer, *Moshe Sharett*, pp. 654–5.
10. Bar-Joseph, *Intelligence Intervention*, p. 179.
11. Sharett conducted secret negotiations with Nasser from 1953 onwards through several back channels. See Moshe Sharett, *Personal Diary* (Tel Aviv: Am Oved, 1978); Sheffer, *Moshe Sharett*, pp. 655–7, 676; and Bar-Joseph, *Intelligence Intervention*, pp. 210–15.
12. Bar-Joseph, *Intelligence Intervention*, pp. 194–5; Gabriel Sheffer, *Resolution Versus Management of the Middle Eastern Conflict: Moshe Sharett and David Ben-Gurion* (Jerusalem: Magnes Press, 1980).
13. Bar-Joseph, *Intelligence Intervention*, pp. 176–9, 182–4.
14. Except the Israeli operator of the spy ring, Avri El-Ad, who escaped from Egypt in early August. El-Ad came under suspicion of having being turned into a double agent by the Egyptian secret service. See Bar-Joseph, *Intelligence Intervention*, pp. 194–201.
15. Bar-Joseph, ibid., p. 210, argues that 'Givli's Egyptian operation of 1954 is a clear-cut case of the crudest type of interference in the conduct of national foreign policy by an intelligence organization...Givli's attempt to decide the fate of Israel looks especially grave; furthermore, when one considers what type that foreign policy was.' This is an exaggeration, however, because the operation was not designed to affect Israel's fate but to intervene in others' domestic affairs. Bar-Joseph is correct in estimating the grave damage this operation caused to Israeli–Egyptian relations.
16. Former head of the Mossad Shabtai Shavit recently revealed another case in this class of intervention. It involved the supply of military equipment and military advisers to the royalist forces in the Yemeni civil war (1962–67), mostly during the 1965–67 period. This help was based on an effort to thwart Egyptian forces in the civil war. This episode will not be discussed here owing to lack of information. Nonetheless, it clearly had little or no effect on the outcome of that war.
17. Black and Morris, *Israel's Secret Wars*, p. 182.
18. Ibid., p. 182.
19. On the Egyptian–Jordanian leg of this subversive activity see Elie Podeh, *The Quest for Hegemony in the Arab World: The Struggle over the Baghdad Pact* (New York: E. J. Brill, 1995); Bin Tilal Hussein, *Uneasy Lies the Head* (London: Heineman, 1962); and Zeev Maoz and Ben D. Mor, 'International Hate Affairs: The Evolution of Enduring International Rivalries', unpublished manuscript, Tel Aviv University, 1999, Ch. 6.

20. Except for the haphazard participation of Israeli agents and diplomats in plots to subvert the Syrian regime in 1957. See Maoz, *Israel and Syria*.
21. On the rebellion in Sudan see Yaakov Shimoni, *The Arab States: Their Contemporary History and Politics* (Tel Aviv: Am Oved, 1977), pp. 612–18 (in Hebrew).
22. Ibid., pp. 617–18.
23. Shlomo Nakdimon, *A Hopeless Hope: The Rise and Fall of the Israeli–Kurdish Alliance* (Tel Aviv: Yediot Aharanot, 1996), p. 43.
24. Ibid., p. 48.
25. Ibid., pp. 56–9.
26. Dana Adams Schmidt, *Journey Among Brave Men* (Boston: Little, Brown, 1964).
27. Nakdimon, *A Hopeless Hope*, pp. 73–9; Edgar O'balance, *The Kurdish Revolt* (London: Faber and Faber, 1973), pp. 110–11; Ofrah Bengio, *The Kurdish Rebellion against Iraq* (Tel Aviv: Ha'Kibbutz Ha'Meuchad, 1989), pp. 22–3 (in Hebrew).
28. Nakdimon, *A Hopeless Hope*, pp. 80–2.
29. Ibid., p. 83.
30. The Iranians advocated a 'low-flame' policy because in 1965 the number of Kurds in Iran was double the number of Kurds in Iraq (four million as opposed to two million). A success by the Kurdish rebellion in Iraq could have fuelled a similar rebellion by the Irainian Kurds. See Bengio, *The Kurdish Rebellion*.
31. Nakdimon, *A Hopeless Hope*, pp. 100–93.
32. Ibid., p. 194.
33. In contrast to other cases of intervention, the Israelis made relatively little effort to hide the aid given to the Kurds. Although the Israeli advisers stationed in Kurdistan were required to wear local uniforms and to avoid speaking in Hebrew, there were numerous reports of Israeli aid to the Kurds in the Arab and international press. Israeli weapons were captured by the Iraqis and captured Kurds disclosed details of the nature of this aid. Barazani's visit to Israel in 1968 involved a number of public receptions, including a meeting with Israeli newspaper editors (ibid., pp. 221–8).
34. In practice, logistical and other problems prevented the actual delivery of these tanks to the Kurds. The decision to upgrade Kurdish capability was because of the intensified relations between Iraq and the Soviet Union and growing Iraqi–Iranian tensions (ibid., pp. 341–3).
35. Ibid., p. 349.
36. The Israeli intelligence community was not aware of the secret Iranian–Iraqi talks to resolve their conflict (ibid., p. 348).
37. Ibid., p. 354.
38. Ibid., pp. 365–71.
39. Ibid., p. 355; Bengio, *The Kurdish Rebellion*, p. 151.
40. Shlomo Gazit, *Trapped* (Tel Aviv: Zmora-Bitan, 1999), pp. 167–71.
41. Shaul Mishal, *The PLO under Arafat: Between Gun and Olive Branch* (New Haven: Yale University Press, 1986), p. 114.
42. Maoz, *Israel and Syria*, p. 147.
43. Emile Shaliyeh, *In Search of Leadership: West Bank Politics Since 1967* (Washington: Brookings Institution Press, 1988), p. 64.
44. Mishal, *The PLO under Arafat*, pp. 107–08; Shaliye, *In Search of Leadership*, p. 64; Maoz, *Palestinian Leadership on the West Bank* (Tel Aviv: Reshafim, 1985), pp. 146–7 (in Hebrew).
45. Maoz, *Palestinian Leadership*, p. 147. The number of eligible voters in 1976 was over 88,000 as opposed to 31,000 in 1972. See Mishal, *The PLO under Arafat*, p. 110; and Maoz, *Palestinian Leadership*, p. 149.
46. Maoz, *Palestinian Leadership*, p. 148. For detailed analyses of the election results see Maoz, ibid.; and Mishal, *The PLO under Arafat*, pp. 114–18.
47. Gazit, *Trapped*, pp. 191–2.
48. Ibid., pp. 237–9.
49. Ibid., p. 191.
50. Maoz, *Palestinian Leadership*, pp. 205–8; Shaliyeh, *In Search of Leadership*, pp. 83–6; Mark Tessler, *A History of the Israeli–Palestinian Conflict* (Bloomington, IN: Indiana University Press, 1994), pp. 552–3.
51. Shaliyeh, *In Search of Leadership*, pp. 69–81.

52. Gazit, *Trapped*, pp. 206–7.
53. Ibid., pp. 207–11; Maoz, *Palestinian Leadership*, p. 209.
54. Gazit, *Trapped*, p. 207.
55. Anat Kurz with Nachman Tal, *Hamas: Radical Islam in a National Struggle* (Tel Aviv: Jaffee Centre for Strategic Studies, 1997), JCSS Memorandum, No. 48, p. 12.
56. Shaliyeh, *In Search of Leadership*, p. 143.
57. Ibid., pp. 144–62.
58. Kurz with Tal, *Hamas*, pp. 11–12, document some of this activity. See also Gazit, *Trapped*, pp. 127–8, who disputes the claim that the Israeli authorities nurtured the Islamic movement as an alternative to the PLO. He claims that Israeli policy was to tolerate this movement in order to avoid being portrayed as anti-Islamic in character, as do Shaul Mishal and Abraham Sella, *The Palestinian Hamas: Vision, Violence, and Coexistence* (New York: Columbia University Press, 2000), p. 26. However, Tessler, *A History of the Israeli–Palestinian Conflict*, p. 675, argues that Israel entertained the notion that Islamic activity would replace nationalist fervour in the occupied territories. See also Ann M. Lesch and Mark Tessler, *Egypt, Israel, and the Palestinians: From Camp David to Intifada* (Bloomington, IN: Indiana University Press, 1989), pp. 260–2.
59. Gazit, *Trapped*, p. 128.
60. This episode has many facets, most of them paradoxical in that they represent causally induced contradictions between goals and intentions on the one hand, and actual outcomes on the other (Zeev Maoz, *Paradoxes of War: On the Art of Self-Entrapment* (Boston: Unwin Hyman, 1990)). Some of these aspects are documented elsewhere. See Zeev Maoz, 'Power, Capabilities, and Paradoxical Conflict Outcomes', *World Politics*, 41, 2, Chs 8, 10; Zeev Maoz, 'Framing the National Interest: The Manipulation of Foreign Policy Decisions in Group Settings', *World Politics*, 43, 1, pp. 77–110; and Maoz and Mor, *International Hate Affairs*, Ch. 8. Here I deal only with the Israeli–Christian–Shi'ite triangle and its implications.
61. The figures are based on data gathered by Dr Ranan Kuperman in the framework of the project on the Quantitative History of the Arab–Israeli conflict. See his 'Dynamics of a Policy: A Comparison of Israel's Military Actions Across Time', PhD dissertation, Tel Aviv University.
62. Yair Evron, *War and Intervention in Lebanon: The Israeli–Syrian Deterrence Dialogue* (London: Croom Helm, 1987), pp. 30–3, 49–50.
63. Avner Yaniv, *Dilemmas of Security: Politics, Strategy, and the Israeli Experience in Lebanon* (New York: Oxford University Press, 1987), p. 57.
64. According to Kuperman, 'Dynamics of a Policy', Israeli fatalities over the 1975–77 period were 14 people killed and 58 wounded.
65. Yaniv, *Dilemmas of Security*, pp. 61, 65.
66. On the Mount Sanin crisis see ibid., pp. 85–90; Patrick Seale, *Asad: The Struggle for the Middle East* (Berkeley and Los Angeles: University of California Press, 1988), pp. 368–70; Evron, *War and Intervention*; Maoz and Mor, *International Hate Affairs*.
67. See Schiff and Yaari, 1984, pp. 33–5, on the Israeli decision-making process.
68. Maoz, 'Framing the National Interest', p. 239; Schiff and Yaari, p. 42; Yaniv, *Dilemmas of Security*, pp. 100–7.
69. Maoz, 'Power, Capabilities' and *Paradoxes of War*, pp. 239–43.
70. For a sober evaluation of this process of establishing local militias see Yaniv, *Dilemmas of Security*, pp. 229–45. Yaniv also hints that this effort may have affected Hizballah activities against Israeli forces.
71. Hala Jaber, *Hezbollah: Born with a Vengeance* (New York: Columbia University Press, 1997), pp. 14–19.
72. The exception that proves the rule is, of course, Allon's *Curtain of Sand* (1968).

# 9 *'Oom-Shmoom'* Revisited: Israeli Attitudes Towards the UN and the Great Powers, 1948–1960

## NEIL CAPLAN

Reviewing his first year in office, and perhaps even foreshadowing the surprise announcement (which would come in September 1993) of the historic mutual recognition between Israel and the Palestine Liberation Organization, the late Prime Minister Yitzhak Rabin declared:

> The train that travels towards peace has stopped this year at many stations that daily refute the time-worn canard – *'the whole world is against us'*. The United States has improved its relations with us...In Europe, our dialogue with the European Community has been improved and deepened. We have been inundated by visiting heads of state – and we have responded to them with friendship and with economic and other links. We are no longer *'a People that dwelleth alone'*.[1]

This optimistic view of the world, and of Israel's place among the family of nations, was part of a deliberate attempt to break away from longstanding negative, cautious and suspicious Israeli and Jewish attitudes reflected in the two quoted (italicized) slogans. Such a negative worldview derives from a sweeping and general Jewish and Israeli alienation from, and sometimes disdain for, the *goyim* – the entire gentile (non-Jewish) world. Some Jews and Israelis, often citing the world's demonstrated indifference to the plight of European Jewry during and immediately after the

Holocaust, truly believe that 'the whole world is against us', and there are many who regard the rebirth of a Jewish state in 1948 as compensation, or even as a 'reprisal', for that tragedy.[2]

Those who share such a pessimistic worldview would no doubt also endorse the rallying call attributed to David Ben-Gurion: 'It matters not what the *goyim* say but [rather] what the Jews do'. Amplifying her discussion of this Ben-Gurionite slogan, one author has written:

> By [1956] Israel was disillusioned with the UN and began to develop a 'Gevald Syndrome', a political paranoia based on the belief that the whole world conspires against Israel... Since 1956 the UN has been stigmatized, called bad names ('UN-Shmum' [sic], translated as UN equals zero) and, at best, ignored in Israeli politics.[3]

Taken together, the slogans cited above constitute something of a syndrome, reflecting a complex set of negative attitudes to the outside world firmly entrenched in Israeli political culture. The colourful phrase *'oom-shmoom'* – expressing utter contempt for the United Nations – has been a well-known one in Israeli public life since the mid-1950s. It is a classic application of the all-purpose Yiddish idiom of repeating a word and adding the prefix 'shm-' the second time, to indicate mockery of the original word. Thus, *'oom'* – the Hebrew abbreviation of *ha-umot ha-me'uhadot* (the United Nations) – becomes, derisively, *'oom-shmoom'*.[4]

Today, the phrase sometimes serves as a useful reference point for explanations of negative Israeli attitudes to the United Nations that appear in English-language textbooks dealing with Israeli society and political culture. As Aharon Klieman has written, '[r]esentment is deep at how Israel fares in world public opinion and in international forums such as the United Nations. Cynicism prevails...The world beyond Israel's borders is often perceived of...as distinctly inhospitable – a dangerous and challenging place.'[5]

The phrase *'oom-shmoom'*, familiar to most Israeli taxi drivers and politicians, has also found expression in contemporary Israeli political discourse. Responding to a UN vote censuring Israel for its construction works in the disputed Har-Homa/Jamal-Gneim area in 1997, former prime minister Benjamin Netanyahu generated newspaper headlines with his comment that, if this was all the *oom* was good for, then it was truly *'shmoom'*. And, in a March 1998 address to the Knesset, UN Secretary-General Kofi Annan impressed listeners with his elementary Hebrew wordplay by arguing that Israel's historical view of his organization as being *'oom-shmoom'* merited some reassessment – since 'without the *oom* we would have *cloom* [nothing]'.[6]

## ORIGINS OF THE *'OOM-SHMOOM'* PHRASE

The first written evidence of the use of the expression *'oom-shmoom'* is not to be found among David Ben-Gurion's writings and speeches but in Moshe Sharett's personal diary, first published in 1978.[7] On 29 March 1955, the Israeli cabinet devoted a marathon six-hour session to a debate over Ben-Gurion's proposal to conquer the Gaza Strip as a way of curtailing *fedayyun* cross-border attacks. According to Sharett's diary account, Ben-Gurion made a point of correcting an earlier remark made by Sharett, to the effect that,

> had it not been for the UN resolution of [29 November] 1947 [recommending the partition of Palestine into an Arab and a Jewish state], the state would not have been created in 1948. 'No, no, no!', he shouted, 'only the daring of the Jews created the state, and not any *oom-shmoom* resolution'.

Sharett, who was then serving as both prime minister and foreign minister, used his diary to register his outrage and to criticize Ben-Gurion, who had only recently been reinstalled as defence minister after 18 months in retreat at Sde Boqer. What seems to have irked Sharett most was Ben-Gurion's narrow-mindedess in resorting to this undignified phrase and his sanctimoniousness in taking to task those who disagreed with him. Two weeks later, Sharett continued his dispute with Ben-Gurion over the UN role in an exchange of letters.[8]

The significance of Ben-Gurion's *'oom-shmoom'* remarks may well have been exaggerated in Moshe Sharett's mind and through his published diaries. Shabtai Teveth, Ben-Gurion's official biographer, believes that – contrary to the Sharett diary account – the *'oom-shmoom'* remark was probably uttered in private, outside the cabinet room. The absence of that colourful phrase from the official stenographic protocol of the late-March 1955 cabinet meeting suggests that Teveth may be right.[9] It is also worth noting that the actual disagreement between the two men in the spring of 1955 was of the narrow, hair-splitting type. Not unlike other Sharett–Ben-Gurion disputes, this one was, in essence, more over timing and tone than substance and principle. While castigating Ben-Gurion for unfairly berating the UN with an undignified but catchy phrase, Sharett pedantically insisted that the United Nations' support for partition *in 1947* had indeed been essential to the creation of the state *in 1948*.

Nonetheless, from this somewhat petty squabble, the phrase *'oom-shmoom'* has become a permanent element in Israeli political folklore, a catch-phrase used to designate a variety of negative attitudes to the UN as a world body. The degree of support for the *'oom-shmoom'* outlook was one of the major variables in the 'attitudinal prism' of Israeli decision-makers interviewed by Michael Brecher in the 1960s, as revealed in his pioneering work, *The Foreign Policy System of Israel*. Brecher found that leaders' views of the United Nations, 'its role in the creation of the State, and its ongoing importance in the Arab Israel conflict were subjects of extreme controversy' within the 'inner circle':

> With rare moments of ambivalence, Ben Gurion dismissed the UN as of no consequence, insisting that Israel's birth and survival owed virtually nothing to any but the people of Israel: 'The State is the result of our daring.' His contempt was best captured in the phrase *'oum–shmoum.'* Sharett strongly opposed this view, going so far as to assert that 'we owe our State to the United Nations.' Correspondingly, Sharett attached significant weight to the UN and to world opinion, while BG largely ignored them.
>
> ... [Moshe] Dayan, [Shimon] Peres, and (to a slightly lesser extent) [Golda] Meir closely emulated Ben Gurion's outlook. [Abba] Eban recognized the UN's shortcomings but insisted on its importance as well; [Pinhas] Sapir followed his lead. [Yigal] Allon tended towards the BG pole on the grounds that no factor could supersede in importance the need for strategically defensible borders. [Levi] Eshkol's (for the most part unarticulated) position was closer to dead centre between the two extreme approaches.[10]

ISRAEL AND THE UNITED NATIONS: POINTS OF CONTACT,
POINTS OF CONFLICT

Through its partition resolution of 29 November 1947, the United
Nations was, in the words of one scholar,

> witness – some would say midwife – to the birth of a modern
> Jewish State. It succeeded in terminating the first round of
> Arab–Israel warfare and assisted the process of negotiations
> leading to the Armistice agreements of 1949. The system of
> Mixed Armistice Commissions [MACs] and the Chief of Staff
> of UNTSO [United Nations Truce Supervisory Organisation]
> eased border tension from time to time. The UNEF helped to
> keep the antagonists apart from 1957 to 1967.[11]

During this period, Israelis viewed their experience of the
United Nations as a mixture of some positive – but mostly negative
– elements. The following overview distinguishes among several
levels of UN activity and points of contact with Israelis:

(a) resolutions of the Security Council and General Assembly;

(b) statements, positions and activities of UN-appointed mediators
    (1948–49) and the Conciliation Commission for Palestine [PCC]
    (1949–51);

(c) statements, positions and behaviour of the UN secretary-
    general;

(d) statements, positions and behaviour of the UNTSO chief of
    staff; and

(e) activity of the MACs and UNTSO personnel.

In the period under discussion (1948–60), points of conflict
between Israel and the United Nations did not yet include the
controversial decision of UN Secretary-General U Thant hastily to
remove the United Nations Emergency Force (UNEF) from the
Egyptian–Israeli frontier in May 1967, or the 1975 General
Assembly (GA) resolution delegitimizing Israel by equating
Zionism with racism. And, prior to 1960, we see only the beginnings of what were later to become two predictable patterns of
United Nations debates: (a) the use or threat of the Soviet veto to
increase the number of Security Council (SC) resolutions critical of

Israel and to reduce or eliminate those that would have been condemnatory of the Arab states; and (b) a blatant and intense East–West polarization within the General Assembly, and the accompanying politicization of non-aligned African and Asian delegations, after 1967, into a predictably pro-Arab and anti-Israel voting bloc.

## (a) Resolutions of the Security Council and the General Assembly

On 29 November 1947, radios in the Yishuv (Palestinian Jewish community in the pre-state period) were all tuned in to the live broadcast from the United Nations as the required two-thirds majority of votes was cast to accept the United Nations Special Committee on Palestine (UNSCOP) recommendation for the partition of Palestine. Yet David Ben-Gurion took a more sober view of the role played by the UN and the great powers in the creation of the state. As minister of defence, he viewed the UN arms embargo, observed all too scrupulously during 1948–49 by the United Kingdom and the United States, as maintaining a deadly imbalance of weaponry between Israel and her Arab enemies. Fifteen years later, expressing the feeling that 'the whole world is against us', Ben-Gurion commemorated the anniversary of the partition resolution with the remark that on 15 May 1948 the United Nations had 'wipe[d] out the credit due to it for its decision on 29 November 1947'.

> If the UN had been worthy of its name it should have defended its honour when certain countries tried to destroy the people of Israel in its Land. But there was not a single state – not even the United States or the Soviet Union – that lifted a finger on the 15th of May. And I am not obliged as a Jew to give them credit for anything. The State of Israel exists thanks only to the people of Israel and, first and foremost, to the Israel Defense Forces.[12]

Among the few early UN resolutions that Israelis could point to with any degree of satisfaction were (a) the GA's vote of 11 May 1949, admitting Israel to membership in the United Nations; (b) the SC resolution of 11 August 1949, expressing appreciation to acting mediator Ralph S. Bunche for his achievement in bringing about General Armistice Agreements (GAAs) between four Arab states and Israel; and (c) the SC resolution of 1 September 1951, calling upon Egypt to terminate restrictions on commercial shipping through the Suez Canal.[13] Yet Israel derived little practical satisfaction from the Canal decision but only recurring frustration at the inability or unwillingness of the world body to force Egypt to comply with it.

On the other hand, between 1948 and 1960, the Security Council and General Assembly adopted a larger number of resolutions considered unfriendly to Israel, dealing with Palestinian refugees, the internationalization of Jerusalem, the legality of Israel's water-diversion project in the Huleh demilitarized zone (DMZ), and the reduction of tension caused by cross-border raids and reprisals. These resolutions, and the debates that preceded them, were presented in ways that conflicted with Israel's national interests and declared policies, increasingly singling out Israel's behaviour for one-sided condemnation.[14] As described by Abba Eban, Israel's ambassador to the United Nations and to Washington during the 1950s, the threat of a Soviet veto meant that the Security Council became 'closed to Israel as a court of appeal or redress' for its complaints against Arab cross-border attacks, blockades against Israeli shipping or other violations of the armistice agreements, while 'there was no such inhibition to resolutions criticizing Israel for retaliating against attacks'.[15]

### (b) UN-appointed Mediators (1948–49) and the Conciliation Commission for Palestine (PCC) (1949–51)

While appreciating the contribution of UN Acting Mediator Ralph Bunche in concluding armistice agreements with Egypt, Jordan, Lebanon and Syria during the first half of 1949, Israelis had feared and fought the imposition of a peace plan formulated by Bunche's predecessor, Count Folke Bernadotte. In fact, Bernadotte's role and proposals had aroused so much suspicion and hostility among Israelis that members of the terrorist LEHI (Fighters for the Freedom of Israel, also known as the Stern Gang) assassinated him in September 1948. During 1949–51, Israeli negotiating teams struggled to avoid substantial concessions by resisting US pressure exerted through the mediation efforts of the Conciliation Commission for Palestine, established after Bernadotte's assassination with the goal of achieving a comprehensive peace settlement involving Israel and all her neighbours.[16]

Following the PCC's failed attempts at conference diplomacy at Lausanne (1949), Geneva (1950) and Paris (1951), Moshe Sharett mounted an unsuccessful campaign to have the UN organ dissolved altogether. The Israeli foreign minister came to Paris to argue that the PCC was not merely useless, but actually harmful. The mere existence of an organ like the Commission, he told US Secretary of State Dean Acheson, had served to retard, rather than accelerate, a settlement. The Arabs, in his view,

> were using the comings and goings between them and the Palestine Conciliation Commission as a make-believe – a cloak to disguise their real attitude which was one of complete refusal to advance towards a settlement. May be [*sic*] if that cloak were taken away and their tactics exposed they might feel under an international compulsion to take a positive step.[17]

In a subsequent memorandum to UN Secretary-General Trygve Lie, Sharett argued that the solution of outstanding problems between Israel and the Arab states should best 'be left to time, which is another way of saying to the growth of a real will for peace in the latter camp'. Revising the 'cloak' metaphor that he had used with Acheson, the foreign minister equated the abolition of the PCC with the 'removal of the fig-leaf now covering the nakedness of the Arab refusal to advance toward peace – a fig-leaf represented so far, quite unintentionally, by the PCC'.[18]

## (c) Statements, Positions and Behaviour of the UN Secretary-General

Israeli attitudes towards the United Nations were also influenced – mostly in a negative way – by leaders' experiences in their dealings and negotiations involving the UN secretary-general. While the first secretary-general, Trygve Lie, was well liked for his solidly pro-Israel attitude, his successor, Dag Hammarskjöld, was a more problematic character, evoking a certain uneasiness and suspicion from most Israelis, even from those, like Abba Eban and Mordecai (Reggie) Kidron, who worked most closely with him, and also from Moshe Sharett and other foreign ministry personnel. In the case of David Ben-Gurion, mutual attitudes were mistrustful and ambivalent, while Golda Meir 'never considered him to be a friend of Israel'.[19]

Hammarskjöld's conflict-management skills, good faith and ability to win the confidence of Israeli officials were put to the test in a number of areas. In 1953–54, he was unsuccessful in responding to Israel's call for the convening of a conference with Jordan under Article XII of the Israel–Jordan GAA.[20] He was also ineffective in his periodic attempts to get Egypt to comply with the September 1951 Security Council resolution calling for unrestricted passage through the Suez Canal. And, most notably, in his handling of the Sinai–Suez war and its aftermath (especially in Gaza) he was resolutely critical of Israel's invasion of Egypt and insisted legalistically on full withdrawal without reference to the Israeli grievances that had contributed to the military operation. With regard to border incidents and *fedayyun* activity, an extensive study commissioned in the summer of 1958 by the research branch of Israel's Military Intelligence (AMAN) characterized the secretary-general's approach as being

> based on a skepticism of Israeli accusations and claims, a tendency to balance responsibility in cases where Egyptian responsibility was beyond any doubt, patient indulgence *vis-à-vis* Egypt, a minimization of the importance of Egyptian incursions into Israeli territory, an exaggerated reliance on assurances given by Egyptian leaders, and an avoidance, for a sustained period, of making serious appeals to those leaders for an end to hostile acts.

Tactically, the report continued, the secretary-general tried to overcome obstacles caused by Israel's objections to his proposals by working for condemnation of Israel by world public opinion and by undertaking diplomatic activity among delegations of the powers at the UN, refuting Israel's claims that Egypt was primarily and solely responsible for border incidents. AMAN's detailed survey led to the conclusion that

> without a doubt the Secretary-General has conducted a clear-cut anti-Israel policy and has in effect advanced the interests of one of the parties to the Israel–Arab conflict... [F]or an extended period the Secretary-General followed a policy which endangered Israel's international standing and its security.[21]

### (d) Statements, Positions and Behaviour of the UNTSO Chief of Staff

Perhaps the most regular channel of Israeli contact with the United Nations was through the day-to-day relations with the UNTSO chief of staff, who was appointed by the UN secretary-general. Both the Ministry of Foreign Affairs (MFA) and the General Staff HQ of the Israel Defence Forces (IDF) designated liaison personnel who worked closely with the UNTSO head and his staff. Of the seven incumbents who served between 1949 and 1960, Israelis developed what they felt was an excellent rapport with William Riley (USA, 1948–53), and a correct and professional relationship with E. L. M. Burns (Canada, 1954–56). But they experienced particular disillusionment and disappointment regarding the competence, objectivity and integrity of Vagn Bennike (Denmark, 1953–54) and Carl von Horn (Sweden, 1958–63).

### (e) Activity of the MACs and UNTSO Personnel[22]

Under the armistice regimes, between 100 and 150 observers were seconded from a dozen UN member-states to serve with UNTSO in Lebanon, Syria, Jordan, Egypt and Israel. The proper channels and methods for Israel's dealings with this UN machinery were a source of frequent behind-the-scenes disagreements between the foreign ministry, on the one hand, and the defence ministry and IDF general staff, on the other. As foreign minister, Moshe Sharett sought to have all Israelis involved with the MACs sensitive to the political importance of the GAA regime; and, in one of his many debates with Ben-Gurion over the appropriate weight to be attached to foreign affairs and defence, he urged cooperation between the two ministries and the IDF, and argued against BG's single-minded insistence on the security imperative:

> The armistice agreements are not purely a security or a military affair, but a political matter of the utmost importance to us. The MACs are the only area of regular contact between us and the Arab countries. MAC matters are the subject of constant contacts and struggles between us and the UN. Our relations with the great powers are also tied to [this matter]. It affects public opinion in the entire world towards Israel.

In his counter-argument for the primacy of defence considerations, Ben-Gurion (who had recently tried unsuccessfully to win cabinet endorsement to abrogate the Egypt–Israel GAA) lectured Sharett on 'the overriding importance of security in the life of the nation and on the need to educate it to understand that its security depends first and foremost on itself – not on the UN or on the great powers'.[23]

The battle-lines were visible several years earlier, and the issue had already come to a head in late 1953, during the UN Security Council's consideration of a complaint about Israel's raid on the Jordanian village of Qibya. Deploring Ben-Gurion's denial of the need for a cabinet discussion on the matter, Sharett had

> voiced concern over the glaring inconsistency between our complete objective dependence on the support and sympathy of the world [on the one hand] and our subjective mental isolation from the world [on the other] – our turning inward upon ourselves and our total insensitivity towards world public opinion with regard to our actions.

Sharett commented in his diary that he 'deplored this narrow-mindedness with which we have become afflicted'.[24]

The progressive deterioration of the armistice regime, with a vicious cycle of increasing *fedayyun* incursions and Israeli reprisal raids, was marked by growing Israeli dissatisfaction with the cumbersome procedures for handling complaints in the MACs. Even worse, from Israel's point of view, was the built-in tendency to more easily identify and condemn the Israelis for a reprisal than the irregulars who crossed the frontiers from Jordan or Egypt to inflict sabotage and terror inside Israel. Doubts about the objectivity and competence of the UNTSO personnel who were charged with the investigation of complaints of armistice violations further poisoned the atmosphere.[25] Perhaps the most egregious examples of anti-Israel bias during this period came from the chairman of the Israel–Jordan Mixed Armistice Commission (IJMAC), Commander E. H. Hutchison, who claimed in March 1954 that he lacked sufficient evidence to condemn Jordan for a murderous attack at Scorpions' Pass (Maaleh Akrabim) on an Israeli bus. This – coupled with reports that the UNTSO chief of staff, General Bennike, seriously considered the outrageous possibility that *Israelis themselves* might have inflicted the attack on their own civilian bus – led to an Israeli boycott of the IJMAC that lasted half a year.[26]

Months and years of such low-intensity 'border wars' had the cumulative effect of undermining both Arab and Israeli moral commitment to the armistice regime. Moshe Sharett's criticism of UN peacekeeping was that 'while Israel view[ed] the armistice agreements as a bridge to peace, the Arab states tr[ied] to use them as cover from behind which they [could] carry on their warfare against Israel by all possible means short of a full-scale war'.[27] Faced with unrelenting *fedayyun* incursions, Ben-Gurion similarly came to regard the armistice regime as fundamentally flawed. While he claimed that he did 'not accuse the UN representatives of bearing us ill will', it was

> obvious that they [were] ineffectual in forcing our neighbors to honor their promise. The chain of murders continues. We have no choice but to act in self-defense... The UN adminis-tration has long exhibited a tendency to turn the Armistice Agreements between ourselves and our neighbors into a unilateral obligation on the part of Israel toward the UN, thereby effectively absolving the other signatory nations of their obligations towards Israel.

Seeing this as an affront to Israeli sovereignty, Ben-Gurion complained of UNTSO's 'tendency to treat Israel as if it were inter-national territory'.[28]

## RHETORICAL SLOGANS AND POLICY DECISIONS

Given the largely negative Israeli experience of the UN and its personnel in the period under review, was the dismissive *'oom-shmoom'* attitude an accurate characterization of the approach actually adopted by the Israeli leadership towards the United Nations? And did Israel's leaders make foreign-policy decisions that reflected a worldview based on defiant slogans like 'the whole world is against us' and 'it matters not what the *goyim* say but what the Jews do'?

The evidence adduced here indicates that the negative and contemptuous attitudes reflected in the *'oom-shmoom'* slogan and the 'it-matters-not-...' dictum were not espoused, in practice, by Ben-Gurion or his followers to the degree suggested by their own, or their critics', rhetorical excesses. On the level of official Israeli policy as endorsed by a majority of cabinet members, these atti-tudes were never translated into decisions that resulted in sustained actions deliberately derisive of the UN and defiant of the great powers.

In his seminal study of the making of Israel's foreign policy during Ben-Gurion's years at the helm, Michael Brecher offers a strong critique of Ben-Gurion's 'single-factor image of the road to statehood', which enjoyed a strong resonance with the majority of Israelis:

> Ben-Gurion's disdain for the UN role in making history, especially in the creation of Israel, carried over into the post-1948 period of high policy: his contempt for the UN, his reliance on the *Yishuv* and, particularly, on *Tzahal* [that is, the IDF], is a logical, an inevitable extension of his image of the events of 1947–8. The United Nations counted for little then in the Middle East, it counts for nothing now – this has long been the essence of Ben Gurion's view, with far-reaching consequences for Israeli foreign policy from 1948 onwards.[29]

The evidence I will point to below suggests that the impact of Ben-Gurion's dismissive attitude to the United Nations was felt far more in the realm of *rhetoric* than on the *operational* level. My presentation also implicitly questions whether the *'oom-shmoom'* slogan did, in fact, have any 'far-reaching consequences for Israeli foreign policy' as formulated by the Israeli cabinet and implemented by its diplomats and soldiers.

A proper treatment of the topic requires two prefatory explanations. We need, first of all, to make an important precision to the Ben-Gurionite slogan 'It matters not what the *goyim* say but [rather] what the Jews do'.[30] Here the operative words are *'goyim* say'. Certainly, no Israelis – or nationals of any other country for that matter – would subscribe to the notion that their own decisions and destiny should be governed by what outsiders might harmlessly think or say. But not even Ben-Gurion was so cavalier or chauvinistic as to extend this dismissal of outside *opinion* to a lack of concern for what the gentiles might actually *do* – that is, actions that might turn out to be harmful to Israeli interests.

A second underlying constant that must be taken into account is the widely acknowledged weakness of the United Nations as a supranational body suffering from what one observer has labelled a 'curious organizational deficiency':

> Despite its endowment (at least theoretically) with devices to punish offenders against the peace, it can offer virtually no

incentives to desirable behaviour. Beyond announcing its moral and political approval, the rewards it offers are hypothetical...The most persuasive implements for resolving conflicts in the Eastern Mediterranean may well be force and reward. The UN system can reliably use neither.[31]

In this respect, Israel was no different from any other member of the world body: 'United Nations resolutions were treated in the manner of all sovereign states: those which served Israeli interests were accepted; those which were perceived as inimical were rejected' or ignored.[32] Yet the UN did have 'teeth' at selected moments, namely, when one or more of the great powers chose to employ incentives or threaten sanctions in support of, or in conjunction with, the world body. And if Israel (correctly) viewed the UN as unable on its own to force compliance with all its declared wishes, her leaders could not help but notice when the United States, Great Britain, the Soviet Union or (to a lesser extent) France stood ready to back the world body. On at least two occasions, American dissatisfaction with Israeli behaviour was clearly linked to an eagerness to support the UN. As we shall see below, the US was, on these occasions, prepared to use its own 'coercive diplomacy' on Israel by holding up consideration of transfer payments and loans until the Israelis complied with a UN ruling.[33] In addition, Israelis were quick to learn that there was, operating within the United Nations, a double standard according to which certain more powerful states might have no cause to fear critical or condemnatory resolutions, or could ignore them more successfully than smaller, weaker states. A glaring example of this was the late-1956 Soviet invasion of Hungary, which never evoked any real threat of international sanctions, while Israel's occupation of Egyptian territory in the wake of the tripartite Anglo-Franco-Israeli attack did.

Most writers presume, along with Avi Shlaim, that 'the dominant school of thought' in Israeli foreign policy-making during this period 'was inspired and led by Ben Gurion' while Moshe Sharett 'was an independent and original thinker on the basic questions of Israeli security' who 'represented a clear and serious alternative, albeit one which was never tested'.[34] The following six examples of actions taken and not taken are evidence that – notwithstanding the mid-1956 ousting of Sharett as foreign minister and the heroic mythology surrounding the Sinai campaign – the dominant trend during this period was *not* a 'Ben-Gurionist' or activist approach, but rather a *blend* of tough reprisals along the frontiers, on the one hand, tempered by a 'Sharettist' sober appreciation of international opinion, on the other.[35]

## Example 1: Bnot Yaacov Water Diversion Project

In October 1953, Ben-Gurion (over Sharett's protests) initially brought Israel into a showdown with the United Nations over the UNTSO chief of staff's recommendation and the UN Security Council's request to cease its water-diversion works at the Bnot Yaacov bridge in the Israel–Syria DMZ. If Israel's decisions had been truly motivated by the syndrome of defiance and rejection illustrated by '*oom-shmoom*' and 'It matters not what the *goyim* say, but what the Jews do', this diversion of the Jordan waters would have gone ahead despite international criticism or even condemnation. Yet, once the US administration suspended financial aid, a pragmatic Ben-Gurion gave in ('without prejudice to Israel's rights, claims or position in the matter') and within two weeks ordered a 'temporary' work stoppage – an action that was immediately followed by a resumption of American aid.[36] This was the first of several illustrations of Ben-Gurion backing down when he realized that he could simply not afford to ignore what the *goyim* associated with '*oom-shmoom*' were saying – largely because of what the *goyim* in the American administration were *doing* in support of the world body.

## Example 2: Cabinet Decisions on Reprisals

Israel's reprisals against neighbouring Arab states were decided by the cabinet. During 1955, it rejected (usually for fear of provoking an international backlash) a number of proposals developed by defence minister Ben-Gurion in concert with his chief of staff, Moshe Dayan, for far-reaching military action against the neighbouring states. In late March 1955, Ben-Gurion urged the cabinet to approve the capture of the Gaza Strip; this proposal was defeated on 3 April. The following day, the cabinet voted down his proposal to abrogate the Egypt–Israel GAA. Later that year, Ben-Gurion and Dayan elaborated a plan to break the Egyptian blockade of Eilat's access to the Red Sea by capturing the Straits of Tiran. On 5 December, a slim majority of the cabinet rejected this proposal. In the spring of 1956, Ben-Gurion himself vetoed an IDF request to respond with reprisals to *fedayyun* provocation from Gaza; the prime minister was, on this occasion, urging restraint in deference to the UN secretary-general's trouble-shooting visit to the region.

Whenever it came to a vote, Ben-Gurion's 'activist' approach was espoused by only a minority of Israel's leaders, both in cabinet and within the Mapai Central Committee.[37] Being thus out-voted on a number of his pet proposals helps explain Ben-Gurion's growing vehemence in denouncing Sharett for what he felt was an exaggerated concern for international opinion.

## Example 3: Reactions to 'Excessive' Reprisals

In the cases of Israeli reprisal attacks on Qibya (October 1953), Gaza (February 1955) and Syrian bases opposite Lake Kinneret (December 1955), the IDF did end up – for various reasons – inflicting greater death and destruction than originally conceived or approved at cabinet level. In light of the resultant international condemnation of Israel, a majority of Israel's cabinet openly or implicitly chastized Ben-Gurion and Dayan. Not only foreign ministry officials, but also many of Israel's leading politicians, were concerned about Israel's standing in world public opinion, whether in the eyes of the United Nations or, more importantly, in Israel's dealings with its Western allies: the US, Britain and France.[38]

Such reaction was especially strong after the Kinneret raid, which resulted in the killing of more than 50 Syrian soldiers and involved a failure to consult the cabinet. Sharett, who was in the United States at the time, wrote mockingly in his diary: 'Ben-Gurion the Defense Minister consulted with Ben-Gurion the [Acting – during Sharett's absence] Foreign Minister and received the green light from Ben-Gurion the Prime Minister'.

Following a storm of protest among the various coalition partners, a cabinet decision demanded that, in future, all reprisal operations be submitted for approval. There is ample evidence of Ben-Gurion being put 'on the defensive' among his colleagues in late December because of the Kinneret raid.[39] While maintaining a confident and unapologetic façade before Israeli and world opinion, Ben-Gurion reportedly confided to one of his commanders that the operation might indeed have been 'excessive' and 'too successful'.[40] The timing of the Lake Kinneret raid – on the eve of Moshe Sharett's return from the US – also seriously compromised the foreign minister's personal credibility with John Foster Dulles, and thus Israel's relations with the US. Both Sharett and Eban complained bitterly at the time that the raid had the effect of undermining Israel's quest for American arms, which they believed (erroneously, it turned out) was on the verge of receiving a positive response.[41]

*Example 4: 'Preventive' War*

Intense worry mounted inside Israel in the months following the Soviet–(Czech–)Egyptian arms deal announced in September 1955. Much public and secret discussion revolved around whether Israel ought to launch a preemptive strike or 'preventive' war against Egypt, at a time of Israel's choosing and before Egypt had successfully absorbed its latest arms acquisitions. During this period Ben-Gurion, serving as both prime minister and defence minister, found himself frequently reining in the more-consistently activist Moshe Dayan and other IDF commanders who believed Israel had to act quickly in initiating such a 'preventive' war. When in mid-November 1955 Dayan recommended a massive military confrontation with Egypt as soon as possible, Ben-Gurion ordered him to hold off until the end of January, claiming there was still a prospect of obtaining arms from the US. As Yaacov Bar-Siman-Tov has argued,

> Ben-Gurion, who usually attributed minimal importance to external constraints in implementing his policy of retaliation against the Arab states, was now more restrained. When the question became one of [initiating a] war with Egypt, he considered the constraints of the great powers more seriously.[42]

Although the main considerations in Ben-Gurion's calculation were timing and arms procurement, his decision against preemptive military action was one which showed respect for what the *goyim* – especially those in Washington – might do or say with regard to Israel's arms requests.

An even more striking illustration of Ben-Gurion in the perhaps-unexpected role of 'restrainer' rather than 'activist' was his mid-December 1955 address to the IDF general staff, conveying and justifying the cabinet's recent rejection of resorting to the 'preventive war' option at that time. Once again, the overriding factors in his analysis were timing and arms procurement, but the Israeli

prime minister and defence minister presented two further reasons
for restraint. The first was the heavy cost of even a victorious war
to Israel's border villages, youth and economy – 'a loss that will set
us back as much as five to seven years'. Ben-Gurion's second reason
was his concern for Israel's image in international opinion:

> Up to now the Arabs have attempted to denounce us as
> expansionists, and aggressors, with varying [degrees of]
> success. If we were to start this war, we would indeed become
> known as the aggressors, and it will not redound to our
> credit... As the victims of aggression they [the Arabs] will
> receive arms from all sides. One thing I am sure of: we will
> receive no arms... Israel will have no arms, and we shall have
> to face the Third Round. We shall be in the same position as
> today, but the circumstances will be much more difficult, and
> whatever satisfaction we may have experienced on the day of
> victory will have been dissipated. It will be much as it is
> today, except that in the eyes of the world we shall have been
> at fault... We must take all these matters into considera-
> tion... [We must] do everything to obtain arms, to improve
> the Army and not become involved in a preventive war. The
> belief that the best thing for us to do now is to attack immedi-
> ately is an emotional and hurried decision which fails to take
> into account all the factors involved.[43]

Such appreciation for Israel's need to be seen by the outside
world as being in a defensive, rather than an aggressive, posture
harked back to Ben-Gurion's preference, since the 1930s, for *havlaga*
(restraint) over activism and revenge in the face of Arab provocation. It displayed a concern for attempting to set Israel on the moral
high ground of international opinion, rather than appearing to
behave as a nation defiantly promoting its narrowly defined security interests.[44]

### Example 5: Preparing for the Sinai Campaign

In September and October 1956, Ben-Gurion considered the possibility of collaboration with France and England in an attack on
Egypt. In elaborating a set of conditions he wanted to place on such
collaboration, Ben-Gurion displayed a remarkable sensitivity for
what at least certain *goyim* might say or do. While the conditions he

sought to lay down did not, in the end, govern Israel's collusion arrangements, the following two diary entries are nevertheless noteworthy illustrations of his approach:

(1) On 27 September 1956, Ben-Gurion wrote:

> I made three negative assumptions: (1) We shall not be the ones to open [hostilities]. (2) We shall not participate unless there is British agreement and their agreement must also include our defence against a Jordanian and Iraqi attack. (We on our part will promise not to attack either Jordan or Syria.) (3) That no action will be taken contrary to US opinion and without it being informed.[45]

(2) During his secret meetings at Sèvres, near Paris, on 22 October, Ben-Gurion recorded in his diary:

> I explained my reasons for rejecting the…proposal that we start the war against Egypt and, 48 hours later, after an ultimatum to both sides, the English and the French would take the Canal. There are ethical, political and military reasons. Why should we all of a sudden become the aggressors – and have our friends in the world denounce us? (Pineau tried to explain that with their veto they will prevent a condemnation in the Security Council.) The US would disapprove, and there's no telling what Russia would do. And most important – Egypt would bomb the airports in Tel Aviv and in Haifa.[46]

Indeed, as Shabtai Teveth has noted,

> Ben Gurion's deep concern over the possibility of aerial bombardments on Israeli population centers was at the heart of his conviction that Israel should not go to war without a strong ally…The need for a powerful ally seemed so vital to Ben Gurion that at one time he thought Israel should join the British Commonwealth and tried to suggest as much to the British Government. Later his aides explored the possibility of Israel joining NATO. Both of these attempts came to naught, and without allies Ben Gurion felt that Israel would gain little or nothing from war with the Arabs.[47]

When finally recommending Operation 'Kadesh' to his cabinet on 28 October 1956, Ben-Gurion realized full well that power would 'be brought to bear to force us to retreat from Sinai', adding the confession that he feared America most of all since it was fully 'capable of forcing us to withdraw. She doesn't need to send an army for that purpose. She has other effective means which are powerful enough.'[48] All in all, the calculations made by Ben-Gurion along his road to Suez hardly seem those of someone who cared not what the *goyim* might say or do.

*Example 6: From 'Victory Speech' to Agreement to Withdraw*

On 7 November 1956, Ben-Gurion congratulated the IDF on its dramatic penetration into Egypt in what was seen as a great 'victory speech' to the Knesset. Expounding his 'new revelation at Sinai', he declared the GAA with Egypt to be null and void, claimed that the Sinai Peninsula had never been recognized as belonging to Egypt, and argued that the Jews had an ancient historic claim to the islands of Sanapir and Tiran at the entrance to the Gulf of Aqaba.[49] Michael Brecher describes the speech as 'a tactical error of the first magnitude', noting that 'it alienated not only '*oum shmoum*' and Israel's enemies – but her friends as well'.[50]

But even as Ben-Gurion was indulging in such bravado there were a number of intersecting external pressures building up on Israel to force her to retreat. These included:

(a) a menacing letter from Soviet Premier Nikolai Bulganin, made worse by French and US indications of a real danger of Soviet missiles being used, and the noteworthy absence of any offer of US protection against such attack;[51]

(b) a request for assurances of Israel's withdrawal from US President Eisenhower, accompanied by not-so-veiled threats of both losing America's international diplomatic support and suffering an embargo on US financial aid;[52]

(c) early indications that American Jewry would not unanimously back Israel in a struggle against the US administration;[53] and

(d) persistent requests for Israel's immediate withdrawal from Egyptian soil made by an impatient and unfriendly UN secretary-general, accompanied by a movement within the General Assembly for condemnatory resolutions with the prospect of sanctions, and Israel's total isolation in world opinion.[54]

'Within less than 48 hours', notes Shlomo Avineri, 'after Bulganin's letter and the clear indication from Eisenhower that Israel would be on its own against a Soviet threat, Ben-Gurion changed course completely.'[55] For purposes of our analysis, Ben-Gurion's about-face illustrates that he was making difficult decisions based on conscious calculations of what the powerful *'goyim'* – including those involved in the UN (*'oom-shmoom'*) – were thinking, saying and threatening to do. Despite his apparently cavalier dismissal of what he called Ambassador Eban's 'frightened' communications of those tense days and Foreign Ministry Director-General Walter Eytan's reports of Israel's near-total isolation in world opinion, even Ben-Gurion was not exempt from sharing the general sense of alarm – including fears of bringing the western world to the brink of a world war involving the Soviet Union – on the day following his 'victory speech'. On 8 November, he instructed Eban to announce Israel's conditional compliance with the UN call to withdraw, while he himself took to the airwaves at 30 minutes after midnight to make the difficult and painful announcement to the Israeli people.[56]

## THE BEN-GURION–SHARETT DISPUTE REVISITED

Much has been written about the differences in temperament and approach which resulted in the breakdown in the mid-1950s of the decades-long political partnership of David Ben-Gurion and Moshe Sharett. One of the most insightful short summaries of this breakdown was penned by Abba Eban:

> [T]he difficulties between Ben-Gurion and Sharett went far beyond quarrels over 'turf'. In theory they should have constituted a balanced harmony. Each posssessed some virtues and had some faults that the other lacked: Ben Gurion was impulsive, imaginative, daring, dynamic; Sharett was prudent, rational, analytical, realistic. Had they been able to work in close harness, an ideal equilibrium might have been achieved. But the contradictions that divided their characters also created an incompatibility of emotion...Far from moving toward a sense of partnership, they had become unable to bear the sight of each other. Ben-Gurion thought that Sharett was talented, but pedantic, excessively meticulous, and

inclined to confuse the vital with the incidental. Sharett, with all his admiration for Ben-Gurion, considered him demagogic, tyrannical, opinionated, devious, and, on some occasions, not quite rational. Their complementary virtues should have been harnessed for the national interest, but their antipathies were too strong for those potentialities to be fulfilled.[57]

Among the issues over which the two leaders clashed was their appraisal of Israel's best ways of dealing with the United Nations and the great powers. As one of Ben-Gurion's biographers has noted, 'the controversy over "what the gentiles will say" was the key to most of the disputes which began to poison the atmosphere between Ben-Gurion and Sharett in the 1950s'.[58] Indeed, belief in a worldview characterized by such slogans as '*oom-shmoom*' and 'it matters not what the *goyim* say...' is one of the defining contrasts used by Brecher, Shlaim, Sheffer, Bar-Siman-Tov and others[59] to distinguish between rival 'activist' and 'diplomatic' schools of Israeli foreign policy-making, associated with Ben-Gurion and Sharett, respectively. Much of the academic analysis of Israel's foreign and security policies is based on this generally sound contrast between the so-called 'Sharett school' favouring caution, moderation and a diplomatic approach and the so-called 'Ben-Gurion school' favouring daring, military prowess and minimizing the importance of outsiders' approval for Israel's behaviour.

Without denying the general usefulness of such contrasts, there is much evidence to suggest that these analyses tend to exaggerate actual *policy* differences between Ben-Gurion and Sharett and their respective supporters. Consider the following two quotations, both from the mid-1950s:

*Quotation 1:*   A decision [must] be reached by the Government for an operational plan aimed at destroying the Nasser régime, either on our own or in cooperation with the Western powers...The Russian–Czech–Egyptian agreement...marks the weakening of Western influence in the region and presents a danger to the very existence of the State of Israel...[We must] begin on the one hand preparing everything necessary for an independent operation, and on the other hand embarking on a campaign in the United States and among the other western powers to acquire defensive weapons and achieve a security treaty as well as a secret agreement for closely coodinated action that would redress the situation in the Middle East.

...If the arming of the enemy's forces is not arrested...I am of the opinion, as are my colleagues...that there is no recourse but to plan a military operation to go hand-in-hand with diplomatic efforts. We must employ our military strength on two levels. First of all, as a threat that will hang over the present situation, and secondly – on the battlefield itself. [60]

While this might sound like a proposal coming straight from the Dayan–Ben-Gurion playbook, it was, in fact, a proposal penned in early October 1955 in the USA by a leading proponent of the 'Sharettist line', Abba Eban, in consultation with Reuven Shiloah, Gideon Rafael (another 'Sharettist') and Katriel Salmon.

*Quotation 2:* The United Nations is certainly still far from perfection. We have bitter and strong objections against it and not only during recent times. But we shall not reject this international institution. The vision embodied in the United Nations is the vision of our prophets. The principles on which it is founded are the principles of peace, justice, and equality among nations. These principles are not less dear to us than to any other nation. In accordance with their heritage, faith, needs, and position in the world, the people of Israel have to adhere to these principles and assist with all their modest strength in preserving them and making them effective in international relations.[61]

While these lofty words might sound like vintage Abba Eban,[62] they were in fact uttered by Prime Minister David Ben-Gurion, addressing the Knesset on 21 February 1957, a week before Israel's formal decision to complete the IDF withdrawal from Gaza.

These statements are, admittedly, not typical of their authors. But they are enough, as exceptions, to form part of a warning against oversimplification and stereotyping in using the 'activist'-versus-'diplomatist' labels. Almost a decade ago, one veteran writer on

Israeli military history concluded that, during the Suez–Sinai crisis, 'Israel's moral standing in the eyes of the world was a decisive consideration, much more than Ben-Gurion's much-publicized derisive reference to the UN ('Um-Sh'mum') suggested',[63] and that, generally speaking, 'the difference between him and Sharett was not as great as one is led to believe'.[64] The evidence summarized here likewise challenges the validity of an exaggerated polarization between the two approaches. Certainly, while we can understand much about Israel's foreign policy by regarding Ben-Gurion and Sharett as personifying 'two broad competing strands of Israeli perceptions and high policy in the period 1948 to 1956',[65] the differences between the 'Ben-Gurionists' – who had a very low opinion of the UN – and the 'Sharettists' – who deplored the *'oom-shmoom'* attitude – were seldom diametrical opposites. Often they were differences of *style, timing, degree* or *emphasis*, rather than fundamental policy.

It would be wrong, for example, to stereotype David Ben-Gurion as boldly dismissing the *'oom-shmoom'* and paying little heed to what the *goyim* say, caring solely for Israeli self-reliance and self-defence. Contradicting the image of a narrowly focused, defence-oriented politician, a diary entry of mid-1950 reveals the Israeli prime minister's nuanced thinking on the interplay between military accomplishments and Israel's international diplomatic posture: 'Foreign policy and defense policy', he wrote,

> both serve the same purpose...If [verbal] explanations do not persuade, [then] use is made of force...Force is not only an army but the creation of the fact...When the state was established it faced three problems: borders, refugees, and Jerusalem. None of them was solved or will be solved by the force of explanation – but on the strength of facts...The creation of a fact in the solution of the three problems takes precedence over explanations, and there must be no holding back from an action [just] because it involves an unfriendly reaction and arouses anger against us.

Even so, Ben-Gurion went on to concede that there was a 'limit' to Israeli 'indifference' to world opinion: '[W]e are dependent on the whole world like every country and more so than every other country. However, a change in relative strength in practice comes before friendly relations [with outside elements].'[66]

Likewise, it would be inaccurate to caricature Moshe Sharett and the MFA as showing little concern for Israel's defence requirements and naïvely exaggerating the importance of international opinion. Sharett, for example, made it clear that he was not opposed to reprisal raids *in principle* and was prepared, if necessary, to risk the disapproval of the UN and the powers. But he regarded resort to military force as acceptable only when it appeared to be the lesser of two evils, and he favoured measured response over excessive retaliation that would only lead, in his view, to a thirst for revenge and an escalation of violence.[67] As one Israeli scholar has summarized it, Sharett's approach called for

> a constant balance between Israel's foreign and defense policies, between self-reliance and awareness of its dependence o[n] international support. Defense policy should be subordinated to foreign policy and be determined by it. Sharett...was highly sensitive not only to 'what the gentiles will say' in response to Israeli action, but even more so to 'what the gentiles will do'.[68]

Like Sharett, Ben-Gurion also showed healthy respect for 'what the gentiles will do'. Even his apparent disinterest in 'what the *goyim* say' is contrary to one of the 'old man's' three constant operating principles, as described by biographer Shabtai Teveth, namely, that Israel will not survive without the sympathy and support of at least one of the free world's major powers.[69] In another sense, the contempt for non-Jews implied in Ben-Gurion's rhetorical dismissal of 'what the *goyim* say' is contradicted by his passionate intellectual interest in the history, cultures, languages, geography and social development of many peoples and countries around the globe. In addition to his patriotic concern for the Zionist 'ingathering of the exiles' and the building up of the IDF, Ben-Gurion was imbued with a broad international outlook that led him in the 1950s and 1960s to foresee the rising power of the countries of Asia and to be among the first to alert Israelis to the need to build bridges with them. In late 1952, for example, Ben-Gurion argued that a worthy Israeli delegation be sent to a conference of Asian countries to be held in Rangoon. Writing to Foreign Minister Sharett, he stressed the fact that he regarded this meeting as being

> of *supreme importance* [emphasis in original]...more important than the UN General Assembly and conferences of that kind (from our point of view)...This is in my opinion an

*historic* [emphasis in original] opportunity of unique political
and moral importance where we can meet with the intelligentsia...of Oriental countries.[70]

As we have seen, the line between haughtily dismissing 'what
the *goyim* say', on the one hand, and acting cautiously out of a fear
of what the stronger nations of the world (whether working
through the United Nations, or on their own) might *do*, on the other,
was wisely crossed by a pragmatic Ben-Gurion at several crucial
moments. The dichotomy set up between *either* diplomacy aimed at
winning world opinion *or* military action against Arab 'terrorists' to
ensure Israel's security was often a false one. Israel's efforts to
acquire armaments from the United States, France and other
sources of supply were, by their very nature, based on a combination of both defence and foreign-policy imperatives. They involved
years of devoted lobbying activity by officials in both the MFA and
the ministry of defence (admittedly not always working in
harmony). Such pleading in Washington, Paris and London was
necessarily accompanied at times by veiled threats that Israel might
be forced to resort to military action, for example, to capture Gaza
or launch a 'preventive war' – threats uttered by 'moderates' like
Sharett and Eban, not just the recognized 'activists' Ben-Gurion and
Dayan.[71]

The tendency to overstate the Ben-Gurion–Sharett differences is
not a *post facto* academic invention, but was promoted and exaggerated during the in-fighting between these two leaders. The
dichotomy was further sharpened in the day-to-day political and
personality struggles and rivalries among members of the defence
and foreign-ministry establishments. Thus, Ben-Gurion often
portrayed Sharett in distorted and caricatured fashion, as though
the foreign minister's 'entire world consist[ed] of nothing but
"What will the gentiles say" and [his] whole approach [was] to find
favour in their eyes'. By contrast, he portrayed his own approach as
being 'to look after the security of the state, its independent status,
and the education of its youth'. Sharett further quotes Ben-Gurion
as arguing, before the Mapai Central Committee in early August
1955, that in his version of a properly run government the minister
of defence would be authorized to determine defence policy, while
the role of the foreign minister would be 'to explain this policy to
the powers and to "*oom-shmoom*"'.[72] This unflattering view carried
over well into the 1960s and 1970s, as Michael Brecher discovered

during his extensive interviews with Israel's leading decision-makers. Army and defence officials, he found, 'persistently ridiculed' the MFA's methods

> and its alleged soft line and concern for 'the *Goyim*': in their preoccupation with foreign reaction, was the charge, they did not contribute to Israel's crucial foreign policy objective – security... To the Army the [MFA] was saturated with 'Sharettism', the policy of caution and exaggerated concern with 'the external factor'.[73]

The 'macho' image of Ben-Gurion as someone uniquely endowed to defend the nation has been fostered, in part, by those who like to romanticize Israel and think of it as a little maverick state standing defiantly alone against a hostile world. But it would be incorrect to conclude, from his association with cavalier, dismissive phrases such as *'oom-shmoom'* and 'it matters not what the goyim say...', that Ben-Gurion and his supporters actually governed the country in accordance with policies based squarely on such attitudes. In practice, these slogans remained mostly in the realm of rhetoric. They were indeed highly emotive reflections of a broad current of Israeli sentiment – a feeling of being in a small country, isolated and beleaguered in a cold and dangerous world. Such slogans were also effective in mobilizing party and public support for Ben-Gurion over Sharett as leader. But when it came to *actions*, Ben-Gurion's superior leadership qualities included the ability to behave, when appropriate, in the moderate 'Sharettist' tradition – all the while consolidating his now-legendary posture as the sole true defender of Israel's security by rhetorically dismissing *'oom-shmoom'* and attacking Moshe Sharett for being too concerned about 'what the *goyim* think'.

In sum, students of Israeli foreign policy should be wary of accepting at face value simplistic and overdrawn applications of the admittedly useful 'activist'–'moderate' dichotomy sometimes popularized through self-serving memoirs, political rivalries, personal backstabbing and electoral rhetoric. Differences over *'oom-shmoom'* and 'It matters not what the *goyim* say...' between the fondly remembered David Ben-Gurion, on the one hand, and his non-charismatic and much-forgotten partner, Moshe Sharett, on the other, were not always the contrasting polar-opposites that have commonly been presented.

NOTES

This essay is based on a paper presented to the 15th annual meeting of the Association for Israel Studies, Washington, DC, 23 May 1999. The author wishes to acknowledge, with thanks, the Harry S. Truman Institute of the Hebrew University for its award of a Visiting Research Fellowship which enabled him to begin work on this subject, and to express his appreciation to Shabtai Teveth and Professors Michael Brecher and Bernard Wasserstein for their critiques of an early draft of the paper; the author remains solely responsible for the result.

 1. Y. Rabin address to the Knesset, 27 June 1993. The biblical reference is to a phrase in Numbers 23:9. Cf. Yaacov Herzog, *A People that Dwells Alone: Speeches and Writings of Yaacov Herzog*, Misha Louvish (ed.) (London: Weidenfeld and Nicolson), 1975.
 2. See, e.g., Amos Oz, 'The State as Reprisal', *Essays*, transl. Nicholas de Lange (New York: Cambridge University Press, 1995), 61–9; cf. Neil Caplan, 'Victimhood and Identity: Psychological Obstacles to Israeli Reconciliation with the Palestinians', in *Israeli and Palestinian Identities in History and Literature*, Kamal Abdel-Malek and David C. Jacobson (eds) (New York: St Martin's Press, 1999), 67–71.
 3. Nitza Nachmias, 'The UN and Israel, 1947–1987: Cooperation and Conflict in Review', *Be'ayot Beinlumiyot, hevra u-medina*, 27, 1–2 (1988), p. 29.
 4. Leo Rosten, *The Joys of Yiddish* (New York: McGraw-Hill, 1968), p. 316. Cf. Michael Brecher, *The Foreign Policy System of Israel: Setting, Images, Process* (London/Toronto/Melbourne: Oxford University Press, 1972), p. 139.
 5. Aaron S. Klieman, *Israel and the World After 40 Years* (Washington: Pergamon-Brassey's, 1990), p. 43. See also ibid., p. 29; Brecher, *Foreign Policy System*, p. 139, and *Decisions in Israel's Foreign Policy* (New Haven: Yale University Press, 1975), p. 622 (Glossary); Adam Garfinkle, *Politics and Society in Modern Israel: Myths and Realities* (Armonk, NY: M.E. Sharpe, 1997), p. 234.
 6. Rafi Mann, *Lo Ya'aleh 'al ha-Da'at [It's Inconceivable]: Quotations, Expressions, Nicknames and Linguistic Phrases* (Or Yehuda: Hed Arzi, 1998), p. 7; Esther Hecht, 'Say It Again, Golda' (review of R. Mann), *Jerusalem Post Magazine*, 18 Sept. 1998, p. 9.
 7. Moshe Sharett, *Yoman Ishi* (Personal Diary, 1953–1957), 8 vols, Yaacov Sharett (ed.) (Tel Aviv: Sifriyat Maariv, 1978). I was unable to find any discussion of '*oom-shmoom*' in the popular biography by Michael Bar-Zohar, *Ben-Gurion*, 3 vols (Tel Aviv: Am Oved, 1977), published a year before Sharett's diaries.
 8. *Yoman Ishi*, Vol. III, p. 874 (29 March 1955); Vol. IV, pp. 931–2 (13 April 1955).
 9. The official stenographic protocol of the last part of the cabinet meeting presents a different, and less pointed, record of Ben-Gurion's remarks. As in Sharett's account, there are frequently reworked phrases about the state emerging as a result of 'Jewish willpower and Jewish strength to remain here until death', and not thanks to the United Nations, except (Ben-Gurion did allow) for the moral support of the 33 countries which voted for partition. 'But, in essence', he went on, 'the UN resolution would have been of no use had there not been Jewish youngsters prepared to kill and be killed.' There are, however, two noteworthy differences from the version given in *Yoman Ishi*: (a) the protocol does not contain any mention at all of the phrase '*oom-shmoom*', and (b) Ben-Gurion's argument is not directed at Sharett in particular, but rather at 'several colleagues who say that the state would not have been created had it not been for the UN resolution'. Israel State Archives (hereafter ISA), Cabinet Meetings, Vol. 21, meeting 37, item 309, pp. 57–74.
10. Brecher, *Foreign Policy System*, pp. 366ff. Cf. ibid., Ch. 12 and pp. 298, 307, 332ff., 338, 342.
11. Brecher, *Foreign Policy System*, p. 544. For a self-consciously untypical positive spin on Israel–UN relations over the years, see Abba Eban, 'Does the U.N. Belong at the Table?', *New York Times*, 13 June 1991, p. A29.
12. Speech to the annual Journalists' Luncheon, Tel Aviv (Jerusalem: Government Printing Office *Press Bulletin*, 30 Nov. 1962), quoted in Brecher, *Foreign Policy System*, pp. 257ff. Cf. Independence Day address, 27 April 1955, quoted and discussed in Bar-Zohar, *Ben-Gurion*, Vol. III, p. 1142.
13. UNGA Resolution 273 (III) and UNSC Resolutions 72 (1949) and 95 (1951), respectively, reproduced in George J. Tomeh (ed.), *United Nations Resolutions on Palestine and*

the *Arab–Israeli Conflict, Vol. I: 1947–1974* (Washington: Institute for Palestine Studies, 1975), pp. 18, 131, 134.

14. See, e.g., UNSC Resolutions 92 (8 May 1951), 93 (18 May 1951), 100 (27 Oct. 1953), 101 (24 Nov. 1953), 106 (29 March 1955), 107 (30 March 1955), 108 (8 Sept. 1955), 111 (19 Jan. 1956), 113 (4 April 1956) and 114 (4 June 1956), and UNGA Resolutions 303 (9 Dec. 1949), 394 (14 Dec. 1950), 997 (2 Nov. 1956), 999 (4 Nov. 1956), 1002 (7 Nov. 1956), 1120 (24 Nov. 1956), 1123 (19 Jan. 1957), and 1124–1125 (2 Feb. 1957), reproduced in *United Nations Resolutions* I, pp. 20–3, 31–40 and 133–9.

15. Abba Eban, *An Autobiography* (New York: Random House, 1977), pp. 176–7.

16. Neil Caplan, *Futile Diplomacy,* Vol. 3: *The United Nations, the Great Powers and Middle East Peacemaking, 1948–1954* (London: Frank Cass, 1997), Chs II–X.

17. Sharett–Acheson meeting, 19 Nov. 1951, in United States Department of State, *Foreign Relations of the United States: 1951,* Vol. V (Washington: USGPO, 1982), pp. 935–40; Israel State Archives, *Documents on the Foreign Policy of Israel,* Vol. 6 (1951), Yemima Rosenthal (ed.) (Jerusalem, 1991), pp. 808–19 (doc. 498) – hereafter ID6. Cf. Caplan, *Futile Diplomacy,* Vol. III, 207–10.

18. Sharett memorandum to UNSG, 29 Nov. 1951, ID6, pp. 836–9 (doc. 509). The PCC never did, in fact, resume any conciliation attempts after November 1951. See David P. Forsythe, *United Nations Peacemaking: The Conciliation Commission for Palestine* (Baltimore / London: Johns Hopkins University Press, 1972), Ch. IV; Shabtai Rosenne, 'Israel and the United Nations: Changed Perspectives, 1945–1976', in M. Fine and M. Himmelfarb (eds), *American Jewish Year Book 1978* (New York and Philadelphia: American Jewish Committee and Jewish Publication Society of America, 1977), pp. 18–20; Caplan, *Futile Diplomacy* Vol. 3, p. 210f.

19. Golda Meir, *My Life: The Autobiography of Golda Meir* (London: Weidenfeld & Nicolson, 1975), p. 243; Michael B. Oren, 'Ambivalent Adversaries: David Ben-Gurion and Israel vs. the United Nations and Dag Hammarskjöld, 1956–57', *Journal of Contemporary History,* 27, 1 (1992), pp. 89–127; Ben-Gurion to Eban, 27 May 1956, reproduced in *David Ben-Gurion, Rosh ha-Memshala ha-Rishon: Mivhar Te'udot (1947–1963) (The First Prime Minister: Selected Documents),* Yemima Rosenthal and Eli Shaltiel (eds) (Jerusalem: Israel State Archives, 1996), pp. 304–7 (doc. 78) (hereafter Mivhar Te'udot); Ben-Gurion remarks, quoted in Mordechai Bar-On, *The Gates of Gaza: Israel's Road to Suez and Back, 1955–1957,* transl. Ruth Rossing (New York: St Martin's Press, 1994), p. 212; Abba Eban, *Personal Witness: Israel Through My Eyes* (New York: G. P. Putnam's Sons, 1992), pp. 266–7; Brecher, *Decisions,* pp. 235–8; Brecher, *Foreign Policy System,* p. 307; Rosenne, 'Israel and the United Nations', p. 27.

20. For a detailed discussion, see Caplan, *Futile Diplomacy,* Vol. III, Ch. XII.

21. AMAN Research Department, 'The Policy of UNSG Dag Hammarskjöld on Middle East Problems', 25 Sept. 1958, forwarded by Bar-Yaacov to Gazit, 20 Sept. 1958, ISA, Foreign Ministry files (herafter: FM), 130.19 / 4316 / 3.

22. For different accounts of UNTSO–Israel relations, see: E. L. M. Burns, *Between Arab and Israeli* (New York: Ivan Obolensky, 1963); Rosalyn Higgins, *United Nations Peacekeeping, 1946–1967: Documents and Commentary,* Vol. I: The Middle East (London/New York/Toronto: Oxford University Press (under the auspices of the Royal Institute of International Affairs), 1969); Benny Morris, *Israel's Border Wars, 1949–1956: Arab Infiltration, Israeli Retaliation, and the Countdown to the Suez War* (New York: Oxford University Press, 1993); Nathan A. Pelcovits, *The Long Armistice: UN Peacekeeping and the Arab–Israeli Conflict, 1948–1960,* foreword by Samuel W. Lewis (Boulder / San Francisco / Oxford: Westview Press, 1993); Caplan, *Futile Diplomacy,* Vol. III, Ch. VIII.

23. *Yoman Ishi,* Vol. IV, pp. 919ff. (11 April 1955).

24. *Yoman Ishi,* Vol. I, pp. 50ff. (18 Oct. 1953). Cf. Gabriel Sheffer, 'The Confrontation Between Moshe Sharett and David Ben-Gurion', in Shmuel Almog (ed.), *Zionism and the Arabs: Essays* (Jerusalem: Historical Society of Israel / Zalman Shazar Center, 1983), p. 127; Sheffer, *Moshe Sharett: Biography of a Political Moderate* (Oxford: Clarendon Press, 1996), pp. 688, 1003.

25. Pelcovits (*Long Armistice,* pp. 44–5) describes a 'fundamental asymmetry' in the 'armistice situation' (emphasis in orig.) that Israelis found prejudicial to their interests. Cf. pp. 78–9, 113–15, 215–20; Eban, *Personal Witness,* pp. 236–7.

26. Report of a Danish priest's conversation with General Bennike, in Erell to Eytan, 23 April 1954, ISA, FM 130.02/2425/8b; E. H. Hutchison, *Violent Truce: A Military Observer Looks at the Arab–Israeli Conflict, 1951–1955* (New York: Devin-Adair, 1956), pp. 47–54, 194–5; Morris, *Israel's Border Wars*, pp. 294–300. A similar situation arose a year earlier, in which Major-General Bennett de Ridder, Chairman of IJMAC and sometimes acting chief of staff of UNTSO, refused to accept tracks leading to the Jordanian border as evidence of Jordanian culpability in an attack which gravely injured a woman in Kfar Saba, raising the possibility that Israeli terrorists had been guilty and had faked the tracks. See Sharett's complaint to Eban and Elath, 11 June 1953, in Israel State Archives, *Documents on the Foreign Policy of Israel*, Vol. 8 (1953), Yemima Rosenthal (ed.) (Jerusalem: 1995), pp. 468–9 (doc. 262) (hereafter ID8).

27. Interview, *US News and World Report*, 17 Sept. 1954, p. 68. Cf. Neil Caplan, *Futile Diplomacy*, Vol. 4: *Operation Alpha and the Failure of Anglo-American Coercive Diplomacy in the Arab–Israeli Conflict, 1954–1956* (London: Frank Cass, 1997), p. 46.

28. Ben-Gurion remarks to the Knesset, 15 Oct. 1956, quoted in Bar-On, *Gates of Gaza*, p. 212. Cf. Brecher, *Decisions*, p. 235. Versions of the text of this important speech are available in *Israel's Foreign Relations: Selected Documents 1947–1974*, Meron Medzini (ed.) (Jerusalem: Ministry of Foreign Affairs, 1976), Vol. I, pp. 357–64; ISA, FM 130.02/2383/18; David Ben-Gurion, *Israel: A Personal History*, trs. Nechemia Meyers and Uzy Nystar (New York: Funk and Wagnalls, 1971), pp. 496–502; *Mivhar Te'udot*, pp. 317–20 (doc. 84).

29. Brecher, *Foreign Policy System*, pp. 258ff. Brecher does, however, recognize evidence of 'rare moments of ambivalence' in Ben-Gurion's *'oom-shmoom'* attitude: 'he had always manifested a mixture of disdain, regarding its role in the Arab–Israel conflict, and hope, concerning its potential contribution to world order', Brecher, *Decisions*, p. 235. Cf. *Foreign Policy System*, pp. 266, 367.

30. This much-misinterpreted slogan is better understood in its proper context, namely, Ben-Gurion's exhortation to Israeli youth to draw more upon their own resources (e.g. in developing the Negev) rather than looking to outsiders for approval or support.

31. Leon Gordenker, 'The United Nations as a Third Party in Arab–Israeli Conflicts', *Jerusalem Journal of International Relations*, 10, 1 (March 1988), p. 65. In 1961 Ben-Gurion recognized that the UN 'has not the power, the authority or the will to put its principles into practice'. David Ben-Gurion, 'Achievements and Tasks of Our Generation', *Israel Government Yearbook 5722 (1961/62)* (Jerusalem: Government Printer, 1962), quoted in Brecher, *Foreign Policy System*, p. 266.

32. Brecher, *Foreign Policy System*, p. 144.

33. The two cases were (a) American endorsement of a UNSC resolution asking Israel to suspend water-diversion works at Bnot Yaacov in late 1953, and (b) Eisenhower's and Dulles's firm backing for Dag Hammarskjöld's repeated calls for Israel to withdraw unconditionally from Egyptian territory captured in the Sinai–Suez war in late 1956 and early 1957. See Abraham Ben-Zvi, *The United States and Israel: The Limits of the Special Relationship* (New York: Columbia University Press, 1993), Chs 2–3.

34. Avi Shlaim, 'Conflicting Approaches to Israel's Relations with the Arabs: Ben Gurion and Sharett, 1953–1956', *Middle East Journal*, 37, 2 (spring 1983), p. 180.

35. In his discussion of the events and debates of the period 1953–1956, even Shlaim himself clearly shows how, on several key occasions, Ben-Gurion suffered setbacks when cabinet majorities rallied behind Sharett, Shlaim, 'Conflicting Approaches', pp. 191, 195, 198. Cf. Example 2, below.

36. Primary documentation from the Israeli and American perspectives can be found, respectively, in ID8, 645–1025 *passim* (docs. 366–620), and United States, Department of State, *Foreign Relations of the United States: 1952–1954*, Vol. IX, Paul Claussen, Joan M. Lee and Carl N. Raether (eds) (Washington: USGPO, 1986), pp. 1303–1434 *passim* (docs. 658–9, 661, 663, 665, 673, 675, 682, 725, 734–6). Critical discussions of the episode are given in: Brecher, *Decisions*, Ch. 5; Stephen Green, *Taking Sides: America's Secret Relations with a Militant Israel* (New York: Morrow, 1984), Ch. 4; Yaacov Bar-Siman-Tov, 'The Limits of Economic Sanctions: The American–Israeli Case of 1953', *Journal of Contemporary History*, 23 (1988), pp. 425–43; Ben-Zvi, *The United States and Israel*, Ch. 2; Sheffer, *Moshe Sharett*, p. 682.

37. Cf. Yaacov Bar-Siman-Tov, 'Ben-Gurion and Sharett: Conflict Management and Great Power Constraints in Israeli Foreign Policy', *Middle Eastern Studies*, 24 (1988), p. 352; Shlaim, 'Conflicting Approaches', pp. 191, 195, 198; Sheffer, 'The Confrontation', pp. 135–40.
38. For primary documentation on the negative fallout in Western capitals, at the United Nations and among Diaspora Jewry after the Qibya raid, see reports and correspondence in ID8, 756-913 *passim* (docs. 433–5, 439, 448, 461, 471–2, 477, 479, 483, 490–1, 495, 499–501, 503–5, 514–5, 518, 533, 539, 544). Cf. Caplan, *Futile Diplomacy*, Vol. III, pp. 222–5; Morris, *Israel's Border Wars*, pp. 244–62.
39. *Yoman Ishi*, Vol. V, p. 1310 (16 Dec. 1955). Cf. ibid., p. 1314 (25 Dec. 1955); Bar-On, *Gates of Gaza*, pp. 62ff.; Ben-Gurion to Eban, 19 Dec. 1955, in *Mivhar Te'udot*, pp. 288–9 (doc. 75); Ben-Gurion speech to Mapai Political Committee, 28 Dec. 1955, pp. 290–2 (doc. 76); Eban, *An Autobiography*, pp. 198–9 and *Personal Witness*, pp. 248–9; Morris, *Israel's Border Wars*, pp. 365–8.
40. Ariel Sharon, with David Chanoff, *Warrior: The Autobiography of Ariel Sharon* (New York: Simon & Schuster, 1989), pp. 126ff. Cf. Mordechai Bar-On, *Sha'arei Aza: Mediniut ha-Bitahon ve-ha-Hutz shel Medinat Yisrael: 1955–1957 (The Gates of Gaza: Israel's Defence and Foreign Policy)* (Tel Aviv: Am Oved, 1992), pp. 78 and 437 n.15; Morris, *Israel's Border Wars*, pp. 366, 368.
41. Isaac Alteras, *Eisenhower and Israel: U.S.–Israeli Relations, 1953–1960* (Gainsville: University Press of Florida, 1993), pp. 154, 161; Bar-On, *Gates of Gaza*, 58–61, 352 n.19; Sharett, *Yoman Ishi*, Vol. V, 1314–15 (25 Dec. 1955); Eban, *An Autobiography*, pp. 198–9 and *Personal Witness*, pp. 248–9; Gideon Rafael, *Destination Peace: Three Decades of Israeli Foreign Policy: A Personal Memoir* (New York: Stein & Day, 1981), pp. 47–8; Herzog, *A People that Dwells Alone*, p. 241; Morris, *Israel's Border Wars*, p. 368.
42. Bar-Siman-Tov, 'Ben-Gurion and Sharett', p. 341, citing Moshe Dayan, *Avnei Derekh: Autobiografia (Stepping Stones: An Autobiography)* (Jerusalem: Edanim (with Dvir, Tel Aviv), 1976), pp. 164–5 (13–14 Nov. 1955). See also Shabtai Teveth, *Moshe Dayan: The Soldier, the Man, the Legend*, transl. Leah and David Zinder (Boston: Houghton Mifflin, 1973), pp. 249, 254–5; Shlaim, 'Conflicting Approaches', p. 194. On the internal debates for and against Israel's launching of a preventive war, see Bar-On, *Gates of Gaza*, Ch. 4, and Motti Golani, *Israel in Search of War: The Sinai Campaign, 1955–1956* (Brighton: Sussex Academic Press, 1998). It should be noted that Ben-Gurion's argument against a war *initiated by Israel* was consistent with the IDF's chosen policy of deliberately attempting to provoke Nasser into being the one to initiate – and be seen by the world to be the one who initiated – full-scale hostilities. See Bar-On, *Gates of Gaza*, Ch. 4; Caplan, *Futile Diplomacy*, Vol. IV, pp. 164–8.
43. Address to General Staff, 16 Dec. 1955, English text as transmitted to Allen W. Dulles, 10 Jan. 1956, USNA, NEA Lot 59 D518 Box 33. Cf. Dayan, *Avnei Derekh*, pp. 174–5; Teveth, *Moshe Dayan*, pp. 248–9, 255; Shlaim, 'Conflicting Approaches', p. 196; Bar-Siman-Tov, 'Ben-Gurion and Sharett', p. 342; Netanel Lorch, 'David Ben-Gurion and the Sinai Campaign, 1956', in Ronald W. Zweig (ed.), *David Ben-Gurion: Politics and Leadership in Israel* (London: Frank Cass, 1991), p. 294; Bar-On, *Gates of Gaza*, pp. 66–8.
44. During the first year of the Palestinian *intifada*, Teveth recalled the arguments that Ben-Gurion had made during the 1936–39 Palestinian–Arab rebellion in favour of *havlaga* as being linked to his understanding of Britain's differing reactions to Jewish and Arab use of force, Shabtai Teveth, 'Ben-Gurion's Three No's', *Ha-aretz*, 5 Feb. 1988.
45. Diary entry, 27 Sept. 1956, in 'Ben-Gurion's Diary: the Suez-Sinai Campaign', ed. and intro. Selwyn Ilan Troen, in Selwyn Ilan Troen and Moshe Shemesh (eds), *The Suez-Sinai Crisis, 1956: Retrospective and Reappraisal*, (London: Frank Cass, 1990), p. 300. In another context, Teveth notes ('Ben-Gurion's Three No's') that, ever since the Mandate period, Ben-Gurion had operated on three negative principles: (1) Israel will not survive without the sympathy and support of the Jewish people; (2) Israel will not survive without the sympathy and support of the free world – then represented by Great Britain, later by the United States; (3) Israel should never contemplate war or embark on one unless the physical existence of its citizens was at stake.
46. Diary entry, 22 Oct. 1956, in Troen, *The Suez–Sinai Crisis*, p. 307.

47. Teveth, *Moshe Dayan*, pp. 248–9.
48. Quoted in Bar-On, *Gates of Gaza*, p. 271.
49. Ben-Gurion, Knesset address, 7 Nov. 1956, ISA, FM 130.03/1965/4; Hebrew text in *Mivhar Te'udot*, 341–6 (doc. 92). Cf. Teveth, *Moshe Dayan*, p. 257.
50. Brecher, *Decisions*, p. 282. A number of writers have drawn upon Abba Eban's report of remarks made to him by Canada's Minister of External Affairs, Lester B. Pearson: 'This speech must have been as offensive to the British, the French, the Americans and to us Canadians as it was to the Arabs. If you people persist with this, you run the risk of losing all your friends.' Eban, *Personal Witness*, p. 275. Cf. Lorch, 'Ben Gurion and Sinai', p. 306; Bar-On, *Gates of Gaza*, p. 274; Shlomo Avineri, 'The Sinai Campaign and the Limits of Power (II)', in Troen, *The Suez–Sinai Crisis*, pp. 246–7; Keith Kyle (New York: St Martin's Press, 1991), pp. 477–8; Pelcovits, *Long Armistice*, pp. 130–1; Alteras, *Eisenhower and Israel*, pp. 246–7.
51. Bulganin to Ben-Gurion, 5 Nov. 1956, text in John Norton Moore (ed.), *The Arab–Israeli Conflict* (Princeton: Princeton University Press, 1974), Vol. III, pp. 622–4. Cf. Ben-Gurion, Diary entry, 7 Nov. 1956, in Troen, 'Ben-Gurion's Diary', pp. 317–18; Ben-Gurion reply to Bulganin, 7 Nov. 1956, in *The Arab–Israeli Conflict*, Vol. III, pp. 624–5; Brecher, *Decisions*, pp. 284–6, 290–1; Netanel Lorch, *Be-Tzvat Maatzamot: Yisrael ve-Lahatzei ha-Maatzamot be-shilhei Milhemet ha-Atzma'ut ve-Maarekhet Kadesh* (In the Grip of the Powers: Israel and the Pressures of the Powers at the End of the War of Independence and the Sinai Campaign) (Tel Aviv: Maarakhot/Ministry of Defence, 1990), Ch. 2; Bar-On, *Gates of Gaza*, pp. 272–4; Alteras, Eisenhower and Israel, pp. 243–4, 247.
52. United States Department of State, Nina J. Noring (ed.), *Foreign Relations of the United States: 1955–1957*, Vol. XVI, *Suez Crisis: July 26–December 31, 1956* (Washington: USGPO, 1990), pp. 821–1096 *passim*; Brecher, *Decisions*, pp. 286–7; Bar-On, *Gates of Gaza*, pp. 274–6; Alteras, *Eisenhower and Israel*, pp. 247–9.
53. Goldmann to Ben-Gurion, 8 Nov. 1956, tgm.870/297, ISA, FM 130.02/2459/1; Bar-On, *Gates of Gaza*, p. 275; Brecher, *Decisions*, pp. 277–8, 287; Alteras, *Eisenhower and Israel*, p. 248 and Ch. 10.
54. Brecher, *Decisions*, pp. 291, 293–6; Bar-On, *Gates of Gaza*, p. 275. On 7 November the UNGA voted 65–1–10 calling on Israel 'once again' to withdraw immediately. Resolution 1002 (ES-1), *United Nations Resolutions*, I, 34.
55. Avineri, 'Limits of Power', p. 247. Avineri continues: 'His response to Bulganin, which Ben-Gurion himself read over Israel radio, while aggressive in tone and language, clearly stated that Israel had no territorial claims on Egypt, and [had gone] to war only in order to secure its border against incursion and to guarantee freedom of navigation in the Gulf of Eilat.'
56. Ben-Gurion, Radio Broadcast, 00:30, 9 Nov. 1956, ISA, FM 130.03/1965/4; Hebrew text in *Mivhar Te'udot*, pp. 348–51 (doc. 94). Cf. Ben-Gurion, Diary entry, 8 Nov. 1956, in Troen, 'Ben-Gurion's Diary', pp. 318–19; Brecher, *Decisions*, pp. 286–9; Bar-On, *Gates of Gaza*, pp. 275–6; Alteras, *Eisenhower and Israel*, pp. 247–9.
57. Eban, *Personal Witness*, pp. 249–50. Cf. *An Autobiography*, p. 202.
58. Michael Bar-Zohar, quoted in Sheffer, 'The Confrontation', p. 102. Cf. Brecher, *Foreign Policy System*, p. 253.
59. Brecher, *Foreign Policy System*, Ch. 12 ('Ben Gurion and Sharett: Contrasting Views of the World'); Shlaim, 'Conflicting Approaches', pp. 180–201; Sheffer, 'The Confrontation', pp. 95–147; Bar-Siman-Tov, 'Ben-Gurion and Sharett', pp. 330–56.
60. Quotations are taken from two documents: Abba Eban to Moshe Sharett, 12 Oct. 1955, and Eban–Shiloah draft proposal, 11 Oct. 1955, both quoted in Haggai Eshed, *Reuven Shiloah: The Man Behind the Mossad: Secret Diplomacy in the Creation of Israel*, transl. by David and Leah Zinder, fwds. by Shimon Peres and Haim Herzog (London: Frank Cass, 1997), pp. 211–12 and 213. Cf. Sharett, *Yoman Ishi*, Vol. IV, p. 1207; Eban, *Personal Witness*, pp. 254–5; Bar-Siman-Tov, 'Ben-Gurion and Sharett', p. 339.
61. Ben-Gurion, Statement to the Knesset, 21 Feb. 1957, in *Israel's Foreign Relations*, I, p. 598. Cf. '…some kind of supreme authority for mankind is taking shape…The UN may yet do great things in drawing the peoples closer and building peace in the world.' Ben-Gurion, 'Achievements and Tasks of Our Generation', *Israel Government Yearbook 5722 (1961/62)* (Jerusalem: Government Printer, 1962), quoted in Brecher, *Foreign Policy System*, p. 266.

62. For Eban's philosophical reasoning behind the need to support a world body like the United Nations, see his article, 'Do we really need the UN?', *Look Magazine*, 29 June 1965, pp. 75–6; Cf. longer draft, 'Do We Need the United Nations?', ISA, 130.02/3/5924/36.
63. Lorch, 'David Ben-Gurion', p. 309. This view would seem to contradict the one advanced by Brecher, who argues (*Decisions*, p. 235) that '[t]hroughout the decision flow on Sinai...it was the denigrating *"oum shmoum"* image which prevailed', and cites as evidence Ben-Gurion's 15 October 1956 speech to the Knesset (n. 24 above). That speech – although it was undeniably a 'most important public *tour d'horizon* before the strategic decision to launch the Sinai Campaign' – was, I would submit, an occasion for rhetorical self-justification and morale-building which had little *operational* impact.
64. Lorch, 'David Ben-Gurion'. This view is shared by Ben-Gurion's official biographer, Shabtai Teveth, among others.
65. Brecher, *Foreign Policy System*, pp. 256ff.
66. Diary entry, 22 July 1950, quoted in Uri Bialer, 'Facts and Pacts', pp. 216–17.
67. On several occasions, Sharett compared his own, restrained approach to Ben-Gurion's 'system of angry reactions designed to bring matters to a crisis point, as if redemption will thereby come about as a result'. *Yoman Ishi*, Vol. IV, p. 920 (11 April 1955). Cf. ibid., Vol. II, p. 455 (12 April 1954); Sheffer, 'The Confrontation', pp. 127, 133.
68. Bar-Siman-Tov, 'Ben-Gurion and Sharett', p. 332, citing Sharett to Ben-Gurion, 22 March 1954, *Yoman Ishi*, Vol. II, pp. 408–10, Sharett to Lavon, 13 Sept. 1954, ibid., p. 577, and Sharett's address to the Mapai young people's 'study group' following his resignation, *Yoman Ishi*, Vol. V, pp. 1515–19 (28 June 1956). Cf. Sheffer, 'The Confrontation', pp. 126ff.; Sheffer, *Moshe Sharett*, pp. 722, 734.
69. Teveth, 'Ben-Gurion's Three No's', *Ha'aretz*, 5 Feb. 1988.
70. Ben-Gurion to Sharett, 23 Dec. 1952, ISA, FM 130.02/2446/11. Cf. David Ben-Gurion, 'Towards a New World', *Israel Government Yearbook 5721 (1960/61)* (Jerusalem: Government Printer, 1961), pp. 23–33, 36–42; Brecher, *Foreign Policy System*, p. 264.
71. Evelyn Shuckburgh of the British foreign office recounts 'an hour of painful and vigorous arguments' in Washington with Reuven Shiloah and Gideon Rafael (the latter of the two being a loyal 'Sharettist'), who were 'quite frantic' about the September 1955 Czech arms deal and who 'told [him] solemnly that Israel will not sit by and see the balance of strength turned against them by Soviet arming of Egypt'. Evelyn Shuckburgh, *Descent to Suez: Diaries 1951–56*, selected for publication by John Charmley (London: Weidenfeld and Nicolson, 1986), pp. 285ff. (diary entry of 2 Oct. 1955). See also Sharett, *Yoman Ishi*, Vol. IV, p. 1203 (11 Oct. 1955), Vol. V, pp. 1249ff. (25 Oct. 1955), pp. 1252ff. (26 Oct. 1955), p. 1266 (30 Oct. 1955), 1272–4 (31 Oct. 1955); Eban, *An Autobiography*, pp. 194–6; Bar-Siman-Tov, 'Ben-Gurion and Sharett', pp. 339ff.
72. *Yoman Ishi*, Vol. IV, p. 1117 (8 Aug. 1955). Cf. Shlaim, 'Conflicting Approaches', p. 192; Sheffer, 'The Confrontation', p. 138; Bar-Siman-Tov, 'Ben-Gurion and Sharett', p. 337f.; Sheffer, *Moshe Sharett*, p. 820.
73. Brecher, *Foreign Policy System*, p. 399.

# 10  Paving the Road to War: Israeli Diplomacy and the 1967 Crisis

## DAVID TAL

Three weeks of waiting in mid-May 1967 and six days of fighting in June changed the entire face of the Middle East. Besides tracing Israel's remarkable victory, scholars have concentrated on these preliminary three weeks of waiting that 'convey the sense of anxiety and indecision then prevailing in Israel'.[1] 'Anxiety' refers to the sense of danger prompted by the sudden, unilateral massing of Arab forces along Israel's borders, and the military pacts signed between Egypt and Syria, and Egypt and Jordan. 'Indecision', in turn, relates to the internal debate between the military and the government over Israel's proper reaction to the entry of Egyptian forces into the Sinai on 14 May 1967.

The debate was sharp and heated, and the forced appointment of former IDF chief of staff General (res.) Moshe Dayan to the defence ministry in place of the prime minister, Levi Eshkol, only further strengthened the impression of a weak government caught totally off guard and blindly seeking a way out of the national crisis in the face of militant army officers and a worried public.[2] This notion misses the true nature of the Israeli government's crisis conduct, however, because, as I shall be arguing here, the waiting period was not a time of hesitation and stumbling, but a necessity. This, for two reasons: war at that time would have served no Israeli interest; and, besides, the waiting period was well used by the government to allow time for diplomacy to overcome tactical and logistical obstacles that might otherwise have precluded later achievements on the battlefield.

The government of Levi Eshkol did not want war. Israel's overall geostrategic environment had improved significantly in the decade following the 1956 Sinai campaign. Infiltrations from the neigh-bouring countries, which had been endemic from 1949 to 1956, ceased. If in the first years of independence Israel had genuine diffi-culty in procuring arms, things changed for the better during the latter half of the 1950s, when it had no problem purchasing the weapons it needed, first from France and later from Britain and other European states. In August 1962 another strategic break-through occurred when the Kennedy administration agreed to sell Israel surface-to-air Hawk missiles, marking the first time the United States was prepared to sell a major weapons system to Israel. The Johnson administration continued the trend by selling Israel combat planes and tanks, thus laying the groundwork for gradually converting the United States into Israel's major arms supplier.

During this pre-crisis period, Israel also began to emerge from its regional and diplomatic isolation. For one thing, the United States and Britain came to accept Israel's perception that the West needed to counter the pro-Soviet Arab camp, led by Egyptian President Gamal Abd al Nasser. This same argument was instrumental in establishing clandestine yet active relations with non-Arab Middle Eastern states like Turkey, Iran, Ethiopia and even Sudan, in what became known as the 'Peripheral Alliance'. To these secret-channel ties one notes the establishment of formal, direct diplomatic rela-tions with Israel by more and more Third World countries.[3] Internally as well, Israel was preoccupied in the 1957–67 decade with the continued absorption of over one million immigrants who had flooded the country since its establishment, and with attempt-ing to stabilize its stagnating economy. For all these reasons, war in 1967 seemed the least desirable scenario.

Not only feelings that war was inexpedient led the Eshkol government to reject the military's demands for an immediate response to Nasser's provocation in favour of a more guarded policy of waiting. Here, the cabinet also adhered to a fundamental tenet of Israel's security perception, stipulated by former prime minister David Ben-Gurion: Israel should not go to war alone and without a great-power ally. Or, as in this case, not without first convincing its allies that it had no alternative but to go to war – unless the crisis could be defused.

Accordingly, the government's strategy emphasized diplomacy as the primary tool for two reasons: finally to resolve the crisis; and to create the external conditions allowing the IDF to carry out its war plan, calling for a preemptive strike against the Arab armies. To that end, Israeli diplomats heightened their interventions in various world capitals. Still, the main theatre of activity was undoubtedly in the United States, because America's importance for a war decision by Israel was fully recognized in Jerusalem.[4] William Quandt describes the internal bureaucratic process from an American perspective, culminating in President Johnson abandoning 'the policy of making an all-out effort to prevent war', and giving Israel a 'yellow light' to launch the war it was seeking.

However, giving Lyndon Johnson the time he would need to authorize the 'yellow light' also forced the government to sustain heavy criticism from internal opposition circles plus a powerful defence establishment and the Israeli army itself. Senior officers tagged the government's decision, sometimes in very brutal language, as a sign of weakness. Withstanding critics and pressure at home, Prime Minister Eshkol and other ministers insisted, however, on looking beyond the immediate crisis. It is this viewpoint, more than any other factor, that determined the nature and direction of government activities during the tense waiting period.

Based on now-declassified Israeli documents, this paper underscores the role Israeli diplomacy played during the crisis, showing how, in the end, it worked to make war possible. Principally, by bringing President Johnson to admit the United States had no other real answer to a crisis initiated by Nasser.

FIRST STAGE: DIPLOMACY PREVAILS

The entry of Egyptian forces into the Sinai on 14 May 1967 came as a distinct surprise to the Israel Defence Forces' (IDF) intelligence branch. Among the experts the predominant assumption since 1963 had been that Egypt was too deeply entangled in the Yemenite civil war for Nasser to open a new front against Israel.[5] Nevertheless, the improbable was now happening, and it remained for Israel to interpret exactly what Nasser's true intentions were. Although General Aharon Yariv, head of the IDF's intelligence branch, postulated that Nasser really did not wish for an all-out war with Israel, he did assume, on the other hand, that (a) Egypt intended to exhaust Israel, and (b) might even initiate some kind of limited military action. Yitzhak Rabin, the IDF chief of staff, reiterated the same themes in front of the cabinet, noting on 22 May that the Egyptian formation in Sinai was defensive and that there were no clear signs that Nasser was intending to go to war with Israel.[6] These professional assessments were, in turn, fully accepted by the cabinet.

Ever since 1967 the true reasons for Nasser's provocative step have been a source of debate. Among historians of the crisis it is agreed that early in May Soviet officials in Cairo and Moscow had told the Egyptians and the Syrians that Israel had amassed military forces along its border with Syria in order to attack it. Trying to bolster his personal position and at a low ebb after the setbacks the Egyptian army had suffered in Yemen, Nasser responded to Soviet warnings by an act largely aimed at supporting the Syrians. Especially since he was bound to do so by the Syrian–Egyptian defence treaty of 4 November 1966.[7] Others explain Nasser's sending Egyptian forces into the Sinai as a well-calculated action by the Egyptian leader who, in fact, really sought to launch a preemptive strike on Israel's secret nuclear plant in Dimona.[8] Not only Egypt's intentions but the reasons for the Soviets' false warning have also remained a source of lively debate. Israeli diplomats, for one, placed their interpretation of the Soviet action within a Cold War context, claiming the Soviets wanted to create a counterpoint to Vietnam and to induce the United States to rearrange the world order more comprehensively.[9]

However, even if Egypt did not plan to launch an actual attack, its flagrant, massive build-up in the Sinai forced Israel to go on a full military alert, with opinions divided only over exactly what eventuality to be prepared for. Eshkol believed the crisis related foremost to inter-Arab affairs, and hence Israel should adopt a wait-and-see policy. Foreign Minister Abba Eban insisted that since the winds of war were blowing, Israel ought to redouble its diplomatic activity in attempting to calm the Arabs. Abraham Harman, Israel's ambassador in Washington, went one step further when he suggested seizing the opportunity to demand from Syria and Jordan strict compliance with the 1949 armistice agreements, and to insist they curb terror attacks launched from their soil. The government accepted Eban's proposed course, which did not necessarily contradict Harman's suggestion,[10] and decided that the main effort for the moment be aimed at defusing the crisis.

Eban then instructed Israeli representatives in Washington, Paris, London and Moscow to call upon the respective governments to convey that Israel had no intention of attacking Syria, and to press the Egyptian leader to pull his forces out of Sinai.[11] The Israeli foreign minister invited the Soviet ambassador in Tel Aviv to visit the border area and to see first-hand that allegations of an Israeli military build-up along the border with Syria were baseless – an invitation the ambassador declined.[12] Backed by their American and British colleagues, Israeli diplomats at the UN also tried – unsuccessfully – to avert redeployment of the UNEF away from the Israeli–Egyptian border. U Thant, however, refused to accept any limits on UNEF, and instead ordered total withdrawal of all UN forces from Sinai – a step not even the Egyptians had asked for.[13]

Israel's responses were based not only on its own interests, but also on the positions adopted by its allies, foremost the United States. Calls were made from Washington urging Israel to show utmost restraint and not to be the first to strike. But it was President Johnson who set the direction of Israel's thinking in coming days. In a message to Eshkol on 17 May, the President expressed 'sympathy and understanding' for Israel in the face of the crisis, yet asked the prime minister to refrain from taking any military action without prior consultation. The president reiterated this point in a personal follow-up letter, adding: 'I am sure that you will understand that I cannot accept any responsibility on behalf of the United States for situations which arise as the result of actions on which we were not consulted'.[14] At this time Israel was still not seriously considering the possibility of war. Even so, the president's carefully couched words were a clear message to Israel to act carefully, even at a stage when war seemed inevitable. On the other hand, Johnson's admonition was also promising, as it implied that under certain circumstances the United States would be prepared to back up an Israeli military action.

Israeli leaders were particularly sensitive to Johnson's messages, since they entertained hopes of completing the slow tilt in US policy towards Israel evident since the late 1950s. Since its establishment Israel had tried, with little success, to bring the United States to make a clear commitment to its security. When the Truman and Eisenhower administrations consistently rejected all such requests, a substitute was found in France, Israel's main ally and major arms supplier since 1954. Nonetheless, feelings towards France remained mixed, as Israeli strategists realized the alliance was the result of a unique constellation of factors rather than reflecting a genuine French national interest. After all, France's traditional interests resided in the Arab world; and its strategic association with Israel resulted from the Algerian revolt, believed in France to be fomented and assisted by Nasser.

It was therefore assumed in Jerusalem and Tel Aviv that the Israeli–French link was one of expedience. This line argued for Israel's relying on the United States, whose interests in, and ties with, Israel arguably transcended ephemeral considerations – the more so in the wake of the July 1958 crisis in the Middle East, when a perceptible change of American attitudes towards Israel had become evident, and security relations between the two states were cemented by JFK's 1962 decision to provide ground-to-air missiles and Johnson's 1966 decision to supply Skyhawk combat aircraft.[15]

There was, in addition, a specific reason for now turning to the United States. It was largely because of brutal American pressure and principled promises given by the Eisenhower administration that Israel had relinquished the Straits of Tiran and the Sinai after the 1956 war. In a 'most important telegram' to Eugene Rostow of the State Department on 19 May, Eban recalled the commitment the United States took upon itself in 1957: 'the most explicit and solemn ever done by our two governments in the framework of a general US commitment to Israel's security and integrity'.[16] Calling in its chips, Israel now sought an American declaration publicly committing the United States to Israel's security, as a counter to Soviet support for Egypt and Syria, and as a powerful superpower deterrent against Egyptian attack.[17]

The arguments used by Israeli spokesmen to extract such an unequivocal American commitment were entirely unexceptional and similar to those used in the past. As during the 1958 crisis, it was again claimed that the current crisis should be viewed not only in the narrow framework of the Arab–Israeli conflict but also in the context of the Cold War. Foreign ministry officials repeatedly argued that the crisis involved Soviet–Egyptian–Syrian collusion directed not only against Israel but also against the United States. Another theme to re-emerge in May 1967 was the suggestion that were the current crisis to further strengthen Nasser's prestige it would dishearten pro-Western forces in the region.[18]

The reaction from Washington to these lines of reasoning and derivative recommendations was confusing, to say the least. On the positive side, the president and his aides tended to accept Israel's basic perception about the origins of the crisis, and Rostow agreed with Israeli diplomats that the Syrian government was to blame for the current tension since it would not prevent terror groups from using bases in Syria to carry out attacks in Israel.[19] As to US commitments stipulated in 1957, Rostow stated clearly: 'There is no misunderstanding. The 1957 agreements are alive...But they should all be read within the terms of the president's letter to the P.M. about consultations before you take any action.'[20]

Johnson's letter and Rostow's response meant the administration was insisting on what was tantamount to a veto regarding Israeli action, but at the same time was unwilling to make an open verbal commitment. Instead, President Johnson would only publicly refer to the May 1950 Tripartite Declaration, which stipulated that the US, Britain and France remained pledged to prevent, even by force, the violation of the demarcation lines between the states in the region.[21] This reference to the earlier Tripartite Declaration worried many policy-makers in Israel, and Eban even went so far as to accuse the administration of being 'insufficiently sensitive to our feelings'. He explained that while past pledges given by Eisenhower and Kennedy implied an active, independent unilateral American step, the Tripartite Declaration meant the 'mere joining' of others' initiative.[22] However, other seasoned Israeli diplomats understood the meaning of what they heard in Washington differently. Ambassador Harman, in particular, was sure that despite the difficulties, even were it to remain alone, the administration would nevertheless stand by Israel.[23]

In spite of Israeli complaints, the two governments were careful to activate and maintain an open channel throughout the crisis. Meetings were held between high-ranking officials from both nations, and the Americans kept Israeli counterparts closely informed. So, too, did the Israelis increase their cooperation with the administration – a necessary step in the immediate context of the crisis, but also because of its potential for the future.

## THE CLOSURE OF THE STRAIT OF TIRAN

The most dramatic point of the crisis was Nasser's announcement at midnight on 22 May of the closure of the Strait of Tiran to Israeli shipping and Israel's clarification that it regarded such an act as a *casus belli*, freeing it to take any measure deemed necessary to ensure the sea passage remained open. In fact, Nasser's move actually played to Israel's advantage, since the really grave problem at the time derived from the growing deployment of Egyptian troops massed in the Sinai. As of 21 May, there were already 80,000 Egyptian soldiers, 600 tanks and 600 cannons tightly deployed in the area. This accumulation of forces compelled the IDF to mobilize 80,000 reserve soldiers.

Israel could not afford to sustain such a force open-endedly, or for an extended period of time, and indications were that Nasser had no intention of bringing the crisis to an end. He announced that Egypt would not attack Israel, yet he seemed determined to exploit fully the gains of his brinkmanship policy without having to go to war.[24] The problem was that it would be difficult to justify an Israeli preemptive attack in response to the Egyptian military build-up alone.

The Egyptian blockade of the Tiran Straits currently offered a way out, considering that Israel's right under international law to free passage was widely accepted. When Israel had complied with the United Nations' demand to withdraw from the Sinai on 2 February 1957, Golda Meir stated that Israel reserved the right to self-defence in accordance with the UN charter's Article 51, if the Straits were ever closed again.[25] Picturing just such a situation, shortly after the May crisis commenced letters were sent to most West European heads of state and to President Johnson in which Prime Minister Eshkol and Foreign Minister Eban recalled Mrs Meir's declaration.[26] In short, closure of Tiran presented Israel with an entirely justifiable pretext to go to war at a time when the real security compulsion to do so was the massive Egyptian build-up of ground forces facing Israel's long, vulnerable land frontier.

At the same time Israel's claim of a *casus belli* put it in a delicate situation, dictating that it *had* to go to war. Chief of Staff Rabin stressed this point to the cabinet: 'What is in question today is not the passage through the Tiran and the freedom of navigation, but Israel's ability to act on what it declared was its right to self-defense... If there is no response, it is impossible to predict the results, as Israel will lose its deterrent capability.'[27] For Rabin this was the time to abandon the policy of restraint and to give the IDF an order – or permission – to attack. However, the chief of staff remained ambiguous when asked if immediate action was essential.

It was Eban who set the tone for a decision, reminding the government that it was essential to achieve 'a warm understanding with the United States... Otherwise, we might win the war, but once again lose the fruits of the victory.' Consequently, the cabinet decided that it 'sees in the closure of the Strait of Tiran to Israeli shipping an act of aggression against Israel', but that the 'decision of the nature of the reaction to this act is to be postponed for 48 hours', giving time 'to check the United States' position toward the new situation'. Towards this end it was decided that Foreign Minister Eban proceed immediately to Washington to see President Johnson, despite fears that the meeting's outcome might only restrict or compromise Israel's own freedom of action.[28]

## EBAN'S MISSION

On his way to Washington, Eban stopped over in Paris and London, presenting Charles de Gaulle and Harold Wilson with Israel's chief desire to see an international flotilla formed to execute the standing commitment the Western great powers had taken upon themselves in 1957 to ensure that the Tiran Straits remained open. The request was phrased in such a manner that were the flotilla initiative not to materialize, the two leaders would have to acknowledge Israel's position that it had a right to go to war.

De Gaulle, for his part, was unequivocal in demanding that Israel not be the first to shoot. He rejected Eban's demand for an international naval force, and called for a discussion of the whole issue in a multilateral meeting to be attended by the United States, Britain, France and the Soviet Union.[29] De Gaulle's response was particularly ominous, signalling Israeli–French special relations were nearing an end. British Prime Minister Wilson's response, on the other hand, was far warmer, although still reflecting Britain's basic power limitations. The prime minister did stress the UK's determination to join an armada were one to be established. He made no comment as to the possibility that Israel would start a war, and expressed Britain's determination not to let Nasser emerge from the crisis with the upper hand. In any case, he made it fairly clear that Britain's response depended wholly on America's leadership and action. On balance, Wilson's response was, in Eban's judgment, 'realistic and mature'.[30]

The ultimately fateful meeting was the one in Washington with Lyndon Johnson. Adding further importance to this crucial encounter, while Eban was en route to Washington the situation on the Israeli–Egyptian front had worsened, increasing Israel's sense of urgency. The Egyptians had steadily strengthened their military build-up, which by 25 May included four infantry and two armoured divisions, bringing the total number of tanks to 800. Troops had been called back from Yemen, and the concentration of Egyptian forces was no longer directed towards the straits, but directly against Israel.

It now seemed that Nasser was planning all-out war against Israel, an assumption reinforced by the massive build-up of the Syrian army along its southern border with Israel. Iraqi forces joined the Syrians, and Jordan asked for Iraqi and Saudi reinforcements. The Egyptian war minister's sudden visit to Moscow heightened Israel's anxiety. As if all of this were not enough, President Nasser addressed a meeting of the Arab Labour Association in which he exposed the unified Arab war aim: destruction of the State of Israel. On Rabin's and Yariv's advice, Eshkol sent a cable to Eban asking that he stress to Johnson that the straits issue had become secondary since a coordinated Arab attack on all fronts against Israel appeared imminent. He instructed the foreign minister specifically to ask LBJ what practical steps he was planning to take in this critical hour.[31]

Eban did as instructed, but knew that in his Washington talks he was on safer ground by addressing the straits issue rather than the less convincing argument about Egypt's amassing of forces and threat of war. In a brief to the president on the eve of his meeting with Eban, Secretary of State Dean Rusk suggested rejecting the option of 'unleashing them'. Instead, he recommended taking 'a positive position, but not a final commitment', on the British proposal, which called for a declaration by the maritime powers that they were ready to enforce free passage through the Straits of Tiran.[32] And indeed the general assumption in Washington at the time of Eban's mission remained that war was not inevitable.

When Eban told the president of Eshkol's estimation that 'Nasser is ready for an imminent all-out attack together with Syria', Secretary of Defense Robert McNamara noted that 'we see neither the capability nor the intention of imminent offensive action' by Nasser. Johnson went further, claiming that even if Israel were attacked, 'our judgment is that the Israelis would lick them'.[33] Other than that, Johnson did agree that Israel should not be banned from the straits, and had a right to self-defence. However, as much as he stood by Israel, he had to gain domestic and international public support for this position, which could be achieved only after diplomatic activity had been exhausted. He therefore encouraged Eban to recruit more and more congressmen to side with Israel, while, in the meantime, he, LBJ, would do all he could to establish an international armada. Even if the effort were doomed, it had to be tried. He consequently approved closer military cooperation and intelligence-sharing between the two states, and concluded: 'I must emphasize the necessity for Israel not to make itself responsible for the initiation of hostilities. Israel will not be alone unless it decides to do it alone. We cannot imagine that it will make this decision.'[34]

Zaki Shalom concludes that the Eban–Johnson meeting did not bear the expected fruits.[35] His conclusion is supported by critics who charge that Eban misled the government about Johnson's exact phrase regarding America's commitment to assist Israel in this time of crisis.[36] The controversy reached a climax with the exchange of letters between Eshkol and Johnson after Eban's return. In his letter to Johnson, Eshkol wrote: 'I welcome the assurances that the United States will take any and all measures to open the Strait of Tiran to international shipping'.[37] Even though the phrase was an accurate citation from Eban's report of the words used by the president in their meeting, Johnson responded by insisting that it was not an accurate quote of what he had said because he was not authorized to make such a commitment.[38]

This difference can be traced to what has already been noted as a divergence of approach between the two governments. Eshkol's citation mirrors the Israeli government's expectation of an American action, even unilaterally, whereas Johnson implied the United States would *join* others in the effort to keep the straits open, but would not act alone.

In the end, these differences amounted to little more than semantics. What Johnson was referring to in correcting Eshkol was the attempt to avoid the appearance of Israeli–American 'collusion'. The Israelis were in fact getting what they wanted. While not receiving direct permission to open war, the president was laying down in precise language the terms for a possible Israeli action. He agreed that Israel was right in its disposition, but felt diplomatic activity had to be exhausted before resorting to other means. If this sequence were kept, the administration would be able to stand by Israel. Similarly, the administration was also implicitly accepting the time limit set by Israel, and was proceeding on the assumption that there was only 'a week or two' – in Eshkol's words to Johnson – to organize an international armada. The president regarded the timetable as a working thesis, not as a threat; and the Israelis were systematically and regularly informed of the administration's activities as well as constraints.[39]

During the following days administration officials were busy with attempts at building an international task force, while at the same time Israel was asked mainly not to give any appearance of direct American cooperation or, even worse, of collusion, with Israel. To that end, the White House told Israel not to make public references to American commitments, and rejected Israel's request to establish a military liaison between the two states.[40] On the other hand, in an attempt to make it easier for Israel to maintain restraint, Johnson himself decided to provide Israel with a special assistance package meant to relieve the heavy burden mass Israeli mobilization was imposing on Israel's strained economy.[41]

## WAITING FOR THE ARMADA

The response in Israel to the Johnson–Eban meeting was mixed. General Yariv estimated that time was now working in Egypt's favour and to Israel's disadvantage, since Nasser had moved 'from a state of reluctance to go to war to a state of reluctance to initiate a war, but readiness to be involved in one'. Consequently, Rabin told the war cabinet that 'our ability to carry out a surprise attack on Egypt' – a crucial element in the IDF war plans – diminished with the passing of time.[42]

Opinions within the government were equally divided between those in favour and those against going to war immediately. Some ministers supported Eshkol's view that diplomatic options should be exhausted, while others called for attacking promptly. Haim Gvati, minister of agriculture, warned, 'if we will not be the first to strike, Nasser will eliminate us'. Other ministers, Yigal Allon and Yisrael Galili among them, agreed. Yet Eshkol insisted on waiting further, his decision reinforced by a series of cables from Johnson and the State Department forcefully counselling Israel not to attack, and stressing continuous intense activity by the US to form the naval armada. On 28 May the prime minister informed the president that the government had indeed decided to prolong the waiting period.[43]

This decision unleashed an unprecedented campaign against Eshkol by the IDF high command and the public at large. He was, in turn, accused of putting Israel in a grave situation, of exposing its weakness, of severely undermining Israel's deterrence ability, and of 'destroying the wonderful people's spirit'. Some of the military charged that the delay endangered Israel and, even though they were confident in the IDF's ability to win in any case, they insisted belated action would be far more costly than prompt action. Eshkol rejected the criticism. Justifying his decision to prolong the waiting period, he said: 'All the IDF's material has been gained by our [diplomatic] exertion. We must not forget that, and we should not see ourselves as Goliaths. With unarmed and unequipped fists, we have no power.' Moreover, Israel's ability to obtain what it needed for its safety and existence was dependent on its link with a great power.[44]

Nevertheless, things proceeded to worsen for Eshkol. Rumours about the harsh confrontation with several of the IDF's top brass circulated around the country, adding further fuel to the general feeling of insecurity and apprehension. Furthermore, just before a meeting with the IDF general staff, the prime minister publicly addressed the nation on radio in order to explain the difficult situation to the people of Israel. In speaking, however, Eshkol stumbled several times, creating the impression of a loss of confidence and wavering on his part. On the external front, Jordan and Egypt escalated the tension by signing a mutual defence agreement on 30 May, which meant that in the event of war it would no longer be restricted solely to Egypt and Syria.[45]

Public opinion in Israel was understandably agitated, with readers sending letters to the daily papers comparing the Eshkol government's handling of the crisis with Chamberlain and Munich. A 'Churchill' was called to take 'Chamberlain's' place, with the former personified by Moshe Dayan, David Ben-Gurion's protégé. In the end, Eshkol had no choice but to yield to public pressure, appointing Dayan defence minister on 1 June.[46]

However, the road to war had already been paved. Officials in Washington were meeting with Israeli diplomats on a daily basis, often more than once a day, providing accurate, up-dated reports on US attempts to launch the armada. But what these briefings actually told Israeli diplomats was that the diplomatic efforts were futile; that Washington and London had failed to mobilize the marine nations in forming a flotilla; and that, by 30 May, as Rostow was forced to admit, 'he saw no way out of the crisis, which seemed today as very severe'.[47]

It was becoming painfully obvious that the administration's

alternative to war was a dismal failure. The time now came to take the final plunge. Eshkol sent a letter to President Johnson in which he recalled how Israel had dutifully adopted the cautious waiting policy, refraining from any military response while it waited for the United States to take concrete measures 'to meet the challenge of the illegal blockade, the aggressive build-up of Egyptian forces on our southern frontier, and the continuation of terrorist incursions into Israeli territory'.[48] What Eshkol in fact was saying was that with the American failure, Israel now free to act independently.

The director of the Mossad, Meir Amit, was dispatched to Washington in order to hear a clear admission of the administration's failure to build an international armada. The fuller implications of such an admission had to be clear to both sides. Amit met with CIA Director Richard Helms and his staff presented Israel's view of the crisis and Nasser's intentions, offering his candid assessment that the diplomatic campaign was leading nowhere. To which his hosts readily concurred.

More important yet was Secretary of Defense McNamara's admission that he, too, saw the situation in the same bleak terms. McNamara responded with great scepticism to Amit's question about the build-up of the armada, and 'read very carefully' Amit's presentation and estimation of the situation and Israel's intentions. Amit returned from his mission on the eve of 3 June, relating to the government his firm impression that there were no tangible indications of any American military or marine build-up, so that if Israel had linked its planned military response to the straits issue, an American blanket approval could be safely expected.[49] With Amit's report, Eshkol and the government now felt Israel could go to war with the tacit blessing of the US.[50]

## CONCLUSION

Tensions between senior diplomats and senior military officers were not exactly unprecedented in Israeli's experience. One precedent can be found in the Ben-Gurion–Sharett debate in the first half of the 1950s over how to calm relations with Israel's neighbours, wherein the former advocated a militant line against the Arabs, while the latter favoured diplomacy.[51] This time though, while dividing the government, the 1967 controversy was not over principle. The prime minister totally agreed with the IDF high command that military action was necessary, but differed with them over the precise timing. Eshkol, Eban and other cabinet members felt a military victory was only a partial achievement. Of no less importance to them was the need to convince Israel's friends that there was simply no alternative to war. This was because Israel's security was fundamentally based, more than anything else, on its association with a supportive great power.

Senior commanders and ministers who disagreed for the most part overlooked this diplomatic point when demanding to go to war regardless of world opinion. Eshkol stood his ground, fighting for a diplomatic–military decision that would transcend the narrower military calculation. He and Eban, and to some extent Rabin, were fully convinced that it was impossible for a small, vulnerable country like Israel to ignore Johnson's warning not to act without first consulting the United States. All efforts were directed at providing the necessary diplomatic circumstances and preconditions that would allow the IDF to act in its best lights.

Israeli leaders and statesmen identified weak points in the American argument and pressed these to advantage. At a certain moment the problem was no longer the blockade of the Straits of Tiran but the great mass of Arab military forces in the Sinai Peninsula. However, in the existing international climate Israel stood on much firmer ground by demanding that the straits be reopened.

Admission by America of its failure to put together the requisite international armada in effect provided Israel with the ironclad legal and moral justification for defining the situation as a *casus belli*. America's response to the Israeli strike on the morning of 5 June proved that those who had advocated waiting had been correct in their assessments. Clearly Israel could not be asked to wait any longer no matter how much Washington did not want to see a resumption of hostilities in the Middle East. While Egypt's military build-up in the Sinai was the more threatening issue, for Israel it was the comparatively less urgent issue – closure of the Straits of Tiran – that in the end provided it with the pretext to go to war with an international diplomatic seal of approval. None too late – but also none too soon.

## NOTES

1. Aaron S. Klieman, *Israel and the World After 40 Years* (Washington, 1990), p. 74.
2. Arie Brown, *Moshe Dayan and the Six Days War* (Tel Aviv, 1997), pp. 12–13; Nadav Safran, *From War to War* (New York, 1969), pp. 303–6.
3. These developments are described in Abraham Ben-Zvi, *Decade of Transition* (New York, 1998); Uri Bialer, *Between East and West* (Cambridge, 1990); David Tal, 'Seizing Opportunities: Israel and the 1958 Crisis in the Middle East', *Middle Eastern Studies* (forthcoming); David Tal, 'Symbol or Substance? Israel's Campaign for U.S. Hawk Missiles, 1960–1962', *International History Review*, 22, 2 (June 2000); Klieman, *Israel and the World After 40 Years*, pp. 73–5; Zach Levey, *Israel and the Western Powers, 1952–1960* (Chapel Hill, 1998).
4. William B. Quandt, 'Lyndon Johnson and the June 1967 War: What Color Was the Light?', *MEJ*, 46, 2 (1992), p. 199. Douglas Little does not explicitly 'color' the nature of Johnson's acquiescence to Israel's first strike, but he seems to see it more as a 'Green light', than a 'Yellow one'. Douglas Little, 'A Fool's Errand: America and the Middle East, 1961–1969', in Diane B. Kunz (ed.), *The Diplomacy of the Crucial Decade* (New York, 1994), p. 302.
5. Haber, pp. 54, 95.
6. Protocol of the IDF General Headquarters Meeting, 19 May 1967, IDFA, 117/70/206; Haber, pp. 151–2, 161–2.
7. David Bukai, 'Who is to Blame in the Eruption of the 1967 War? Jordan and the Six Day War', *Iyunim Bitkumat Yisrael*, 9, 1999, pp. 247–53.
8. The most fervent advocates of this thesis are Shlomo Aronson and Oded Brosh, *The Politics and Strategy of Nuclear Weapons in the Middle East* (Albany, 1992), pp. 107–11. For an opposing view on this matter see Avner Cohen, *Israel and the Bomb* (New York, 1998), pp. 260–5.
9. See a discussion on the various scholastic opinions over the Soviets' conduct in Bukai, 'Who is to Blame in the Eruption of the 1967 War?', pp. 255–9; Telegram 183 from Foreign Office, Jerusalem to Israel Delegation, Paris, 23 May 1967, FO 4084/2. FO documents are from the Israel State Archives, Jerusalem, unless cited otherwise. Klinghoffer made this line of explanation the thesis of her book: Judith A. Klinghoffer, *Vietnam, Jews and the Middle East* (New York, 1999), pp. 1–5, 103–4.
10. Telegram 146 from Israel delegation, Washington to Foreign Office, Jerusalem, May 17, 1967, FO 4078/4/; Telegram 13 from FO, Jerusalem to various Israeli Embassies, May 19, 1967, FO 6447/4; Telegram 348 from FO, Tel Aviv to the FO, Jerusalem, May 1967, ibid.
11. Telegram 952 from FO, Jerusalem, to Israel's embassy, Washington, 16 May 1967, FO 4078/4; Telegram 117 from Israel's embassy, Paris to Foreign Office, Jerusalem, 17 May 1967, FO 4084/2; Telegram 83 from the Office in Tel Aviv to the Office in Jerusalem, 18 May 1983, FO 4080/50. The telegram is a report of a conversation between Foreign Minister Eban and British Ambassador Michael Hadow; Message from Foreign Minister Eban to Secretary of State for Foreign Affairs, H. Brown, 20 May 1967, FO 4091/23.
12. Telegram 40 from Foreign Office, Jerusalem to Israel's Delegation, Moscow, 17 May 1967, FO 5937/30; Eban, pp. 313–15, 319–20.
13. Telegram 156 from Israel's embassy, Washington to Foreign Office, Jerusalem, 17 May 1967, FO 4078/4; Telegram 987 from Foreign Office, Jerusalem, to Israel's Delegation, New York and Washington, 18 May 1967, FO 6447/4.
14. Telegram 155 from Israel's embassy, Washington, to Foreign Office, Jerusalem, 16 May 1967, FO 4078/4; Telegram 156 from Israel's embassy, Washington, to Foreign Office, Jerusalem, 17 May 1967, ibid.; Telegram 80 from the Office in Tel Aviv to the Office in 18 May 1967, ibid.; Haber, pp. 152–3.
15. Ben-Zvi, *Decade of Transition*, pp. 59–129; Bialer, *Between East and West*, pp. 197–275; D. Tal, 'The American–Israeli Security Treaty: Sequel or Means to the Relief of Israeli-Arab Tensions, 1954–1955', *Middle Eastern Studies*, 31, 4 (1995), pp. 828–48; D. Tal, 'Seizing Opportunities: Israel and the 1958 Crisis in the Middle East', (forthcoming); Tal, 'Symbol or Substance?'.
16. Telegram 22 from the office, Jerusalem, to Israel's embassy, Washington and Israel's

delegation, New York, 19 May 1967, FO 4078/4. On US commitment to Israel in 1957 see Aide-Mémoire from the Department of State to the Israeli embassy, 11 February 1967, *FRUS 1955-57 XVII*, pp. 132–4; Message from President Eisenhower to Prime Minister Ben-Gurion, March 1957, ibid., pp. 347–48.

17. Report of a meeting between A. Eban and W. Barbour, Tel Aviv, in Foreign Office, Tel Aviv to Foreign Office, Jerusalem, 18 May 1967, FO 4078/4.
18. L. Eshkol letter to L. B. Johnson, in Telegram 80 from Foreign Office, Tel Aviv to Foreign Office, Jerusalem, 18 May 1967, FO 4078/4; Telegram 60 from FO, Jerusalem to Israel's embassy, Washington and Israel's Delegation, New York, 21 May 1967, FO 4078/4; Tal, 'Seizing Opportunities: Israel and the 1958 Crisis in the Middle East'.
19. Telegram 142 from Israel's embassy, Washington, to Foreign Office, Jerusalem, 16 May 1967, FO 4078/4; Telegram 156 from Israel's embassy, Washington, to Foreign Office, Jerusalem, 17 May 1967, FO 4078/4.
20. Telegram 191 from Israel's embassy, Washington to Foreign Office, Jerusalem, 20 May 1967, FO 4078/4.
21. L. B. Johnson to L. Eshkol, 22 May 1967, FO 4091/23; 'Joint Statement by the Governments of the United Kingdom, France and the United States, 25 May 1950', *Department of State Bulletin*, 5 June 1950, p. 886.
22. Telegram 211 from Israel's embassy, Washington to Foreign Office, Jerusalem, 21 May 1967, FO 4078/4; Telegram 67 from FO, Jerusalem to various Israeli delegations, 21 May 1967, ibid.; Eban, pp. 324–5.
23. Telegram 217 from Israel's embassy, Washington, to Foreign Office, Jerusalem, 21 May 1967, FO 4078/4.
24. Telegram 65 from Liaison Department/FO, Jerusalem to various delegations, 21 May 1967, FO 6447/4; Haber, p. 161.
25. Mordehai Bar-On, *Shaarei Gaza* (The Gates of Gaza) (Tel Aviv, 1992), p. 365.
26. Message from Prime Minister Eshkol to President De Gaulle, 19 May 1967, FO 4091/23; Telegram 22 from the Foreign Office, Jerusalem, to Israel's embassy, Washington and Israel's delegation, New York, 19 May 1967, FO 4078/4; Message from Foreign Minister A. Eban to Foreign Minister H. Brown, 20 May 1967, FO 4091/23.
27. Haber, p. 166.
28. Telegram 125 from Israel's embassy, Washington, to Foreign Ministry, Jerusalem, 23 May 1967, FO 5937/30; Eban, pp. 331–3; Haber, pp. 167–70.
29. The Eban–De Gaulle Memo of Conversation is in Telegram 426 from Israel's delegation, New York, to Foreign Office, Jerusalem, 25 May 1967, FO 4078/4.
30. The Eban–Wilson Memo of Conversations is in Telegram 121 from Israel's embassy, London, to Foreign Office, Jerusalem, 24 May 1967, FO 4080/50; Telegram 131 from Eban, London, to Eshkol, 25 May 1967, FO 4080/50; Eban, pp. 335–43.
31. Telegram 358 from Eshkol, Tel Aviv, to Eban, Washington, 25 May 1967, FO 6445/6; Nasser's speech in Telegram 287 from FO/Research to various Israeli Delegations, 26 May 1967, FO 6445/6; Y. Rabin, *Pinkas Sherut* (Service Notebook) (Tel Aviv, 1979), pp. 160–1.
32. Memo for the President, 26 May 1967, L. B. J[ohnson] L[ibrary, Austin, TX], N[ational] S[ecurity] F[iles], NSC History, M[iddle] E[ast] Crisis, Vol. 2, Tabs. 31–42.
33. Notes of a meeting with President L. B. Johnson and Foreign Minister Eban at the White House, 26 May 1967, FO 5937/30; the American protocol is in Memo of Conversation, 26 May 1967, LBJL, NSF, NSC History, ME Crisis, Vol. 2, Tabs. 43–59.
34. Notes of a meeting with President Lyndon B. Johnson and Foreign Minister A. Eban at the White House, 26 May 1967, FO 5937/30.
35. Zaki Shalom, 'Foreign Minister Abba Eban's Meeting with President Lyndon B. Johnson on the Eve of Six Day War', *Yahadut Zmanenu*, 11–12 (1998), pp. 314–18. Shalom is also wrong when he claims that President Johnson tried to avoid the meeting with Eban, ibid., pp. 313–14.
36. See the implied criticism by the prime minister's military adjutant: Haber, p. 201. Eban also refers to the criticism directed against him: Eban, pp. 368–70.
37. L. Eshkol to L. B. Johnson, 30 May 1967, FO 4091/23.
38. Telegram 444 from Israel's embassy, Washington to Foreign Office, Jerusalem, 31 May 1967, FO 5937/30.

39. Telegram 314 from Israel's embassy, Washington to Foreign Office, Jerusalem, 27 May 1967, FO 6445/6; Prime Minister Eshkol, 3 June 1967, ibid.; Johnson, *The Vantage Point*, pp. 294–5.
40. Telegram 334 from Israel's embassy, Washington to Foreign Office, Jerusalem, 27 May 1967, FO 5937/30.
41. Telegram 402 from Israel's embassy, Washington, to Foreign Office, Jerusalem, 29 May 1967, FO 5937/30. The Israeli implied threat was made to Walt Rostow: Telegram 408 from Israel's embassy, Washington, to Foreign Office, Jerusalem, 29 May 1967, FO 5937/30.
42. Haber, p. 190.
43. President Johnson to Prime Minister Eshkol, 28 May 1967, FO 4091/23; Prime Minister Eshkol to President Johnson, 30 May 1967, ibid.; Telegram 423 from FO, Jerusalem, to Israel's delegations, 30 May 1967, FO 6444/5; Eban, pp. 364–9; Haber, pp. 190–3; Brecher, *Decisions in Israel's Foreign Policy*, p. 396. Brecher's description of the government meeting is inaccurate, as the government did not officially vote.
44. Haber, pp. 194–7, 211; Rabin, *Pinkas Sherut*, pp. 171–5.
45. Telegram 517 from FO, Jerusalem, to Israel's delegations, 30 May 1967, FO 6444/5.
46. Haber, pp. 199–203.
47. Telegram 431 from Israel's embassy, Washington, to Foreign Office, Jerusalem, 30 May 1967, FO 5937/30; Schoenbaum, *The United States and the State of Israel*, p. 152.
48. L. Eshkol letter to L. B. Johnson, 30 May 1967, FO 4091/23.
49. Eban, p. 379; Meir Amit, Report of the Visit to the United States, 4 June 1967, FO 6445/7.
50. Eban, pp. 388–91; Haber, pp. 216–22.
51. David Tal, *Israel's Conception of Current Security – Origins and Development, 1949–1956* (Be'er Sheva, 1998), pp. 139–205.

# 11 Dynamics of the US–Israel Special Relationship

## ABRAHAM BEN-ZVI

In a recent analysis,[1] Yaacov Bar-Siman-Tov explains the formation of the American–Israeli alliance primarily in terms of certain 'hard' factors such as common security interests, which became fully manifested in the aftermath of the Six Day War of June 1967. While acknowledging the role of 'soft' factors such as shared values and ideals (promoted most notably by the American Jewish community) in forging the alliance, he assigns priority to a set of 'hard' global and regional strategic interests and considerations which – in the wake of the war – provided the main impetus for the creation of a security partnership of unprecedented and genuine uniqueness:[2]

> The watershed in establishing the special relationship was Israel's military victory in 1967, which not only increased Israel's strategic importance but created a new political and strategic situation in the Middle East, especially in the Arab–Israeli conflict.[3]

Bar-Siman-Tov asserts that Israel's decisive military victory in the 1967 conflagration consolidated its status as the most formidable military power in the region. This 'new military and strategic importance', he further claims, made political and strategic cooperation with it 'more attractive to the United States than in the past'.[4]

Predicated largely upon 'common political, ideological, security, and strategic interests',[5] a special patron–client relationship between the US and Israel therefore emerged in 1967, transforming an amorphous and opaque cluster of attitudes and feelings of sympathy and empathy towards Israel in American public opinion into a more concrete and effective strategic–security relationship.

Against the backdrop of this focus on the 'hard' complex of strategic components as the main source of the American–Israel informal alliance, and in order to better elucidate the basic structure and dynamics of American–Israeli relations as they actually unfolded, the following analysis will provide an overview of this partnership while employing a set of definitions and categories which differ from those developed by Bar-Siman-Tov. Specifically, whereas Bar-Siman-Tov views the special relationship as the combination of both soft and hard factors (while really underscoring the importance and centrality of security–strategic factors),[6] the following analysis will treat the special relationship as a distinct and separate category, as a source – rather than an outcome – of the process of alliance-formation within the American–Israeli sphere. It is hoped that by treating the special relationship as a discrete category (in juxtaposition with the 'hard' components of the alliance), a more nuanced picture of the forces which continuously shape the American–Israeli scene will emerge.

American policy towards Israel was never formulated in a political, social and ideological vacuum. In seeking to accomplish both its regional and bilateral goals, the architects of American Middle East diplomacy were repeatedly faced with a complex of domestic constraints, which either aborted or severely circumscribed the effective pursuit of certain highly desired strategic objectives. Given the centrality of these constraints, the entire course of American–Israeli relations can be analysed in terms of the specific dynamics of interaction between the forces comprising this cluster, and those which have been inextricably related to American regional strategic objectives. These clusters or paradigms are (a) the 'special-relationship' paradigm, which incorporates the entire web of domestic constraints on American diplomacy, deriving from a sentimental and emotional set of attitudes towards Israel; and (b) the 'American national-interest' paradigm, predicated upon purely 'hard' geo-strategic perceptions of American interests in the Middle East.[7]

The national-interest orientation, patterned on a strategic vision of the international system, concerns a broad complex of well-defined vital interests that US policy-makers believed the nation needed to promote. The traditional objectives derived from these interests included (with varying degrees of emphasis and dominance) the desire to mitigate the Arab–Israeli conflict; the wish to maintain political and economic access to Arab oil; and the quest –

during most of the Cold War era – to increase American influence in the area at the expense of the Soviet Union.

Predicated upon a complex of affective rather than merely cognitive beliefs, the elements that merge into the special-relationship paradigm reflect 'a widespread fund of goodwill toward Israel that is not restricted to the Jewish community', and an equally strong and persistent commitment to Israel's continued national existence, integrity and security. A complex of broadly based attitudes that underscores the affinity and similarity between the two states in terms of their pioneering nature, historical legacy and commitment to democracy,[8] this paradigm emerged as a legitimate and pervasive concept as soon as Israel was established in 1948.

On the whole, the examination of the prevailing attitudes of the American public, as well as of assorted leadership groups, to Middle Eastern issues over the last five decades, suggests that among those who had opinions on these matters, sympathy for Israel far outweighed support for the Arab cause, and cannot be explained solely as a continued residue of guilt feelings related to the plight of European Jewry during the Second World War.

Notwithstanding the existence of this broadly based core of supportive attitudes in American public opinion, it became increasingly apparent during the early 1950s that a basic asymmetry existed between the two paradigms, with the Eisenhower presidency perceiving the special-relationship orientation as incompatible with American national security. Seeking to incorporate the Arab world into Washington's containment designs in the early 1950s, American decision-makers were predisposed to endorse at least some of the basic Arab positions concerning the appropriate means of resolving the Arab–Israeli conflict, and at the same time to refrain from any pro-Israeli move or gesture. In the thinking of Washington's policy-makers, the fear of Arab defection and alienation clearly overshadowed any considerations patterned as yet on the special-relationship paradigm.[9]

In this context of perceived incompatibility between the premises of the special-relationship paradigm and the American national interest, the role of the representatives of the special-relationship orientation (and particularly of the leadership of the American Jewish community) was marginal. Not only did President Eisenhower and his entourage repeatedly express their determination to ignore the premises of the special relationship in the shaping of American policy towards Israel, but they deprived the leadership of the American Jewish community of continuous access to the top levels of the administration. The fact that the American Jewish community was not yet a cohesive political force during this period further contributed to the failure of its sporadic efforts to reorient the course of American diplomacy towards Israel. And indeed, during both the 'water crisis' of October 1953 and the 'Suez crisis' of 1956–57, faced with a highly determined and motivated admin-istration, the forces constituting the core of the paradigm were incapable of constraining President Eisenhower's margin of manoeuvrability and thus of redirecting the course of American Middle East diplomacy.[10]

It was only during the late 1950s that this incompatibility and asymmetry between the two paradigms began to evaporate. With the hope of achieving Arab unity and of consolidating a wide, intensive regional coalition against the Soviet Union receding against the backdrop of incessant inter-Arab cleavages and perva-sive hostility towards the West, there was no need to persist any longer in the effort to secure Arab goodwill while remaining obliv-ious to the basic premises of the special-relationship orientation.

Indeed, with the acutely menacing vision of Arab defection to the Soviet orbit becoming at least partially realized (in the wake of such developments as Egypt's defection to the East and the July 1958 Iraqi revolution), President Eisenhower became increasingly prepared to reassess his pre-existing premises, including the view of Israel as a strategic liability and an impediment to Washington's regional plans. Contrary to Bar-Siman-Tov's excessive emphasis on the Six Day War as the trigger event or impetus to the establishment of the American–Israeli partnership, it was the revised regional context almost a *decade earlier* which laid the groundwork for the eventual development of security ties between Washington and Jerusalem.

Confronted with a recalcitrant regional landscape, the adminis-tration ultimately became predisposed, in the aftermath of the Suez Crisis, to abandon its original perception of Israel 'as an obstacle to the attainment of American objectives'.[11] Instead, the belief that Israel could provide invaluable assistance to the US and Britain in their efforts to protect the remaining pro-Western strongholds in the area came to increasingly permeate the thinking of Washington's high-policy élite as the decade approached its end. And while the Six Day War can legitimately be viewed as the culmination of this process of reassessing American priorities and preferences in the area, it by no means initiated this shift. Nor was it responsible for the growing convergence between the two central tenets of the American–Israeli dyad: the national-security orientation and the special-relationship paradigm, which became fully manifested in May and June 1967.

In concluding this section, with Soviet involvement in the Middle East becoming an integral part of the regional landscape in the late 1950s, the establishment of security ties between Washington and Jerusalem was no longer looked upon as a dangerous liability. In this respect, President Kennedy's decision, in August 1962, to sell to Israel the Hawk anti-aircraft missile closed the gap that had separated the operational from the perceptual and thus demonstrated – five years before the outbreak of the Six Day War – that the US was now fully prepared to predicate its Israeli posture upon the vision of the Jewish state as a close ally in the struggle 'to contain Soviet-backed revolutionary Arab nationalism'.[12] In other words, while 'the community of strategic interests' was indeed crucial to the formation of the alliance as maintained by Bar-Siman-Tov, the turning point in establishing this partnership was not 'Israel's military victory in 1967',[13] but the earlier collapse of Washington's strategic designs, which had been shaped in the 1950s and had been closely patterned on the desire to solicit the support of all major Arab powers in a joint defence posture against Soviet encroachment.

For all this emphasis on the role which 'hard' strategic factors played in forging the American–Israeli alliance, there remains the question as to the relative contribution of various considerations and factors, which were inextricably related to the special-relationship paradigm, to this partnership. In contrast to Bar-Siman-Tov's analysis, which views the cluster of 'soft' factors as marginal to both the formation and preservation of this alliance,[14] the historical evidence suggests that the institutional representatives of the special relationship (and primarily Jewish organizations and the US Congress) did manage to perform (from the early 1960s onwards) the highly significant function of constraining successive administrations and thus of repeatedly forcing them to scale down, modify or abandon certain courses of action *vis-à-vis* Israel. Indeed, in view of the persuasiveness of the images incorporated into the special-relationship paradigm, it is hardly surprising that pro-Israeli organizations were frequently successful in promoting favourable policies and legislation.

To the extent that American Jews have been able (since the 1960s) to advance their interest in Israel, their success has depended on the sympathy or at least acquiescence of the public at large. And indeed, in seeking to exert pressure on Israel, American policy-makers – who were committed to the premises of the American national-interest paradigm – were significantly constrained by the organized representatives of the special-relationship paradigm who, by and large, fully shared Jerusalem's concerns, priorities and objectives.

Thus, far from comprising a complex of abstract, disjointed images invariably subordinated to strategic requirements, the cluster of beliefs and attitudes incorporated into the special-relationship paradigm was in fact continuously converted (since the early 1960s) into powerful interest-group activity on behalf of Israel.[15] For these accurately reflected 'the beliefs and values of most Americans'.

Notwithstanding the fact that the initial gap separating the two paradigms largely disappeared towards the end of the Eisenhower era, this growing convergence could by no means guarantee that successive later administrations would refrain at some point from applying coercive strategies *vis-à-vis* Israel. It is against this backdrop of Washington's repeated efforts to broaden its margin of manoeuvrability in the Arab–Israeli sphere by exerting pressure on Israel that the constraining role of the representatives of the special-relationship paradigm unfolded. It is to an examination of this constraining role in the context of several crises in American–Israeli relations that we now turn.

A clear illustration of the role played by representatives of the special-relationship paradigm in constraining Washington's policies (which were perceived as incompatible with the logic and basic premises of the special-relationship orientation) is provided by a review of the 'reassessment crisis' of 1975. In this crisis episode, Secretary of State Henry Kissinger's desire to rapidly conclude an interim agreement between Israel and Egypt in the Sinai Peninsula regardless of its territorial costs to Israel (and thus to guarantee that Egypt's President Anwar Sadat was fully and irreversibly drawn into the Western bloc at the direct expense of the Soviet Union), conflicted with the Israeli insistence on specific trade-offs and linkages with Egypt (for example, between the scope of Israel's withdrawal from the Sinai Peninsula and the nature of Egyptian commitments regarding such issues as non-belligerency) as the main prerequisite for an acceptable agreement incorporating a partial Israeli withdrawal from Sinai. The subsequent 'reassessment' posture, which was initiated in late March 1975 by the Ford administration in view of the failure of its initial mediating effort, was viewed by Kissinger as a means of softening the Israeli position through 'the threat of economic pressure and diplomatic isolation'.[16] However, in pursuing its coercive drive (which included the threat of reconvening the Geneva peace conference with Soviet participation), the administration could not remain totally and continuously oblivious to a number of domestic factors and actors, particularly Congress, which ultimately severely narrowed its margin of manoeuvrability. And indeed by May 1975 it had become abundantly clear to President Ford and Secretary Kissinger that the administration lacked the domestic support necessary for the accomplishment of their objectives.[17]

The most powerful indication of this domestic discontent, which infuriated and frustrated President Ford and Secretary Kissinger,[18] and played a major role in affecting Washington's perceptions and expectations, was conveyed to the administration on 21 May 1975. Incensed by what they perceived as the exertion of 'too much pressure on Israel', 76 Senators responded to an AIPAC (American–Israeli Public Affairs Committee) initiative and sent a strongly worded letter to the president, urging him to be 'responsive to Israel's economic and military needs'.[19] Further reinforced by the spate of messages sent to the president by most Jewish organizations, including the Conference of Presidents of Major American Jewish Organizations and the National Jewish Community Relations Advisory Council (NJCRAC), which demanded that the administration 'stands firmly with Israel in the search for peace in future negotiations',[20] the 21 May letter provided the main precipitant for change in the administration's attitude.

Lacking the necessary infrastructure of public and Congressional support for the effective pursuit of its 'reassessment' policy, President Ford and Secretary Kissinger decided to soften the American course of action *vis-à-vis* Israel by incorporating significant inducements and incentives into their strategy. While both leaders had hitherto been reluctant to compensate Israel for the concessions it was called upon to make to Egypt, they were now prepared to offer Israel a wide assortment of incentives (incorporated into the 1 September 1975, US–Israeli Memorandum of Understanding) in order to coax it into abandoning most of its demands *vis-à-vis* Egypt (these incentives included the promise of large-scale economic and military aid as well as several far-reaching strategic guarantees).

It was this 'sweetener' or 'carrot' – American compensation to Israel – that led Prime Minister Rabin to modify his position and sign the Sinai Interim Agreement (or Sinai II as it is commonly known). This, despite its significant imbalance within the narrow parameters of the Israeli–Egyptian dyad; even now, the Israeli withdrawal from the Mitla and Gidi passes was not reciprocated by any Egyptian commitment to formally terminate the state of belligerence. But Rabin was ultimately induced to sign an agreement in which the mediator rather than the opponent offered the necessary compensation for Israel's territorial concessions to Egypt.[21]

Far from being an isolated and unique event, the 'reassessment crisis' of 1975 was but one illustration in which representatives of the special-relationship paradigm, both in Congress and the Jewish community, succeeded in aborting or significantly modifying American initiatives and moves in the Arab–Israeli sphere.

For example, two years after the resolution of the 'reassessment crisis', the Carter administration also came to recognize that it lacked the necessary margin of domestic support in order to implement the 1 October 1977 US–Soviet Joint Declaration on the Middle East. As was the case with the 'reassessment crisis', the release of a document which sought to involve the Soviets in the peace-making process and to compel Israel to agree to the participation of the PLO in the Geneva peace conference, which President Carter hoped to convene before the end of 1977, precipitated a storm of domestic protest in the US. The Congress, which took a leading role in challenging the superpower initiative, reacted with defiance, with 150 members of the House expressing 'grave concern' over the matter.

Incensed by both geostrategic considerations (opposition to the invitation issued to the Soviet Union to re-enter the scene of Middle East negotiations) and considerations premised on the special-relationship paradigm, Senators Henry Jackson, Robert Dole, Daniel Patrick Moynihan, Howard Baker, Clifford Case and Jacob Javits forged a broadly based 'blocking coalition', composed of both conservatives and liberals. As was the case during the 'reassessment crisis', this strong Congressional constraint was further reinforced by the leadership of the Jewish community, which acted swiftly and unanimously in support of the Israeli opposition to the superpower initiative. Fully committed to the Israeli posture of refusing to recognize the PLO unless the organization recognized Security Council Resolution 242, the Conference of Presidents of Major Jewish Organizations, headed by Rabbi Alexander Schindler, labelled the 1 October communiqué 'an abandonment of America's historical commitment to the security and survival of Israel', and an avalanche of angry telephone calls and telegrams descended on the White House, mostly from aroused Jewish groups.[22]

Confronted with these mounting signs of domestic dissent and defiance, and faced with an irreconcilable Israeli refusal to acquiesce in the PLO's participation at Geneva, the Carter administration was forced to shift gear and offer Israel compensation of such magnitude as to render obsolete most aspects of its new strategy. Ultimately, in a US–Israeli working paper which was signed on 5 October 1977, the administration agreed to radically modify the 1 October statement, and reaffirmed its 1975 commitment to Israel not to accept any new participant in the peace process without the consent of *all* the parties.

Deprived, as had been the case during the 'reassessment crisis', of an adequate base of domestic support, and faced with a cohesive Jewish community, the besieged Carter administration ultimately agreed to 'interpretations [of the 1 October statement] that seriously diluted the mandate of the proposed [peace] conference'.[23] This development, and the acquiescence of the Carter administration in the pressures exerted by proponents of the special-relationship paradigm, infuriated the Soviets, who 'did not hide their disappointment' with the apparent about-face in the American position.[24]

As these two crises in American–Israeli relations sought to demonstrate, in their efforts to predicate American Middle East policy exclusively upon the premises of the national-interest paradigm while ignoring certain basic tenets of the special-relationship paradigm, Presidents Ford and Carter were confronted with a defiant domestic front, with the leadership of *all* major Jewish organizations cooperating with AIPAC and with Congressional leaders in an effort to abort – or significantly modify – the American posture or initiative. Fully and irrevocably committed to the official Israeli position, these representatives of the special-relationship paradigm, who enjoyed a broad base of support in American public opinion, forced the administration, both in 1975 and 1977, to reassess its own strategy and ultimately set aside some of its fundamental premises.

It was only at the beginning of the 1990s that this capacity of the organized representatives of the special-relationship paradigm to constrain the administration was called into question. In most crises which strained American–Israeli relations in the three previous decades (despite the progressively intensifying strategic ties within the dyad), it was the cohesion among nearly all the groups supporting Israel which helped the advocates of this orientation to prevail in their encounters with an occasionally divided and vacillating administration. The picture began to change in the course of the Bush presidency, with the special-relationship paradigm itself becoming increasingly susceptible to cleavage and division. Paradoxically, at the time when the level of strategic cooperation between the two allies reached new peaks, indications of erosion came increasingly to cloud the very core of the special-relationship orientation, with the backbone of the paradigm no longer able to perform effectively its traditional function of setting severe limits on Washington's ability to exert influence on Israel's behaviour.

These signs of strain surfaced most clearly onto the landscape of American–Israeli relations during 1991 and early 1992 in the context of the crisis over Israel's request for $400 million (and later $10 billion) in housing-loan guarantees to accommodate the wave of immigration to Israel from the former Soviet Union. Insisting on a specific trade-off between approval of the loan guarantees for Israel and a revision of the Shamir government's position on such issues as Resolution 242 in general and Israel's settlement activity in the West Bank and Gaza in particular, in September 1991 the Bush administration adopted a posture of procrastination given the Israeli rejection of its plan to establish a joint machinery for ascertaining that the funds appropriated would not be used directly or indirectly in the occupied territories.[25]

In late February 1992, the 'loan guarantees crisis' escalated into a bitter confrontation between the two governments when President Bush announced that unless Israel formally and unequivocally agreed to freeze all settlement activities in the West Bank (and not merely to refrain from using the loan guarantees for constructing new housing units there or to provide Washington with detailed information concerning its planned settlement activity), it could not expect to receive even a fraction of the requested loans. Shamir's intensive effort, in subsequent months, to secure at least a portion of the requested loan guarantees without acquiescing in the new American demand proved futile. It was only with the return of the Labour Government to power, in the summer of 1992, and in view of its new order of national priorities, that President Bush announced, on 11 August 1992, his decision to approve the Israeli request for $10 billion in loan guarantees.

An examination of the role of the forces associated with the special-relationship paradigm in the course of the 'loan guarantees crisis' clearly indicates that, contrary to the image of unity which Congress and the leadership of the Jewish community had projected in a variety of past confrontations, the 'loan guarantees crisis' exposed a picture of sharp divisions among the traditional, and most determined, representatives of the special-relationship paradigm. Indeed, by linking the loan guarantees issue to the highly unpopular question of foreign aid, the Bush administration forced Israel's Congressional allies to acquiesce so as to avoid a direct confrontation not only with the president but with broad segments of American public opinion which fully supported the administration's position.

Thus, unlike the intensive Congressional drive to force the Ford administration to terminate its reassessment course, and unlike the vigorous Congressional *modus operandi* in the course of the October 1977 crisis, no such defiant position was forthcoming in 1991 or 1992. Furthermore, the leadership of the American Jewish community, which in 1975 and 1977 had expressed unanimous support for the positions taken by the Rabin and Begin governments and forged, together with Congress, a most effective 'blocking coalition', was now sharply divided over Israel's settlement policy. Combined with the reluctance of Israel's Congressional allies to become associated with a course that could be construed, rightly or wrongly, as incompatible with America's economic needs, significant segments of the Jewish leadership remained highly critical, in 1991 and early 1992, of Israel's settlement policy. Rather than challenge the administration, they forcefully urged the Israeli government to refrain from any action which might precipitate a confrontation with President Bush.[26]

Ultimately, with the backbone of the special-relationship paradigm becoming increasingly critical of Israel's settlement policy, President Bush's February 1992 decision to make the loan guarantees contingent upon an ironclad Israeli assurance that it would freeze *all* construction in the occupied territories, did not encounter much domestic opposition. As a result, the Shamir government found itself (in the course of the fruitless negotiations over the specific terms of the loan guarantees which followed the February

1992 decision) deprived of much of its traditional base of support in American public opinion which, in the not too distant past, had repeatedly restricted Washington's margin of manoeuvrability in the Arab–Israeli sphere.

In terms of both its structure and outcome, the 'loan guarantees crisis' was by no means an isolated episode. Rather, it was an early and partial manifestation of the growing centrifugal forces which progressively converted what had traditionally been a cohesive and highly effective paradigm into an emotion-laden, highly strained and fractured framework, whose main representatives differed sharply from one another not merely over the tactics to be employed, but over the target of their organized activity. It is to an analysis of this process, which was fully manifested during the period 1993–99, that we now turn.

During the 1990s, Congress continued to be highly supportive of Israel, granting lenient loan payment terms and converting loans to grants, and initiating new foreign aid programmes for Israel's bene-fit. However, it is within the confines of another core component of the special-relationship paradigm – the Jewish community – that the continued process of transformation of the relationship from the pole of internal unity, cohesion and unabated support of Israel's policies, to the extreme of dissent, friction and alienation, became most clearly manifest. Whereas previous crises within the American–Israeli framework had developed between an assertive American administration and a defiant Israeli government, with the Jewish leadership rallying almost unanimously in support of Israel, the picture changed dramatically during the period 1992–96. Now, both governments were endeavouring to constrain a growing segment of the Jewish community that was highly critical of the Oslo accords and the policy of accommodation with the Palestinians.

Increasingly disposed to abandon the traditional Jewish policy of providing full support for Israel's peace-making strategies, a salient and vocal segment of American Jewry embarked upon a defiant posture *vis-à-vis* both the Rabin and Peres governments. Thus, while most Jewish umbrella organizations, including the Council of Jewish Federations, the National Jewish Community Relations Advisory Council, and the Conference of Presidents of Major Jewish Organizations, have remained continuously commit-ted to the peace process, the more determined opposition groups, like the Rabbinical Council of America (which represents Orthodox rabbis), have become increasingly prominent on the American scene by virtue of their arguments as well as their combative rhetoric. The stormy confrontations that took place from 1993 to 1996 between such opposition leaders and spokesmen as Harvey Friedman and Rabbi Steven Pruzansky, on the one hand, and several Jewish and Israeli representatives, including the national ADL director, Abraham Foxman, and the Israeli ambassador to Washington, Itamar Rabinovich, on the other, were but a few illustrations of the deepening divisions which, on the eve of the assassination of Prime Minister Rabin, threatened the very core of the special relationship.[27]

The election of Benjamin Netanyahu as Israel's prime minister on 29 May 1996 provided yet another impetus for accelerating the shift from unity and consensus to dissent within the Jewish community, with the core of the special relationship rapidly becoming a highly fractured framework, whose components were continuously engaged in incessant disputes with the Netanyahu government over such issues as Israel's peace strategy and the conversion law, rather than in more traditional activities in support of official Israeli policies and strategies. During the Rabin and Peres era, it was the Orthodox critics of the Oslo process within American Jewry who vociferously attacked Israeli policies from the right of the political spectrum. Following the election of Benjamin Netanyahu, it was the liberal mainstream of the Jewish community (composed largely of Reform and Conservative Jews) that increasingly became the source of protest and opposition to Jerusalem's peace policies and legislative initiatives.

It is true that Netanyahu's election momentarily helped to defuse the tension between critics of the peace process within American Jewry and the Israeli government. However, Netanyahu's decisions to open the Hashmonean tunnel, to construct the Har-Homa neighbourhood in eastern Jerusalem and to suspend the implementation of the Wye agreement quickly became the source of bitter disputes within the American Jewish community, with numerous groups and organizations expressing strong and open reservations about the Israeli *modus operandi* and commitment to peace in the Palestinian sphere. Clearly, so deep were the divisions in the traditional pro-Israeli base of support that they could not be eliminated overnight as a result of leadership changes in Israel. They were thus destined to cloud American–Israeli ties and vastly complicate any renewed Israeli effort to use the Jewish community as a lever to thwart American attempts to redefine its margin of manoeuvrability in the Arab–Israeli sphere.[28]

In numerous crises that had clouded American–Israeli relations since the 1960s, leaders of the Jewish community had been unequivocal (and sometimes outspoken) in their support of the Israeli position. But the 1990s witnessed the emergence of a new behavioural pattern on the part of broad components of the American Jewish community, whose objective now was to constrain the Israeli government rather than the Clinton administration. Indeed, whereas in the past, most – if not all – initiatives designed 'to save Israel from itself' had originated with individuals who were consistently critical of the essence of the special relationship, during the years 1996–99 the demand that the administration raise the profile of its involvement in the Arab–Israeli conflict and apply coercive measures towards Israel was made by individuals and groups most intimately associated with the core of the special relationship (including Robert Lifton, the former president of the American Jewish Congress, and Henry Siegman, its former executive director), who were previously considered part of the mainstream of American Jewry.

This picture of political and ideological fragmentation, with significant segments of the Jewish representatives of the special-relationship paradigm becoming increasingly predisposed to openly criticize the Israeli government, was further compounded during the 1990s by indications of a growing cultural, demographic and religious crisis within the American Jewish community, dramatically manifested in an intermarriage rate of 52 per cent in 1990, as compared with only 6.7 per cent during the 1940s and 1950s, as well as a steady decline in the fertility rate of the non-Orthodox communities, which averaged between 1.5 and 1.6 children per couple in 1998. These indications raise doubts as to the future of this community as a viable, vibrant and influential pressure group. The recent decline in the percentage of the Jewish vote in both the presidential elections of 1996 and the Congressional elections of 1994 and 1998 is another indication of the potential erosion in the political power and influence of the American–Jewish community.[29]

Despite its continued skirmishes and clashes with the Netanyahu government (on matters pertaining to the Palestinian–Israeli peace process), the Clinton administration did not seek to take advantage of the Jewish–Israeli framework in order to broaden its margin of manoeuvrability *vis-à-vis* the Israeli government. Furthermore, in contrast to the processes of erosion which, during the 1990s, had significantly weakened the cluster of 'soft' components that comprised the backbone of the special-relationship paradigm, the complex of 'hard' factors which were inextricably patterned on the premises of the national-interest orientation gained dominance in the course of the Clinton era, as the president intensified strategic cooperation with Israel.[30]

Indeed, concurrent with the growing fragmentation of the forces affiliated with the special-relationship paradigm, the level of strategic cooperation between Washington and Jerusalem reached new heights during the 1990s. Not only did the administration grant Israel a status equal to that of NATO members with regard to defence technology transfers, but it also authorized the transfer to Israel of advanced computers and surplus military equipment, renewed its commitment to pre-position in Israel military supply stocks for use in wartime, continued the Arrow missile project, authorized joint developments and pilot training programmes, and provided military hardware including F-16 and F15I long-range bombers as well as AMRAAM missiles.[31]

Notwithstanding this unshattered American vision of Israel as a strategic asset to the US and as a close ally in the effort to contain the threat of Islamic fundamentalism, the possibility of sharp American–Israeli disagreements over such issues as the terms of a permanent Israeli–Palestinian settlement should not be discounted (regardless of the specific composition of the Israeli government). Thus, whereas the first Oslo accord and the Wye agreement temporarily obfuscated parts of the ideological, political, territorial and national core of the Palestinian predicament, no such decoupling between the centre and periphery of the conundrum will be possible as the parties prepared to face the most arduous task of defining the parameters of lasting accommodation between them. Notwithstanding the defeat of Prime Minister Netanyahu in the Israeli elections of 17 May 1999, and the rise to power of a more accommodating government headed by Ehud Barak, it is entirely possible that the inevitable encounter with all the thorniest components of the Israeli–Palestinian dispute will inject its strain into the American–Israeli scene by exposing the traditional American interpretations of at least some of the parameters of a permanent settlement (such as those pertaining to the status of Jerusalem), which have remained essentially incompatible with basic Israeli views (adhered to by both Labour and Likud governments).

If this scenario does indeed materialize, then the Barak government may find itself in the unenviable situation of having to face the administration without at least part of the traditional infrastructure of support in American public opinion which, in the not too distant past, repeatedly forced successive administrations to scale down, abandon or significantly revise their designs. Indeed, with the backbone of the special-relationship paradigm deeply fraught with disunity, the administration may find itself ultimately able to broaden significantly its margin of manoeuvrability *vis-à-vis* the Israeli government. With major representatives of the paradigm either drifting into passivity and reticence or actively supporting the administration, a window of opportunity may therefore be opened for Washington to accomplish an objective which has eluded American diplomacy for more than five decades: a permanent settlement in the Palestinian sphere.

## NOTES

1. Yaacov Bar-Siman-Tov, 'The United States and Israel Since 1948: A 'Special Relationship'?', *Diplomatic History*, 22, 2 (spring 1998), pp. 231–62.
2. Ibid., p. 232; Peter L. Hahn, 'Commentary: Special Relationships', *Diplomatic History*, 22, 2 (spring 1998), p. 262.
3. Bar-Siman-Tov, 'The United States and Israel Since 1948', p. 232.
4. Ibid., p. 232.
5. Ibid.
6. Ibid.
7. For a detailed analysis of these paradigms, see Abraham Ben-Zvi, *The United States and Israel: The Limits of the Special Relationship* (New York: Columbia University Press, 1993), p. 14.
8. Bernard Reich, *The United States and Israel: Influence in the Special Relationship* (New York: Praeger, 1984), p. 183.
9. Abraham Ben-Zvi, *Decade of Transition: Eisenhower, Kennedy, and the Origins of the American–Israeli Alliance* (New York: Columbia University Press, 1998), pp. 30–3.
10. Ibid., pp. 44–5.
11. Steven L. Spiegel, *The Other Arab-Israeli Conflict: Making America's Middle East Policy, from Truman to Reagan* (Chicago: University of Chicago Press, 1987), p. 87.
12. Ben-Zvi, *Decade of Transition*, p. 67.
13. Bar-Siman-Tov, 'The United States and Israel Since 1948', p. 232.
14. Ibid.
15. Michael, N. Barnett, 'Identity and Alliances in the Middle East', in Peter J. Katzenstein (ed.), *The Culture of National Security: Norms and Identity in World Politics* (New York: Columbia University Press, 1996), p. 433. See also James Lee Ray, *The Future of American–Israeli Relations* (Lexington: University of Kentucky Press, 1985), p. 25.
16. Henry Kissinger, *Years of Renewal* (New York: Simon & Schuster, 1999), p. 428.
17. Ibid., pp. 385–459.
18. Ibid., p. 434.

19. Quoted by Spiegel, *The Other Arab–Israeli Conflict*, p. 296.
20. Ibid.
21. Kissinger, *Years of Renewal*, p. 454.
22. Raymond Cohen, 'Israel and the Soviet–American Statement of October 1, 1977', *Orbis*, 22, 4 (Fall 1978), p. 624.
23. Raymond Garthoff, *Detente and Confrontation: American–Soviet Relations from Nixon to Reagan* (Washington, DC: Brookings Institution, 1985), p. 581.
24. Zbigniew Brzezinski, *Power and Principle: Memoirs of the National Security Adviser, 1977–1981* (New York: Farrer, Straus, Giroux, 1983), p. 175.
25. Ben-Zvi, 'Paradigm Lost?', p. 7; James A. Baker, *The Politics of Diplomacy: Resolution, War, and Peace, 1989–1992* (New York: Putnam's Sons, 1995), p. 540.
26. Ben-Zvi, 'Paradigm Lost?', pp. 7–8.
27. Abraham Ben-Zvi, *Partnership Under Stress: The American Jewish Community* (Tel Aviv University: Jaffee Centre for Strategic Studies, Memorandum No. 52, August 1998), p. 24.
28. Ibid., p. 27.
29. Ibid., p. 30.
30. Bar-Siman-Tov, 'The United States and Israel Since 1948', p. 258.
31. Ibid.

# 12  Contending Narratives: The Israeli Peace Movement's Role in the Oslo Process

## TAMAR HERMANN

Political narratives are noticeably fast to evolve. This is probably because they are usually meant to sustain contemporaneous political agendas. The conveyers of such political narratives, however, usually deny their functional nature,[1] since the more transparent the linkage between a specific political agenda and the political narrative, the more the audience tends to take the narrative with a grain of salt. Both the functionalist character and the rapid construction of political narratives seem to gain further momentum in times of dramatic political transformations, apparently because highly elaborated narratives enable the political actors to implant and interpret the unfolding strategic developments and select the proper responses to them without delay.

The strategic transformation that occurred in the Middle East from the early 1990s onwards, best known as the Oslo process, indeed generated within Israel – and quite rapidly – a variety of narratives which explain this unprecedented process and identify its initiators. Three main distinctive narratives in this regard can be identified: the first was constructed by the Labour Party; the second by the right, or the Likud-led national camp; and the last – by the left or, more precisely, by the peace movement.[2]

This chapter is meant first and foremost to analyse these three narratives and elaborate on the reasons for the fact that while the first narrative completely ignores the peace movement's role in the launching of the process, the latter two, although developed by political camps holding antithetical political agendas, magnify the role it played in preparing the background and the initiation of this strategic transformation. Labour's narrative of the launching of the Oslo process not only ignored the peace movement but in the same spirit almost no use was made of the peace activists' connections with the Palestinian side, even when the negotiations slowed down or neared a dead-end. The narrative developed by the rightist opponents of the process, on the other hand, indeed recognized the peace movement's role: it blamed the movement for propelling the Labour government into making dangerous moves and taking overly high risks in the context of this process. As expected, the peace movement developed a narrative emphasizing its unique contribution to the Oslo process, presenting it as a highly positive development of its own making. It should be mentioned at the outset that in all three political camps' discourse some variations could indeed be noticed. However, in all three of them a 'mainstream' narrative has also been developed and it is on these three central narratives that the analysis below will focus.

Focusing on the Israeli peace movement in this context is not arbitrary, taking into consideration the striking similarity between the underlying premises of the Oslo process and those the peace movement had been promoting for a number of years before this process was launched. Four premises had been fostered by the peace movement and gradually embraced by Israel's official decision-makers in the years 1992–95: (a) definition of the Israeli–Palestinian conflict as a potentially win–win rather than a zero-sum situation; (b) recognition of the Palestinians' right to national self-determination and the PLO as their legitimate representative; (c) affirmation of the desirability – from the Israeli point of view – of a political solution to the conflict rather than relying on military strategic advantage both because such a solution is lower-cost in terms of human suffering and Israel's likely inability to achieve a decisive military victory; (d) acknowledgment that achieving a peace agreement entails considerable territorial concessions, and that painful as they may be such, concessions are worthwhile in terms of Israel's long-range security.

The Israeli case dealt with here may also be of importance on a more general level as it pertains to a recent 'hot' issue in the study of foreign-policy formation, namely the relations between the political centre and the periphery as far as foreign-policy decision-making is concerned.[3] What we are looking at here is a situation, perhaps not so unique but indeed of an under-investigated type, in which a nation's leaders tacitly adopted a political strategy formerly advocated only by a peripheral actor, thereby transforming the long-held viewpoint of the centre on a crucial aspect of the nation's external relations.

Thus, the second aim of this paper is to shed some light on the way in which such crucial political transformations occur and how they are rationalized by political actors with different political positions. In this context, and based on the Israeli case, an effort will be made to analyse how the transformation was explained: (a) by the decision-makers who made the dramatic decision and then had to justify it and expunge its original non-consensual image; (b) by their challengers, close to the power centre and eager to gain control of it by, among other means, delegitimizing the policies of the incumbent government; and, (c) by the political actors in the periphery, who wished to be recognized as the originators of the new strategy in order to improve their political positioning. In other words, it is maintained here that while Labour leaders' narrative was meant to help them in their struggle to justify the radical policy change the Oslo process entailed,[4] the narrative of the Likud-led camp of the right was meant to strengthen its position as a substantial alternative to the ruling party by exposing the defects in its innovative policy,[5] while the peace movement's narrative was aimed at using the transformation in the 'political structure of opportunities' to improve its extra-parliamentary political status and enable it to get closer to the decision-making process.[6]

To understand better the argument presented above regarding the influence of the political positioning of the three political streams on the content of their respective narratives and on the links constructed in these narratives between the Oslo process and the peace movement, a short historical overview of this movement's relations *vis-à-vis* the Israeli political centre is required.[7]

## PEACE ACTIVISM AND THE DISCOURSE ON THE ISRAELI–PALESTINIAN CONFLICT

Since the establishment of the State of Israel in 1948 and until the opening of the peace negotiations in the early 1990s, Israel's relations with the Arab world were mostly hostile and often violent (with the exception of the Israel–Egypt peace treaty of 1979). However, the intractable conflict failed to encourage the emergence of a significant peace camp in Israel for several decades. While now and again individual peace activists and tiny peace groups did appear, most of them faded away without leaving any significant political traces or legacies.[8] The feeble peace activism prior to the late 1970s can be attributed to various factors, starting with the scarcity of pacifist legacies in the Jewish tradition and ending with the rejection in the newly independent Israel of the 1950s and 1960s of the extra-parliamentary *modus operandi* employed by most peace movements.[9] The fundamental explanation, however, seems to lie in the nature of the Israeli public discourse on peace and war that developed under the shadow of an imminent – real or perceived – external existential threat.

Apparently, systematic and organized peace advocacy was slow to develop in Israel as it was strongly at odds with the dominant security ethos shared by almost all major Zionist political actors in the country – left, centre and right. This security ethos, extensively analyzed in recent years mainly in the context of 'the new-historian debate',[10] had several postulates which are relevant to this discussion. The first was its stress on the centrality of power politics, according to which the Israeli–Palestinian relationship was interpreted as a basically zero-sum, life-and-death struggle of two peoples over the same piece of land. Second is the perception that the State of Israel, as a Jewish state, is but one link in the catastrophe-filled chain of Jewish history. Israel is thus envisaged as the target of hostile intentions and deeds of the Arabs, and as the utterly defensive side in the conflict. This underlying existential anxiety, together with the painful and still fresh experience of the Holocaust, laid the foundations for the Israeli mainstream's attribution of major importance to the military, which at certain times and in certain contexts was even presented as the epitome of the national spirit. Strategic superiority was perceived in this context as the most important guarantee for Israel's national security both in the short and long run, while political agreements were looked upon as much less satisfactory and reliable for that purpose.

These prevalent perceptions apparently precluded the emergence of a significant peace camp, as peace activists normally reject the notion of power politics; they uphold universalistic values while undermining particularistic ones, exalt the notion of compromise or win–win solutions to international and intercommunal disputes, and usually consider the use of military means for the strengthening of the national security and the resolution of international conflict as more costly and less effective than political ones.

The mainstream security postulate regarding Israel's position *vis-à-vis* the Arab world as 'David against Goliath', or the 'few against the many', was first shaken by the 1967 war, the main outcome of which was the occupation of the Sinai, Golan Heights, West Bank and Gaza Strip. Another outcome was the pronounced decrease in the collective sense of external threat that followed the sweeping victory of the Israeli Defence Forces (IDF) over the armies of Syria, Jordan and Egypt. These changes together with the emergence of the Movement for a Greater Israel, which advocated the immediate, full annexation of the occupied territories, served as catalysts for the appearance in early 1968 of the Movement for Peace and Security (MPS), the first Israeli grass-roots peace movement.[11]

This movement, which numbered at the peak of its activity in 1970–71 a few hundred hard-core activists and a few thousand activists in its outer circle, was the first to publicly warn of the political, military and social dangers inherent in the occupation. It strongly recommended putting an end to it, before it become rooted in Israel's political and economic reality and, more importantly, in its psychological mindset, thus endangering the country's democratic nature. For that purpose the MPS advocated the opening of a direct dialogue with any Arab leader or group willing to talk peace, regardless of their earlier deeds or former positions. The MPS also tried to convince the Israeli decision-makers and the broad public that significant territorial concessions were a necessary and reasonable price to pay for a peace settlement with the Arab states and the Palestinians. Last but not least, the movement warned that should Israel administer the occupied territories too harshly, a violent rebellion of the Palestinians would break out sooner or later.

Nonetheless, the immense military victory, interpreted by many euphoric Israelis as divine intervention on behalf of the Jewish people, along with the fact that MPS could not single out any actual Arab partners for peace talks,[12] played into the hands of its opponents. They maintained that the movement's ideas were totally unrealistic and, if realized, might critically jeopardize Israel's security. The strongest attacks on the movement came, as expected, from the right. However, no less harmful to its efforts to gain public support was the caustic criticism of Labour, then the dominant political party in Israel and the pillar of the mainstream, and of the United Worker (Mapam) Party, both of which were apprehensive of the MPS's significant public appeal, particularly with the younger cohorts of the left camp. The MPS, badly stigmatized and isolated because of the established parties' antagonism, vanished in the early 1970s. However, its critique of Israeli power politics and of the country's self-righteousness with regard to the causes and cures of the regional conflict, as well as its advocacy of territorial compromise, left indelible traces on the Israeli public discourse to be found in particular in the Peace Now agenda less than a decade later.

The fractures in the Israeli national consensus on such matters became more conspicuous with the massive wave of protest that followed the 1973 October War. The Arabs' well-coordinated surprise attack and the apparent malfunctioning of Israel's political and military decision-makers shocked many Israelis, eroding their former solid belief that military might could guarantee the state's safety in the long run and convincing them that a political solution to the conflict should be sought without delay. This notion was fully elaborated by a new peace organization – the Israeli Council for Israeli–Palestinian Peace (ICIPP), established in 1976. This organization was actually a think-tank which numbered some tens of participants, most of whom were well-known public figures from the political arena, civil administration and even retired IDF officers. It was the first to dare to state that Israel should negotiate directly with the PLO and recognize it as the legitimate representative of the Palestinian people. However, at that time, most Israelis did not consider the Palestinians a significant partner for a peace dialogue and the PLO was still being overwhelmingly denounced as a terrorist organization of the worst kind. Nevertheless, the ICIPP activists continued to develop close relations with certain prominent Palestinian leaders, meeting them mostly in European countries such as France or Italy. All of these meetings were declared private as the ICIPP activists had no official authority to negotiate with their Palestinian counterparts, who, by the way, were usually PLO officials. The contents of these meetings, however, were often reported directly to the most prominent Israeli decision-makers.[13] By accepting these reports and not taking any action to stop the meetings, these decision-makers, including the then prime minister Yitzhak Rabin, implicitly acknowledged that some value accrued to this channel of communication between Israel and the PLO. Still, the ICIPP remained a tiny and exclusive body with only marginal political status.

The status of Israeli peace activism improved dramatically in early 1978, with the emergence of Peace Now (PN), the largest and most significant Israeli peace movement to arise to date. This movement emerged less than a year after the first electoral defeat of the Labour Party (May 1977) and the establishment of a right-wing government by the Likud Party. Only a few months later, as is widely known, the new government, under the leadership of Prime Minister Menachem Begin, began negotiations for peace with Egypt. Within a short time, however, the talks seemed to be reaching a dead-end. The growing fear that the Likud-led government had no genuine interest in concluding these talks helped PN to mobilize unprecedented public support for its demand that the talks continue until a peace agreement was reached. It was backed by hundreds of thousands of Israelis who openly supported Israeli withdrawal from the Sinai in return for such a peace, thereby, intentionally or unintentionally, opening the door for a similar step if peace talks with the Palestinians were to begin some time in the future.

After the signing of the peace treaty with Egypt, PN, by then a large mass movement, shifted its protest, aiming it against the Jewish settlements which were rapidly spreading and taking root in the West Bank. PN warned that not only did these settlements constitute a sore grievance at the time, but that they would also be a huge obstacle if and when peace talks with the Palestinians were launched. The movement also protested against the harsh measures taken by the army against the Palestinians in the occupied territories, claiming that these acts proved that, contrary to the government's propaganda, the occupation was far from benign and that no occupation, by its very definition, could be truly 'enlightened'. At the same time, the appeal of PN's agenda regarding the possibility of establishing positive relations with the Palestinians was significantly undermined by the reccurrence at that time of fatal terrorist acts by Palestinian organizations against Israeli civilians, such as the armed attack on a bus on the coastline highway full of unarmed men, women and children (April 1978).

PN was clearly successful in breaking the taboo on mobilizing Israeli citizens for protest against the government when it took questionable steps affecting foreign and security matters, a realm hitherto virtually out of bounds to the public. However, against the over optimistic expectations of a large number of Israelis, Palestinians and others, fostered by the extensive positive media coverage of its massive demonstrations and articulated statements, the movement could not slow down the expansion of the Jewish settlements in the occupied territories, nor could it do much to ameliorate the Palestinians' grim living conditions under the occupation. PN was also unable to moderate the 'peace-resistant' policy of the Likud governments nor, owing to the stigma of 'naive and dangerous to the nation's interest' stamped on peace activism by the mainstream, could it obtain full legitimization as an actor with a say on national security matters. Even the fact that the founders and leaders of PN repeated declarations of their unwavering allegiance to the state and the Zionist cause, as proved by their military service and opposition to unlawful acts of protest, was insufficient to attain the desired legitimization. PN's unchallenged position within the peace camp was severely damaged in 1982, following the launching of the Lebanon War, when many peace activists looked to it to lead the opposition to that war, but its leaders refrained from doing so for almost two weeks. This hiatus left the stage clear for new, and significantly less conformist, peace groups to emerge and gain saliency by advocating formerly taboo acts, such as objection to military service on political grounds.

The authorities' rejection of the peace activists as 'dangerous to the nation's interest' was translated into deeds in 1986 when they passed a law that prohibited meetings between Israeli citizens and PLO officials and, in fact, some peace activists were sentenced to prison for disobeying it. This law, however, did not halt the vigorous wave of radical peace activism that emerged following the eruption of the Palestinian uprising, the *intifada*, in late 1987.[14] The groups which emerged were all small but often very conspicuous. The most visible were, perhaps, the women-only groups, in particular Women in Black. Between 1988 and 1993 this group held weekly Friday-noon vigils in central squares and at crossroads throughout the country. Each of the women demonstrators was dressed in black and stood silently holding a placard that called for an end to the occupation.[15] This unequivocal and uncompromising demand was fostered by other pro-peace/anti-occupation groups as well, some of which identified openly with the Palestinian national liberation struggle. Although the mainstream, broad public and decision-makers alike, viewed this sort of peace activities negatively, their message was heard and seen in most Israeli homes via the intensive media coverage they were given. These reports, along with disturbing scenes of the *intifada* and its repression by IDF soldiers and of the frequently violent attacks on Israeli civilians by Palestinian terrorists, apparently eroded the formerly prevalent conviction that force should be met by greater force, making a political resolution of the conflict increasingly attractive.

The regional situation changed radically with the convening of the Madrid conference in 1991, for this conference marked the beginning of multi-channel peace negotiations which, within less than two years, generated the Oslo process.[16] It should be emphasized, however, that the Likud government, then headed by Yitzhak Shamir, agreed to participate in this conference only because of the tremendous pressure put on it by the American administration. Labour's victory in the 1992 elections, although by only a very small majority, marked a turning point in Israel's formal attitude towards the peace talks. The new government, headed by Yitzhak Rabin, made the achievement of a political solution to the conflict in general, and in particular to the Israeli–Palestinian strife its main goal. It was also the first time that an Israeli government had publicly acknowledged – to the vociferous dismay of the right – that the territorial and other compromises a political solution entailed, painful as they might be, were justified. This was, indeed, a strategic transformation, and it necessitated a convincing explanation. The three narratives analysed in this chapter are meant to provide such an explanation.

## THE OSLO PROCESS NARRATIVES

Before describing the three Oslo process narratives – of the Labour Party, the right and the peace movement – and bringing into focus the differences between them, it is important to note that they have several common denominators. First, all three narratives recognized that the Oslo process marked a sharp departure from former Israeli–Arab relationships. Each of the narratives was therefore constructed to provide a compelling answer to the major question of what – if anything – had changed to justify replacing the long held zero-sum definition of the situation by a new interpretation of these relations. Was it a result of the nation's leaders' realization that the former interpretation had gradually became dysfunctional or was, perhaps, unsound from the start? Was the transformation inescapable following certain socio-demographic and socio-cultural changes that had eroded Israeli society's willingness and ability to fight wars? Was it perhaps that the global environment had changed so much in the early 1990s that a fundamental revision of some of Israel's basic political premises, as well as those of the Arab states and the Palestinians, was necessary? Or was it perhaps the intentions of the Arabs that had essentially changed? In addition to searching for the sources of the change marked by the Oslo process, each narrative presented a certain scenario of the future, depending to a large extent on the answer it gave to the former questions. In this context they all tried to answer whether the Oslo process would serve as a step towards a stable and secure peace or as a step towards the collapse of the whole Zionist dream. Last but not least, all three narratives tried to identify the initiators of the Oslo Process, so they could be either praised or blamed for its potential and actual consequences.

## THE LABOUR PARTY'S NARRATIVE

The Labour Party's narrative was developed in 1992–96 when the party was in power, that is, at the heart of the political centre. It was therefore very different in content and function from the narrative of the right-wing opposition that was developed on the outskirts of the centre and from narrative of the peace movement which was developed at the political periphery. For that reason it was essential that it be unifying and non-confrontational in order to make it acceptable to the broad public. Furthermore, like the initiators of the Oslo process on the Israeli side, Labour's leaders developed a narrative highly supportive of the transformation it represented while undermining the risks it entailed.[17] This had to be done with great care and subtlety, because as already mentioned their own party had for years rejected the ideas on which this process was based, when these were raised by the peace movement and other political actors of the left. Labour's narrative was therefore meant to rationalize the Oslo transformation without admitting that the party had made mistakes in this regard in the past. Another diffi-culty that Labour's narrative had to overcome was the natural reluctance of most people to abandon their long-held beliefs. Labor's new policy contradicted several major aspects of the national consensus mainly by acknowledging the national rights of the Palestinian people, negotiating directly with the PLO and recog-nizing it as the Palestinians' legitimate representative, and being prepared to make significant territorial concessions as implied by the Rabin government's participation in the process. Finally, this narrative had to ensure that the Labour Party received the full and sole credit for the process if successful, to be cashed in on election day. In particular, Labour could not afford to let the peace movement be credited with originating or leading to the Oslo process. Owing to the stigma of unpatriotic capitulation that had marked the peace movement, such recognition could easily delegitimize the entire process in the public's eyes. Moreover, such a sharing of credit might electorally strengthen the Meretz Party, next in line to Labour in the centre–left political camp.

The cognitive shift inherent in the Oslo process was evidently more difficult for Rabin, a former IDF chief of staff, than for Shimon Peres, with his less military-oriented mentality. Thus, whereas Rabin often rationalized the Oslo process by the pressing need to reduce both Israel's military burden and the number of Israeli soldiers and civilians killed and injured, Peres emphasized the far-reaching economic benefits of the Oslo process, as well as its potential to promote the cultural integration of Israel into the region – his famous vision of a 'New Middle East'. Moreover, while Peres seemed to be almost euphoric in the years 1994–95 concerning the positive outcomes of the Oslo process, Rabin was obviously concerned with the possible dangers of the course of action his government was undertaking. However, despite these cognitive differences between them, the two Labour leaders joined forces in outlining a new narrative, one which rationalized the Oslo process and endowed it with its *raison d'être*. This narrative described the Labour's government's decision to join the process both as a very difficult one to make in view of the Arabs' hostile attitude towards Israel since, and even before, 1948, and, concomitantly, as a rational and pragmatic decision, based on a reading of the early 1990s global, regional and domestic political map. It was this updated reading, Labour's narrative argued, in addition to the high price that Israel was paying for the protracted conflict, which led to the realization that negotiating peace with the Palestinians had now become a timely solution. The cessation of bloodshed was a central theme in this narrative and, when informing the Knesset of the self-rule agreement Israel had signed with the Palestinians, Rabin referred at length to it (although no compassion towards the Palestinians is to be found in this speech):

> We have lived all our lives in this land under the barrage of shells and the explosions of mines and hand grenades. We

planted, and they [the Palestinians] uprooted; we built while they ruined; we defended, as they attacked. Almost every day we had to bury our dead. One hundred years of war and terror have indeed hurt us, but did not destroy our dream. We have been dreaming of peace for one hundred years... This government has made up its mind therefore to try and put an end to the hatred, so that our children and grandchildren will not suffer the painful cost of war, terror and violence. This government has decided to protect their lives and security, and to bring solace to the pain and grievous memories, to pray and hope for peace.[18]

This pragmatism was not Rabin's alone. Shimon Peres, the more optimistic and visionary of the two leaders, also emphasized the matter-of-fact nature of the Labour government's decision to pursue the Oslo process and negotiate with the formerly ostracized PLO. In his well-known book *The New Middle East* he says:

There was no point in waiting any longer. The Likud government had run its course and the political freeze – the product of its ideological beliefs – was over. Terrorism continued, and the demographics were changing fast. If Israel was not careful, it would lose its lead in population growth between the sea and the Jordan River, and thereby invite a tragedy – the same sort of ethnic conflict that destabilized Yugoslavia.[19]

This reading of the situation as one that had now changed from a zero-sum situation to a mixed-motive one integrated well in the context of Labour's narrative, which was to explain why the launching of the peace process in the early 1990s did not imply that mistakes had been made by the party's leaders in the past. On the contrary, it actually sustained the validity of the party's earlier definition of the situation. It also served Labour's effort to undermine the argument, often made by the right, that Rabin's government had betrayed not only the Zionist mission but even the traditional policy of the Labour Party itself, thereby misleading its voters. Last but not least, presenting the situation as a very recent change allowed Labour to refute the peace movement's argument that the new policy could or should have been adopted years sooner.

One of Labour's primary needs when back in power in 1992, after 15 long years in opposition, was to show that it was competent to make rational and innovative decisions in matters of the greatest national importance. Therefore, in order to confute the right's arguments that it had made erroneous and dangerous decisions in the realm of national security, deserted the Zionist dream, and been soft and naïve when negotiating with the Palestinian side, Labour had to dissociate itself from any non-mainstream allies. Close and overt relations with the peace movement at that time could have sustained the allegations of Labour's rivals that it was a tool in the hands of certain non-governmental interest groups. This may explain why Rabin was said to have been much annoyed by a sticker disseminated by the left in the autumn of 1995 bearing the clever word-play: 'Peace is Meretz's work'.[20] Always disaffected by the peace movement, Rabin was also annoyed by the large number of its placards prominently displayed at peace rallies at which he spoke, including the one on 4 November 1995 at the conclusion of which he was assassinated.

Labour's public distancing of itself from the peace movement was also manifested by party politicians who were in fact well connected with it both before and after the Oslo process was launched. Yossi Beilin, for example, one of the 'Oslo architects', took part in a number of the movement's leadership meetings. However, in a book in which he describes the unfolding of the events that led to the Oslo process, the peace movement is mentioned only once, and even then in a rather detached, critical manner:

> Shortly after the [1992] elections I met with Peace Now leaders while in the US. Apparently they felt then that they had already reached their destination, that a peace-oriented government had taken over and that things would take care of themselves. When they realized that I didn't share their euphoria, they wondered why. I told them that nothing would happen by itself. Four years could be either a short or a long period of time. It would be possible to change the world in these years but it would also be possible to more or less go on along the already paved and familiar road leading nowhere.[21]

## The Narrative of the Right

Israeli right-wing parties and groups have all been strongly opposed to the Oslo process since its inception. In fact, their speakers often refer to it indistinctly as 'the political process', not as 'the peace process', thereby indicating their conviction that the negotiations will not lead to a real peace at all. This position of the right had two major motivations: the first was their automatic negative response, as the major body of the opposition, to all the Labour government's policies, while the second, and more substantial one, had to do with their authentic perception of Israeli–Arab relations as inevitably antagonistic.[22]

The Oslo process runs against the right's well-known fundamental opposition to an Israeli withdrawal from the entire West Bank (or Judea and Samaria as it prefers to call it) which was fostered by all Likud governments.[23] This policy considered the maintaining of this part of the land in Israeli hands as a *sine qua non* as far as the state's security is considered. The anti-withdrawal policy is also based on a number of equally important and cherished religio-nationalist values, the first of which is the precept that the territory claimed as their own by the Palestinians is and has always been part of the God-given, and thus immutable, patrimony of the Jewish people.[24] Furthermore, from the right's perspective the peace negotiations clearly jeopardize the future of the Jewish settlements in the West Bank and on the Golan Heights. Not only are these settlements of utmost ideological importance to the right, and considered the genuine fulfilment of the Zionist mission, but they are also populated by voters of the parties of the right. Therefore, their removal, an unavoidable step in the context of the Oslo framework, would clearly damage a critical interest of this political camp.

The right had other factors to take into consideration besides their security-based and national–religious reservations towards the Oslo process. The process and the rationale given to it by the incumbent Labour government pointed to the failure of the right-wing governments which preceded it to bring the Palestinian uprising under control and to mitigate the severe impact it had on the Israeli collective psyche. In other words, the Israeli public's growing war fatigue, which had clearly served as a catalyst to Labour's decision to try another way of managing the conflict, was taken as evidence of the right's failure to strengthen the nation's sense of security. In addition, the legitimacy given to the PLO in its capacity as the main partner to the Oslo negotiations was heinous in the eyes of the right. This is understandable given the ongoing demonization of this organization by the leaders of the right (and, in fact, in the past, also by those of Labour). The right's leaders often described the PLO, and its leader Yassir Arafat, as the worst enemies of Israel, some of then even going so far as to defame the PLO as the successor of the Nazis. Last but not least, the Oslo process was viewed by the international community, as well as by many Israelis, as a tremendous political achievement of the Labour Party and its leaders, Rabin and Peres, who had defeated Likud in the 1992 elections.

The Oslo narrative adopted by the right-wing parties and groups reflected all these reservations about the process: the unreasonable security risk it involved, the impairment of the Zionist endeavour it entailed, the religious transgression it implied, and the dangerous achievement of Labour it signified. This narrative also maintained that although peace *per se* was a desirable aim, the peace the Oslo process would bring about was only a mirage. How, then, did one explain why so many Israelis were taken in by it? Shortly after the signing of the 1993 DOP, Dore Gold, then a political analyst and later a political adviser to Prime Minister Netanyahu and Israel's ambassador to the UN, explained this allegedly strange phenomenon:

> For a society that has sustained conflict for so many years, when the taste of peace is put on the table, the immediate reaction is that we have reached the days of the messianic era, and that perhaps explains the kick-off of the euphoria that initially accompanied the signing of the September 13th arrangements.[25]

The right's narrative attributed the major blame for taking this ill-conceived step to the decision-makers of the Labour Party. However, the fact that most of the Labour leaders who had launched the process were widely known for their patriotism and their long experience in dealing with Israel's national security matters (it should be recalled that Rabin was elected in 1992 precisely because of this 'Mr Security' image) could not be denied, and they could not be accused of neglecting the important issue of security. The right-wing's narrative therefore had to present another miscreant who was responsible for the critically mistaken strategic change the process allegedly entailed. Under the given circumstances, putting the major blame on the left in general, and on the peace movement in particular, made perfect tactical sense.

Paradoxical as it may seem recalling the prolonged antagonistic relations between these two political camps, the narrative developed by the right, much like that of the peace movement itself (which will be discussed below), maintained that the Labour government's decision to start the peace negotiations and agree to far-reaching territorial and other concessions had been strongly influenced by this movement. Obviously, unlike the latter narrative, that of the right considered this influence to have been completely negative, and used the alleged impact of the movement on the process to delegitimize it altogether. As mentioned earlier, the right's antagonism towards the peace movement was by no means new. For many years right-wing politicians and publicists had portrayed peace activists as obsessed with abstract moralistic ideals, unpatriotic and lacking a sense of solidarity with the Jewish people's history and destiny. Furthermore, in the eyes of many supporters of the right, the peace movement was viewed as both the source and the embodiment of the many weaknesses of Israel's modern society. Thus, it has often been argued that the excessive individualism, scepticism and pampering of the younger generation that the peace movement manifested and even promoted by, for example, its demand to pull out of Lebanon in the early 1980s had eroded the survival instincts and capabilities of Israeli society as a whole. Israelis, in particular the secular sector, it is then claimed, had therefore become unwilling to make the individual sacrifices necessary for achieving the primary national collective goals, although the latter are clearly of greater importance to the nation's life in the long run.[26]

The right's narrative delineated some of the peace movement's tainted ideas, which allegedly 'contaminated' Labour, formerly the spearhead of the Zionist enterprise. This 'contamination' was allegedly manifested by the Labour leaders' readiness to give up national assets of the highest religious significance and military importance in return for a dubious peace agreement, referred to in this context as 'a piece of paper'. Yoash Tzidon, an MK of the right-wing Tzomet Party, analysed the destructive impact of the peace movement as follows:

> The term 'peace now' is being translated at the present into the language of policy as 'territories for peace'. The aim of those who demand 'peace now' is to disengage themselves from the control over [a part of] another people, as soon as possible, even if this is paid for in the form of certain Zionist values, national assets, and a significant deterioration of the state's security and economic potential.[27]

Some proponents of the right were even more scornful than Tzidon. In January 1996, a couple of months after Rabin was assassinated by an activist of the radical right, an article in a right-wing journal described the late prime minister's way of making decisions concerning the Oslo process:

> For the first time in his entire political career Rabin put himself in the front line of a political camp located outside of the national consensus. Furthermore, with the help of a parliamentary minority he tried to impose on Israel a radical political move unacceptable to the majority of the Israeli public... From a Zionist activist he turned into the messenger of leftist demagoguery.[28]

For the same reason that the peace movement could not claim to have had direct influence on the decisions made by the Labour government – the Labour leaders' manifest dislike of this movement – the narrative of the right also had to deal with the issue of such influence in its argument that the peace movement had actually pushed Rabin and Peres into launching the process. The right's narrative found that the missing link was the Meretz Party:

> Meretz, the umbrella movement of Peace Now and its descendants 'Bezelem', 'Women in Black', and the like, sees itself as a 'post-Zionist' stream... What Uri Avnery put forward some decades ago has become the present political program of Shulamit Aloni and Yossi Sarid... In the first week of June 1993, the representative of the United Kibbutz Movement, MK Hagai Marom, laid bare the great secret, that seven ministers of the Labor government supported the idea of negotiating with Yassir Arafat. In other words, the [difference] between the Labor party and Meretz has ceased completely to exist.[29]

The narrative developed by the right thus delegitimized the Oslo process by describing it as the handiwork of the unpatriotic, post-Zionist and marginal peace movement, which had succeeded in manipulating the Labour government. This narrative was meant to expose this government as spineless and non-democratic, thereby substantiating the right's opposition to the Oslo process without its taking the risk of being denounced for war-mongering.

## The Peace Movement's Narrative

This is how Tzali Reshef, one of the leaders of Peace Now, described his feelings while Israeli and Palestinian peace activists were together watching the White House lawn ceremony in which the first Israeli–Palestinian agreement was signed:

> For us, September 13th 1993 was the day when the…goals, for which we had struggled so many years, finally material-ized…The fact that we chose to be there together, Israeli and Palestinian activists, reflected our success in establishing rela-tions of mutual confidence, as well as the end of a complicated process by which we learned to identify our common inter-ests. This process had its ups and downs, its exciting peaks, and more than a few crises. But all these together – at least this was how I felt that day – made our bond one of our greatest achievements, giving us the full right to be very proud.[30]

The occasion undoubtedly brought much pride and satisfaction to the peace movement's members who, for years, had called for Israel to undertake a direct dialogue with the Palestinians. Having failed to change the official Israeli policy prior to 1993, they now justified their years of seemingly futile grass-roots activity by argu-ing that the dialogue they had been conducting since the mid-1970s with Palestinian pro-peace activists was meant to prepare the ground for the future official negotiations: by establishing some degree of mutual confidence, the official representatives found it easier to sit together at the negotiation table when the time came. Thus not only did the peace movement openly and strongly support the launching of the Oslo process, but it perceived the process as a victory of its own making. In particular, it applauded Labour's unprecedented decision to negotiate formally with the Palestinians. It should be noted that there were some radical peace groups that criticized the Oslo agreement owing to their scepticism regarding the true intentions of Labour, the party they considered the originator of the Israeli zero-sum security ethos. These critics on the far left maintained that the agreements signed by Rabin and Arafat virtually deprived the Palestinians of their natural right to an independent state, leaving them with a Bantustan-type semi-state. Moreover, these agreements, according to their interpretation, did not ensure a full Israeli withdrawal from all of the territories occupied in the 1967 war, without which the noxious occupation could not be abolished.[31] The narrative adopted by the peace movement at large, however, emphasized the positive side of the process, as well as its own role in setting in motion this highly desirable change in the regional political reality.

However, as mentioned earlier, the peace movement's narrative could not claim to have had direct influence on the official decision-making process which brought about the Oslo process since it was widely known that its practical access to the national decision-making circles had always been minimal, and that it had not increased very much during the years 1992–96, when Labour was in power. The members of the movement were indeed troubled by the question of how important was the role they had filled as far as the launching of the peace process was concerned: 'What was our contribution to this historic occurrence? Was Israeli public opinion ready to accept the agreement without the untiring activities of the groups that had maintained that this was the only possible solution? What would have happened had we not joined forces to nourish the flames of the demand for peace negotiations?'[32]

With this uncertainty in mind, the movement's narrative portrayed the historical development as follows. The peace activists were a small vanguard of realists (not naive idealists as people tend to think) who understood, well before everyone else in Israel, that the protracted regional conflict could be successfully and finally resolved only by political means, and never by military force. They were also the first to see the moral and practical justification of the Palestinians' demand for self-determination and to realize that it would eventually obtain worldwide recognition.[33] Neither the broad public nor the national leaders accepted the logic of their analysis until the early 1990s, when the Labour Party and its followers, formerly convinced of the exclusive validity of the zero-sum nature of the Israeli–Arab relationship, began to realize that there was some truth to the peace movement's ideas. The party's leaders and those who voted for them in the 1992 elections sensed that structural and cognitive critical changes in the global, regional and domestic environments necessitated changes in the definition of the situation and in its now outdated and dysfunctional programme. Nevertheless, captives to their long-held confrontational argumentation, Labour leaders and supporters found it very difficult to admit to the obsolesce of their interpretation. The peace movement's narrative therefore stressed that its most significant

accomplishment was 'to influence public opinion by broadening
the scope of public debate...the insistent advocacy of the peace
movement gradually led many people, both in the center and on
the left, to modify their views and accept the need for mutual recognition and compromise'.[34]

To refute the right's allegation of deviation from the Zionist
endeavour, the peace movement's narrative linked the Oslo process
with the original, mainstream Zionist creed and its advocacy of
peace. This explains the argument made by Haim Oron, then a
Meretz MK and one of Peace Now's prominent leaders, in the
Knesset debate on the Oslo DOP in the summer of 1993:

> These days we are returning to the true Zionist path from
> which we were drifting away for the last twenty-six years or
> so because of the total eclipse of the sun [that is, since the 1967
> war]. For the true Zionist way was leading to a real compro-
> mise with the Arab people.[35]

The narrative of the peace movement also openly called for
broad public recognition for having opened the communication
channels to the Palestinian side. To counter Labour's narrative, it
maintained that the sitting together of Israeli and Palestinian delegates at the negotiation table, in Oslo and afterwards, was
facilitated – if not made possible – by the movement's members'
previous meetings and ice-breaking discussions with their
Palestinian counterparts. The peace movement's narrative also
extolled the movement for having been the first to see and admit
openly that extensive territorial concessions were not only
unavoidable, but were a fair price for Israel to pay for a stable
peace.

People close to the peace movement also disclosed that Rabin
and Peres had more than once hesitated before taking the necessary
decisive steps towards reconciliation. They were often described as
quite shaky when having to pay the price demanded by the process:
'The fact is that Yitzhak Rabin got cold feet when faced with the
necessity to withdraw Israeli forces from populated Palestinian
centers prior to Palestinian self-rule elections, as specified by the
Oslo Declaration of Principles'.[36] It was the peace movement that,
according to this narrative, furnished the indispensable grass-roots
pressures that encouraged – and sometimes even forced – the
Labour government into making the necessary though painful

concessions that it might otherwise not have had the courage to make.[37] Still, these revelations can be attributed not only to the impatience of the peace activists with the slow pace of the process and with the overly cautious positions of the government, but also to their difficulty in coming to terms with the fact that the government had now appropriated the dialogue with the Palestinian side, leaving the peace movement virtually bereft of its *raison d'être*.

And yet, fairly soon after the signing of the Oslo accord, the peace movement realized that overtly close relations between itself and the Labour government might actually damage, or even destroy, the chances of the process obtaining wide public support. Thus, in 1994–95, in their desperate effort to see the process continue, the movement's leaders virtually abstained from promoting some of their own interests, putting practical considerations far ahead of ideological ones. First and foremost, they suppressed their criticism of the process even when they realized that Rabin and his government were reluctant to go 'all the way' to a Palestinian state and that the government's iron-fist policy towards the Palestinians of the West Bank was not much softened:

> Much as we refrained from openly assisting the government in other matters connected to the process, we should now avoid criticizing it, as such criticism may well eventually conjoin the criticism of the right...There is so sense in discussing dreams and desires...I only ask what is attainable providing that this government would stay in power at all.[38]

The peace camp paid a high price for this tolerant treatment of the Labour government: not only did it not help Labour to mobilize wide public support as it lost the 1996 elections and Likud came back to power, but the peace movement lost much of its credibility as a political and moral actor. Its lenient position created a confidence crisis between the movement and its Palestinian counterparts and between Israeli Jewish and Arab activists, as expressed by the reaction of Amir Machul, an Israeli Arab peace activist, to the above warning of Dayan: 'The Left today is a captive of the Labor party. The peace movements have also been taken captive, and no longer present an alternative. By and large our dream has been broken.'[39]

## SUMMARY AND CONCLUSIONS

Discourse can never be abstracted from the conditions of its
production and circulation... The most significant relations of
any piece of discourse are to the social conditions of its use,
not to the signifying system in general, and its analysis exem-
plifies not an instance of that system in practice, but its
function in deploying power within those conditions.[40]

This quotation from Fiske's theoretical analysis of discourse
construction condenses very well the central theme of this paper.
The deployment of power is indeed the name of the game in the
case analysed here. The primary feature of the structure of political
power in Israel in the early to mid-1990s was the competition
between two, almost identically sized, political blocs – the left, led
by Labour, and the right, led by Likud. Although Labour won the
1992 elections, its victory was not decisive, as proved by the Likud
comeback in the 1996 elections. Thus, along with the launching of
the Oslo process, these two political blocs were competing with
everything they had for the support of the middle-of-the-road
voters – who comprise the largest Israeli sector of the public.

At that time many people in the broad centre part of the Israeli
political map were bewildered. Most Israelis found it very difficult
to grasp fully the rapid political changes that were taking place,
while the cognitive transformation innate in the Oslo process was
even more unfathomable. Moreover, the new peace agenda ran
against the deeply rooted and long-held zero-sum security ethos. At
the same time, after over five decades of violent conflict many
Israelis suffered from depressing war fatigue, leading them to put
much hope, together with a good dose of fear, in the unfolding
peace process.[41] In its effort to win the support of the non-commit-
ted sector, the Labour government played on this sensitive cord,
painting a rosy picture of the tranquil future the peace accords
would bring, while exposing the Likud leaders as war-mongers
mired in atavistic frightening scenarios. The Likud-led bloc, for its
part, trying to delegitimize the entire Oslo process, enlarged on the
security dangers to which the signed agreement would expose the
country. It also reiterated the 'irresponsibility' of the Labour leaders
who signed them. However, while attacking each other, both
Labour and the right did not fail to disparage the peace movement,
although for different reasons and by different means.

Labour was afraid that if the peace movement's agenda materialized, it would gradually win wide public support. This might erode the party's dominance within its own bloc, forcing it, against the will of Rabin and Peres, to rely more on the parties of the left, particularly Meretz, associated with the movement. The Likud-led right, poised on the other side, was apprehensive of a united, well-functioning and increasingly popular Labour-led left block that might gain enough power to defeat it again in the 1996 elections. Both of the large political bodies thus had a common interest and tacitly joined forces in preventing the peace movement from establishing itself in the centre of the national political arena. This explains why the peace movement, despite the evident similarities between its long-held ideas and the underlying principles of the Oslo process, was not able even at that time to succeed in getting closer to the political centre.

However, the methods used by the two large blocs to keep the peace movement at the periphery differed. Labour disregarded the similarities in their favoured policies and ignored the peace movement's overt desire to help it in pushing the process forward, for example, by declining to use the peace movement's well-established connections to the Palestinian side. The Likud and the national camp, on the other hand, raised some leading questions as to the peace movement's real motivations, thereby compelling the Labour government to distance itself from the movement to avoid being 'tainted' by association with it.

Somewhat paradoxically, the same political power structure also accounted for the fact that the ideological antagonism between the left-wing peace movement and the right-wing national camp did not prevent their narratives from attributing to this movement very great influence over the launching of the Oslo process. These two political streams, despite their different views and very different size and status, were each trying to occupy the political centre, occupied at the time by Labour. From this point of view, the most relevant division was between the position of Labour as the ruling elite and the position of the other two bodies outside of the power centre.

After losing the 1992 elections, the Likud-led camp was about to spend at least four years in opposition, thereby becoming a typical 'dissident elite'.[42] However, contrary to the positive relations that Lofland predicted will develop between dissident élites and peripheral social movements, emerging from the fact that both

sides are challenging the party at the centre, the character of relations between the right and the Israeli peace movement remained
antagonistic: between their diametrically opposed ideologies there
was no common ground whatsoever, not even for some pragmatic
*ad hoc* cooperation, particularly as the movement was strongly
supportive of the newly elected Labour government's peace policy.
In addition, the Likud-led camp was already campaigning for a
political comeback, by various means, including the delegitimization of the incumbent Labour government by exposing its affinity
to, and its alleged close relations with, the peace movement.
Arguing that the peace movement was the real power behind the
'disastrous' peace process was an integral part of the right's strategy and its narrative. Therefore it could never join forces with this
movement.

The peace movement, on the other hand, was mired in a kind of
a limbo, unwilling to join the right-wing opposition on ideological
grounds and constrained from getting closer to the decision-
makers. Meretz, the party ideologically closest to the movement,
was indeed in the relevant years a prominent partner to the coalition government. In this sense, the peace movement was, perhaps,
closer than ever before to the decision-making process. However,
the leaders of the main partner of this coalition, the Labour Party,
thwarted any such proximity, partly because of their unwillingness
to share power, as mentioned above, but also because they feared
playing into the hands of the right by having the peace movement
so close to them.[43] These complex power relationships were
reflected in the contesting narratives of the Oslo process that each
of the three players developed as presented above.

Are there any general lessons to be learned from this Israeli case
study insofar as political narrative-building is concerned? First, it
seems to substantiate the argument that political narratives are
often strongly geared to specific political agendas and are meant to
serve them. It also seems to demonstrate how quickly political
narratives develop. The Israeli case could also contribute to the
understanding of the process by which political ideas, particularly
those calling for strategic changes, are conveyed from the political
periphery to the centre, that is, 'bottom-to-top'.

The analysis of this case was meant to produce some sense of
what happens and how and when, owing to unforeseen developments, ideas and values developed at the periphery and rejected by
the centre become acceptable as they appear to be more useful than

those adhered to by the mainstream for years. Our findings in this regard do not seem to confirm the prevalent hypothesis that in times of massive political transition in the relevant realms, the political opportunities structure is necessarily more open to extra-parliamentary actors, such as the peace movement, to enter the political process.

On the contrary, they suggest that, at least in the case of premeditated transition, skilful policy-makers may reshape their policies extensively without losing control over the political centre or over the access of actors on the periphery to the decision-making process. When the overall political system stays intact – that is when the transition does not involve a substantial change of the political regime – such access is rather easily denied even to those actors whose proposals underlie the transition after their ideas have been embraced by the decision-makers. The decision-makers may have good reason for pushing these aspiring partners aside. First, leaders operating in democratic systems take a great risk of severely damaging their image as 'consistent', and hence trustworthy, by making dramatic ideological and practical shifts. This risk is even greater should they admit that a 'bottom-to-top' flow of ideas has taken place. Furthermore, their political rivals, striving to take over, would probably exploit this precarious situation to oust them from the centre by blaming them of inconsistency and of acting in the interests of some political actors with extremely dubious goals, as supposedly proved by adopting these actors' ideas.

This brings us to our last issue of how extra-parliamentary actors react when their ideas are appropriated by the centre, an occurrence observed fairly often in the last few decades. The case of the Israeli peace movement, as well as those of some 'green' and other grass-roots movements around the world, suggest that the members of such movements have to accept that realizing their goals often requires relinquishing their due recognition and appreciation. In the specific case of peace activists, when formal peace talks are at last launched, its true pioneering sponsors are likely to be repudiated by the formal decision-makers. Refusing to come to terms with this reality could well help one's opponents not only to destroy the still fragile process but also the movement's very *raison d'être*. This is an extremely difficult lot to accept, but it may very well be part of the price for peace.

NOTES

1. Allan Spitzer, *Historical Truth and Lies about the Past* (Chapel Hill: University of North Carolina Press, 1996), p. 2.
2. The term 'Israeli peace movement' as used here designates various non-governmental bodies whose common denominators are: (a) activity for promoting mutual recognition of the right to national self-determination of both the Israeli and the Palestinian people; (b) seeking a non-violent solution to the Arab–Israeli conflict and making efforts to assuage the injustices and grievances caused by this conflict to all people involved in it. Some scholars have correctly observed that the Israeli peace movement is actually composed of the larger Zionist camp and the much smaller non-Zionist, or even anti-Zionist, one (see, for example, Mohammed Abu Nimer, 'Dialogue and National Consensus in the Pre-Madrid Period: Dilemmas of Israeli and Palestinian Peace Activists', in Kevin Avruch and Walter Zenner (eds), *Critical Essays on Israeli Society, Religion, and Government*, Vol. IV (Albany, New York: SUNY Press, 1997), p. 45). The following discussion refers mostly to the narrative developed by the Zionist component with some references to the version adopted by the non-Zionist one.
3. For comprehensive analyses of the various theoretical approaches to this issue see, for example, Bruce Russett, *Controlling the Sword: The Democratic Government of National Security* (Cambridge, MA: Harvard University Press, 1990); Ole Holsti, 'Public Opinion and Foreign Policy: Challenges to the Almond–Lippman Consensus', *International Sudies Quarterly*, 36, 4 (1992), pp. 439–66; Miroslav Nincic, 'A Sensible Public: New Perspectives on Popular Opinion and Foreign Policy', *Journal of Conflict Resolution*, 36, 4 (1992), pp. 772–89.
4. The difficulties the decision-makers have to deal with when changing some long-held policy, particularly in the realm of foreign affairs, is very well analysed by Alexander George. See his 'Domestic Constraints on Regime Change in U.S. Foreign Policy: The Need for Policy Legitimacy', in Ole Holsti, Randolph Siverson and Alexander George (eds), *Change in the International System* (Boulder, CO: Westview Press, 1980), pp. 233–62.
5. On the tactics used by the opposition see, for example, Hagen, 1993.
6. See, for example, Peter Eisinger, 'The Conditions of Protest Behaviour in American Cities', *Political Science Review*, 67, 1 (1973), pp. 11–28.
7. The analysis presented below is an outgrowth of an international comparative study of the contribution of peace-oriented non-governmental organizations (NGOs) to the launching and effectiveness of conflict-resolution processes. This comprehensive study has focused on three case studies: Northern Ireland, South Africa and Israel/Palestine – in all of which the pivotal socio-economic conflict arrived at a critical turning point in the early 1990s. For an overall analysis of the Israeli case see Hermann, 2000.
8. For a detailed historical analysis of Israeli peace activism from the 1930s to the mid-1980s see Tamar Hermann, 'Between the Peace Covenant and Peace Now: The Pragmatic Pacifism of the Israeli Peace Movement in a Comparative Perspective', PhD dissertation (Tel Aviv University, 1989) (in Hebrew). For the later period see Mordechai Bar On, *In Pursuit of Peace – A History of the Israeli Peace Movement* (Washington, DC: US Institute of Peace, 1996).
9. Tamar Hermann, 'Do They Have a Chance? Protest and Political Structure of Opportunities in Israel', *Israel Studies*, 1, 1 (1996).
10. See, for example, Ilan Pappé, 'The New History and Sociology of Israel: A Challenge to the Old Version', *Palestine–Israel Journal*, 2, 3 (1995), pp. 70–6; and Ephraim Karsh, *Fabricating Israeli History* (London: Frank Cass, 1997).
11. On these two movements see Real Isaac, *Israel Divided: Ideological Politics in the Jewish State* (Baltimore, MD: Johns Hopkins University Press, 1976).
12. In late 1970 President Sadat of Egypt responded positively to the basic premises of the peace initiative launched by the UN special emissary to the Middle East, Dr Gunnar Yarring. However, to the frustration and anger of the MPS, the Israeli government, then led by Golda Meir, declined to recognize Sadat's response as a potential starting point for peace talks, convincing most Israelis that it was nothing more than a hot-air balloon.

13. Uri Avnery, *My Friend the Enemy* (London: Zed Books, 1986).
14. A complete list of the groups which emerged at this time can be found in Tamar Hermann, Peter Lemish and Yuval Label, *Cultivating the Ground: The Israeli Peace Movement and the Peace Process*, Report submitted to the Aspen Institute, Non-Profit Sector, Washington, DC, 1996.
15. Sara Hellman and Tamar Rapoport, 'Women in Black and the Challenging of the Social Order', *Theory and Criticism*, 10 (summer 1997), pp. 175–92 (in Hebrew).
16. Ben Tzur, 1998.
17. Indeed, the Labour Party was not completely unanimous in its support for the Oslo process, which was promoted by its then leaders, Rabin and Peres. However, Labour politicians who were sceptical of the justification for the strategic shift this process implied did not put forward an organized internal opposition to the government's policy or develop a discernable alternative narrative to the process.
18. Yitzhak Rabin, *The Knesset Protocols*, 21 September 1993 (in Hebrew).
19. Shimon Peres, *The New Middle East* (Shaftsbury, UK: Element, 1993), p. 16.
20. Work and labour are the same word in Hebrew.
21. Yossi Beilin, *To Touch Peace* (Tel Aviv: Yediot Aharanot, 1997), p. 15 (in Hebrew).
22. It is not surprising then that in 1993, when the Arab–Israeli peace talks were resumed in Washington, someone scribbled graffiti over the highway near Tel Aviv saying: 'Once All The World Was Against Us. Now It's The [Israeli[ Government As Well'. See Akiva Orr, *1993 – Palestine: Occupied Territory to Become a Bantustan. Israel: Politics, Myths and Identity Crises* (Boulder, CO: Pluto Press, 1994), p. 48.
23. This concern was manifested most clearly by Prime Minister Begin who in 1978–79, when negotiating a peace agreement with Egypt, made a major effort to maintain Israel's rule in the West Bank, including his surprising acceptance of Egypt's demand for a full withdrawal from Sinai apparently in the hope that this would alleviate the external pressures regarding Israel's presence in the West Bank.
24. For example, Benjamin Netanyahu, *A Place Among the Nations* (New York: Bantam Books, 1993), pp. 48–50.
25. Dore Gold, 'Changing Political Dynamics between Israelis and Palestinians', in *Political and Structural Arrangements in the New Era of Israeli–Palestinian Relations* (Conference Proceedings, Jerusalem Centre for Public Affairs and Konrad Adenauer Stiftung, December 1993), p. 55.
26. See, for example, Mordechai Nissan, 'The PLO and the Israeli Left: The Common Aim', *Nativ* (February 1994), p. 10 (in Hebrew).
27. Yoash Tzidon, 'Peace Now or a Stable Peace', *Nativ* (April 1994), p. 22 (in Hebrew).
28. Arie Stav, 'Praising the Dead, Condemning the Living', *Nativ* (January 1996), pp. 6–7.
29. Shiloah, p. 26.
30. Tzaly Reshef, *Shalom Achshav* (Peace Now) (Jerusalem: Keter, 1996), p. 10.
31. Orr, *1993 – Palestine*, pp. 160–70.
32. Reshef, *Shalom Achshav*, p. 12.
33. Some observers attribute this accurate forecasting to the non-Zionist left only: 'Recognition of the Palestinians as a political entity was a victory for the anti-Zionist left in Israel, which had fought for this recognition since 1948. This left, which was attacked in hysterical tones by the entire Israeli media, proved not only its moral integrity but also the validity of its political analysis. All the 'Arab specialists' of the Israeli establishment, all its 'think tanks' and 'brain trusts' failed to foresee what a handful of Israeli anti-Zionists had predicted for years – the re-emergence of the Palestinians as a political factor and the slow but inevitable decline of Zionist policies' (Orr, *1993 – Palestine*, p. 127).
34. Bar On, *In Pursuit of Peace*, pp. 323–34.
35. Haim Oron, *The Knesset Protocols*, 30 August 1993, p. 7756 (in Hebrew).
36. Victor Cygielman, 'No, Oslo is Not Dead', *Palestine–Israel Journal*, 2, 1 (winter 1995), p. 3.
37. The often-heard slogan '*Rumratz Rabin*' ('Rabin should be energized') in the context of the Oslo process, which for all Hebrew speakers clearly alluded to the name of the pro-peace Meretz Party, was but one example of the peace movement's image and self-perception as the mainstay of the process.
38. Dayan, Round Table, p. 6.

39. Machul, Round Table, p. 7.
40. John Fiske, 'Introduction', in *Media Matters: Everyday Culture and Political Change* (Minnesota, MN: University of Minnesota Press, 1994), p. 3.
41. For some empirical data on Israelis' attitudes towards the Oslo process see the collected findings of the Peace Index, published by the Tami Steinmetz Centre, Vols 1–4 (1994–99). The data can also be retrieved from the Centre's website: http://www.tau.ac.il/peace.
42. John Lofland, *Social Movement Organizations: Guide to Research on Insurgent Realities* (Hawthorne, NY: Aladine De Gruyter, 1996), p. 307.
43. For a general account of such centre–margin problematic relations see David Kowalewski and Dean Hoover, *Dynamic Models of Conflict and Pacification: Dissenters, Officials and Peace Makers* (Westport, CN and London: Praeger, 1995); and Michael Morgan and Susan Leggett (eds), *Mainstream(s) and Margins: Cultural Politics in the 90s* (Westport, CN: Greenwood Press, 1996).

# PART THREE

# Zionism and Modern Jewish History

# 13 Ahad Ha'am and the Jewish '*Volkgeist*'

EYAL CHOWERS

## INTRODUCTION

Ahad Ha'am has been described by David Vital not only as the 'sage of Zionism',[1] but as perhaps the only genuine thinker of this national movement. As Vital notes, the interest in Ahad Ha'am has been continuous throughout the twentieth century, and his writings remain pertinent to current debates. In fact, these writings possess particular significance for Jews and Israelis as they enter the twenty-first century and address pressing concerns about the meaning of Jewish identity, the best ways of preserving and cultivating this identity, and the overall place of literary culture in contemporary life. But while Ahad Ha'am's thinking is highly relevant to these debates, his thought is often misconstrued, since it is examined through lenses focused too tightly on the early ideological polemics of the early Zionist movement and exclusively within its compass.

My purpose is to expand this interpretive horizon to include the wider, European intellectual milieu by examining the profound affinity between Ahad Ha'am and J. G. Herder. This affinity is apparently not accidental. In writing his intellectual autobiography, Ahad Ha'am remarks that he read German literature at an early stage, and that he especially admired 'books written by Enlightenment thinkers, such as Herder and the like'.[2] Despite this revealing statement, Ahad Ha'am hardly refers explicitly (let alone in any detail) to Herder in his writings. Thus, one is unable to prove *conclusively* that he conceived his *main* ideas under the *direct* influence of the German philosopher (the secondary literature, indeed, hardly mentions them together). But reading the two thinkers, one

nevertheless cannot but take due note of the deep-seated similarities in their thinking about language and culture, time and
nationalism.

At the very least, I would argue that Ahad Ha'am conducted an
intense dialogue with the intellectual tradition originating in
Herder, and that his 'cultural Zionism' is intrinsically related to this
background. At issue, however, is not only the need to interpret
Ahad Ha'am anew, but to see that such an interpretation calls for an
overarching reflection on the singular complexities and novelty of
Jewish nationalism.

Recent studies of Zionism such as those of Sternhell and
Hobsbawm (who follow Kohn and Kedourie)[3] have argued that this
movement wholly espoused the nationalism that dominated
Eastern and Central Europe, and that this nationalism originated in
Germany with the thought of Herder. Sternhell in particular claims
that Herder's organic nationalism is much more relevant to our
understanding of Zionism than liberalism or even socialism. In
Sternhell's view, the appeal of Herder's thought to Zionists lay in
'the definition of the nation not in political or judicial terms but
cultural, historical, linguistic, and religious terms'. This definition

> raised the stature of all those peoples who had lost their polit-
> ical independence hundreds of years earlier. The idea that the
> individual owed his being to the nation, that unique cultural
> unit which derived its existence from nature and was rooted
> in the soil of the motherland, created a human identity
> independent of a person's political or social status.[4]

This interpretation of the affinity between Zionism (as it evolved
in practice) and Herderianism is questionable. In order to establish
a Jewish state, Zionists had to reject central tenets of Herder's and
Ahad Ha'am's thinking. These included the notion that identity is
cultivated through language; the conception of social change as
occurring through slow evolution; the faith that time is ontologically continuous; and the belief in an essential *Volksgeist* that
dominates the nation's life and binds it to a particular ethos (an
ethos that, in the Jewish case according to Ahad Ha'am, involved
heightened moral norms and the spurning of force in human interaction).

But as it developed in Palestine, Zionism celebrated the human
capacity to shape history anew through power and productivity,

and no longer presented moral conduct as the highest measure of human life. This Zionism rejected Herder's and Ahad Ha'am's conception of a collective narrative that is pregiven and unalterable, language-centred and spiritually guided, evolving gradually and without temporal leaps. The marginal place Ahad Ha'am occupies in the actual development of Zionism signifies that – contrary to the prevailing view – Zionist self-definition was incommensurable with key elements of Herderian thought, and that Zionism consti-tuted a new type of nationalism that symbolized precisely the *collapse* of this thought.

Herder's view of the nation marries biological with idealistic approaches to social reality, both of which would become promi-nent during the nineteenth century. In this view, the nation – and each of its people – is akin to a living being or plant that develops according to both an innate idea and influences from the external environment (*Klima*). Regarding the latter, Herder comments that some people

> feel to intimately close to their native country, are so much attached to its soil, that they can scarcely live if separated from it. The constitution of their body, their way of life, the nature of work and play to which they have been accustomed from their infancy, indeed their whole mentality, are climatic.[5]

On a larger scale, Herder sees the nation as a body whose char-acter is affected by its absorption of the external environment (for example, soil, climate, flora).[6] The *Volk* unfolds like any living crea-ture: each stage follows naturally from the previous one and brings to fruition what was present in an undeveloped form from the start. The life of the nation cannot be viewed in static terms, with its iden-tity and culture fixed at some historical point. Identity involves a delicate play among elements that are changeable and those that are lasting; between secondary attributes and essential ones without which the nation cannot remain itself. What is true for the human being ('at no single moment', writes Herder, 'can he be said to be the whole man, rather he is always in a state of development, of progress, of becoming')[7] holds even more so for the nation, which engulfs the lives of many individuals.

But this vista of *continuous becoming* means that change is necessarily a gradual phenomenon, a piecemeal affair. For Herder, there are no leaps or radical transformations in historical processes.

Each moment can be explained in terms of the pre-given materials and spiritual contents of the social body. In the same way that the concept of revolution has no place in explicating processes of biological bodies, the Herderian position entails that nations distort and injure themselves if they revolutionize their culture and institutions.

Despite his emphasis on environment, matter and bodies, Herder gives clear priority to the *Geist* of the nation in explicating the nation's journey through time. For him, the nation materializes in history a potential spirit that was given in embryonic form in its first days. This spirit is reflected in the nation's laws, social and political institutions, customs, religion, culture and more. Each realm echoes the others, creating a living and coherent totality. Without reference to this spirit, one cannot make sense of the various spheres of the nation's life (both in and of themselves and in relation to each other). Only a grasp of the spirit puts everything in context, forming a coherent picture out of an otherwise perplexing array of puzzle pieces.

Herder insists there is no point in comparing national spirits as each is wholly unique, shaping a distinct culture and singular patterns of evolution. As Sir Isaiah Berlin notes, Herder dreaded the Enlightenment's attempt to present nations as essentially artificial-contractual creations, ones that should embrace universal norms, rights, political institutions and even language;[8] instead, he asserts that nations should be authentic, should defend and cultivate their unique spirits. For Herder, the human world (and the natural world) is plural – and it is meant to be this way. The multiplicity of nations and cultures has value for him both ontologically and aesthetically. Each nation articulates another possibility of being in human history. And the richness and complexity that is thereby instituted can be experienced as nothing but beautiful.

Herder celebrates language as the most important feature of collective life, since it both shapes and expresses the nation's spirit. Language joins both reason and emotions; it is a testimony to the ways we comprehend and experience the external world. In contrast to Condillac and Rousseau, Herder claims that language is intrinsic to human existence – that we cannot think without it or be bound as a people. Language testifies to our thoughts and experience. Herder suggests that a transparency and a correspondence exist between the history of national life and that of language, and that the liveliness of a language reflects the intensity of collective life and culture. A dead language (one frozen in rules and conventions) is an ominous sign for a culture, and the more 'vitality it [the language] has, the less it can be written at all'.[9] Hence the critical role Herder assigns to poetry and folk culture.

Both the mentality of the nation and this mentality's narration are preserved in language: 'The language is its [the nation's] collective treasure, the source of its social wisdom'. Nations guard their national languages and see them as the source of their 'communal self-respect',[10] not because of narrow-minded tribalism, but rather because of the cultural achievements that languages shelter. To replace the language of one's ancestors is to lose our anchor and orientation:

> Our mother tongue embodies the first universe we saw, the first sensations we felt, the first activities and pleasure we enjoyed. Secondary ideas of time and place, of love and hate, and all the flaming impetuous thoughts of youth are perpetuated by it. This perpetuation of thoughts and feelings through language is the essence of tradition.[11]

Herder views the nation, then, as a *genetisches Individuum*, a coherent unit that, like an organic body, develops through an interaction of inner and outer forces. In deciphering this body, Herder presents material and spiritual elements that complement each other. A community cannot be termed a nation if it does not possess (a) a distinctive spirit and language, and (b) if it is not attached to a particular area of land. In fact, spirit, language and land are essentially interdependent. A people's spirit and language affect the way it interacts with the environment, while the latter plays a critical role in forming the substance of national memory, myths, habits, speech – in short, the nation's distinctive identity.

Ahad Ha'am's understanding of nationalism in general and his celebration of language in particular manifest a deep affinity to these aspects of Herder's thought. For Ahad Ha'am, modernity had a centrifugal effect on Jews. On a demographic level, communities dispersed as the Jewish population moved from country to city, from enclosed community to urban anonymity, from European *shtetl* to roomy America and elsewhere. Worse was the spiritual confusion: there were religious Jews and ambivalent *maskilim*, cautious traditionalists and ardent Nietzscheans, socialists who rejected their Jewishness as well as those who embraced it, a multiplicity of nationalists each adhering to his or her own adopted country and culture, and more.

Ahad Ha'am believed that, in this context, the main problem of the Jews was a breakdown of identity and the impending collapse of the entire diasporic way of life. Not economic impoverishment or political insecurity concerned him, but rather the evaporation of Jewish culture in an increasingly unfenced, secular world freed of the ghetto's walls. Ahad Ha'am's response was to espouse a centripetal philosophy that pictured two centres in need of reconstruction: a physical one in Palestine and a spiritual one at the heart of the nation. In his view, these two centres cannot be separated, since spiritual invigoration can take place only on the original soil of the Jews, and since no settlement project in Palestine would be possible without the prior recognition of the national spirit and self.

In conceiving of a *Volksgeist* (in Hebrew: *ruach ha'am*) Ahad Ha'am presupposes a body of people, the supra-subject that carries this spirit. How is this body maintained, given that it does not have the inborn bodily integrity of an animal, for example? Following the nineteenth-century fashion of using biology to explicate social phenomena, Ahad Ha'am argues that the nation has an 'instinct' for perpetuation, one that belies reason and its ostentatious designs. The source of the power that allows people to further Zionists causes

> is not in reason, but rather in the lower department of the soul, a place where the national instincts propel a person to fulfill their interests regardless of her own good ... This driving power is 'a national sense of preservation' [*chush kiyum l'eumi*] that induces us to do whatever is needed for safeguarding our national existence.[12]

Individuals may think that they struggle to satisfy their own narrow goals, but their individual actions (which, from their personal perspectives, might miserably languish) unknowingly combine to form a trajectory that steers the community away from harm and promotes its existence. Moreover, communal continuity and unity are also preserved by the irrational fabric of emotions. In effect, Ahad Ha'am insists that membership of a community does not result from collective deliberations and considerations of utility but is founded upon the Jew's profound passion for the community, upon an emotional make-up that belies calculations.[13]

These instincts and emotions are the forces that assiduously maintain the integrity and consistency of something higher: the nation's shared consciousness. In the same manner that individual identity is secured by continuity in time – by the ability to hold together past impressions, existence in the moment, and hopes for and fears of the future – the national ego (*ani l'eumi*) secures such an identity throughout the ages. Yet the national ego is able to transcend the limited temporality that binds the individual body. For Ahad Ha'am, it is this national ego, 'in its historical shape, that wishes to exist, this ego and not another, entirely as it is, with all its memories and hopes'.[14]

In these and other pronouncements about instincts, emotions and consciousness Ahad Ha'am emerges as one of the most essentialist and collectivist Zionist thinkers. The nation is like a person, possessing a core (ego) that is critical for its identity. Moreover, while even Herder had a prominent place for the individual – seriously contemplating how he or she could best materialize his or her uniqueness, happiness and freedom – for Ahad Ha'am the individual is for the most part a passing moment in the life of the nation's collective, semi-body:

> One is the people across generations. Individuals that come and go in each generation are like those diminutive parts in the living body, which are renewed every day, without having any ability to unsettle the overall unity of the entire body.[15]

In his Zionist vision, Ahad Ha'am is haunted by the impression that those traditional elements preserving the Jewish people in the past might not hold any longer, a recognition that leads him to ponder the key role of spatial, geographic Palestine in modern times. So much so that his attitude towards Palestine perplexed many in the movement. Why, they wondered, does he insist on a Jewish community in Palestine if he takes every opportunity to ridicule their grand plans of settlement and their political aspirations? The answer to this question cannot be found merely by looking at Ahad Ha'am's own declarations. Here, again, we must also view his Herderian presuppositions, which posit an essentialist connection between land, language and spirit.

On the one hand, Ahad Ha'am does not have any illusions about Palestine becoming a home for the entire Jewish people. He adamantly criticizes the belief that a Jewish state can be established in the foreseeable future. Among the stumbling blocks are, in his view: the fact that Jews control only a small segment of the territory in Palestine; the land is not empty of inhabitants (in contrast to what many Zionists professed) and one was duty-bound to respect this Arab population and its rights; economic infrastructure, resources and potential for growth in Palestine are severely limited. For these and other reasons, then, Ahad Ha'am does not see Palestine as the full or sole solution for the Jewish masses.

Yet Ahad Ha'am does see the union of the people and the land as critical for Zionism. A Jewish elite living on the ancient land and breathing its history would create a spiritual centre, one that would inject new substance into Jewish identity everywhere:

> The predicament of our nation...propels us to recognize the need to return and join the coalesced elements that have been divorced, the two critical pillars of our national life, both of which are so close to us yet so remote: our country and our language. By establishing a true literary center in Palestine, we would marry them into a national horn of plenty, one that would overflow into all the countries of our dispersion.[16]

For him, the land is the womb of language: geography and the associations and memories that the landscape begets shape the character of the language. In contrast to Gershom Sholem – who fears that the Hebrew words 'are about to explode' and the mooring of language and land would open a catastrophic abyss for Israelis[17] – Ahad Ha'am believes that cultural revival, the gist of Zionism, must begin by rebinding the Jews to the only place where their language can be whetted.

For Ahad Ha'am, however, a spiritual centre and settlement projects are not the ends of Zionism, but merely the means for galvanizing the ebbing Jewish spirit.[18] This spirit, which used to envelop the entire life of the Jew (through law, political institutions, private life, and so on) is now pertinent merely to the narrow sphere of moral convictions and conduct. But this sphere remains emblematic of the entire Jewish mentality, just as any morality is emblematic of its people's character and approach to life. In trying to shed light on the development of the national spirit, Ahad Ha'am claims that it was formed by the accumulated activities of individuals living together, with each epoch elaborating and refining principles formed during the nation's first days. Adhering to his centripetal vision, he suggests that this spirit is the true cement of a culture: 'Not systemic agreement among the various departments of *praxis* fosters internal true bonds among people, but only the unity of the spiritual root from which everything branches off'.[19]

Elsewhere Ahad Ha'am submits an even more totalistic vision of collective life and its idealistic foundation: 'The national spirit creates its products in its own image, and these products and spirit are one'.[20] For him, the most important product of the Jewish national spirit was the Jewish religion, and Ahad Ha'am is adamant that religion should be seen as a cultural achievement, not as the gift of God.[21] This interpretative move allows him to construct a cultural continuity between the normative contents of the Jewish religion and the normative world he foresaw for modern Judaism.

At the centre of both stand a few critical moral convictions: an uncompromising search for justice and a faith in its supremacy over all other considerations; a disposition towards abstract thinking that leads Jews to espouse a 'view from nowhere' (to use Thomas Nagel's phrase to describe ethical deliberations that are conducted irrespective of personal interests, communal membership and any particular situatedness); reluctance to glorify human beings and to view them as Promethean semi-gods; and the spurning of altruism and uncritical forgiveness. Most importantly, these moral convictions also included the commitment to avoid the use of force in human conflict ('ever since the days of the prophets, our fathers learned to scorn in their hearts the power of the fist, and respect only spiritual power').[22] In short, Ahad Ha'am sees the gist of the Jewish *Volksgeist* as advancing a heightened morality that serves as an example for other nations. 'There should be in the world one nation', he writes, 'whose national attributes will prepare it for moral development, more than any other nation.'[23]

How does the nation's spirit evolve? Through what means is it first articulated and then refined? Ahad Ha'am has a decisive answer: through the nation's language. He posits a dual relation whereby the spirit is disclosed in the language and the language shapes the spirit. On the one hand, faithful to his Herderianism ('What is the whole structure of language', the German thinker asks, 'but a mode of development of man's spirit, the history of his discoveries?'[24]), Ahad Ha'am suggests that language is the vast container of culture and meanings, and that the intricate record of words reflects the history of a nation's mentality. 'Language is on many occasions the finest key for fathoming the nation's spirit',[25] he writes, since the thoughts and soul of the people urge them to choose a certain vocabulary to express themselves. Corresponding to the development of the Jewish spirit, the history of Hebrew reveals a steady movement: from poetic and emotional elements predominant during its ancient, independent political life, towards a more abstract and reflective language (ever since the destruction of the Second Temple and the composition of the *Mishna* and the *Talmud*). Such modifications in language – in its vocabulary, grammar, morphology and so on – are inevitable, because language is intertwined with both the movement of the nation in time and the progression of its spirit.[26] Even more decisive for Jews was the overall alteration in the status of language in the nation's life. Ahad Ha'am believes that, in the absence of a fixed territory and a shared public life, language becomes the sole bond of the Jewish people: in fact, 'we barely have any remnant; only our language itself still shows signs of life'.[27] Whoever longs to vitalize the Jewish culture must pay heed to this historically formed, splicing role of language.

For Ahad Ha'am, then, language mirrors the spirit. But it is also the sphere by which the nation's culture can be revived, its identity cemented, its self-respect enshrined. Nor, for him, is this merely technical. He rejects both the artificial invention of words (the path embarked on by the great hero of Zionism, Eliezer Ben-Yehuda) and the emulation of European modern literature, with its preoccupation with the individual and aesthetics (as practised, for example, by Berdyczewski). Rather, language has an integrity of its own and is emphatically not a political tool, an ideological means, an entity to be constructed at will. Words are to be added in a natural, spontaneous way, each very gradually enlarging the potentially roomy terrain called human experience. Moreover, the integrity of language implies that these new words and phrases should be in line with the nation's spirit.[28] In the case of the Jewish people, this means that literature – the arena, for Ha'am, where language is truly renewed – should be preoccupied with philosophical and contemplative attitudes: 'In Israel, literature must submit to reflective thought if it wishes to be respected by the people'. Therefore, 'if you desire to enliven the language, strive to enliven the literature; and if you would like to enliven the literature, inject it with living thoughts'.[29] To be sure, this perspective was increasingly ridiculed in Zionism, especially by the actual architect of the movement, Ben-Gurion. 'Not by the power of literature, but by the power of intrepid people of action', Ben-Gurion declares, 'is this enchanted castle being erected.'[30]

## CONCLUSION

Applied to Zionism by Ahad Ha'am, Herder's tradition of nation-alism established a paradox. As we saw, Herder upheld an organic, prepolitical and territorial conception of nationalism. He professed that each nation has a unique spirit, and that the nation's ultimate obligations to itself are (a) to remain true to this spirit, and (b) to cultivate it in public life. Moreover, Herder suggested that language is the critical sphere through which culture is produced, as well as being the primary bond between people. This pluralistic and language-centred view legitimized a wide variety of national types, each determined by the character of the nation's spirit, language and land. A nation could act either like a primordial tribe or a cosmopolitan society, could be either belligerent or peace-seeking, and so on.

This Herderian vista propelled Ahad Ha'am to construct an essentialist picture of Jewish culture that celebrated high moral standards, including a non-situated ethical mode of deliberations, as well as an adamant refusal to recommend force in human inter-action. Parenthetically, let us note that in reconstructing Jewish culture in this fashion Ahad Ha'am was not alone. The German Reform movement presented a similar position during the nine-teenth century, as have Jewish scholars throughout the ages. But precisely this essentialist picture of Jewish culture made Ahad Ha'am the first major critic of Jewish attitudes towards the Arabs and their lands.

He noticed early the unbridgeable gap between the Jewish spirit and the political practice required by state-centred nationalism, asking, 'If Palestinian Jewry is unable to exercise restraint and decency now that it holds a little power, how much worse will it be when we control the land and its Arab inhabitants?'.[31] Contrary to Ahad Ha'am's notion that territory is merely a means to cultural inspiration, mainstream Zionists saw territory as a political resource whose control and integrity become necessary precondi-tions for sovereignty, the latter conferring, one assumes, security and normalcy. This *political* anchoring to the land – reinforced by the increasingly conflictual nature of Arab–Jewish relations in Palestine – propelled Israelis to invent a model of virile citizenship, naturalness and heroism. In other words, the emerging Israeli ethos neglected precisely what Ahad Ha'am considered most essential – the distinctive Jewish, moral spirit.

A second feature of Ahad Ha'am's Herderianism that brought him into conflict with the form of Zionism that actually evolved in Palestine was its view of language as the theatre of cultural preservation and elaboration. To be sure, Zionists in Palestine (especially the pioneers of the Second *Aliya*) were certainly no less committed to promoting the Hebrew language as the sole vernacular, as demonstrated by their teaching modern Hebrew in schools and kindergartens, by their using it in political debates and public spaces, by their literary and journalistic composition in Hebrew, and more. Nevertheless, I would argue that the new Hebrew society that emerged in the *Yishuv* during the first decades of the twentieth century perceived the Hebrew language, first and foremost, as a political tool. Hebrew's revival, to be sure, supported the claims of Jews to sovereignty over the land by evoking ancient names. It distinguished the Jews in Palestine from Yiddish-speaking Jews of the Diaspora (as well as from the Arab population). And it promised an authentic expression of the new mode of life and experience. 'The existence of the new Hebrew society had nothing but an ideological justification', writes Benjamin Harshav. 'That ideology saw *Eretz-Israel* (Land of Israel) as an embryo Jewish state belonging to the immigrants and sanctioned as a Jewish "homeland" by the League of Nations.'[32]

Ahad Ha'am held a rather different conception. According to him, language should not create a gulf between Palestinian Jews and Diaspora Jews. On the contrary, it ought to serve constructively as a bridge between them. Similarly, language (and especially its vocabulary) ought to bridge the present and the past by establishing an unbroken cultural chain. For Ha'am, language is not a tool of the will that can express a new mode of life through artificially invented words; rather, it is constantly exhuming what has transpired into the present, transmuting the 'has been' into a continuous becoming.

But the chief difference between Palestinian Zionism and Ahad Ha'am is this. The people of the Second *Aliya* demanded that pioneers (and later citizens) invest their energies in the world of the seen, the tangible and the measurable: by establishing *kibbutzim* and *moshavim*; by paving roads; by working and taking control of the land; by creating military power; by increasing the population, and so on. In distinction, Ahad Ha'am celebrated the audible, intangible world established by words. What interested him was not the sphere in which human beings compete for power and resources, but the collective sphere that human beings are capable of instituting among themselves by writing, reading, speaking, debating and interacting with each other as interpretive beings, as *homo-hermeneut*.

In point of practice, the activist nationalism that evolved in Palestine departed not only from Ahad Ha'am's vision, but also from Herderianism in general. While political Zionism shared with Herderianism an emphasis on common ethnic origins and a prepolitical conception of communal membership, it rejected the Herderian notions of language and culture as the highest achievements of the community and of an essential, immutable national spirit. Instead, the Zionist national movement is distinguished by its temporal ontology, which celebrates the amorphous nature of social life and the opportunity for discontinuous transfiguration offered at unique historical junctures.

While Western European nation-states emerged from the modern period in a piecemeal fashion, with monarchies and other central institutions gradually imposing their authority upon pre-existing populations, and while Central and Eastern European communities based their claims for nationhood upon hundreds of years of rootedness and cultural perpetuity, Zionism possessed at first neither an organizational foundation nor a geographically concentrated and anchored population. In making its claim for Jewish nationhood (a claim that required Zionists to establish political, legal, military, economic and other institutions; to bring masses of people to Palestine; and to introduce a wholly novel ethos into Jewish life), secular Zionists announced a revolution in the modern conception of time as it formed during the late eighteenth and nineteenth centuries. For them, history came asunder: it was a void lacking any binding meta-narratives, and indifferent to notions of both progress and decline. This void invited precisely the type of cultural discontinuity (and grand, revolutionary human action) that Herder and Ahad Ha'am both saw as lethal for any worthy nationalism.[33]

## NOTES

1. David Vital, 'Ahad Ha'am as the Sage of Zionism', *Jewish History*, IV, 2 (autumn 1990). For recent works on Ahad Ha'am, see Steven I. Zipperstein, *Elusive Prophet: Ahad Ha'am and the Origins of Zionism* (Berkeley: University of California Press, 1993); Yehiel A. Gottschalk, *Ahad Ha'am and the Jewish National Spirit* (Jerusalem: Hassifriya Haziyonit, 1992, Hebrew edition); and Yosef Goldstein, *Ahad Ha'am* (Jerusalem: Keter, 1992).

2. Ahad Ha'am, *'perkai zichronot'*, in *Kol kitvei Ahad Ha'am* (Jerusalem: Achozaath Ivrith, 1947), p. 495. The translations from Hebrew are mine, and henceforth I shall refer to this text as *KK*. It should be noted that Ahad Ha'am was also influenced by nineteenth-century writers such as Spencer and Krochmal, whose organic–biological and idealist philosophies (respectively) partly resemble Herder's. This resemblance points to the difficulty in distinguishing the exact sources of influence on Ahad Ha'am and in mapping their genealogy.

3. In his acclaimed study of nationalism, Hans Kohn distinguishes between two types of nationalism. The first type (modelled after the French Revolution and liberal thought) presents the nation as a political entity born at a definite moment: a number of individuals rationally decide to join their fates and establish a set of institutions, a constitution, and laws to regulate their shared lives. The members of this polity are citizens who preserve their natural rights; their bond does not negate but guards their individuality. Kohn's second type of nationalism (modelled after the German experience and Herderian thought) pictures the nation as a political entity, distinguished by shared soil and landscape, language and literature, and ethnic origins and folk culture. Human beings do not choose to join such an organic body; they are born into and inescapably shaped by it. In fact, individuals cannot fathom themselves without this engulfing whole and its collective meanings and purposes. Naturally, in this vision, the nation has no distinct moment of formation; it is a creature that gradually unfolds in history according to its distinct and incommensurable spirit and character. See Hans Kohn, *The Idea of Nationalism* (New York: Collier Books, 1967); Elie Kedourie, *Nationalism* (Oxford: Blackwell, 1993); Eric Hobsbawm, *Nations and Nationalism Since 1780* (Cambridge: Cambridge University Press, 1990); Zeev Sternhell, *The Founding Myths of Israel* (Princeton: Princeton University Press, 1998).

4. Sternhell, *The Founding Myths of Israel*, p. 55.

5. J. G. Herder, 'Ideas for a Philosophy of History', in F. M. Bernard (ed.), *J. G. Herder on Social and Political Culture* (Cambridge: Cambridge University Press, 1969), p. 285 (henceforth *HS*). My discussion on Herder has benefited from the work of F. M. Bernard, *Herder's Social and Political Thought: From Enlightenment to Nationalism* (Oxford: Clarendon Press, 1965). I also draw here on my discussion of Herder in my article 'Time in Zionism: The Life and Afterlife of a Temporal Revolution', *Political Theory*, 26, 5 (Oct. 1998), pp. 6520–85.

6. 'Whatever the influence of the (external) climate, every man, every animal, every plant, has its own climate. For every living being absorbs all the external influences in a manner peculiar to itself and modifies them according to its organic powers'. See 'Ideas for a Philosophy of History', *HS*, p. 293.

7. Ibid., p. 156.

8. Isaiah Berlin, *The Crooked Timber of Humanity: Chapters in the History of Ideas* (London: John Murray, 1990), pp. 37–40.

9. 'Essay on the Origin of Language', *HS*, p. 120.

10. Ibid., p. 165.

11. Ibid., p. 164.

12. Ahad Ha'am, 'Sach Ha'kol', *KK*, p. 421.

13. 'Lo zo haderech', *KK*, p. 12.

14. 'Avar v'atid', *KK*, p. 82.

15. 'Lo zo haderech', *KK*, p. 12.

16. 'Higiya hasha'a', *KK*, p. 379.

17. While Ahad Ha'am believes that the renewal of the Hebrew language will promise the integration and coherence of Jewish culture and history, Sholem believes this renewal invites a bold leap to the distant past, a leap that could entrap Zionists in ancient meanings and symbols. In his famous letter to Franz Rosenzweig (1926), Sholem writes: 'People here do not know the meaning of endeavors...They think they have made Hebrew into a secular language, that they have successfully eradicated its apocalyptic sting. But this is untrue. Secularization of language is nonsense, a hollow proclamation. There is no way to flatten the words that are about to explode – except perhaps if one forsakes the language itself' (p. 59). Living in the Hebrew language means dwelling on the edge of an abyss: 'A language is composed of names. The power of the language is entangled in the name, and its abyss is enclosed

within the name. Having summoned up the ancient names day after day, we can no longer suppress their potencies. We have roused them and they will reveal themselves, for we have invoked them with immense power.' Gershom Sholem, *Od Davar* (Tel Aviv: Am Oved, 1986), p. 59.

18. '*Al devar ozar h'yhadot belashon ivrit*', *KK*, p. 108. According to Zipperstein's illuminating interpretation, Ahad Ha'am's vision of a spiritual centre was inspired by his years in Odessa, where, with friends such as Dubnow and Lilienblum, he orchestrated a vivid intellectual community. See *Illusive Prophet*, Ch. 3.
19. '*Derech haruach*', *KK*, p. 152. For an inclusive discussion of Ahad Ha'am's conception of the Jewish spirit, see Gottschalk's *Ahad Ha'am and the Jewish National Spirit*, Ch. 7.
20. Ahad Ha'am continues to claim that 'the spirit is the internal force by which they [i.e. culture's products] are formed, live, and develop. And these products are the external world through which the spirit is materialized and exposed.' See *Techia u'beriah*, p. 292.
21. '*Hamusar hal'eumi*', *KK*, p. 161.
22. '*Chikui v'hitbolelut*', *KK*, p. 88.
23. '*Shinui arachim*', *KK*, p. 156.
24. Ibid., p. 142.
25. '*Al devar otzar hayahadut belashon ivrit*', *KK*, p. 113.
26. Like Herder, Ahad Ha'am criticizes the tendency to freeze the Hebrew language into outdated grammatical structures and vocabulary and rejects the notion of 'pure' language. See '*Halashon v'dikduka*', *KK*, p. 99.
27. '*Etza tova*', *KK*, p. 133.
28. To be sure, translations from other languages are important (since no nation should be immune to the teachings of others), but all the new materials should be 'absorbed' by the nation and made germane to its spirit. See '*Chikui v'hitbolelut*', *KK*, pp. 88–9.
29. '*Halashon v'dikduka*', *KK*, p. 97. This view, incidentally, leads Ahad Ha'am to invest immense energies in editing the *Ha-Shiloach*. It also explains his (unfulfilled) desire to write a major book that would be a sort of *Guide to the Perplexed* for modern times.
30. I owe this quote to Anita Shapira. See her 'Ben Gurion and the Bible: The Creation of a New Historical Narrative?', in *New Jews, Old Jews* (Tel Aviv: Am Oved, 1997), p. 239. To be sure, one could find conflicting proclamations of Ben-Gurion in this matter, but I believe the quote given above best reflects his overall attitude.
31. *Igrot Ahad Ha'am*, Vol. 5, 12 February 1914, pp. 160–1. Quoted here from Zipperstein, *Elusive Prophet*, pp. 246–7.
32. Benjamin Harshav, *Language in Time of Revolution* (Berkeley: University of California Press, 1993), p. 142.
33. I draw, in this last paragraph, on my discussion of Zionist temporal ontology in 'Time in Zionism', pp. 673–74.

# 14  First Encounters:
# East European Jewry Discovers
# Pre-Balfour England

## YAACOV SHAVIT

'Ashkenaz – Thought; England – Action; France – Pleasure.'
Morris Vinchevsky (Benzion Novakhovichi),
'A Letter from the Diaspora', *HaKol*, 27:4, 1879[1]

'Their modern culture is of no importance, empty
and frivolous are their periodicals, and yet spirituality is
not lacking for the more spiritual among them: the legacy of
generations – Byron and Shakespeare, Shelley and Carlyle.'
Yosef Haim Brenner[2]

Professor David Vital's second published book, *The Making of British Foreign Policy* (1968), analysed the mechanisms involved in shaping British foreign policy. Long before that, because the Balfour Declaration committed England to support for a Jewish national home in Palestine and Britain's League of Nations mandate gave it responsibility for governing the Holy Land, Zionist leaders during the interwar period were very interested in learning how British foreign policy was determined. For example, in 1930, Chaim Arlosoroff wrote an article entitled 'The Colonial Office' based on Sir George V. Fiddes's 1926 book *The Dominions and the Colonial Office*, one of the volumes in his Whitehall Series. Arlosoroff also translated into Hebrew Barth Williams's book, *The British Empire* (in Hebrew, 1930). It is obvious, then, that the early shaping of pre-Zionist Jewish attitudes to England seems particularly appropriate to this jubilee book.

In his satirical novel, *The Travels of Benjamin the Third*, published in 1896, Mendele Mokher Seforim (Shalom Jacob Abramowitsch) describes a conversation between idlers sitting in a house of study in the city of Zalmona, where two travellers, Benjamin and Sandril, the heroes of the story, arrive in the midst of the 1853–56 Crimean War. The men in the house of study (*Bet midrash*) exchange items of news and rumours of events in the big world. They tell wondrous tales about 'Lady Vita, the world-renowned Queen Victoria, praise her exceedingly for her ingenuity and wisdom, and find great purpose in all her deeds', and in the marvels of the 'machines of England'.

There is, of course, no reason to wonder at the fact that reports about Queen Victoria and the industrial revolution penetrated as far as small Jewish towns in Eastern Europe in the 1850s. But it is clear that if this conversation had taken place a decade or two later, the men in the house of study would have known a great deal more about England. This additional information would result from the expanded horizons of geographical and historical knowledge of the 'average' contemporary Jew in Eastern Europe insofar as the world at large was concerned, including remote countries like England and far more distant ones.[3]

My intention is not to review the information about events in England and the British Empire received by Jewish newspaper readers in Eastern Europe during the mid-nineteenth century but to examine how these same Jews formed an opinion about England and whether the resulting image played any part, first in shaping their modern consciousness and later in affecting political decisions.

As is well known, German culture was the non-Jewish culture which played a key role in the modernization of Jewish consciousness. Alongside it, France and French culture served as a 'secondary model', according to Israel Bartal's definition. He describes France as a political model, for instance, towards which the Jew had an ambivalent attitude. Certain ideas of French origin were absorbed into Jewish society, generally in an indirect manner, and various literary models were adopted by Jewish authors.[4] Besides the fact that political ideas, originating in the France of the Enlightenment and the Revolution, and of later generations, reverberated widely, France also had a real presence in the culture of the higher classes in Eastern Europe; and some elements of French culture (first and foremost, a knowledge of French) passed from them to small circles in the Jewish community.

But what of England? Was she, too, a 'secondary model'?

Unquestionably, the ideas of English and Scottish philosophers were widely disseminated in Eastern Europe, where the educated Jew of the mid-nineteenth century would have heard the ideas of John Stuart Mill and Jeremy Bentham, of Charles Darwin and Herbert Spencer,[5] Thomas Carlyle, Thomas Henry Buckle, John William Draper,[6] and other English thinkers. Each of them influenced the Russian or the Polish intelligentsia in general, and also had a profound effect on some members of the Jewish intelligentsia in particular.[7] An educated Jewish public might very well have read English literature in translation – from Shakespeare and Byron to Dickens and Oliver Goldsmith, and others.[8] But English culture, aside from philosophy and literature, had a very limited presence, and hence could only serve as a 'marginal' – not a 'secondary' – model for the East European Jew.

Nonetheless, the image of England formed in the minds of the Jewish reading public in Eastern Europe is not a marginal chapter in describing how the Jewish knowledge of the world was shaped in modern times. A discussion of this topic does not merely constitute an academic study of the connection between the development of available knowledge, transmitted through various agents (the press, rumours and the like), or the formation of images and perceptions on any given subject. Despite England's marginal status, the attitude towards it in the Jewish press reflects the way in which Jews learned about the contemporary world and formulated an opinion about the forces acting in it. Needless to say, England's central and determining status in the contemporary world – as a power in the European constellation; as a world-embracing empire, with deeply rooted interests in the Middle East (including Palestine); as the generator of the industrial revolution and a formidable industrial power; as a constitutional monarchy and a parliamentary democracy which granted Jews full political rights; and as a destination for Jews emigrating from the east – could not help but arouse a desire to know as much as possible, to understand her nature, the secret of her strength, what made her unique and the way in which she operated.

The activity of English philanthropists and gentile Zionists in the second half of the nineteenth century, expressed in the aid given to the Jews of Eastern Europe and the millenarian ideas of the redemption of the Land of Israel which arose during that period also aroused interest in the nature of the mother country in the organizations involved in these movements. Towards the end of the nineteenth century and up to the First World War, this interest grew once Herzlian Zionist diplomacy made England a target country and even obtained her agreement to establishing a Jewish settlement in Uganda. As expectations of England increased, interest in that country became less theoretical and more pragmatic.

In order to know what one could expect, it was desirable to know as much as possible about the object of these expectations. Having said this, I nevertheless believe that had it not been for the Balfour Declaration and British rule over Palestine after the First World War, the perception or image of England, and the reconstruction of the development of knowledge about her, as well as the attitude adopted towards her, would have been relegated to the sidelines of historical interest. The facts that the destiny of Zionism is closely and fatefully bound up with Britain and that Britain ruled Palestine from 1918 to 1948 are what make the attitude of East European Jews towards England so important. In other words, since knowledge about England had already developed before 1917, it was not a totally strange land to the Jews; they already had certain images of it as well as certain expectations.

By no means was this a negative view from the outset, one that engendered a suspicious or hostile attitude towards England. Nor was it an image that made her into a negative political model.[9] It is true that the Zionist attitude towards England was often mingled with harsh criticism. Those adhering to socialist (and Marxist) views were critical of British capitalism and the status of workers in England. So, too, were they opposed to British imperialism and its treatment of the populations it ruled imperially. However, in general, East European Jews had a positive attitude towards England. One might even describe it as one of sympathy and admiration.

This positive attitude endured in Zionist public opinion in Europe and in Palestine, with certain exceptions, until nearly the mid-1940s, namely until the period of the *Yishuv's* 'struggle' against British rule in Palestine. Only then did an Anglophobic attitude begin to develop within certain circles. Although from the end of 1944 the majority did consider England a political enemy, it did not develop a hostile attitude towards her or her culture. The hostile, at times acrimonious, views voiced by public opinion in Palestine from 1944 to 1948 should not gloss over the fact that the greater part of this public clearly appreciated, even admired, several traits regarded as characteristic of Great Britain.

In any event, the fundamental difference between knowledge about England and the way it was understood before 1917 and after is clear. Until 1917 the knowledge was theoretical, and the image was of a distant political society and an unknown culture. After 1917, it became nothing less than critical to understand England and its image.

Zionist politics and statesmanship were largely based on the views and images Zionist leaders had of the nature of English political culture, the way England's dominant mechanisms operated, the interests that drove the country, and what characterized the 'English mentality' – both in England itself and in the officialdom that conducted British imperial rule overseas.

From 1917 onwards, there was daily contact with English politics and English political culture by permanent Zionist representatives in London and Jerusalem; the ties to English culture were not only direct but also tangible as a result of Britain's rule and presence in Palestine. After 1917 we are no longer referring to an attitude towards 'spiritual England',[10] namely, towards 'high British culture' expressed in political principles, philosophical ideas and *belles-lettres*. It becomes an attitude towards 'concrete' England: towards patterns of government and administration, rules of conduct and lifestyle as expressed in Palestine, as well as ties and attitudes to various aspects of English culture (film, sport, popular culture and the like). Jewish society in Palestine was introduced to all these elements as a result of the growing number of its members who studied and knew English, and the open, receptive nature of the cultural market in Palestine, which enabled the importation of books, films, and the like.

The process by which knowledge of the 'other' expands into an image, or a repertoire of stereotypes, is dynamic and complex. As we shall see, a great deal of news about England and events taking place in that country was published by the Jewish press in Eastern Europe, often accompanied by commentary. This commentary stemmed from preconceived images and, at one and the same time, created and disseminated new images in turn. The news from England – and about England – was part of the ongoing reporting about events in the world, while the images reflected understanding and interpretation, which created a conventional pattern. Often, the image is more influential than the knowledge because it determines an *a priori* attitude towards the imagined object, and sometimes also dictates modes of action and behaviour towards it, which, as noted, was important mainly in relation to shaping Zionist policy years later, at the time of the British mandate.

The news sections of the Jewish press reported on numerous subjects, while the editorials selected a particular dimension, usable both in determining a stance towards the overall East European society and in debating the desirable character of the Jewish society. England, as the 'other', was a multifaceted entity, and the Jews who wrote about it were able to discern four major facets. They saw England as: a distinctive *political* culture and a unique *political* tradition in contrast to the continental countries, including the special tradition of English liberalism on the one hand, and of English socialism on the other; the ruler of an empire; a land of singular culture; and the birthplace of the industrial revolution and the leading power in international trade and commerce. From the 1920s onwards, an attempt was also made by some Zionist writers to explain the riddle of the English character and single out its particular traits. In addition to these four emphases, great attention was devoted to the special and inspiring history of Jewish emancipation in England.

In terms of the time and place – East European Jewry in the Enlightenment era of proto-nationalism until the emergence of the Zionist movement in the late 1880s – the Jews formulated an image and a stance towards each of the four or five major facets on the basis of the admittedly only fragmentary, sometimes superficial, knowledge at their disposal, but also according to how they might be able to use this accumulated knowledge in their own local and distinctively internal Jewish context. Regarding the latter, the images and knowledge found expression in the manner in which England was used as a role model and how various Jewish writers hoped to learn lessons and derive inspiration from it.

Two brief methodical comments are necessary at this point:

1. A group of quotations taken from the press, periodicals and philosophical observations as well as from correspondence provides information about the views of the writers, but cannot represent those of the public. When we speak of a perception, we are referring to an image expressed in the writings of a very small group within the public-at-large. Yet it is entirely reasonable to assume that the articles regularly published in the daily press – journalistic writings and literature – were read by a large public as their major source of information and had to have had

some influence in shaping the perceptions and understanding of at least large segments of this public. At the very least, readers took the object – England – and transformed it from a distant, unfamiliar land and culture into a fairly well-known one, so that the later encounter with her politics and statesmanship, officials, army, and various sections of her culture was not an encounter with *Anglia incognita*.[11]

2. Educated Jewish *maskilim* and the Jewish intelligentsia could garner information from the press in languages such as Russian or German (a knowledge of English was not widespread among East European Jews), from literature written in these languages and from translations of English literature into these languages. But there is no way to reconstruct the sources of their knowledge – with the exception of several testimonies about the manner in which they read English philosophical literature, or about it. On the other hand, again, we can reasonably assume that the average Jewish reader gained most of his knowledge from the press and literature in Hebrew or Yiddish. What was written in them therefore constituted for most Jews their window on the world – and the prism through which they looked out at that external, often exotic and uncharted world.

The weekly, *Ha-Maggid* (The Declarer), the first Hebrew newspaper and mouthpiece of moderate *Haskalah* and Jewish proto-Zionism in Eastern Europe from the 1850s to the 1980s, was founded in 1856, the year in which the Crimean War ended. Its continued to appear until 1903. It was published in the Prussian city of Lyck on the Russian–East Prussian border, then for two years in Berlin, and then, until closure, under the name *Ha-Maggid Ha'chadash* (The New Declarer), in Cracow. Hence, while most of its readers were subjects of the tsarist empire, in practice it never came under the scrutinizing eye of the tsar's censor. Still, because most of the paper's readers lived in Russia, and Prussia was itself an autocratic state, the journalists freedom to write what they wished was restricted in more subtle ways. Its editors, for example, practised self-censorship on any item of a critical nature relating to Russia and autocratic Prussia. On the other hand, this did not preclude their praising parliamentary democracy in England, so that these words of commendation were an indirect way of criticizing, by unfavourable comparison, the autocratic regimes in Russia and Prussia.

The number of the paper's subscribers ranged, according to various estimates, from 400 to 2,000, although the number of its readers was much greater. *Ha-Maggid* was, therefore, a central fount of information about events in the Jewish world and in the world at large for Hebrew readers in Eastern Europe. The paper translated telegraphic items of news received from London which were frequently edited summaries of news published in *The Times* of London. In its worldview, too, the paper ardently supported Western Europe's first and foremost nation, England. Disseminated worldwide, the weekly also served as a harbinger of proto-nationalist ideas. In this way, the information and images *Ha-Maggid* created and disseminated were, on the one hand, a part-modernization of the process Jewish public opinion in Eastern Europe was undergoing and, on the other, contributed to the very development of the process Itself.[12] From its first issues, the paper devoted space to reports about England as part of its political reviews of world events, and several times devoted editorials to England. I will not examine the current news the paper published, but will sum up the basic images of England that are reflected in its issues over a period of nearly half-a-century.

Another source of information available to the educated Hebrew reader from the 1860s onwards was Kalman Schulman's popular universal history. Schulman (1819–99), the most outstanding popularizer of Hebrew literature in the second half of the nineteenth century, made an immense contribution to the development of the East European Hebrew reader's knowledge of the world – past and present – since his books sold in several editions and were enormously popular.[13] In his six-volume work, *Divrei yemei olam* (World History) (Vilna, 1867–84), adapted from a German source, Schulman devoted a great deal of space to the history of England, from the mid-twelfth century to the early 1880s. For instance, in his book *Sefer mosadei eretz* (A Geography Book) (Vilna, 1875) he included a detailed description of governance in England.

On the pages of *Ha-Maggid* and in Schulman's book, England was portrayed as a model of political rule and political culture. Government in England was the antithesis of the absolutist regimes in Russia and Prussia, as well as of the tradition of the French Revolution. England's democratic form of government placed her 'at the highest point among all the peoples of the globe' – an exemplar for them (together with the political system in the United States).

On 10 July 1862, the newspaper wrote:

> Yes, dear reader, this House of Commons is an ideal exemplar
> for the entire universe, a beacon for many nations to follow in
> its light and path. And the earth will be full of knowledge and
> justice as the waters cover the sea. Not merely do the British
> legislators show their concern for their own people, but they
> are the benefactors of other peoples as well, for as their own
> people's strength grows, so do the happiness and welfare of
> others.

The civil liberties of every citizen – including the Jewish citizen –
are assured. Unlike in other countries, government ministers are
elected by Parliament and need its support.[14] Members of
Parliament have the right to respond to the Queen's speech at the
annual opening session of the Parliament – something unthinkable
in tsarist Russia. Schulman writes: 'All those familiar with the
customs of England will cover her with praise, and indeed she is
deserving of praise, for she lays judgement by a plumb-line and
righteousness by a plummet'.[15] Even the king himself is not above
the law in England, Schulman writes. Since King Charles I tried to
undermine the *Magna Carta*, Schulman does not criticize the Puritan
revolution as he so harshly does the French Revolution.[16] The
reason is simple: the French Revolution brought the mob to power,
whereas the Puritan revolution was followed by the restoration of
the monarchy and the supremacy of law. England, in Schulman's
eyes, is the very embodiment of democracy, while the prosperity
and strength she enjoys are directly attributed to the political and
civil freedom prevailing in that land.

*Ha-Maggid* and Schulman did not marvel only at the processes of
English government but also at the country's democratic political
culture, wherein the principles of liberty and justice were put into
practice and the rights of the citizen anchored in a long-standing
historical tradition:

> Here, in the free land of England, judgement prevails in the
> market place, and truth and justice lodge in the streets. Here
> the small and the large are judged alike, and a member of no
> faith is given precedence over a member of another.

Ignoring the Puritan revolution, both stressed the fact that this political culture had developed in an evolutionary manner, without its traditional institutions being destroyed. In a formulation also accepted by the Russian intelligentsia, *Ha-Maggid* and Schulman created an interdependence between the political form of government in England and its industrial–technological progress, international trade ('the peddler of the nations'), and the material wealth endowing her with political power and greatness. England was a blessed land that had become the cradle of progress.

It is interesting that neither *Ha-Maggid* nor Schulman devoted any space to a description of the condition of the working class in England or to the negative aspects of English capitalism. The poet and man-of-letters, Judah Leib Levin (*Yahalel*, 1844–1925), in contrast, was well aware of England's dual nature. In a letter in April 1883, he wrote: 'You ought to know, my friend, that while England has the most favoured government of all nations, the proletariat and pauperism have increased in it sevenfold compared to all other countries'.

Nonetheless, Levin regards England as a land to be envied:

> And would not your heart rejoice to see the Jews settled in their land, happy and blessed with only one-eighth the good and happiness of England? The general poverty is a separate issue, and the people as a whole, unprotected and open to plunder, is a separate issue.[17]

The sympathetic attitude towards England is also reflected in *Ha-Maggid's* and Schulman's position in relation to British imperialism. Although at times there is an undertone of criticism in relation to the tyranny of imperialist rule, insofar as the domination of non-white peoples in Asia and Africa was concerned, both the paper and Schulman were ardent advocates of England's civilizing mission ('the white man's burden') in the world, as a representative of the West. British imperialism was portrayed by them as an 'enlightened occupation', motivated not only by considerations of trade but also by a sense of moral mission: England is bringing progress to a 'backward' world. England, Schulman writes:

> planted the seeds of the sciences in other lands and distant isles too, for her sons, who found too little room for themselves in that country, scattered throughout the lands of the East and the islands of the seas, and wherever they resided,

they spread the light of wisdom and knowledge, of crafts-manship and the practical arts. 'The ways of England are pleasant, all her paths lead to peace.' Only to Ireland did she say: 'There is no peace'.[18]

The Indian rebellion in 1857, for example, is depicted as an upris-ing against progress. Both *Ha-Maggid* and Schulman did in fact criticize England's intolerance in this affair. However, since the reli-gions of the Far East were regarded as idolatrous, the suppression of the Indian revolt was seen in a positive light, and the newspaper called on England 'to better its ways in India, and seek to spread light in this vast country... but not to expand her government and treas-ures' (30 October 1857). Observing more broadly, the weekly expressed its opinion that England had played a positive role in India and China by making these countries, which until then had been outside the 'civilized world', a part of that world (17 April 1857).[19]

Now the Queen of England also rules over India, and the ministers of her government render judgement and compas-sion in the lands of India, a just sentence to the rebels and compassion to the inhabitants by giving them good and just laws according to which they will live happy lives so they will no longer rise up in rebellion.[20]

In the same vein, Schulman writes about the British occupation of Ethiopia in 1867–68:

This war too will testify to the fact that the enlightened sons of Europe will always rule over the sons of benighted Asia and Africa, and... the Enlightenment will overcome all folly with all its might and power. Since then the Kingdom of England has positioned a large army in Abyssinia to put an end to the tyranny of her rulers and ministers, and perhaps that kingdom will also succeed in opening the gates of that land to European enlightenment and civilization until it unites with the lands of Europe in the practice of the sciences, industry and trade.[21]

*Ha-Maggid* also wrote during the war that it was England's duty to introduce order into an uncivilized country like Abyssinia.[22]

Criticism was only voiced on those occasions when England was perceived as trying to undermine religious tradition. Although *Ha-Maggid* showed no sympathy for the 'idolatrous' religions, and could not openly express opposition to the spread of Christianity, it apparently perceived the suppression of religious rites *per se* as a condemnable act. On the other hand, *Ha-Maggid* did denounce England's policy in Ireland and South Africa and, in the latter instance, revealed clear sympathy for the Boers.

This overall favourable attitude towards England's cultural 'mission' in Asia and Africa, the description of British imperialism as tolerant and enlightened, and the distinction drawn between the manner of British and French rule in their respective colonies found ample expression in Zionist literature up to the First World War, and doubtless prepared Zionist public opinion for accepting England as the enlighted holder of the mandate over Palestine. A perfect illustration of this is Ahad Ha'Am's comment about English rule in South Africa after England won the Boer War. In the summer of 1909, he wrote:

> The English, for example, surely know how to use force – of the fist and the cannon. They have conquered a whole world with these, and founded an empire on which the sun never sets. But at the same time, they know that their empire will endure 'not by armies nor by force, but by the spirit'. Therefore, wherever possible, they try to replace the force of the fist with the force of the spirit...the spirit of 'liberty, equality and brotherhood'.[23]

As a rule *Ha-Maggid* devoted no space to reports about English literature or thought. Thus, the controversy over Darwin's book *The Origin of Species*, published in 1856, is not mentioned at all in the paper. Nor did Schulman devote any space in his book to a description of English culture, except to mention Shakespeare: 'The light of the aspiring writer, unparalleled among the authors of all the peoples under the sun, is the sublime, famous writer called Shakespeare'.[24]

*Ha-Maggid* and Schulman's books reflect perceptions based on second-hand, indirect knowledge acquired from the foreign press and literature. A similar perception can be found in Jewish publicist writings in Eastern Europe by authors whose image of England was formed through a distant mirror. It will be interesting shortly to see whether closer, more personal and direct acquaintance – a stay in England, for instance – reinforced or altered these perceptions.

For the most part, we do not find England serving as a model or argument in internal Eastern European Jewish debates. For much of the nineteenth century, after all, the question of the character of political government in any future Jewish society was not yet on the public agenda; therefore, a discussion of political rule in England had no effect whatsoever. Two noteworthy examples, however, in which England was used as a standard serving internal Jewish aims can be found in Peretz Smolenskin's publicistic historical writings.

Smolenskin (1842–85), a nationalist *maskil*, author and publicist, settled in Vienna in 1868, and for 17 years edited the periodical *Ha-Shachar* (*Dawn*) there.[25] In his view, England was the first country in Europe in which, even in the time of Henry VIII, the spirit of toler-ance and freedom had overcome religious clericalism and political despotism. Not France, but England, was the first country to accept and apply the ideas of emancipation. Not because it had no anti-Semitism, but because it had a tolerant political system. Smolenskin was of the same opinion as Schulman, that England had succeeded in changing her political system while preserving her social stabil-ity, without resorting to terror or violence, without giving the mob any power, and without undermining the institution of the monar-chy. This English precedent was undoubtedly the model of change that the enlightened Jews would have liked to see emulated in tsarist Russia. Furthermore, Smolenskin regarded the English expe-rience as an instrument by which one could resolve the '*kulturkampf*' between the 'religious' and the 'free-thinkers' in Jewish society. The English model rejects the rule of the church but, at the same time, provides a way of introducing reforms in religion and society through consensus, not by the indiscriminate destruc-tion of tradition and the 'old world'.

One could say that Smolenskin envisioned a kind of 'praisewor-thy revolution' in Jewish society, leading to structural changes without impairing its framework and organic continuity. In his long article, '*Am Olam*' (An Eternal People), published in 1872, he wrote:

> There is only one nation whose heart is set upon sublime knowledge and which has also applied it to man's actions. This nation is that of the British people, this people of both thought and deed, who will act, but will first think before doing so. This people has risen high on the ladder of this sublime knowledge until it now stands at the head of all the nations. This people did not seek to embrace and kiss all

humankind with its thought, like the Germans, nor did it wish to bring them under its wings and rule them like the French. It knew that first of all man must see to his own life, and only then act for the sake of humankind, for only in this manner will men achieve the lofty aim of benefitting all mankind.[26]

These words were directed against assimilated Jews in the West, the members of *Wissenschaft des Judentums* and the believers. In England's historical trajectory, Smolenskin found a commendable example of a state whose first concern was for its own welfare and which had not succumbed to a self-imposed mission to spread good throughout the world. The English, he wrote, first of all love their own people, and through this love they benefit the entire world. In other words, in England Smolenskin found an exemplar of nationalism and patriotism, free of any missionary tidings like the revolutionary ideas borne by France, conclusively proving that a nation can contribute to world civilization without giving up its national assets.

In English history Smolenskin found a model worthy of emulation for the proper separation between government (politics and civil society) and religion. The English people, he wrote, remained believers even when the clergy had no ruling power; nor was the English government the sworn enemy of the faith.[27] It confirmed that religious reforms could be introduced by the sovereign legislator – a procedure, incidentally which he believed had support in Jewish tradition.[28] From McCaulay, Smolenskin learned that partisan divisions and controversies could be resolved by majority opinion.[29] In other words, England, the only place in which a blend of liberalism, tolerance, a democratic system of government changes according to the decision of the majority, and national unity had been successful, was the optimal (and utopian) model for the reforms required by Jewish religion and society: 'And to this great thing we must also cast our eyes whenever we desire to introduce innovations or reforms in Judaism'.

In Smolenskin's novel, *Hato'eh bedarkei ha'chayim* (The Perplexed in the Paths of Life) (Vilna, 1876–68), the hero writes a letter to his sister after having arrived in Paris from London:

> Unlike London, which is only work and action, this city [Paris] is full. Here the hubbub of life overpowers the hubbub of work and labour in the great streets ... but my heart will not

be captivated by her, the crowd and the commotion in her streets. I cannot endure it, nor do its people capture my heart. The people living in this land are as far removed from the people of Britain as the skies from the earth. A man of Britain is like an ox to his yoke and will wholeheartedly do his work.[30]

In contrast to the image of French culture and society as superficial and even licentious, which was widespread in Jewish literature in Eastern Europe, England is described as a serious, staid society and culture. For a nationalist and positivist like Smolenskin, the revival of Jewry in its land would be realistic only if the Jews were as sober and industrious as the English.

Until the inception of Herzlian diplomacy, England and the British Empire were depicted as a political culture and a great power worthy of admiration. But the East European Jewish mirror in which England was reflected was a distorted mirror, one that revealed only a few aspects of its character.

During the second half of the nineteenth century, the Jews became better acquainted with England and events occurring there, and began to speak her praises; and yet this was a distant, platonic kind of love. Only later, when the intelligentsia and Zionist activists began to arrive in England as immigrants, and spent some time there, did their acquaintance with England deepen. Then the mirror drew closer to the object reflected in it: England increasingly came to be reflected with greater clarity, with growing attempts to understand her true nature.

'I must confess', wrote Chaim Weizmann to his fiancée, Vera, on 2 February 1905, 'that we used to have false notions about the English and England.'[31] These words accurately reflect the first encounters of Eastern European Zionist leaders with England in the pre-First World War period. Their early exposure confronted partial, even superficial knowledge and a stereotyped image of England face-to-face with reality; this gave rise, in turn, to confused mixed reactions, as well as to a longer process of familiarization and learning.

This learning process would be entirely different for Zionist activists settling permanently in England than for those spending only a short time there. For the former, their attitude towards everything English was understandably affected by the sense of foreignness felt by any immigrant on encountering an unfamiliar cultural environment whose codes of conduct he finds strange.[32]

My point is that their early, superficial acquaintance with England, based on information acquired from the 'old country' press and literature, did little to blunt the shock of the encounter or the problems of adaptation, particularly since the newcomers knew little or no English, certainly not on a level that could serve as an entry ticket to English culture.

What matters most is the adjustment process: how first impressions changed over time and led to an improved and in some cases – like that of Weizmann himself – even a sophisticated understanding of England and the English. Several examples will suffice.

Ahad Ha-Am resided from 1907 to 1921 in London,[33] where he was employed as a clerk in the Wissotsky tea company. We have already remarked that his thinking had been much influenced by British philosophers (Spencer, John Stuart Mill and others), but England itself was totally foreign to him. London seemed like 'Babylonia', an anonymous, noisy city that 'confuses the mind and stupefies the heart', and 'the City seemed like Hell, an accursed place that destroys the spirit'.[34] On 17 December 1907, he wrote to Mordechai ben Hillel HaCohen in Jaffa about the 'vast sea known as London', and about how difficult he was finding it to take leave of 'the world you have lived in most of your life and with which your best memories are linked, and to move "on the eve of old age" to a new, strange world'.[35] Nonetheless, Ahad Ha-Am was not oblivious to the enormous power held by a city like London, and when he left it to settle in little Tel Aviv he began to miss the large city, despite 'its crowded streets and markets, the dark City, where I spent so many years without light or air'.[36]

It is not his nostalgia for London that is important to us, but the fact that Ahad Ha-Am marvelled at the political freedom prevailing in England and at the character of its political culture, which was marked by self-discipline and was deeply rooted in tradition. It is hard to say that he felt any emotional link to England; on the contrary, it always remained alien to him, but rational analysis led him to conclude that modern Jewry certainly had a lot to learn from Britain.

Yosef Chaim Brenner's impression of London, where he arrived penniless in early 1904,[37] was similar to that of Ahad Ha-Am:

> London ... is a very large city. And dark, very dark, with many crooked and twisting streets and lanes, filled with smoke and grime by day and night, and many people wander in them,

naked and hungry, searching and searching for something, but, in fact, no longer expecting to find anything. On their backs stand a fair number of very busy creatures, reading newspapers, travelling in carriages, wearing large black top hats. There are, of course, some pleasant aspects to the city that the local citizens can enjoy. It has many tree-filled parks, it has peaceful suburbs, it has culture wherever you look.[38]

Brenner stressed the deep division between the social classes that characterized English society, and described the life of the bourgeois society as superficial and flighty. However, he greatly appreciated the political freedom prevailing in England, although he defined it as external freedom.

A third Zionist with socialist views who lived in London for a short time early in 1914 was Dov Ber Borochov. His sojourn was spent mostly in libraries, and his letters indicate hardly any interest in English society and culture or any attempt to learn anything about them, other than a sketchy impression of the British national character. In his view, that character was best reflected in the library of the British Museum, which was a 'centre of world culture', its rules and regulations reflecting 'British order and England's ability to rule. An analogy, if you will, of the way Britain rules the seas.' Borochov also mentions the Stock Exchange in the City as a centre of world trade.[39] We might, perhaps, have expected a more profound impression from a theoretician with such wide-ranging interests, but Borochov, like Brenner, was only a sojourner in England, unlike Weizmann, who came to feel at home in British society.

In Chaim Weizmann's first letters, as noted, he reveals a negative impression and a sense of foreignness in England. In March 1905, for example, he wrote from Manchester, where he had recently moved, to his fiancée in Geneva: 'England is a country of large-scale social contradictions; nowhere is this felt so strongly as here. I myself work hard, harder than ever, yet I see people around me working even harder and living less well.'

He goes on:

The insincerity, sham and hollowness of the surroundings is somehow more obvious nowadays. Everything is covered by a superficial polish but the inner reality is frightfully nasty. England is a country of apparent 'respectability', but evil deeds are committed beneath the cloak. Politics, personal intrigues, interests, they all blend, and it is difficult to determine where one ends and another begins.[40]

In other letters Weizmann writes about his impressions of the gloomy nature of life in England, of the English lifestyle, which was totally antithetical to his own ideas and feelings, and of his deep sense of foreignness despite his outward adjustment.[41] He also takes pains to stress that the reality he describes is not the product of a melancholy mood, or of a tendency to see everything in dismal colours, but rather a result of his observation of reality. England, he opines, is characterized by a materialistic, commercial existence, lacking in poetry and depth. In his eyes, English culture is inferior to German culture, representing the *Weltkultur*,[42] because 'English society as such lacks the intellectual vigor one finds in Germany or France'.[43]

After some time, however, he states that students of British universities are on a far superior level to those on the continent. Like Ahad Ha-Am and Brenner, he marvels at London, which he depicts as 'a giant, the city of cities'.[44]

His biographer, Jeudah Reinharz, has written that

> Weizmann could not have known that in England, he would encounter a culture that would forever stamp his character. For nearly all the remaining years of his life, England would be his physical and intellectual anchor.[45]

But, like Brenner and Ahad Ha'Am's biographers, he did not reconstruct the process in which these men became more familiar with and acclimatized to the English culture in which they lived. What, for example, did they read, other than newspapers? What theatre performances did they attend? Did they live in a kind of Jewish–Zionist bubble without paying heed to what was going on outside Jewish and Zionist circles? It is hard to believe these otherwise astute observers could have been indifferent to the larger surroundings.

David Vital writes that Weizmann's appreciation – but not his love – for England was accompanied by deferential esteem, and that 'it is doubtful whether he ever understood English ways as thoroughly as he believed he did'.[46]

Weizmann's copious letters, at least from the earlier period, suggest that this 'deferential esteem' arose from the sense of superiority of a man who was the product of a deeply rooted, rich Jewish culture and felt at home, as well, in continental European culture. Vital, of course, is right when he says that Weizmann 'like so many other members of the Russian-Jewish intelligentsia, held Britain in exceedingly high esteem: a free, liberal society that stood in strongest contrast to virtually all other societies and regimes in early twentieth-century Europe'.[47]

The examples cited here lead us to conclude that this essentially positive acquired attitude was shared by all parts of the Jewish–Russian intelligentsia, including liberals and socialists.[48] This does not mean that they felt a sense of spiritual affinity towards England or its history and culture; feelings were not involved in rationally taking stock of the positive foundations of English government and society.

What instilled in Weizmann his British orientation was less a growing sympathy for English culture, the first buds of his later Anglophilism, than his first-hand observation of the growing power of the British Empire and its standing in the international arena. This is what soon led him to recognize that (a) Zionism had to seek a way to win England's heart, and (b) any cooperation between Britain and Zionism had to be based on common interests. By the First World War, Weizmann had shaped more fully his perception of the character and workings of English politics, anchored in what has been defined as the English empiricist genius: namely, that the English did not necessarily operate on the basis of written documents, abstract formulas or a predetermined plan.[49]

This profound insight would underpin Zionist policy towards England in the coming years. If 'the English act slowly, are empirical, and it is difficult to bind them down to a formula', he wrote, then 'life' will have to be stronger than any formula or any promise.[50]

Another important insight Weizmann gained in the first years of his stay in England, shared by his rival Zeev Jabotinsky, was that England was led by an 'oligarchy of the ancient hereditary nobility', and everything was decided not in a party framework or by public opinion but by interests and personal relations within this closed circle. This meant that if it wanted to find the key to England's heart, Zionist diplomacy needed to make its way into this élite circle.

It is interesting to compare this with England's image in the

eyes of Herzl. English culture was not completely foreign to Herzl
– he had books by British philosophers as well as English literary
works in his personal library – but he did not feel any affinity to it.
Similarly, Herzl had only a superficial acquaintance with British
political affairs, certainly when compared to his deeper familiarity
with French politics, which he described as a laboratory of all the
political innovations in the modern world.[51] He also knew very
little about English culture. The only comparison he was able to
draw between France and England in England's favour was the
British parliamentary system. In his view, the rational parliamentary government of England had none of the flaws of the French
republican form of government, which he had covered as a journalist.[52]

What led Herzl to see England as a possible ally was not his
preference for the English political model and political tradition,
but rather Britain's imperial interests in the Near East. Upon
analysing these interests, Herzl concluded it might be possible to
persuade Britain that for ensuring the vital sea route to India it
would be important to have a buffer state under Jewish auspices in
Palestine.[53] This was in addition to his appreciation of England as a
conveyer of civilization to backward societies. As he wrote, British
imperialism 'is cleansing the East' and 'destroying benighted
customs'.[54] To support his pro-British orientation, Herzl claimed
that in 1896 he had seen England as the Archimedean lever one
must grasp in order to get Zionism moving on the right track. While
Israel Zangwill, too, explained this far-sighted approach as based
on recognition of England as the only European country free of
anti-Semitism and noted for its practical genius and financial stability,[55] there is no evidence in Herzl's earlier writings supporting
either this contention in early 1898 or Zangwill's explanation.

Jabotinsky's spiritual and cultural world was also consummately
'continental', although, like the contemporary Russian intelligentsia, he was familiar with the writings of British philosophers.
However, unlike Ahad Ha-Am or Weizmann, Jabotinsky was a journalist writing about cultural and political affairs. Hence his writings
on the new English environment differed from those of others, who
lived in a kind of Zionist–Jewish bubble and whose correspondence
with relatives and Zionist associates 'abroad' was far more intensive
than their contact with their English surroundings. When
Jabotinsky first arrived in England, as a war correspondent for the
Russian newspaper *Russkie Vedomosti*, in 1915 he began not only to

submit articles and news items on the Irish question, England at war and the British army and navy, but also on the theatre and literature, on English secondary schools, and the like.[56]

Two years later, Jabotinsky wrote from a Zionist-political vantage point – an intelligent Russian with a Westernized orientation. In his book *Turkey and the War*, published in London in 1917 by Fisher and Unwin, he insisted that the Zionists had no particular affection for France or England but, emotionally, their sympathy tended towards the French more than the British. Any Zionist preference for England as a political ally was therefore based on a realistic view of the world balance of power and on purely pragmatic long-term considerations. Unlike the French, the English did not tend to impose cultural standards on their colonies, while their rule was comparatively liberal. He later stated that another insight he had arrived at in those years regarding the English 'mentality' or, as he put it, 'their philosophy of life', was that the English tend to see everything as a 'game'. By which he meant they did not take even the most important things too seriously.[57]

Given this background, it would be wrong to say that East European Zionists arrived at the Balfour Declaration with a negative attitude towards Britain. But, on the other hand, they scarcely felt any special affinity either. The most one can say is that England was known to them through a selective mirror of images, some of which changed over time, while others remained fixed. Still, for purposes of diplomatic intercourse in the circumstances prevailing on the eve of the First World War, it was enough to have acquaintances and personal contacts in élite political and public circles. Entrée was crucial in order to place Zionism on Britain's political agenda and to turn it into a playing card.

Perhaps having a profound knowledge of the complexity of the political culture with which one is negotiating is not vital. Certainly, it carries less weight than the common interests that emerge in particular historical situations. Nor is psychological affinity to a familiar culture essential for rational analysis of political reality or in the choice of an ally. What truly matters is defining one's goal, accompanied by the political acumen to discern and then exploit opportunities that have opened.

In all the statements and writings of the Jewish intelligentsia and Zionist activists until 1917, there is no greater sign of deep spiritual affinity between Jews and England than the 19 November 1917 letter to Lord Balfour from Chaim Weizmann and Nachum

Sokolow. Writing in reaction to the Balfour Declaration, they state, among other things, that

> The Jewish people always regarded Great Britain as a bulwark of right and justice and of the defence of the weak against the strong. [Therefore,] no Government is more qualified and no people more called upon by its noble traditions to take the leading part in this work of civilization and national justice than are the people and Government of Great Britain.[58]

This rhetoric and the invented history accompanying it were meant to endow the pragmatic partnership with Britain created under the exigencies of the First World War with a moral and historical dimension. After the war it was also easier to regard Britain – not Germany – as the embodiment *par excellence* of the essential values of European civilization. Indeed, from a psychological standpoint, most Zionist leaders and activists continued to feel a close link to the continent. But after 1917 their appreciation of England grew as well – the inevitable result of political cooperation and deepening first-hand acquaintance. The need to understand character traits dictating its behaviour towards the Jewish national home in Palestine now became vital for Zionist aspirations.

## NOTES

I wish to thank Chava Modrick and Savion Roth-Liron whose works on this subject were of great assistance to me.

1. Benzion Novakhovichi (1856–1930), also known by the names Morris Vinchevsky and Leopold Benedict, was a socialist publicist, a native of the Kovno district, who lived in London for many years. See Yosef Klausner, *The History of Modern Hebrew Literature*, Vol. VI (Jerusalem, 1950), pp. 307–50.
2. *Kol Kitvei Y. C. Brenner* (Collected Writings of Y. C. Brenner), Vol. II (Tel Aviv, 1960), p. 10.
3. On the 'discovery of America' in Jewish nineteenth-century literature and public opinion, see Ben-Ami Feingold, 'The Haskalah Literature Discovered America', in Michal Oron (ed.), *Between History and Literature* (Tel Aviv University, 1983), pp. 91–104 (in Hebrew); Israel Bartal, 'Heavenly America: The USA as an Ideal Model for Nineteenth-Century East European Jews', in Mairiam Eliav-Feldon (ed.), *Following Columbus: America 1492–1992* (Jerusalem, 1996), pp. 511–22 (in Hebrew).
4. Israel Bartal, 'An Alternative Model' – France as a source of Influence for the modernization of East European Jewry (1772–1863), in Richard I. Cohen (ed.), *The French Revolution and its Impact* (Jerusalem, 1991), pp. 271–85 (in Hebrew).
5. See my previous essay, 'The Works of H. T. Buckle and Their Application by the Maskilim in Eastern Europe', *Zion*, NS 49, 4 (1984), pp. 401–12 (in Hebrew) It is interesting to note an unknown detail from Benjamin Zeev Herzl's biography. When he finished writing his booklet, 'The State of the Jews', on 21 March 1897, he sent a copy to Herbert Spencer, with a note saying that Spencer's great spirit was reflected in it.

Spenser's secretary replied, on 26 March, that owing to Spencer's poor state of health, he was unable to respond. See notes to the Hebrew translation of Herzl's journals, Theodor Herzl, *Die Judensache*, Vol. I (Jerusalem, 1997), p. 632, note 185. It seems to me that Herzl's desire to obtain reaction from Spenser indicates that there was a profound positivistic dimension in his worldview, one that contrasted with the romantic dimension, which also pervades his approach.

6. See his *A History of the Intellectual Development of Europe* (1861).
7. The impact of various writings by English intellectuals from the eighteenth century onwards on Jewish thought has been discussed in various works, but has not been the subject of a comprehensive study. For example, in the early 1970s, the radical *maskil* Judah Leib Levin read Adam Smith, Darwin, Spenser and Buckle and, inspired by them, formulated his own radical positivistic stance.
8. One example: David Yellin's Hebrew translation of Goldsmith's novel *Hamokhiach mivikfild (The Vicar of Wakefield)*, based on the German translation, was published in Warsaw in 1897. Ahad Ha'Am was critical of the choice and offered the opinion that it would have been preferable to translate Goldsmith's *The Citizen of the World*, Ahad Ha'Am, 'Sifrei Am', in *Al Parashat Derakhim* (At the Parting of the Ways) (Berlin, 1930), pp. 12–13 (in Hebrew). Benjamin Disraeli's novel *Tancred* was translated into Hebrew from the German translation, by Judah Leib Levin (Yehalel, 1844–1925) and published in Warsaw in two parts (1883/1884) under the title *Nes lagoyim*. On the debate about the book in the Jewish press and its influence, see Shmuel Werses, 'Nachman's Last Speech and its Sources', *Moznaim*, Jubilee issue, 1929–79 (April–May 1979), pp. 280–91 (in Hebrew)
9. This is the view of Anita Shapira, who writes that the labour movement in Palestine was imbued with 'a long-standing East European Jewish tradition' of hostility towards the West (including England), which was depicted as 'heartless, cold-tempered and unwilling to make any self-sacrifice'. She cites no support for this description, which is far from the truth, as we will see here. In any event, the Jews of Eastern Europe, including members of socialist movements, admired English rationalism and pragmatism, the English talent for getting things done, and the like. See Anita Shapira, 'Elements of the National Ethos in the Transition to Statehood', J. Reinharz *et al.* (eds), *Jewish Nationalism and Politics: New Perspectives* (Jerusalem/ Boston, 1996), p. 265 (in Hebrew).
10. On this distinction in the context of a familiarity with French culture and its influence see Yaacov Shavit, 'The Spirit of France' and 'French Culture', in 'The Jewish Yishuv in Eretz Yisrael (1882–1914)', *Cathedra*, 62 (Dec. 1991), pp. 37–53 (in Hebrew).
11. *Anglia* – the Hebrew name for England.
12. See J. Salmon, 'David Gordon and the Periodical *Ha-Maggid*', *Zion*, 40, 2 (1982), pp. 145–64; Yaacov Shavit, 'Window on the World', *Qesher*, 4 (November 1998), pp. 3–119 (in Hebrew).
13. See Shmuel Feiner, *Haskalah and History: The Emergence of a Modern Jewish Awareness of the Past* (Jerusalem, 1995), pp. 339–73 (in Hebrew); J. Klausner, *History of Modern Hebrew Literature*, Vol. III (Jerusalem, 1953), pp. 416–30 (in Hebrew).
14. Ibid., 24 February 1874.
15. Schulman, Part V, p. 49 (allusion to Isaiah 28:17).
16. Ibid., Part III, p. 22.
17. J. L. Levin, *Zikhronot vehegiyonot* (Memories and Studies), edited by Y. Sluzky (Jerusalem, 1968), p. 122 (in Hebrew).
18. Schulman, Part V, p. 49.
19. See also a series of articles entitled 'Observing the Actions of Britain in the Eastern Land, in 1857', whose publication began with the fifth issue in February 1858.
20. *Ha-Maggid*, 13 April 1859.
21. Schulman, Part V, p. 52.
22. Ibid., 1 January 1868. On the war against Emperor Theodore and British public opinion during the time, see Richard Pankhurst, 'Popular Opposition in Britain to British Intervention against Emperor Theodore of Ethiopia (1867–1868)', *Ethiopian Observer*, 16, 3 (1972), pp. 141–203. See also his article, 'The Emperor Theodore', ibid., 8, 3 (1964), pp. 267–72.
23. Ahad Ha'Am, *Kol kitvei Ahad Ha'Am*, (new edition, Berlin, 1930), Vol. 4, p. 84.

24. Part III, p. 176. But in a note, Schulman points to the anti-Semitic nature of *The Merchant of Venice*.
25. On Smolenskin, see Feiner, *Haskalah and History*, pp. 430–57.
26. P. Smolenskin, 'Am Olam', in *Ma'amarim* (Articles), Vol. I (Jerusalem, 1925), p. 138.
27. Ibid., pp. 22–3.
28. He writes: 'For in the House of Israel, the Torah was not given into the hands of the priests...and the rabbis are but the elected from among the people and they must do whatever is asked of them, and hence if the entire people wishes to reform or cancel, it has the authority to do so and no one has the right to protest'. Ibid., p. 32.
29. See his description of the Tories and the Whigs, ibid., p. 40 and note 1.
30. Ibid., Part 4, pp. 9–11.
31. Weizmann to Vera, *Weizmann Letters* (hereafter *WL*), Vol. 4 (Oxford University Press and Israel Universities Press, 1973), p. 41.
32. 'And I must pay visits to Westerners in accordance with all the rules of English "etiquette" (and don't imagine that is such a slight thing; there is a special "Shulchan Arukh" for such things – when to come and how to come and what to wear, etc.)', Ahad Ha-Am, *Igrot* (Letters), Vol. 4 (Tel Aviv, 1958), p. 101 (letter to J. C. Ravnizky of 20 Dec. 1907).
33. On Ahad Ha-Am in London, see Joseph Goldstein, *Ahad Ha-Am* (Jerusalem: Keter), 1992), pp. 327–92 (in Hebrew).
34. Letter dated 2 January 1908, *Igrot*, p. 102.
35. Ibid., pp. 97–8.
36. Ahad Ha-Am, *Igrot*, Vol. V (1959), p. 252. His description of the City as 'dark' is merely a figure of speech. Ahad Ha-Am's office near the Bank of England and his apartment in Gilford Street, in Bloomsbury, were large and comfortable. See Goldstein, ibid., pp. 328–9.
37. On Brenner in London, see Yizhak Baron, *The Life and Works of Brenner until the Publication of 'Hameorer' in London*, Vol. 1 (Tel Aviv: HaKibbutz Hameuchad, 1975), pp. 121–237 (in Hebrew)
38. *Kol kitvei Y. C. Brenner*, Vol. II, p. 10 (in Hebrew).
39. *Igrot B. Borochov* (Letters of B. Borochov) (1897–1917), M. Minz and Avia Balsahn (eds) (Tel Aviv, 1989), pp. 614–15.
40. *WL*, 3 (1972), p. 66.
41. See, for example, his letter to Vera dated 20 June 1905, *WL*, 4, p. 110: 'I can't acclimatize myself to the life here, nor can I imagine that we shall live here permanently.'
42. In September 1898, Herzl said to Philipp Zu Eulenburg, the German ambassador in Vienna, that 'the majority of Jews now belong to German culture' (26 Sept. 1898) and to the Grand Duke of Baden, he had previously explained (3 Sept.) that the Jews in Palestine would be an 'element of German culture in the Orient' (26 Sept. 1898), *Theodor Herzel's Tagebücher, Sweiter Band* (Berlin 1923), p. 117; 3 September, ibid., p. 110.
43. Letter 124, dated 8 September 1905, *WL*, 4, p. 142.
44. Letter dated 10 Oct. 1903, *WL*, 3, p. 48.
45. J. Reinharz, *Chaim Weizmann: The Making of a Zionist Leader* (Oxford University Press, 1985), p. 210.
46. David Vital, *Zionism: The Crucial Phase* (Oxford: Clarendon Press, 1987), p. 163.
47. Ibid., p. 361.
48. The Jewish Russian intelligentsia, like the Russians themselves, were pleased with the British historian Buckle's explanation of the causes of the despotism and backwardness of tsarist Russia in comparison to the freedom and progress of Britain. See Y. Shavit, *Zion*, 49, 4 (1984), pp. 401–12 (in Hebrew).
49. For one example which shows that this perception of the British mode of thinking, as based on empiricism rather than on 'abstract thought', had become a universal insight, see the article by the Chinese author and translator Lin Yutang entitled 'The English Think in Chinese'. He writes that the Chinese and English are noted for their, 'profound distrust in logic and extreme suspicion of arguments that are too perfect'. Moreover, he says that the British Empire was a product of the 'wonderfully robust common sense of the English and their utter freedom from logical reasoning', *Confucius Saw Nancy and Essays about Nothing* (Shanghai, 1937), pp. 92–111. I am

grateful to my colleague, Professor Yoav Ariel, who gave me the biographical details about the author of this book, which I was fortunate to come across in a bookstore during a visit to Beijing.

50. *WL*, 9, No. 108, p. 126; *WL*, 9, p. 98 (1977).

51. Herzl, 'France in 1894', an article written at the end of December 1894, in Theodor Herzl, *From Boulanger to Dreyfus 1891–1895*, Vol. III (Jerusalem, 1974), p. 935 (in Hebrew).

52. Ibid., Vol. I, p. 235. I have no evidence that Herzl or Weizmann read Edmund Burke, but their favourable attitude towards the dimension of tradition in British politics is essentially Burkean.

53. *Theodor Herzel's Tagebücher, Erster Band: Viertes Buch* (Berlin, 1922), pp. 571–3.

54. During a tour in Egypt he also wrote that British rule was bringing 'freedom and progress to the East, which in the end will arouse the subjects to rebel against [their rulers]'.

55. Quoted in Elhannan Oren, *Hibbat-Zion in Britain 1878–1898* (Tel Aviv, 1974), p. 11 (in Hebrew).

56. Unfortunately, the relevant issues have disappeared from the Jabotinsky Institute and I was unable to locate other copies. Therefore, at least for the moment, I cannot quote from their contents.

57. Jabotinsky, *Megillat hagedud* (Jerusalem, 1929). It may also be worth noting that this image of a nation which views 'life as a game' was widespread in European (including English) literature, in relation to the Italians.

58. *WL*, 8 (1977), No. 10, p. 8.

# 15 Jewish Political Culture and Zionist Foreign Policy

## ALAN DOWTY

In the course of a larger study of Israeli politics[1] even a convinced 'realist' comes to appreciate the continuity of a Jewish political culture colouring both internal and external relations. Admittedly, the impact of this culture is intangible, making it exceedingly difficult to measure, especially when it often parallels and reinforces outcomes that in any case realism would predict. The latter happens to be the case in the history of Zionism and Israel.

Since the larger earlier study focuses on the Israeli political system rather than foreign policy, this essay is suggestive and not definitive. It first identifies pre-Zionist patterns of Jewish politics, then traces these patterns in the early Zionist movement, and finally addresses aspects of Israel's foreign policy that are at least consistent with, and perhaps expressions of, this political culture.

Continuities in Jewish and Israeli historical annals and political outlooks have been overlooked, in part, because of the compartmentalization of both histories. Traditional Jewish historians such as Salo Baron, Jacob Katz, David Biale and Eli Lederhendler have very convincingly delineated the political milieu of Eastern European Jewry from which Zionism emerged, but usually without explicit linkage to later periods. Early Zionists, seeking to make a clean break with the Jewish past, attributed their own ideas and practices to prevailing non-Jewish ideologies of the time and saw themselves as beginning from a *tabula rasa*. Later Zionist historians have tended to write in this tradition, though some – Shmuel Almog, Daniel Elazar and Aharon Klieman, for example – have been especially sensitive to the pre-Zionist roots of Zionist theory and practice.

In this regard David Vital's three-volume history of Zionism stands out as a body of work that convincingly locates early Zionism in its Jewish historical context, and in so doing underlines both the continuities and the discontinuities between Jewish and Zionist history. It is only fitting, therefore, that in this *festschrift* in Vital's honour, special reference be made to evidence drawn from his work. In its own small way, this chapter demonstrates the riches to be mined from Vital's landmark study.

## BEFORE ZIONISM

Twentieth-century Jewish historians have challenged the notion that Jews have no political history apart from a lamentable chronicle of persecution suffering and powerlessness. The noted Jewish historian Salo Baron attacked the 'lachrymose' depiction of the Jewish past in 1928; an important recent study argues that Jews were not powerless, but exhibited 'a wide spectrum of persistent and ongoing political activism'.[2] To survive two millennia of hostility required not only spiritual strength but also a capacity for organization and for the assertion of collective interests – in other words, a capacity for politics. As David Biale contends, 'without some modicum of political strength and the ability to use it, the Jewish people would certainly have vanished'.[3]

Jews have often managed their own self-contained political system. The *Encyclopedia Judaica* lists dozens of cases of Jewish autonomy, in various forms, over the ages. 'The Jewish people', it has been argued,

> is most probably the only people which has realized the principle of personal autonomy in its life, creating in different countries under different political regimes certain forms of national autonomy and national organizations recognized in public law as state institutions.[4]

Wherever Jews lived, they held in common not only normative Jewish institutions but also patterns that arose from their position as a beleaguered minority: contention with a hostile environment; provision of needs that could be met only within the community; self-organization to minimize the intervention of outside authorities; and maintenance of relations with those authorities. Long before the modern concept of a 'nation', Jews acquired many of the attributes of nationality, including a sense of community and a felt need for collective expression.

The content of Jewish political culture as described in standard histories can be summarized in the following points:[5]

1. *Struggle for survival on both community and individual levels in a hostile environment.* The basic fact of Jewish politics was the very tenuousness of the framework within which politics was conducted. In the past, even the basic right of residence had been subject to petition and negotiation with local rulers. Jewish history generated a psychology characterized by 'the hypervigilance of the haunted, the alert scanning of the insecure, and the continuous suspiciousness of the vulnerable'.[6] Jews learned to dread events over which they had no control, and perfected great skill in detecting the potentially disastrous side of seemingly benign developments internally and externally. This *'gevalt syndrome'*, or 'doomsday' mentality, expresses as well as anything the deep-seated pessimism and anxiety rooted in the vicissitudes of Jewish history. In the traditional mindset, the outside was seen as 'totally strange and alien, the terrestrial manifestation of the *sitra ahara* or forces of evil'.[7]

2. *Self-regulation through well-developed legal, judicial and legislative mechanisms.* The other side of closure was the forging of a remarkable cohesion within Jewish communities. In Vital's words, 'the hold of the community over its individual members – possibly the greatest of the forces making for Jewish survival through centuries of the Dispersion – remained extremely potent for the majority of Jews well into the present century'.[8]

   There is no systematic political theory in Jewish thought, but the separateness of Jewish life was to prove fertile ground for acceptance of the principle of the nation-state as the basic unit of world politics. Jews already had extensive experience in organizing their communal life, and in maintaining boundaries between it and the larger world. One aspect of this was a strong presumption against revelations likely to damage the Jewish community. Habits of secrecy, and of intimate and confidential modes of operation, were deeply ingrained. Special contempt is reserved in tradition for the informer (*malshin*) who reveals damaging information to outside authorities; Jewish law provides for the trial and punishment of those guilty of this threatening act. The right of recourse to outside authority was reserved for community officials only, and this right was in a sense the defining attribute of their superior authority within that community.[9]

3. *Enforcement without recourse, in most cases, to coercive authority.* The voluntary character of Jewish self-government was of decisive importance. Jewish communities in tsarist Russia were backed by state enforcement in some cases – mainly the collection of taxes – and were sometimes granted other means of compulsion such as the seizure of property or the imposition of fines. The organized Jewish community could also impose a *herem*, or excommunication, which was a very serious sanction in the pre-Emancipation period when there was no Jewish life outside the community. Thus, 'communal elders could still force a rebellious member to his knees by refusing him certain religious services, such as circumcision, rabbinical wedding, or the religious burial in consecrated ground'.[10] But enforcement depended less on formal sanctions than on the reputation of the rabbis issuing decrees, on public opinion and pressure, and on the shared interest in offering no pretext for outside intervention. This sufficed to maintain a modicum of public order, but it rested on a large measure of voluntary consent. The fact was that there was no obligatory final authority within the Jewish community.[11]

4. *The development of formal and informal power-sharing.* Since it was voluntary, Jewish self-government also had to be inclusive. Given the need for unity against a hostile environment, there was a strong incentive to give all groups in the community a stake in the system. The principle of proportionality in power and benefits was widely understood and applied; elections were regularly conducted even though electoral politics was unknown in the surrounding societies. Elections to important positions were for fixed terms, thus upholding the accountability of those elected and providing for rotation in office.[12] Human rights were also relevant. For example, Jewish law protects the right to liberty and security of person, the right to property, freedom of speech and of movement, and even social and cultural rights such as the right to work, the right to an education, and the right to rest and leisure. Jewish law is especially strong on legal and judicial safeguards, with provisions that match or surpass those in modern liberal democratic states.[13]

5. *A pluralistic politics, often with serious gaps between the formal power structure and actual influence patterns.* The co-existence of an over-arching external system and a sphere of communal politics guaranteed the existence of competing laws, jurisdictions and authorities. Also, each community chose 'secular' officials as well as a rabbinic leadership, and the lines of authority between the two were often unclear. Further divisions within the Jewish communities came in the eighteenth and nineteenth centuries as a result of new spiritual and intellectual currents such as *hasidism* and the *haskala*. The pluralism of late nineteenth-century Jewish life, in the Russian setting, was striking. Groups of all types proliferated: artisan guilds, mutual aid societies, cultural associations, political parties, educational groups, savings and loan associations, defence organizations, charitable associations, burial societies, and workers' groups. In the late tsarist period, according to one estimate, each Jewish community had on the average some 20 different associations, while the large city of Vilna, in 1916, had a total of 160.[14]

6. *A contentious style of politics.* As Shlomo Avineri has pointed out, earlier habits help to explain not only the origins of Israeli democracy but also 'some of the lack of elegance which accompanies it...the Israeli Knesset sometimes resembles an unruly synagogue meeting more than the serene atmosphere of Westminster'.[15] The tradition of opposition to power, or basic disrespect for authority, goes beyond matters of parliamentary procedure. Jewish law also put clear limits on majority rule, providing that the minority must be heard and even institutionalizing the role of dissent; it had a tendency towards 'principled political anarchism'.[16] The pluralism of institutions, plus a prevailing suspicion of all centralized power, gave rise to an attitude of expediency towards authority *within* the community as well as that outside, defined by Ehud Sprinzak as a pattern of 'illegalism', or of expediency towards the law.[17] Vital quotes from an 'uncharacteristically frank' admission by an 1888 Russian government commission that, in the light of official repression,

> it is not surprising, therefore, that the Jews, trained in the spirit of a century-long repressive legislation, have remained in the category of those subjects who are less exact in the

discharge of their civic duty, who shirk their obligations towards the state, and do not fully join Russian life.[18]

7. *Lack of guidelines for non-Jewish minorities.* Jewish law and Jewish politics within the community applied only to Jews. The essence of Jewish law towards 'strangers' was humanity; the idea of civic equality of Jews and non-Jews in a Jewish society was as unthinkable as the idea of equal status for Jews in non-Jewish society was at that time. Furthermore, the injunction of humane treatment was geared to the *individual* and not to non-Jewish groups who might claim recognition of their collective identity. Recognition of the rights of individual aliens to humane treatment did not provide for any collective legal or political expression of non-Jewish identity, and the matter was never seriously tested under Diaspora conditions. Jewish communities never had under their jurisdiction large non-Jewish populations seeking to maintain their own collective identity, and thus Jewish political traditions were singularly unequipped to deal with such a situation.

Though not 'democratic' by modern standards, these governing practices did provide a foundation for the growth of democratic institutions. They accomplished this by providing modes of participation that reflected the essentially voluntary nature of community membership, by fostering (before the appearance of modern liberal political theory) an attitude of scepticism towards all authority, and by developing a body of law that *de facto* mandated important basic human rights. However, Jewish politics also contained serious sources of weakness. One was the long habit of secrecy, of concealment and closing off from the outside. A second was the absence of 'civic habits' developed elsewhere, and the development, instead, of an attitude of expediency towards the law. But perhaps the most glaring weakness of Jewish politics derived from the very strength of its sense of community; there was little guidance or experience in dealing with groups who were not an integral part of this community.

## JEWISH POLITICS IN EARLY ZIONISM

Whatever the strengths or weaknesses of this legacy, however, the Zionist movement in theory sought to erase it. Whether subscribing to nationalist, socialist or liberal ideologies, Jews of Central and Eastern Europe in the late nineteenth century were seeking a sharp break with the past.

They filled the ranks of non-Jewish revolutionary movements in disproportionate numbers, and those who rallied to the Zionist call also saw themselves as being in 'revolt' against past patterns of Jewish history. Zionists sought to escape from the particularism of the Jewish past and to rejoin history by recasting Jewish life in new universal moulds provided by modern ideology. In David Vital's apt phrase, they wished 'to extricate the Jews from a rhythm of national history such that the quality of their life at all levels was determined in the first instance by the treatment meted out to them by others ... to cease to be object and become subject'. They felt that 'the course of Jewish history must be reversed'; the significance of Zionism was nothing less than 'the re-entry of the Jewish people into the world political arena'.[19]

Traditional Jewish life was seen, with considerable exaggeration, as politically impotent, as a manifestation of weakness inseparable from the condition of exile. In some cases, the dissociation with the Jewish past reached extreme proportions. Theodor Herzl himself largely accepted the antisemitic portrait of Jews as avaricious, unprincipled, parasitic and vulgar, while arguing that it was Christian oppression that had so deformed the Jewish character.[20] The basic logic of this orientation is best demonstrated, perhaps, by those who took it to the very limit. The Canaanite movement, active in the *Yishuv* (the Jewish community in Palestine) during the 1940s, rejected any connection with Jews or Judaism and sought to assimilate with the indigenous Arabs as a new Hebrew nation. On the other hand, one of the most common themes of Israeli literature has been an attack on Zionism for having detached Jews from their roots; a well-known example is Yudkeh's long and anguished 'sermon' against Zionism's failings in a famous short story by Haim Hazaz.[21]

Furthermore, while Herzl and some of the more Westernized Zionists may have had little feel or regard for Jewish tradition, their followers in Eastern Europe were far closer to it. As Vital reminds us, most of Russian Jewry's traditional and established leaders 'remained opposed to any attempt at a *radical* reordering of Jewish life'.[22] Indeed,

> every settled thing in Jewry militated against a radical approach to its ills: habit of mind, precedent, the Tradition

itself in its most explicit forms, the invertebrate, powerless (and partly voluntary) structure of the nation, and the private views and purposes of a majority...of the Jews themselves.[23]

This set the stage for the protracted struggle between Herzl's 'political' approach, uninformed by Jewish habits and experience, and the 'practical' approach of Russian Zionists whose caution reflected the harsh realities and traditionalism of their milieu.

One of the major contributions of Vital's work on Zionism has been to put Herzl's role, as central and decisive as it was, into more modest perspective. The *Hibbat Zion* tradition of practical settlement work that preceded Herzl continued to dominate Eastern European Zionism – its largest branch – after his emergence, given the decentralized character of the movement. Eventually it again dominated the entire movement, even before Herzl's death, when he lost control of the day-to-day affairs of the movement following the bitter sixth congress (the 'Uganda' congress) of 1903. Herzl's reign was in a sense a brief deviation from the movement's major thrust:

> The six years of Herzl's supremacy may be regarded as an interlude between two much more extended periods, an interlude of peculiarity and abnormality in which the true nature of the movement and the real wishes of its adepts were temporarily swept out of sight and mind by the extraordinary man who had placed himself so unexpectedly at its head.[24]

After Herzl, the Zionist movement, 'hitherto so different from most other contemporary Jewish movements and tendencies by virtue of the coherence which he imposed on it, came somewhat to resemble its rivals'.[25] The centre of gravity shifted back to Russia. Local branches became more autonomous. The scope of the 'revolution' was drastically reduced. As Ahad Ha'Am wrote in 1911, 'a new generation has arisen...for which Zionism is *the very same national ideal in all its ramifications* for which we fought Herzlism all those years'.[26]

Eastern European Zionists did not reject the past outright, but combed it for what might be useful in building the future; 'continuity was crucial: the Jewish society at which they aimed...had to contain within it the major elements of the Jewish heritage'.[27] Furthermore, this was 'in an age when it was extremely rare for a

Jew in Russia and Poland, however much of a secularist in conscious thought, to be without some grounding – and for the most part, a very solid grounding – in the law, traditions, and history of his people'.[28] The past was invoked and reinterpreted in order to restore Jewish dignity (as in the cults of the Maccabees, Masada or Bar-Kochba); precedents for 'new' Zionist departures were sought in the historical sources. The relationship to history may very well be selective, and there was a marked tendency to revere antiquity while reviling Diaspora life, but on the whole few Zionists rejected all connection with Jewish history. As the leading study of the subject concludes, 'between the two poles of continuity and rejection, Zionism established itself on a broad common base best described as dialectical continuity with the past'.[29]

It was unrealistic to believe that a Jewish state could be established without reference to four millennia of Jewish history. Tradition supplied Zion itself as the focus of Zionism; even for the most secular of Jews, only Palestine had the power to mobilize the imagination of would-be settlers. Holidays and national symbols were inevitably drawn from the past, even if attempts were made to alter their content and significance. The very legitimacy of the entire enterprise rested, in the end, on Jewish history and religion, a factor that grew in importance as conflict with the Arab population developed. And if this was the case for the secular Eastern European Zionists who settled in Palestine during the early days, it was that much more the case for religious and non-European Jews who were already settled there, or who came later. Among these populations, the primordial tie to Judaism was strong, while the impact of revolutionary ideologies, including the model of the civic state, was very faint.

The 'dialectical continuity' with the past was often obscured by the rhetoric of revolution and universalism. But even Herzl himself was capable of relapsing 'into the set and mode of thought in which particularity and specificity are celebrated as a matter of course' (with the dialectical process also reflected in Herzl's depiction of his utopian state of the future as an 'Old–New' land).[30] Cultural Zionists, following Ahad Ha'am, also sought to revolutionize Jewish life, but by drawing explicitly on Jewish sources of spiritual renewal, and thus founding 'not merely a state of Jews but truly a Jewish state'.[31] Even the most radical Zionist revolutionaries demonstrated links to tradition in subtle ways: in focusing on a redemptive process (albeit a secular one), in showing little interest in political programmes not centred on Jewish interests, and in their 'mildness' as revolutionaries in the Jewish context (where the emphasis was on building rather than destroying).[32]

There were also certain senses in which Zionism, for all its universalist aspirations, could never escape the particularist mould in which it was shaped. One of Vital's most arresting insights, drawn in part from Max Nordau, was that 'Jews were now faced with a dilemma from which there was no escape. They had no choice but finally to decide whether they wished to remain a nation or not.'[33] In other words, the reality of their pre-existing 'nation-hood' would be entirely lost if assimilation as individuals into the new order of nation-states took place without a Jewish state.

Zionism was also closely attuned to one of the deepest well-springs of Jewish feeling in its assumption of a hostile external world and its stress on the need for self-reliance. The Russian pogroms of 1881–84, with the May laws of 1882 that pushed Jews further into pauperization and alienation, undercut the hopes for reform in Russia or support from non-Jewish sources. The pogroms of 1905, with an even heavier hand of governmental sponsorship, were followed by the outlawing of the Zionist movement in Russia in 1907. All of this only reinforced 'the cardinal, very ancient rule of conduct in Jewish public affairs that Jews as a category and Jewry as a group should strive to avoid involvements in the conflicts of other nations – of *the nations (ha-goyim)*, as the Jews traditionally termed them'.[34] This was reflected in the reaction to the First World War, when Zionist leaders were very slow to respond to the strategic potential in pursuing a course of action designed to bring about the collapse of the Ottoman Empire and open up new possibilities in *Eretz-Yisrael* (the biblical Land of Israel).

In a similar manner the early settlers, and more so the Zionist leaders abroad, demonstrated a striking disregard for the presence of a non-Jewish population in *Eretz-Yisrael*. Speaking of the first *aliya*, Vital notes that 'the question of the future relations between the Jews of *Eretz-Yisrael* on the one hand and the members of other ethnic and religious communities in the country on the other did not register in their minds.'[35] When frictions developed between Jewish settlements and the Arab population, the tendency was to attribute it to local and isolated causes and to 'damp down conflict as it arose'; until the Young Turks' revolution of 1908 brought general Arab hostility to Jewish immigration into the open, Zionist leaders remained on the whole 'sanguine and uncomprehending'.[36]

Their naivety was demonstrated in quaint efforts to influence Arab opinion by purchasing advertisements in Arab newspapers, as though the differences between the two communities were nothing but a matter of misunderstanding.[37]

The revolutionary content of Zionism was attenuated in the new settlements of *Eretz-Yisrael* not only by the habits and traditions that new immigrants brought with them, but also by new realities to which doctrine was ambivalent or even irrelevant. In the early settlements of *Hibbat Zion*, 'there was far too smooth a carry-over... of the mental and organizational habits of the properly philanthropic institutions of the community – which often represented everything that Hibbat Zion was in revolution against'.[38] The structure of the new *Yishuv* 'was analogous to the old pattern of the informal rabbinical hierarchy'; the early attempts to coordinate among *Hibbat Zion* branches in Russia, at the Kattowitz conference in 1884, produced a loose organization dependent on consensus and divided, like the Jewish communities from which it emerged, between the traditionalists and the modernists.[39]

Indeed, the very fact of Jewish settlement in Palestine was more a product of circumstance than of ideological appeal. As Jacob Katz notes, the aim of uprooting a people and replanting them elsewhere 'was beyond the strength of the National idea in itself'.[40] It took place only when persecutions and pogroms in Eastern Europe accomplished the uprooting. Even then, very little of the 'replanting' was shaped by the national idea; of the two and a half million Jews forced out of Russia between 1880 and 1914, only about 70,000 arrived in Palestine, and many of these did not remain.

This process of self-selection had crucial implications. So long as other destinations were available to the vast majority of uprooted Jews who were not devout Zionists, then the new *Yishuv* would represent a high concentration of the most ideologically committed. Thus the more revolutionary elements of the Jewish intelligentsia were able to establish the conceptual and institutional framework that prevailed for decades and absorbed later mass immigrations of non-ideologized Jews who arrived simply because they had nowhere else to go. In a sense, the gap was not closed until the 'breakthrough of society' in the 1977 electoral upheaval.[41] At this point, it could be said that Zionism had met Vital's definition of 'this last great effort to erect a bridge for Jewry between past and future'.[42]

## CONTINUITY IN FOREIGN POLICY

Among the aspects of Israeli foreign and defence policy that might be linked illustratively to Jewish political culture, two stand out most prominently: attitudes towards security, and the theme of separation.

The primacy of security concerns in Israel needs little comment, and clearly it meshes very well with proclivities rooted in the Jewish past. The threat of danger from the outside was to a great extent what made consensus and voluntarism work in Jewish communities. Increased threat usually forced Jews to bond more closely together. Finding themselves surrounded by enemies did not strike Israelis as a novel occurrence; to the contrary, it evoked a long collective memory of similar threats, or threats seen as similar. It may also help explain why 64 per cent of Israelis sampled in 1969, and 72 per cent in 1981, said that they preferred strong leadership over 'all the laws and debates', and why in 1990, 34 per cent agreed that Israel was 'too democratic' to a very large or certain extent.[43] The high value placed on national consensus has been reflected in various ways: in the formation of national unity governments, in the call for a 'Jewish majority' on sensitive issues, and in repeated efforts by members of different parties to formulate agreed principles for the future of the peace process.

The sense of an unfriendly world also influenced the interpretation of international conflict. There was a tendency to deny any objective reason for Arab hostility. Wars with Arab states were not seen as events in international politics rooted in a territorial dispute, but as acts of primordial hostility that evoked images of the Holocaust and other historical attempts simply to kill Jews. Acts of terror against Israeli civilians were seen not as *political* actions designed (however brutally) to achieve Palestinian national aims, but as plain and simple acts of antisemitism. On a broader scale, 68 per cent of Israelis surveyed in 1987 agreed that 'world criticism of Israeli policy stems mainly from antisemitism'.[44] As Asher Arian summarizes,

> even mainstream Zionist parties still tend to reject a geopolitical explanation of international conflict and persist in analysing the Israeli–Arab conflict in the spirit, and often in the lexicon, of the persecution suffered by Jews in most European countries and in some of the countries of the Moslem world.[45]

Given perceived vulnerability and self-reliance, Israelis adopted an active defence. They stressed the need to anticipate, to seize the initiative, and to take the war to the other's territory. But if Israel tended to active defence on a military level, it showed an aversion to risk-taking in politics or diplomacy. Israeli diplomacy tended to be reactive, responding to events and shunning bold initiatives. There was a distinct distaste for diplomatic methods in general, given the meager resources that Israel possessed for playing the diplomatic game and natural suspicion of a process in which Jews had little experience and for which history had not taught them to have high regard.[46]

Because of this ingrained distrust of the outside world, both Zionist and Israeli diplomacy have also typically (and somewhat illogically) sought a sympathetic outside patron or protector. David Ben-Gurion, in what has been termed 'the Ben-Gurion complex', felt that Israel should not go to war without the backing of at least one outside power.[47] The centrality of the US connection in more recent years needs no emphasis.

Israeli scepticism in foreign policy, rooted in traditional Jewish insecurity, also fits well with 'realist' interpretations of international relations. Brecher refers to it as 'the triumph of realism in the foreign policy élites – the acceptance of self-interest as the supreme basis of foreign policy'.[48] But this needs to be qualified. While Israeli attitudes correspond to realism in the common senses of pragmatism and lack of illusions, as well as the political-scientific sense of the importance of power and of self-interest, they contradict realist assumptions on the importance of objective factors over subjective forces such as racial hatreds, misperceptions and ideology. In their more extreme ultra-nationalist versions, they even create a 'meta-reality' totally divorced from the reality they purportedly evoke.

The theme of insecurity in Jewish life is in fact intertwined with the second theme of separation. Despite the search for a powerful patron or protector, Jews must in the end rely on themselves. International support or guarantees cannot be trusted as a reliable basis for national security. The only reliable outside allies were the Jewish communities of the world. Michael Brecher refers to this deep-seated attitude as the 'two-camp' thesis: the bifurcation of the world into Jewish and non-Jewish camps, with the latter seen as basically hostile.[49] Connected to this is the denigration of international bodies such as the United Nations, which Ben-Gurion dismissed as '*oom-shmoom*'.[50] A typical expression was that of Prime

Minister Yitzhak Shamir in 1988 when an international tribunal ruled in Egypt's favour on the Taba dispute: 'The UN, the world court, international arbitration, or international conference – it's always against us'.[51] Paradoxically, the Israeli public and media often display great sensitivity to external opinion even while denigrating its importance. In addition, the focus on the 'friendliness' or 'hostility' of outsiders, seen as an index of their basic attitudes towards Jews, leads to an extraordinary focus on the attributes of specific foreign leaders rather than on impersonal forces driving policy.

The 'two-camp' thesis also has important implications for relations with Jewish communities outside Israel. This goes beyond the maintenance of close ties; there is a sense of mutual responsibility. Israeli diplomats are viewed as emissaries also to local Jewish communities, in a way that has no exact parallel elsewhere. Israel's relations with other nations have often been affected by the interests of local Jewish communities. Its attitude towards other nations has, in fact, been greatly influenced by whether ongoing close relationships with Jews within that nation are possible.

Control of the media also evokes the traditional sensitivity to how the community is seen on the outside. Amos Elon calls this 'a provincial determination not to let the skeletons out', reminiscent of the biblical injunction 'to tell it not in Gath and publish it not on the streets of Ashkelon'.[52] A striking parallel to this verse was expressed by an Israeli chief of staff, Rafael Eytan, who declared that 'nothing which might give satisfaction to an Arab should be allowed to be published by the Israeli news media'.[53] The role of secrecy is also expressed in an oft-noted attachment to 'backstage diplomacy'. Klieman recounts, for example, the fact that Moshe Dayan as foreign minister in 1977 undertook four secret foreign trips within one month.[54] This also ties in with the penchant for reliance on personalized diplomacy and unofficial special emissaries, as seen in the activities of Herzl, Weizmann, Nahum Goldman, Samuel Bronfman and others.

The impact of Jewish politics is also clear in relations with non-Jews. Just as Zionism had no clear guidelines for dealing with Palestinian Arabs, the State of Israel never settled on a clear choice between integration or separate development for the Arab minority within Israel. The willingness to deny civil rights to Arab citizens has been confirmed in a broad range of studies, sometimes in striking fashion. A 1985 survey carried out by Sammy Smooha, found that 50 per cent of Jewish respondents favoured encouraging Arabs to leave Israel, and only 27 per cent clearly opposed a ban on Arab political demonstrations.[55] A Modi'in Ezrahi poll in June 1989 found that 73 per cent of the Israeli Jewish public believed there should be 'one law' for Jews and Arabs in Israeli courts – but 53 per cent, nevertheless, favoured a then-current idea (later dropped) to establish fenced compounds to hold Arab workers from the West Bank and Gaza as they entered or left Israel![56]

Obviously the situation was even more difficult in the West Bank and Gaza Strip, occupied by Israel since 1967. Integrating these territories threatened to dilute the Jewishness of Israel itself. Continuing rule over another people also runs counter to the traditional Jewish suspicion of power and resistance to strong authority, from within or without. Though the experience of being powerless and persecuted does not necessarily produce tolerance and virtue once one has acquired power, the weight of Jewish history could not be entirely ignored. It is no surprise that the most telling critiques of Israeli occupation came from within Israel itself.

Even in the realm of security, the case for separation rather than integration looked stronger with the passage of time. While an independent Palestinian state in the West Bank and Gaza would pose serious strategic issues, so did continued occupation of that area. Strategists pointed out that a settlement with the Palestinians, by furthering the trend among Arab states to drop out of the conflict, would lessen the greater dangers that Israel faced. It would also strengthen Israel's international position immeasurably, leading to final universal acceptance and legitimacy. At some point, security arguments alone became a strong incentive for 'territorial compromise' (under the right conditions) in the territories.[57]

By the mid-1990s it was clear that, in the words of one study, 'the overall tendency among the Israeli political elites is to support greater separation between Israelis and Palestinians'.[58] Even the Likud was not totally assimilationist, in that its proposed programme of autonomy aimed for maximum separation consistent with continued Israeli sovereignty over the West Bank and Gaza. The strategy of separation was also a strategy for reducing the Arab–Israeli conflict to its pre-1948 intra-Palestinian core. By allowing Palestinian Arab self-determination to be realized within Palestine, alongside Israel, the major cause and incentive for external Arab involvement would be neutralized. Israel would remain in a very strong position in dealing with a separate Palestinian entity that in itself posed no military threat (apart from the problem of terrorism, to which continued occupation was also not a solution). The Israeli public has returned to the conventional wisdom that good fences make good neighbours; roughly 75 per cent agreed in 1995 with the statement that 'from Israel's point of view, also in a state of peace, it is preferable to have a clear and closed border between it and the Palestinian entity, in order to create maximum separation between Israelis and Palestinians'.[59]

Insecurity still permeates Jewish politics. The establishment of a Jewish state transferred this fear and mistrust onto a new and unaccustomed plane. Nevertheless, the sense of being 'a people that dwells alone' still pervades the nation. Israelis are reluctant to recognize success even when it is apparent. The historic achievement of at least *de facto* acceptance by most of the Arab world and contractual peace on the country's two longest borders are hardly felt. Despite tremendous change for the better in Israel's security position, and enviable success economically and otherwise, the *gevalt* syndrome still prevails. The capacity to extract gloomy premonitions from even the most promising turn of events remains undiminished.

## NOTES

1. Alan Dowty, *The Jewish State: A Century Later* (University of California Press, 1998).
2. David Biale, *Power and Powerlessness in Jewish History* (Schocken Books, 1986), p. 6; Biale cites Baron's views (from 'Ghetto and Emancipation', *Menorah Journal*, 14 (June 1928), pp. 515–26) on p. 211, fn. 4.
3. Biale, *Power and Powerlessness*, p. 6.
4. M. Silberfarb, *The Kehillah Work, Its Potentialities and Prospects* (1911) (in Yiddish), quoted in A. L. Patkin, *The Origins of the Russian-Jewish Labour Movement* (F. W. Cheshire, 1947), p. 246; see also Dan V. Segre, *A Crisis of Identity: Israel and Zionism* (Oxford University Press, 1980), pp. 58–9; and Mitchell Cohen, *Zion and State Nation: Class and the Shaping of Modern Israel* (Basil Blackwell, 1987) pp. 47–8.
5. For a fuller account of 'Jewish Politics', see Dowty, *The Jewish State*, Chapter 2.
6. Jay Y. Gonen, *A Psychohistory of Zionism* (Mason / Charter, 1975), p. 32.
7. Jacob Katz, *Tradition and Crisis: Jewish Society at the End of the Middle Ages* (Schocken Books, 1971), p. 27.
8. David Vital, *The Origins of Zionism* (Clarendon Press, 1975), p. 33.
9. Eli Lederhendler, *The Road to Modern Jewish Politics* (Oxford University Press, 1989), pp. 12–13.
10. Salo W. Baron, *The Russian Jew Under Tsars and Soviets* (Macmillan, 1976), p. 105; see also Katz, *Tradition and Crisis*, pp. 98–101.
11. Katz, *Tradition and Crisis*, pp. 83, 170–1; Isaac Levitats, *The Jewish Community in Russia, 1844–1917* (Posner and Sons, 1981), pp. 202–3; Mark Zborowski and Elizabeth Herzog, *Life Is with People: The Culture of the Shtetl* (Schocken Books, 1952), pp. 219–20.
12. Katz, *Tradition and Crisis*, pp. 87–8, 106–10; Daniel J. Elazar, 'The Kehillah: From its Beginning to the End of the Modern Epoch', in Sam N. Lehman-Wilzig and Bernard Susser (eds), *Public Life in Israel and the Diaspora* (Bar-Ilan University Press, 1981),

p. 39. While this description applies to Eastern Europe, Jewish communities in the Islamic world also had democratic and competitive elements in their internal governance. See S. D. Goitein, 'Political Conflict and the Use of Power in the World of the Geniza', in Daniel J. Elazar, *Kinship and Consent: The Jewish Political Tradition and its Contemporary Uses* (University Press of America, 1983), pp. 169–81.

13. Haim H. Cohn, *Human Rights in Jewish Law* (Ktav Publishing House, 1984), pp. 17–19 and *passim*.
14. Levitats *The Jewish Community in Russia*, pp. 70–1, 204–5; Baron, *The Russian Jew*, p. 100.
15. Shlomo Avineri, *The Historical Roots of Israel Democracy* (Second Annual Guest Lecture, Kaplan Centre for Jewish Studies and Research, University of Cape Town, 31 March 1985), p. 8.
16. S. N. Eisenstadt, *Jewish Civilization: The Jewish Historical Experience in a Comparative Perspective* (State University of New York Press, 1992), p. 75.
17. Sprinzak, 'Every Man Whatsoever is Right in His Own Eyes – Illegalism in Israeli Political Culture: Theoretical and Historical Footnotes to the Pollard Affair and the Shin Beth Cover Up', in Gregory S. Mahler (ed.), *Israel after Begin* (State University of New York Press, 1990), pp. 55–7; Jacob Katz, *Exclusiveness and Tolerance: Studies in Jewish–Gentile Relations in Medieval and Modern Times* (Oxford University Press, 1961), p. 52; Zborowski and Herzog, pp. 232–3.
18. S. M. Dubnov, *History of the Jews in Russia and Poland* (Philadelphia, 1916–20), Vol. II, p. 364, quoted in Vital, p. 30.
19. Vital, *The Origin of Zionism* pp. 5, 349–50; Vital, *Zionism: The Crucial Phase* (Clarendon Press, 1987), p. vii; see also Biale, p. 4. On Zionism as collective assimilation, see Boas Evron, *Jewish State or Israeli Nation?* (Indiana University Press, 1995), pp. 108, 207.
20. Jacques Kornberg, *Theodore Herzl: From Assimilation to Zionism* (Indiana University Press, 1993), pp. 21, 66, 154, 162.
21. Haim Hazaz, 'The Sermon', in Hazaz, *Seething Stones: Stories, Collected Writings of Haim Hazaz* (Am Oved, 1980). For an analysis from a right-wing perspective see Dov Landau, 'Who's Afraid of Yudkeh's Sermon', *Nativ*, 2 (January 1989), pp. 71–81.
22. Vital, *The Origins of Zionism*, p. 72.
23. Vital, *Zionism: The Crucial Phase*, p. 4.
24. Vital, *Zionism: The Formative Years* (Clarendon Press, 1982), pp. 45–6; see also pp. vi–vii, 9, 313, 315, 344–5, 411.
25. Ibid., p. 367.
26. Quoted in Vital, *Zionism: The Crucial Phase*, p. 59; see also Vital, *Zionism: The Formative Years*, pp. 367, 411, 414, 417, 477.
27. Vital, *Zionism: The Formative Years*, pp. 228–9, 356–7.
28. Vital, *The Origins of Zionism*, p. 148.
29. Shmuel Almog, *Zionism and History: The Rise of a New Jewish Consciousness* (St Martin's Press and the Magnes Press, 1987), pp. 309, 305–8.
30. Vital, *Zionism: The Formative Years*, p. 353; see also Kornberg, *Herzl*, pp. 131, 160–1.
31. Ahad Ha'am, 'The Jewish State and the Jewish Problem' (1897), in Hans Kohn (ed.), *Nationalism and the Jewish Ethic: Basic Writings of Ahad Ha'am* (Schocken Books, 1962), p. 79; see also Steven Zipperstein, *Elusive Prophet: Ahad Ha'am and the Origins of Zionism* (University of California Press, 1993), pp. 138–9.
32. Vital, *Zionism: The Formative Years*, pp. 172–3, 398; Daniel J. Elazar, *Israel: Building a New Society* (Indiana University Press, 1986), p. 134. Elazar maintains that, given the intensity of their ideological fervour, 'only their common Jewishness, which led them to certain perceptions about the necessity for unity at some point and which gave them a useful cultural inheritance for the promotion of the requisite unity, kept them from going the divisive or repressive way of their non-Jewish peers from the same Eastern European milieu', ibid., p. 40.
33. Vital, *Zionism: The Crucial Phase*, p. 9.
34. Ibid., p.121; see also pp. 129, 136, 365.
35. Vital, *The Origins of Zionism*, p. 87.
36. Vital, *Zionism: The Crucial Phase*, pp. 377, 379.
37. Vital, *The Origins of Zionism*, p. 73.
38. Vital, *The Origins of Zionism*, p. 150.

39. Ibid., pp. 155, 167, 172–4.
40. Jacob Katz, *Emancipation and Assimilation: Studies in Modern Jewish History* (Gregg International, 1972), p. 142.
41. Peter Medding, *The Founding of Israeli Democracy 1948–1967* (Oxford University Press, 1990), p. 229.
42. Vital, *Zionism: The Crucial Phase*, p. 375.
43. Asher Arian, *Security Threatened: Surveying Israeli Opinion on Peace and War* (Cambridge University Press, 1995), pp. 233, 237.
44. Ibid., p. 174.
45. Ibid., p. 27.
46. Avi Shlaim and Avner Yaniv, 'Domestic Politics and Foreign Policy in Israel', *International Affairs,* 56 (April 1980), pp. 242–62, emphasize the internal causes of a conservative, risk-averse diplomacy.
47. Michael Brecher, *Decisions in Crisis: Israel, 1967 and 1973* (University of California Press, 1980), pp. 37–8.
48. Brecher, *The Foreign Policy System of Israel: Setting, Images, Processes* (Oxford University Press, 1972), p. 247.
49. Ibid., pp. 274ff., 290, 298, 314, 339, 502.
50. *Oum* is the Hebrew acronym for UN, and the construction *'oom-shmoom'* is a Yiddish form of belittlement.
51. Aaron S. Klieman, *Israel and the World after 40 Years* (Pergamon-Brassey's, 1989), p. 45.
52. Elon, *The Israelis: Founders and Sons* (Holt, Rinehart and Winston, 1971), p. 297.
53. Dina Goren, *Secrecy and the Right to Know* (Turtledove Publishing, 1979), p. 164.
54. Klieman, p. 169; see also p. 88.
55. Sammy Smooha, *Arabs and Jews in Israel*, Vol. 1 (Westview, 1989), p. 141.
56. Data supplied to the author by Modi'in Ezrahi.
57. On security policy see Avner Yaniv, *Deterrence without the Bomb* (Lexington Books, 1987); and Yaniv, 'Israel National Security in the 1980s: The Crisis of Overload', in Mahler, *Israel after Begin,* pp. 93–109.
58. Gad Barzilai and Ilan Peleg, 'Israel and Future Borders: An Assessment of a Dynamic Process', *Journal of Peace Research,* 31, 1 (1994), p. 69; for a vivid portrait of this period of transition see Glenn Frankel, *Beyond the Promised Land: Jews and Arabs on the Hard Road to a New Israel* (Simon and Schuster, 1994).
59. Polls of 27 March and 25 April 1995, supplied by Tami Steinmetz Centre for Peace Research, Tel Aviv University.

# 16  Whose Israel?[1] Jewish-Americans and the Transnational Battle for Jewish Identity

YOSSI SHAIN

## INTRODUCTION

In September 1999, on the eve of the Jewish New Year, members of the Reform and Conservative Jewish movements funded a public campaign on Israel's city billboards and in the Israeli media, calling on secular Israelis to experience their religious identity afresh. In a backlash against the monopoly and religious coercion of religious orthodoxy – which has led many Israelis to shed their religious identities even beyond their socialization to do so by secular Zionism – the campaign called upon Israelis to embrace religious pluralism under the slogan 'there is more than one way to be a Jew'. The campaign, financed by a grant from a Jewish family foundation in San Francisco, met with a harsh and somewhat violent response from the Israeli ultra-Orthodox sector. A leading ultra-Orthodox figure stated: 'If this situation continues, we will have a cultural war here, the likes of which we have not seen in a hundred years'.[2]

This latest campaign, and similar ones in recent years, are parts of a growing liberal Jewish-American involvement in the battle over Israel's Jewish identity. This battle, often described in general terms as the struggle between secular and religious Jews, or between 'Israeliness' and 'Jewishness', is one of the most intense domestic issues in Israeli politics and civic culture, with far-reaching economic and legal ramifications. The struggle over Israel's Jewish character has also become one of the most contentious issues within the American Jewish community, which is grappling with its own identity. This paper examines how contemporary controversies over Jewish identity represent the tightening of the interdependent relationship between the Diaspora and the historic homeland in a way that fosters re-evaluation of identities in both communities and may open the way for greater negotiation and coordination over the meaning and purpose of Judaism in the twenty-first century.

As early as 1988, Israeli Orthodox and ultra-Orthodox parties moved to redefine 'Who is a Jew?' in a manner that invalidated Reform and Conservative rabbis in the United States. Subsequently, leaders of the organized American Jewry declared 'open revolt against Israel'[3] and forced Prime Minister Shamir to dissolve his coalition government. The affair became a 'wrenching trauma' for many Jewish-Americans and paved the way for the emergence of a 'post-Zionist' posture in Diaspora–Israeli relations.[4] When in 1997, Benjamin Netanyahu's government and the Israeli religious establishment tried once again to enact a Conversion Law, 'designed to formalize and institutionalize the prevailing norm, according to which the only acceptable conversions in Israel would be those performed by Orthodox rabbinical authorities',[5] stormy controversy ensued which brought Israeli–Diaspora relations to its lowest point.

Certainly, American Judaism and internal Jewish-American debates regarding the standard of gauging Jewish identity are mostly informed by the reality of Jewish life in the United States and the challenges of contemporary American culture.[6] They are thus somewhat distant from internal Israeli debates.[7] Yet the Jewish-American and the Jewish-Israeli contexts are closely interconnected, as principles and practices in both places nourish and impinge upon each other. Today when the scholarly interest in disporas and 'transnational communities' is blooming, an exploration of American Jews, American Judaism and the linkages between them and Israel – their kin homeland – can further underscore how people negotiate their boundaries and shape their identities in transnational ways.

This essay examines the evolution of Jewish-American–Israeli relations through the prism of Diaspora politics in the US and conflicting Jewish identities. It argues that changes in the Israeli–Diaspora relationship are rooted not only in Israeli domestic developments and the role of Jewish-Americans in US foreign policy, but also in changes in Jewish-American identity – in itself a product of the evolution of Jewish-American religion and ethnicity, the general role of group identity in American civic culture, and Jewish-American encounter with Israel. The struggle over the Jewish character of the State of Israel and the continuing insistence of American Jews to perceive Israel as a critical source of their own disposition, and therefore as a crucial target of their influence, create a dynamic in which reciprocal influences mutually constitute evolving Jewish identity. While many see a widening 'gulf between the two centres of world Jewry' because of 'divergence of identities',[8] I contend quite the opposite. Today American Jewry tries to influence the nature of Jewish identity in Israel perhaps more than ever before, in a process that intends to reinvigorate American Jewish identity itself. This mutual reinforcement may draw the two communities closer rather than drive them apart.

I also maintain that tensions over the meaning of Jewish-American identity in general and the position of the Israeli state in defining the boundaries of Jewish belonging in particular may be better understood if evaluated from the point of view of general ethno-diasporic dynamics in the American context. These are broadly determined by the following factors: developments in American identity, separate from the homeland element; American identity as influenced by homeland-related affairs; the influence on diasporic identity and politics, stemming from changing American foreign policy goals.

All the above factors are interrelated and dynamic. They evolved in the case of Jewish-American–Israeli relations in four main stages:

1. From the late 1940s until the early 1960, American Jewry developed its identity and gained social acceptance as a result of the opening provided by the postwar 'golden age'. The major drive of Jewish identity in the United States during this period was towards integration. The post-war Jewish-American was 'characteristically American, reflecting a far-reaching and systematic accommodation of the East European tradition to American reality'.[9] With the decline of Jewish neighbourhoods, as Jews began to spread out geographically, they lost their distinctive ethnic traits. With the exception of Orthodox Jews it became increasingly impossible to tell them apart from other Americans. Although American Jews were enthusiastic about the birth of Israel as a place of asylum for displaced Jews, Zionism and

Israel's perception of the Diaspora were less significant 'to their own personal Jewish identity'.[10] During this time, Israel had focused on nation-building and security and was not as attentive to its US-based Diaspora as it was to become later. Diasporic institutions were only beginning to change to accommodate Israel's needs. Moreover, US foreign policy-makers under Truman and Eisenhower viewed Israel as at best a benign presence in the Middle East, and more commonly as an irritant in American strategic planning for the region in defence against communist penetration. This in itself hindered Jewish-American organization in support of Israel. AIPAC was created only in 1959. The focus of American Jewry in terms of Jewish identity was on preserving whatever was possible of the lost European Jewish culture.

2. From the mid-1960s until the late 1970s, one can identify the 'Israelization' or 'Zionization' of Jewish-American identity. The domestic assertion of Jewish ethnic identity, which grew as a result of the civil rights movement and its recognition of minority cultures, was magnified and took a dramatic turn after Israel's victory in the Six Day War. As American Judaism began to undergo religious divisions, Israel's victory gave a unifying impetus. It brought about the most powerful transformation in Jewish-American life and invigorated the domestic empowerment of Jewish activists and organizations, in the direction of defining American Judaism along the parameters of helping Israel. The most important development in terms of Jewish-American religion was the introduction of changes in the 'conceptions of gender roles, sexual morality and the nature of individual autonomy'.[11] Friction within Jewish denominations was similar in nature to that in American Protestantism and Catholicism.[12] At the same time, however, the individualization of the community manifested itself in the growth of intermarriage.

3. Beginning in the early 1980s and continuing until the early 1990s, this period is characterized by a consolidation of relations, although with 'deep cracks in the unilateral support of Diaspora Jews for the State of Israel'.[13] It is a time of growing tensions between Israel and the Diaspora, in terms of the nature of each community and culture, internal Israeli divisions over politics and identity, and a weaker identity of foreign-policy interests between Israel and the United States, especially towards the end

of the Cold War. Camps appeared in the form of supporters or opponents of the left or right in Israel, manifesting themselves in new and different lobby activity in the United States. By 1989 a survey of Jewish leaders uncovered that they generally

> may have strong views on how Israel should conduct its foreign policy and they may even vigorously defend the right of others to criticize that policy, but they think it inappropriate for themselves to exert pressure on Israel or to allow others [for example, American officials] to do so as well.[14]

At the same time, the survey findings indicated that 'the principle of non-intervention [in foreign policy] in no way precludes an interest in supporting those Israeli non-party groups that advance one's vision of Israeli society'.[15]

4. Roughly from the first Oslo peace agreement in 1993 to the present has been a time of transformation internationally and internally within both the Israeli and American Jewish communities. It is influenced by the global surge of democratic values and pluralism; peace negotiations in the Middle East and the lack of coherence in American foreign-policy goals and strategic interests in the region; intense religious and political differences and increasing cultural polarization inside Israel. These developments, which heighten the debates over the nature of Israeli Jewish identity, propel, coincide and are nurtured by internal diasporic changes of Jewish identity, thus requiring 'a redefinition of the entire relationship between Israel and the Jewish communities in the Diaspora'.[16]

## DIASPORA, ZIONISM AND THE JEWISH RELIGION

Since Zionism prescribes Jewish identity as a prerequisite for membership of the Jewish state, it falls into a 'trap' whereby religion remains the only characteristic to define national belonging. Thus, it seems that Jews inside Israel cannot separate themselves fully *qua* Jews from the Jewish community abroad, just as diasporic Jews cannot escape from the realities of the State of Israel. Overall, the Diaspora and Jews in Israel cannot disconnect their identity from their religion broadly defined, religion being a more fundamental unifying element than kinship, common histories of persecution, ethnic characteristics, use of the sacred language and so on.

Israeli sociologist Baruch Kimmerling argues that the Zionist 'hegemony' which dominated the State of Israel in its first three decades was able to keep the 'strain between secularism and religion...dormant' by exploiting the 'us' versus 'them' equation in the prolonged Israeli–Arab conflict. The Israeli state also manipulated religious symbols selectively in order to enhance nationalist conformity and collaboration among the nationalist Orthodox community and the traditional Mizrahim (Oriental Jews). With the gradual erosion of the Zionist 'hegemonic coalition' and in the light of drastic changes in Israel's population make-up, owing to the large influx of Jewish immigrants from the former Soviet Union, the country has witnessed the emergence of new coalitions or 'countercultures', each vying to build a new power base in Israeli politics and society.[17] These groups put a special premium on gaining influence over culture, education and identity. A major divide between these competing coalitions is the issue of state and religion. At one end of the spectrum there are those who 'envisioned Israel as a Jewish State, ruled by the Jewish Orthodox religious codex'. At the other extreme there are those who aspire 'to turn Israel into a liberal, secular and civic state for all its present Jews and Arab citizens'.[18] Exported from the United States, the Conservative and Reform movements are part of these new competing segments. They have made significant inroads into Israeli society and have become the nemesis of Israeli Orthodoxy which has long dominated the state's religious establishment but only in the last two decades was able to muster enough political clout to enhance its power through resource allocation from the state in other aspects of Israeli society. In the eyes of the Orthodox and ultra-Orthodox, the Reform and Conservative Jews are at various times 'non-religious', 'anti-religious', 'enemies of Judaism and the Jewish State' and even 'more dangerous to the Jewish nation than the Holocaust' as they allegedly encourage assimilation. Orthodox leaders also charged that the Reform and Conservative movements represent an 'American phenomenon', foreign to the aspirations and needs of Israeli society.[19]

Although the Orthodox camp (a broad term that here includes religious nationalists and the ultra-Orthodox) represents a minority of the Israeli Jewish population, their authorities maintain a monopoly over marriage, burial, conversion and other services and functions that govern life in Israel. The exercise of this domination, and the strong political activism of Israeli Orthodox parties – which, to some extent, grew out of their perception that Israel's Jewishness was under assault – are the cause of broad resentment among non-Orthodox Israelis. They have caused a backlash against Judaism in general.[20] In the 1999 Israeli elections, one of the main issues to galvanize support for the Barak campaign was opposition to religious Orthodoxy. Many polls in Israel rated the religious–secular cleavage as the country's most dangerous crisis – above security concerns.

Despite all of these developments, survey data shows that most Israelis continue to value their ties to their ancestral faith, and in fact are eager to fill its content with modern practices. In other words, they are not necessarily really secular, but they label themselves such.[21] Charles Liebman has written that while most Israelis participate 'in a patterned form of [Jewish] observance that is not *halakhah*, but that they have transformed into the folkways of secular Jewishness ... [they tend to] label themselves "secular" [rather] than "traditional" [because of] the animus they feel toward the religious establishment and the religious parties'.[22] Indeed, the relatively small part of the religious continuum of Israeli society occupied by the Orthodox and ultra-Orthodox leaves the majority of the Israeli Jewish population open to the influence of Jewish denominations that do not suffer from the negative perceptions and accumulated 'baggage' of orthodoxy. In this vacuum, the American-financed and ideologically sourced Reform and Conservative movements have appeared in Israel as the only groups trying to confront the Orthodox in the battleground over Judaism. Recent developments have shown that Reform and Conservative Judaism have had success in gaining Israeli adherents because they seem to provide a meaningful framework for existing 'folk ways' and simultaneously allow Israelis to differentiate themselves from the Orthodox.[23] These US-based movements and their growing branches inside Israel have united forces in their efforts to appeal to the desire of many Israelis to integrate Jewish religious belief and practice into their lives, without being subject to those aspects of religious authority and observance which they find outmoded, unjust and unnecessarily restrictive. Moreover, the large influx of post-Soviet immigrants, many of them not Jewish according to *halacha*, has introduced a large bloc of non-religious citizens into Israeli society who cry out for non-Orthodox religious options.[24] The question of how these movements could most effectively approach the Israeli public remains unresolved.[25]

Confronting the Orthodox monopoly with outright secularism, which denies Israel's Jewish character as a *sine qua non* of the state's identity, seems unrealistic even to some leading secularized and staunchly anti-religious sectors of Israeli society.[26] Indeed, many secular Israelis who shy away from Jewish practices – that have become associated with the Orthodox monopoly they despise – do not wish to become 'post-Jews', devoid of any connection with religion. Thus when leading secular Israeli writers, like Amos Oz, A. B. Yehoshua, Sami Michael, Yehuda Amichai and David Grossman, paraded their opposition to the ultra-Orthodox attack on Israeli liberal-democratic institutions in early 1999, they called on Israelis to join the Reform and Conservative movements in order to 'save Judaism from the enemies of democracy' and to generate 'a new dynamic which will renew Israel's spiritual and cultural landscape'.[27] A. B. Yehoshua added that 'to stand with the Reform and Conservative movements is to defend ourselves'.[28] Certainly, the idea that American Judaism can give Israel 'the greatest gift...a sense of pluralism in Jewish expression',[29] to quote the American Conservative rabbi, Elliot N. Dorff, has been gaining momentum among the liberal segments of American Jewry with a growing foothold inside Israel. Rabbi Ammiel Hirsch, a director of the Association of Reform Zionists of America (ARZA), said that in view of the 'virtual explosion of our popularity [inside Israel]...it is time for us to...build more synagogues...more schools...train more teachers...[and] educate an entire generation of Israelis'.[30]

While some of the new generation of American Jews have become distant and even alienated from Israel in recent years, others, especially active members of the Reform and Conservative denominations, have rediscovered a new source of Jewish involvement and mobilization in the contest over Israel's Jewish identity. Being the vanguard in the combat against ultra-Orthodox power in Israel is perceived by Reform and Conservative leaders as an affirmation of their own movements' validity inside the United States. At a time when their own liberal-universalist content in the United States has seemed to dilute and overshadow the religiosity of their message, the foothold they have acquired within Israeli Judaism has renewed their religious vigour and infused their movement with traditional practices. To some extent they exchange American universalism for greater Israeli/Jewish particularism.

Thus, just as Israeli internal debates have spilled over to the Diaspora and have affected intra-Jewish relations inside the United States, Jewish-American responses have become more and more critical in the shaping of Israeli reality. US-based Conservative and Reform groups have been instrumental in the struggle to alter the Israeli-Orthodox monopoly over Jewish marriage and conversion in Israel and the Orthodox domination of religious councils. They have also played a role in the fight for the rights of non-Orthodox Jews to be buried in non-denominational cemeteries, and have taken the lead in redirecting Jewish diasporic funds from general fundraising for Israel to educational institutions and sociopolitical programmes aimed at promoting tolerance, democracy, civil and human rights and religious pluralism.[31]

Certainly, the efforts of liberal Jews in the US to influence Israel's Jewish identity are not new. As early as 1964 leading Jewish-American groups, including the American Jewish Committee, the American Jewish Congress and B'nai Brith, as well as the Conservative and Reform movements, urged Israel's prime minister, Levi Eshkol, to combat Orthodox imposition.[32] Yet, until recently, non-Orthodox diasporic intervention in Israeli affairs had been sporadic and certainly not vigorous (for reasons explained below). However, Orthodox and ultra-Orthodox (or *haredi*) American Jewry were always eager to intervene in Israeli life even when they sharply opposed its governmental policies.[33] To begin with, a disproportionate number of Jewish-American immigrants to Israel are Orthodox.[34] Moreover, 'while the demographic, financial, and spiritual center of gravity of non-Orthodox movements is in the United States, Israel is the world center for almost every Orthodox group – Hasidim and *mitnagdim* Zionist and ultra-Orthodox alike'.[35] The Orthodox camp in the US is divided between those who advocate greater modernism in Judaism – including in Israeli culture and politics – as a way of halting the growing drift of secular Israelis away from religious practices, and those who distance themselves from modernity and refuse to participate in Jewish communal organization or forums which include non-Orthodox rabbis. Indeed, the disenchantment of large segments of Israeli-based Orthodox with their original alliance with secular Zionism[36] galvanized their kin in the United States to adopt a more aggressive posture in support of stricter Jewish laws and the right-wing politics of Israel's national–religious camp in a process that weakened the voice of modern Orthodoxy in the United States, and accelerated Orthodox separation from Jewish-American liberal streams.[37] Yet the more the American Orthodox affirm their Jewish exclusivity, the more they may question their roots in American society.[38] Indeed, Jewish 'transnationalism' has consequences not only for the beleaguered homeland, but also for the future direction of American Judaism itself.

Some may ask why Reform and Conservative Jews, who have always considered the United States their chosen country, are so passionately involved in shaping Jewish identity inside Israel. There are many answers to this question. Some have emphasized the comforting aspect of having a place to which you can always move should conditions in the United States become unfriendly. Periodic episodes of anti-Semitism serve as reminders to older generations of American Jews of the precariousness of being a Jew in a Christian culture. Yet it is not the danger but rather the absence of it that drives the current attention of liberal Jewish-American leaders to Israel. As they accomplish full integration and great triumphs in all aspects of American life, perhaps beyond all expectations, American Jews have become victims of their own success. From a 'Jewish identity' point of view the community is facing a demographic peril as half of its members marry non-Jews, assimilate or drift. Moreover, American Jewish ethnicity (as a cultural trait) has been in perpetual decline and is certainly not sufficient to sustain Jewish existence in the Diaspora, especially when anti-Semitism is no longer a constant fact of life as it was earlier in this century.[39] The most liberal streams in American Jewish leadership acknowledge that 'without the synagogue Jewish life in the U.S. cannot endure'.[40] Indeed, in the era of growing assimilation, religion has remained the most distinctive attribute of most Jewish-Americans.[41] As Zvi Gitelman has noted, 'In the modern period one may be a non-believer and a Jew, though it is unlikely that one can be an active practitioner of a religion other than Judaism and still be considered by other Jews as a Jew'.[42]

Furthermore, of all major religious communities, Jews are quite distinctive in the sense that their theology includes the concept of a homeland as a central tenet of their belief. The concept of 'the Land of Israel' made the character of the Jewish Diaspora unique, since by religious definition living outside the Land is a sign of Jewish failings, and an eventual return to Zion is viewed as an integral part of God's plan. David Vital has written that '[The Land has] formed a central part of their cosmology and theology, their Law, their history, and their world-view. It was a component of the supremely important realm reserved in Jewish belief, culture, literature, and conduct for elegy and lament, for nostalgia and yearning, but also for hope and for release.'[43] The vision of returning to the homeland is built into the very nature of all Jewish communities *qua* Diaspora. Thus, while most religions do not define themselves according to 'political maps' and are not bound by membership of states or nations, one of the major components of Judaism is indeed the concept of return to the Land. This means that Judaism lends itself more to nationalism than to transnationalism.[44] This reality is now recognized even by the Reform movement which has undergone a dramatic shift from its early anti-Zionist position towards endorsing Zionism and recognizing the State of Israel as the spiritual and cultural centre of world Jewry.[45]

To be sure, some modern Jewish thinkers give the *Galut* (Exile) a permanent ontological status and go so far as to describe Jewish diasporic life as the ultimate moral mission of the 'chosen people'. Their attempt to play down the religious importance of Jewish life in the historic homeland by these 'universalists' – including Jewish-American intellectuals like Leslie Fiedler, Arthur Cohen and Will Herberg – led them to consider Judaism a world religion in which the idea of a 'covenant folk' is much more critical than the recovery of the promised land. Consequently, they have adopted a neutral if not hostile position regarding the centrality of Zionism and modern Israel to Jewish life. Yet, as Yosef Gorny documented, these voices remained marginal in Jewish-American theological thinking.[46] Albert Vorspan and David Saperstein, two leading shapers of the political ideology of the Reform movement, have written recently:

> We are a proud people, and our peoplehood transcends our religious and racial differences. In moments of peril for Israel, as well as in moments of exaltation, we are not Reform, Conservative, Reconstructionist, Yiddishist, Zionist, Orthodox, or atheist. We are Jews, a united people sharing a common destiny, knowing in our bones that what happens to Israel will shape much of our future as Jews.[47]

Even more critical is the growing understanding of leaders of Reform and Conservative rabbis in the United States that their ability to develop and disseminate their creed inside Israel is the 'ultimate test of Jewish authenticity for Progressive Judaism' in the

Diaspora. These words were uttered by Rabbi Richard Hirsch, executive director of the World Union of Progressive Judaism, in his keynote address to the 29th International Convention of the movement held (notably) in Jerusalem in March 1999. Rabbi Hirsch also declared that

> to support the movement in Israel is not philanthropy toward other Jews, such as is Diaspora support for universities, hospitals, *yeshivot*, and a host of other worthy Israeli causes. To support Progressive Judaism in Israel is inseparable from investing in liberal Judaism in the Diaspora.[48]

Similarly, Professor Ismar Schorsch, leader of the American Conservative movement, has acknowledged that building a strong presence of the Conservative (*Masorti*) stream inside Israel is essential for 'revitalizing the Conservative movement in North America'.[49] To sum up, when Orthodox and more liberal Jewish denominations in Israel and the Diaspora clash over the central question of 'Who is a Jew?' they are fighting not only to decide the character of the modern Jewish homeland but also over the right to claim and determine religious and national identity for Jews no matter where they reside.

## THE AFTERMATH OF THE HOLOCAUST AND THE CREATION OF THE JEWISH STATE

Given the strong and complex ties between Israel and American Jewry that have developed over the last decades, it may be easy to forget that Israel was not always the primary focus of Jewish-American life. The migration of Israel towards the centre of American Jewish consciousness and identity did not occur overnight. The divisions among American Jews over the legitimacy and necessity of the Zionist experiment in Palestine largely ended with the establishment of the State of Israel. Jewish-Americans rejoiced following the 1947 UN partition resolution. They organized large rallies on behalf of the new state, pleaded with the Truman government to recognize and stand behind it, and raised tens of millions of dollars for arms procurement in support of its 1948 war efforts.[50] Many volunteered to serve in Israel's War of Independence, during which 37 combatants and an Hadassah medical team lost their lives. Yet Israel did not immediately become the centre of attention of Jewish life in America. In the late 1940s and the 1950s Jews in the United States focused on integrating themselves and European Jewish newcomers into American society, and in encouraging that society to continue to develop along more liberal and inclusive lines while eradicating anti-Semitism. Peter Novick has argued that in their drive to integrate, American Jews after the Second World War preferred to remain relatively quiet about the Holocaust. They did not want to be seen as victims by their fellow Americans. Moreover, during the McCarthy era, when public perception was dominated by a belief in an international communist conspiracy, the Jewish community, like other 'foreign' minorities, wished to lower its profile – especially since many of them fell into the liberal camp.[51] Although Israel's birth largely ended Jewish-American anti-Zionism,[52] many American Jews were contemptuous of the idea that they owed their loyalty or, more troubling, their physical presence, to the new State of Israel. Even with the very real emotional attachment they felt for Israel, and their view of Israel as a centre of spiritual identity and authority, they feared that political expressions of support for the new state would bring charges of dual loyalty that could not be allowed. Rabbi Morris Kertzer, President of the Jewish Chaplains Organization, exemplified the American Jew's desire to erase any suspicion of dual loyalty when, in a 1952 interview to the widely circulated weekly *Look Magazine*, he said:

> The only loyalty of an American Jew is to the United States of America without any ifs, ands or buts. The state of Israel is the ancestral home of his forefathers, the birthplace of his faith. As a haven for over a million Jews after the agonies of the past 20 years it has special meaning for Jews all over the world. But spiritual bonds and emotional ties are quite different from political loyalty.[53]

Samuel Heilman has pointed out that in this era of acculturation and conformity, 'even the Orthodox Jews, who by their unyielding attachments to religious traditions and observances seemed more separatist and ethnic than their coreligionists…emphasized their American allegiances'.[54]

Indeed, from its founding Israel sought to dominate the terms of Jewish interests and of Jewish identity. Israeli Zionist leaders felt they had the right to demand obedience and support from

Jewish-Americans in making Israel strong, secure and economically sound. The fact that Israel considered its version of Jewish existence superior was translated *de facto* into the total negation of diasporic life as inferior, the containment of diasporic voice on policy and the imposition of a 'loyalty burden' on kin who had yet to make the necessary move to become 'normal Jews'. David Ben-Gurion's 'Israelocentrism' considered the 'weaknesses the Jews have acquired in Diaspora life' a major peril in the efforts to secure the Jewish state, and assigned the Israel Defence Force (IDF) the role of erasing these character flaws of new arrivals.[55] Ben Gurion also considered American Zionist organizations potentially disruptive to Israel's sovereignty and sought to curtail the influence of foreign Zionist funds on policy-making.[56] He maintained that only those Jews who were already dwelling in Israel or in the process of emigration to Israel could be regarded as Zionists, while all others, regardless of their deep attachment to and help for the Jewish state, must be regarded, at best, only as 'friends of Israel'. This distinction was compounded with a 'civil religion' that magnified the Bible as the spirit of Jewish independence and played down post-biblical rabbini-cal–exilic Judaism as 'apolitical, particularistic, prone to an exaggerated spiritualism and withdrawal'.[57] The Bible, no less, could only be truly valued by Jews who had returned to their homeland. Arthur Hertzberg has pointed out that the Zionist narrative ignored diasporic contributions to Israel's War of Independence and relegated Diaspora Zionist efforts 'no matter how... helpful they might be to the Jewish State ... [to] lower status in the hierarchy of Jewish values'.[58]

American Jewry generally did not dispute this categorization, either because they were too preoccupied with becoming Americans, or because of feelings of obligation and guilt in the years following the Holocaust. They believed that unlike other Jewish centres in the world the Jewish-American experience was not going to recede into insignificance, but would continue to develop alongside the newly established state. The definitions of this duality vary according to ideological camps. In terms of finan-cial aid to the new state, it is important to note that local needs dominated Jewish fundraising. Pledges to the UJA (led in the early 1950s by non-Zionists) dropped steadily from a high of $150 million in 1948 to a low of $60 million in 1955.[59] Nathan Glazer has pointed out that the raising and managing of funds at this time were 'almost exclusively in the hands of secular institutions in which rabbis and religious groups played little part'.[60]

As for religious identity, from the beginning of the century until the 1950s, Jewish-Americans were generally removed from regular religious observance, and had little exposure to synagogue life: 'To be a Jew was primarily a matter of association with fellow Jews, not an act of affiliation with a synagogue, let alone a commitment to pay membership dues'.[61] Only with the move to suburbia did synagogues begin to grow and proliferate, and Jewish community institutions to thrive. As religion took a more central place in American public life, Jews in suburban America began to enter the mainstream. The social radicalism of the second generation of descendants of Jewish immigrants did not find favour among the third generation which came to the fore at this time. The new generation, following the pattern of their non-Jewish neighbours, expressed a greater interest in the religious element of their identity, but in a distinctly 'American' way. Synagogue services and organizational structures borrowed heavily from mainline Protestant practices, with the creation of Sunday schools, sisterhoods, and so on. This was also the period when Jewish day schools throughout the United States began to proliferate: in 1940 only 33 such institutions existed in the United States, in 1960 there were 237 and by 1990 there were 604. The growing number of day schools included the Conservative and Reform movements, whose leaders gradually subscribed to the Orthodox view 'that only through day school education can Judaism survive [in the United States]'.[62] The increase in the number of Jewish day schools produced internal Jewish debates over government aid to parochial institutions, leading to a rift between liberal proponents of complete separation between state and religion, and mainly Orthodox leaders claiming that Jewish education could not survive without tax aid.[63] Altogether, the return to religious worship, based in large part on a search for 'roots' and authenticity that could in other circumstances have denoted a retreat into cultural isolationism or separatism, was in post-Second World War America a clear signal of Jewish acculturation and integration into the broader society, which adopted religious practices informed by American values. At the same time that synagogues were thriving in new suburbs, Jews were becoming more involved culturally, socially and professionally in their wider communities. Yet American Judaism at this juncture had little to do with the new State of Israel. Nathan Glazer has written that Conservative and Reform American rabbis who visited Israel 'to find out what they could learn discovered an unchanged

Orthodoxy that was almost completely irrelevant to [Jewish-American] contemporary interests and problems. [Hence]...the idea that Israel, once it was established, could in any serious way affect Judaism in America...appeared in the 1950's largely illusory.'[64] Yet, Jewish-American integration, and greater acceptance among other Americans, came with a price. Growing rates of inter-marriage and other manifestations of assimilation became clear trends by the 1960s, developments that caused some in the Jewish community to turn more to Conservative and Orthodox worship as a means of holding on to their Jewish identity. This did not, however, alter the general course of American Jewry, which was towards greater assimilation and integration.

In terms of US policy towards Israel and the Middle East, the 1950s were characterized by the American desire to win the good-will and support of the Arab world in the American effort to contain the Soviet Union, meaning that Israel was excluded from member-ship of regional security alliances initiated by the United States. The particularly unsympathetic stance of the Eisenhower administra-tion towards Israel stifled Jewish-American Zionists politically, and undermined their lobbying power. Ben-Zvi has documented the weakness of Jewish-American leaders in the face of US criticism of Israel during this period. In 1956, the US Jewish community lacked a strong lobbying apparatus and Jewish influence in the White House was less of a factor than during the Truman era. The Jewish lobby was fragmented in the face of confrontational relations between Jerusalem and Washington following the Suez crisis. Nahum Goldmann, President of the World Jewish Congress, told Prime Minster Ben-Gurion that, in view of Israel's reluctance to withdraw from Sinai,

> I must tell you that it is impossible to mobilize an American Jewish front to support this posture. If there will be an open dispute between Israel and the U.S. Government on this point [and] if this should lead to cessation of the [United Jewish Appeal] and the Bonds, I foresee great difficulties in renewing these enterprises.[65]

It was in the late 1950s that the Jewish lobby began to enjoy some success in Washington, as US policy-makers began to recognize Israel as a strategic asset within a turbulent and changing Arab regional environment.[66] Nonetheless, 'not until the mid-1960s did overt organized Jewish political activity on behalf of the state of Israel come to its own'.[67]

## THE ISRAELIZATION OF AMERICAN JEWRY

The 1960s, and especially the Six Day War in 1967, are regarded by many observers as a watershed in terms of Diaspora–Israeli relations. The fact that ethnicity was becoming more legitimate in American public life at that time led to the growing politicization of US Jews and brought to the fore the diasporic component of their identity. The openness of American society and the assertion of identity that came with it had several important influences on the community. On the one hand, Jewish intermarriage rates, which had held steady at 4–6 per cent for half a century, rose dramatically, reaching 50 per cent or more today. On the other hand, differences of many kinds became more acceptable in American society, in ways that enabled younger Jews to claim their distinctiveness in a much bolder manner than their parents' generation had done. The push for gender desegregation in American religion led to Jewish women challenging traditional practices and claiming roles as cantors and rabbis: 'The resulting adaptations include ordination of women in Reform and Conservative branches, the synagogue reform movement known as egalitarian Minyan, and the house based groups known as Havurot'.[68] Jewish Orthodoxy gained confidence and rose significantly in the American Jewish community. Its younger representatives were no longer hesitant in expressing their opposition to Jewish liberal views and publicly contested the strict separation of synagogue and state 'which has become one of the hallmarks of American Jewry'.[69] The *'haredization'* of Orthodox Jews and their growing distance from the rest of American Jewry also expressed itself in the increasing emphasis on foundational texts upon which they based a more rigorous religious observance.[70]

The new politicization and attitudes were evident in the manner in which the energy and emotions released by the 1967 war among American Jews were channelled into the establishment of pro-Israeli organizations and the reorganization of traditional Jewish-American institutions with greater emphasis on the Israeli dimension. The events and reactions surrounding the war gave credence to the thesis of a dual existence of homeland and Diaspora, based on mutual interests and support. Israel gained active diasporic support and, in turn, legitimized the normalized status of the Diaspora and provided it with a much-needed sense of community identity. Israel also provided American Jews with a source of pride and an achievement to focus on that was in accordance with 'American values', a point that was reinforced by the increasingly close defence and security ties between the US and Israel. Commenting on the unique unifying role of Israel among the diverse elements of American Jewry at this time, Melvin Urofsky wrote that, 'within American Jewry, there is one primary concern, namely Israel... Every effort to coordinate Jewish activities in other areas has failed miserably.'[71] Peter Novick charged that the Six Day War had unleashed Jewish obsession with the Holocaust which had been played down until the mid-1960s. The institutionalization of Holocaust memorials became instrumental in garnering support for Israel by creating a linkage between the dangers facing the Jewish state and the Jewish experience of genocide; a vehicle in the struggle to discourage growing Jewish assimilation; and, above all, as part of the Jewish effort to capture the moral centre of American public life.[72]

Israel's victory symbolized the zenith of heroic Zionism for Jews searching for a new identity with the opening of American society for minorities. It was a redemption from the image of the weak Jew. Martin Peretz characterized the war as 'the return of power to the Jewish people'.[73] Alan Dershowitz wrote that the war was the pinnacle event in his life that enabled him to express his Jewishness openly: 'I never stepped back into the closet or even the shadows'.[74] The famous Rabbi Joshua Herschel wrote that 'America's Jews would never be the same'.[75] The fact that Israel grew more dependent on America made American Jews more important to the maintenance of Jewish existence in the homeland, and gave them a strong and clear purpose around which to lobby and organize. The 1967 war 'produced the greatest flood of financial contributions in American Jewish history'.[76] Since the war many Jewish-Americans have lived vicariously through the State of Israel. They underwent 'a kind of a mass conversion to Zionism', and the UJA, through Israel, has evolved into 'America's Jewish religion'.[77] The late Lord Beloff wrote that 'Israel had become the new religion of American Jews... Jews were to be found less often praying to God than raising funds, mobilizing support and engaging in political lobbying on behalf of Israel.'[78] 'The eyes of world Jewry are now consistently upon us [Israel]', wrote David Vital, 'a Mecca to which, if Jews do not make pilgrimage they do tend to make a form – a very mild form – of obeisance.'[79]

The 1967 war also embellished the religious character of the homeland. The strong identification with Israel has transformed Jewish education in America. Israel began to figure prominently in the curricula of Jewish schools and the Sephardic pronunciation of Hebrew also prevailed, although not in Orthodox synagogues. To a large extent, Israel allowed Conservative and Reform Jewish-Americans to find alternatives to Orthodox categories of Judaism. The Israeli flag was placed next to the ark, and blessings for the well-being of the people in the government and armed forces of Israel were added to the Sabbath services. For Reform Jews, in particular, this was a significant departure from their earlier opposition to Zionism, and part of their recognition that their fate as Diaspora Jews was intimately – and legitimately – intertwined with that of the State of Israel. In July 1968, the Reform movement held, for the first time, its international conference in Israel. It was a dramatic milestone in the movement's evolution towards Zionism.[80] Altogether, the modernization of Jewish religion among the Reform and Conservatives, and especially the feminist revolution, were not yet asked of Israel, since in Israel there seemed to appear a new modern Zionist Jew intent on his own version of liberation. In fact, the new religious posture of American Jews – directing the centre of attention of their spiritual lives exclusively towards a land in which they do not live, to paraphrase Jacob Neusner – raised questions as to the political implications of their Jewish faith.[81]

The 1967 war and Israel's new relations with the United States – after the Franco-Israeli alliance collapsed in the mid-1960s – allowed many American Jews to distance themselves from their previous partners in the desegregation movement and the American left. Israel-bashing, especially among radical black activists, was generally perceived by American Jews as a barely disguised form of anti-Semitism. Paul Berman has written that 'it was sometimes believed that Palestinian skin tone was darker than that of the Israeli Jews, as if in pigmental confirmation of the proposed new link between Palestinians and African-Americans'.[82] 'New Left' publications and slogans that equated the Israeli government with dictatorial and genocidal regimes, and indirectly or overtly questioned Israel's right to exist, left many Jewish activists alienated from erstwhile 'allies' for whom every struggle and assertion of identity seemed legitimate, except those of the Jews: 'For many, the insight that as Jews they were still excluded came as a searing revelation'.[83] When forced to choose between safeguarding their own identity and a solidarity with others that required the rejection or destruction of this identity, they would choose to stand up for themselves. In reply to the traditional litany of accusations against Israel which supporters of the New Left were increasingly expected to articulate, Jewish-American authors Sleeper and Mintz declared, 'No Jew need rationalize his support of Israel. And if the existence of Israel is a thorn in the side of the "Third World", then so be it. If the fact of Jewish self-rule in the Middle East serves "imperialist" interests, let it',[84] and so on. Israel's victory in 1967 also produced powerful Christian allies especially among American evangelists. As they view the world through the prism of dispensationalist Bible theology, Israel's triumphs appeared as proof of God's determination. Indeed, American evangelists have been enlisted on many occasions on Israel's side when America's foreign policy was at odds with Israel's perceived interest. Yet this alliance remain tenuous because of suspicion of anti-Semitism.[85]

In response to these social and political developments, a significant minority of American Jews and Jewish organizations began to move rightward politically, a phenomenon which had been virtually unimaginable ten or 20 years before. A major indication of this was the Jewish approach to the Jackson–Vanik Amendment, which linked the issues of trade with the Soviet Union to Soviet willingness to permit Jewish emigration. Although some Jewish leaders were hesitant about supporting the measure at first, most came to support it eventually. This amendment clearly ran counter to the emerging spirit of *détente* between East and West, was compatible with the agenda of conservatives who opposed any accommodation of Soviet interests, and marked a watershed in terms of Jewish-American involvement in the Cold War. J. J. Goldberg has written that 'Jews became the poster children of a renewed Cold War'.[86] The effort to free Soviet Jews gave American anti-communism 'a new moral argument' sorely needed after the disaster of Vietnam, and increased Jewish visibility in and influence on US foreign policy. This higher profile was enhanced by Jewish-American campaigns against the Arab economic boycott of Israel (and of those dealing with Israel), and against the anti-Zionist propaganda prevalent among third world and communist countries which culminated in the 1975 UN vote equating Zionism with racism. Jewish activists were largely successful in communicating the message to American audiences that these ostensibly anti-Israeli actions were in fact directed against all Jews, regardless of citizenship, and were therefore thoroughly racist in character and unacceptable. Organizationally, these campaigns gave new energy to Jewish institutions, and increased the centrality of Israel in their activity and self-definition. Involvement with Israel became a mark of involvement in and allegiance to the Jewish-American community in general.[87]

The new Israeli–Jewish-American alliance of the 1970s pushed aside the Israeli demands that Diaspora Jews emigrate to Israel. Israel accepted the fact that a Jewish-American community would continue to exist, and for diasporic Jews the way was open to legitimize their distinct identity inside the United States. The dilemmas over Israel's democratic character, the position of religion within the state, or the treatment of Palestinians could be minimized when commonality between the two communities was stressed.

## POLITICAL RIFTS AND NEW DIASPORA VOICES

From the late 1970s, with the rise to power of the Likud Party, and the growing divisions within Israel regarding peace with the Arabs and the Palestinian issue, diasporic political positions became more diverse with regard to Israeli policies and US initiatives in the Middle East. The Diaspora also began to assert its right to a voice on Israeli affairs and Jewish identity inside Israel. Although the internal rift was largely kept quiet, it was brought to the surface whenever the American government collided with Israel's Likud-led government. This was the case with the 1982 Reagan plan, and most dramatically, in 1991–92, with the issue of loan guarantees under the Bush administration, and throughout this period the controversial subject of Jewish settlements in the occupied territories. Yet, in situations where criticism of Israel was perceived by American Jews to come from sources traditionally, or even categorically, hostile to Israel or to Jews in general, American Jews were reluctant to voice criticism of Israeli policy, even when it conflicted with the interests, views and widely expressed principles of American Jews themselves. In an environment of broadly based and harsh criticism by the United States, other governments, the media and other institutions and organizations, most Jewish-American spokespeople declined to give what they saw as aid and comfort to enemies of Jews and of Israel. When in 1982 Israel invaded Lebanon in a war that resulted in Phalangist massacres of Palestinians in the Sabra and Shatila refugee camps, some Jewish-American leaders spoke out against the Israeli government. Yet 'the fact is that there was far less criticism among American Jewry of the war in Lebanon than there was in Israel itself... [anti-Israeli US press coverage] created the feeling [among American Jews] that, despite their own disapproval of Israeli policy... they must nevertheless come to Israel's aid in the face of.unfair attacks in the American media'.[88] With the Palestinian intifada the diversification and erosion of Diaspora support for Israel became evident.[89] Yet the gap between Israel and American Jews in terms of politics, culture and interpretations of Jewish life was intensified most acutely in 1988 with the first Israeli Orthodox attempt to alter legislation defining 'Who is a Jew?'. It was the first time that many American Jews had felt obliged to intervene directly in Israeli politics. David Landau describes how the bitter hostility between American non-Orthodox leaders and the New York-based Lubavitch Hasidic movement, led by Rabbi Menahem Mendel Schneerson, was injected into the Israeli drama. The Lubavitchers' ardour and money ignited Israeli Orthodox zealousness and left its mark on the direction of Israeli politics in the 1990s. Conservative leader Ismar Schorch, commented at the time:

> This is not an Israeli affair. This is a personal affair of the Lubavitcher Rebbe. He is trying to use the Law of Return in order to discomfit Conservative and Reform Judaism. His concern is not the purity of immigrants to Israel, but rather the strength of Conservative and Reform in America. This is an American affair which the Lubavitcher Rebbe is forcing upon Israel... Israel is the battlefield; but the war is in America... If the State of Israel declares that [our] conversion is no conversion, that means that [our] rabbis are no rabbis. This is the instrument through which the Lubavitcher Rebbe proposes to declare that Conservative and Reform Judaism in America are not authentic Judaism.[90]

This early episode of identity rupture, which would grow to dominate the Diaspora's political agenda in the late 1990s, signalled the rise in diasporic intervention in Israeli domestic and foreign affairs. It also brought into the open the divergence between Diaspora 'hawks' and 'doves' regarding the peace process. Overall, the breaking point between Orthodoxy and non-Orthodoxy in the Diaspora was the separation of men and women in the synagogue, and this will continue to be the symbolic barrier between American Jewish identity and the Israeli Orthodox monopoly.

As the question of Israel's moral standing also became disputed in the years of the *intifada*, more and more American Jews felt that Israeli affairs might interfere in their own American life. The Pollard case intensified these feelings. Philip Roth wrote in *Operation Shylock* that,

> Pollard is just another Jewish victim of the existence of Israel...I don't hold Pollard responsible. I hold Israel responsible – Israel, which with its all-embracing Jewish totalism has replaced the goyim as the greatest intimidator of Jews in the world; Israel, which today, with its hunger for Jews, is in many, many terrible ways, deforming and disfiguring Jews as only our anti-Semitic enemies once had the power to do.[91]

By 1990 the deep penetration of Israel into Jewish-American life and organizational structures raised concerns about Israeli 'arrogance' in meddling in and manipulating diasporic affairs. By that time a web of over 70 pro-Israel political action committees had been established which channelled $4.7million to pro-Israel candidates during the 1987–88 election cycle.[92] Looking from an Israeli foreign policy perspective, Aaron Klieman wrote in 1990 that an 'Israel-Centric perspective' in mobilizing the Diaspora had reached a dangerous level when AIPAC and other Jewish organizations felt so empowered that they began to adopt an independent foreign policy agenda in the Middle East. He predicted growing friction in Israeli–Diaspora relations 'with each side resentful at what it views as being used by the other and being taken for granted'.[93] Remarking on the Israeli government's pressure on American Jewry to stand behind the homeland, even against the US government official position, David Vital has written:

> the greater Israel's reliance on the Diaspora, the more it necessarily involves the Diaspora in its affairs. The more it involves it in its affairs, the more it endangers it by leading it into conflicts and contestation of which otherwise the Diaspora might be free.[94]

Thus, 'Israel and its affairs tend to continuously rob [American Jewry] of their long sought for and so very recently acquired peace of mind'.[95] Indeed, it was in the late 1980s when the pattern of automatic diasporic support for Israel began to erode, with the highly contentious policy of building Jewish settlements in the occupied territories and the increasingly controversial Israeli relationship with South Africa's apartheid government taking centre stage.

This analysis is also valid for the Diaspora's attempt to lean on Israel for its own domestic purposes. Thus, the more closely the Diaspora affiliates itself with Israeli affairs and policies, the more likely it is to be affected by Israel's conduct. This has been evident with regard to the treatment of Ethiopian Jews. When in 1984 and 1991 Israel airlifted Ethiopian Jews to Israel in Operations Moses and Solomon, the Jewish-Americans felt pride and vindication. The campaign for Ethiopian Jews enabled the Diaspora to argue that the Jews, both abroad and in Israel, were not racists. The Anti-Defamation League, for example, sponsored visits by young Ethiopian Jews to schools across America to meet black youngsters and 'deliver' the positive message about Israel and the Jews. 'Let them know that Israel is not a country of violence, discrimination and oppression, as is often being portrayed in the media',[96] Marjorie Green instructed the Ethiopian Jewish delegation. As long as their campaign strategy was effective and Israel's behaviour was seen favourably, the utilization of Black Jewry was a success. Yet, when the world discovered that the life of Ethiopian Jews in Israel was not so rosy, the shock waves reached the American Jewish community. This was the case during the blood-spilling scandal of 1996. When it was revealed that blood donations by Ethiopian Jews were being discarded regularly because of fear of AIDS or other contamination, Ethiopian Jews rioted, and American Jews had to contend with the fallout.[97] Israel was quick to appoint the first Ethiopian graduate of its school for the diplomatic corps to its consulate in Chicago, directed to spread the message that 'Israel is not a racist country, it is the only country in the world which brought in Blacks not for enslavement but as equal brothers'.[98]

THE DIASPORA LEADING THE WAY?

The dismantling of the friend/foe pattern of the Cold War was reflected in a blurring of similar boundaries in the Middle East, and in the changing dynamics of the relationship between Israel and American Jews. The 1993 Oslo peace accords were welcomed by a majority of American Jews.[99] They were however received by outright hostility by right-wing Jewish groups and Jewish Orthodox. The divergent positions on the peace process overlapped with the rift between religious denominations. These contentious relations have exhibited themselves most recently in the public campaign to enlist Jewish-American support (or opposition) for Israel's peace negotiations with Syria. While Orthodox and right-wing American Jews protested against Prime Minster Barak's intention to trade land for peace and chanted 'traitor, go home!', leaders of the Reform movement visited the Israeli embassy and Israeli consulates across America to show their support for the Israeli prime minister.[100]

In general, the Middle East peace process allowed mainstream diasporic organizations to continue to claim the moral high ground in their support for a country that 'respects the principle of self-determination, even at such a high cost'. Yet, as the peace process was unfolding, Jewish-Americans began to grapple with their diasporic identity. Some voices began admonishing the Diaspora for its failure to find internal sustenance in a Jewish-American identity independent of Israel. They maintained that Judaism in the United States had become ephemeral owing to its overwhelming concentration on the Jewish state. Indeed, after Oslo, mainstream Jewish organizations began to ask, what would be their source of political recruitment in the era of peace? What would compel them to remain Jews if the danger to Israel receded?[101] Right-wing American Jews, primarily nationalist-Orthodox, saw in Oslo, however, a betrayal of the historic/messianic role of the Jewish state. Their rabbis in Israel and the United States joined in virulent attacks to discredit Rabin's government and a few of them went as far as instructing Israeli soldiers to disobey orders if called upon to evacuate Jewish settlements in the occupied territories. They also issued religious injunctions which could be construed as licensing the assassination of Rabin by a religious ultra-nationalist law student in November 1995. Together with conservative lawmakers, right-wing Jewish groups and Israel's Likud Party attempted to forestall the peace process by encouraging Congress to adopt initiatives that could undermine Israeli–Arab negotiations. Thomas Friedman described these actions as bold attempts to subvert Israeli democratic process via Congress by Jewish-American organizations which 'could only thrive if they have an enemy, someone to fight. They have no positive vision to offer American Jews on the central question of American-Jewish identity or the fate of Israel–Diaspora relations in this new era.'[102]

After the victory of the Six Day War (described by many in the Orthodox community in messianic terms) leading ultra-Orthodox segments in Israel and the Diaspora moved away from their opposition to Jewish nationalism. Nationalism was no longer perceived as inherently antagonistic to traditional Judaism. Its triumphs in the modern State of Israel embellished the theory, propagated by Orthodox nationalists, that the Zionists might be the catalysts of the redemption process, serving as the Messiah's messengers in an unseen hand in history that would ultimately result in Israeli Zionist secularism's own demise.[103] Subsequently, we are witnessing a process that grows in intensity and scope of Orthodox and ultra-Orthodox segments – using their power as a swing voting bloc in the Israeli parliament and drawing greatly upon state resources for their own sectarian needs – advancing a divisive agenda via the secular law on issues of dietary restriction, Sabbath observance and the legal definition of Judaism in Israeli civil law. This heavy involvement in domestic policy – while at the same time the ultra-Orthodox enjoy draft deferments and exemptions from military service to attend subsidized *yeshiva* studies – bred resentment among secular and modern Orthodox Israelis alike.[104] Yet the ultra-Orthodox are 'committed not only to disputes and positions concerning Israel's domestic arrangements...but in respect of matters of high policy as well: the disposition of the occupied territories, relations with the Arab states and the Arab peoples, and so, by extension, questions of peace and war, of life and death for all'.[105] Such involvement runs counter to the inherent inability of Jewish ultra-Orthodoxy to recognize the modern credo of national sovereignty and the democratic state. As Hayim Soloveitchik pointed out, these concepts were unknown to traditional rabbinic Judaism and

> are not capable of being expressed in traditional halakhic, or even Rabbinic categories...The state is irredeemably alien, and, not surprisingly, it has been founded and run by atheists...For [the *haredim* (ultra-Orthodox)] there is no essential difference between a Jewish state in Israel and a Gentile one in Exile. There may be a state *in* Israel, but it is not, nor even can it be, the state *of* Israel.[106]

In theory, Jewish ultra-Orthodoxy is a 'transnational civil society', to use Susanne Hoeber Rudolph's term, as it 'respects no political frontiers…least of all those of modern Israel'.[107] Yet ultra-Orthodoxy's growing political activism in Israeli politics and its dependence on state subsidies push it to adopt the values of 'power' and 'violent enforcement' which are the hallmarks of the modern state. By choosing political activism to enforce religious norms in the State of Israel, the ultra-Orthodox have placed themselves in the nationalist 'godless' entrapment: 'Power presumes numbers, force needs critical mass, and Jews never possessed that mass. Exile means to be a minority, and thus adopting the "virtue" of a majority and its modus operandi is not only wrong but suicidal.'[108]

Soloveitchick's appraisal of the ultra-Orthodox community in Israel is also applicable to Jewish Orthodoxy in the United States. Inspired by the political empowerment of their nationalist–Orthodox kin in Israel, Jewish-American Orthodox began seeking political influence in the United States both locally and nationally – 'in sharp contrast to the timidity that often characterized the movement in the first two thirds of this century'.[109] Samuel Heilman has described the growing sense of self-confidence of many young Orthodox who are taking dogmatic positions on religious issues and developing intolerance towards other denominations. This *haredization* manifests itself in the proliferation of Orthodox and ultra-Orthodox institutions and in extended *yeshiva* attendance. The young men are subsidized by philanthropic sources and their lower income gradually produces a community that outgrows its resources. The growing economic needs cultivate ultra-Orthodox immigration in order to benefit from Israeli economic subsides. It also produces a new trend of eliciting public American support in the form of welfare, medicare and other funds for the poor, in a process that may undermine Orthodox institution-building with 'the very source of its [own] undoing'.[110] Heilman argues that as the Orthodox contemplate the idea of tax vouchers to support their parochial schools, they may erode 'the boundary between religion and state…[and thus] run against one of the cardinal principles of American Jewry and American law, both of which have always sought to keep that boundary very clear'.[111] This principle, however, has been contested by Orthodox (and other Jews) since as early as the mid-1960s. Positions have been influenced by a mixture of factors, including class and attitudes on intra-Jewish matters, on Israeli foreign policy and on 'American' questions of state and society (conservative versus liberal).[112]

While from the late 1960s Israel provided a unifying focus for American Jews, more recently it has seemed to fragment and divide the Diaspora, whose identity is less cohesive than ever before. To begin with, the retreat of anti-Semitism has removed the emphasis on the need for Jewish unity. Moreover, the realization that America is evolving into a 'multicultural' society has generally enhanced American Jewish adherence to the pluralist model and marked a retreat from the older position of trying to integrate themselves into the Christian–White paradigm. This means, among other things, a growing rejection by most Jewish-Americans of the isolationist course of the ultra-Orthodox in the US and in Israel. The split between Jewish particularists and universalists now dominates intra-Diasporic relations. The divide in Israel reinforces the divide in the United States and vice versa, especially since the ultra-Orthodox leadership in both countries is truly transnational, having no obligation to either Israel or the United States but to their kin religious community. In addition, Israeli socio-political movements and parties began to build 'American Friends of' organizations for fundraising, in effect expanding their constituencies to include non-voters in the Diaspora.

The Rabin assassination in November 1995, the ascent to power of Benjamin Netanyahu in 1996, and the 1997 explosion of the 'Who is a Jew?' debate reinforced these layers of identity crisis, whose ramifications in terms of politics, economics and religion are vast and yet to be fully realized. In the past, the argument that pressure should be exercised to 'save Israel from itself' was heard from groups or persons perceived by American Jews as adversaries of Israel, such as William Fulbright, George Bull and the Council on Foreign Relations. Such criticisms of Israel can now be heard from those within the mainstream, indeed the backbone, of the 'special-relationship' paradigm.[113] What has long seemed like automatic Jewish-American endorsement of Israeli policy no longer exists. Splits within Israel regarding the direction of peace negotiations have helped to divide the US Jewish community in terms of both varying preferences for American policy in the region and differing assessments of the degree to which Israel's moral claims continue to coincide with American values of democracy, pluralism and human rights. Some important mainstream American Jewish leaders considered Netanyahu responsible for the collapse of the peace process at the time and urged President Clinton to exert pressure on Israel. They have also urged Washington to make it clear to Israel that the United States has other interests in the Middle East, such as the flow of oil and the stability of friendly Arab governments.'[114] Altogether, the era of a unified American diasporic identification with the Homeland has come to an end.[115]

It is still the case that American Jews respond with unparalleled generosity, and without regard to internal political considerations, to particular major events or national crises in Israel such as the huge financial outlay needed to absorb the large wave of Soviet Jewish immigrants at the beginning of the 1990s. However, in the absence of such momentous events, the era of the blank cheque is coming to an end. Just as American Jews who identify with right-wing or ultra-Orthodox political elements in Israel express their views through financial support, Jews in America who support a more pluralistic future for Israeli society have begun, over the last few years, to target their philanthropic efforts accordingly. As early as 1989, a survey by Steven Cohen of American Jewish leaders identified a growing trend of 'supporting those Israeli non-party groups that advance one's vision of Israeli society'.[116] In the 1990s this pattern was reflected in the call of many Jewish organizations and individuals to stop contributions to Israeli bodies not recognizing non-Orthodox movements.[117] In November 1999, activists of the general assembly of America's Jewry held in Atlanta moved to establish a single umbrella organization, the United Jewish Communities (UJC). In what was described by one Israeli journalist as 'more than a bureaucratic upheaval', the new body not only unified all Jewish communities across America – through a merger of the UJA, the United Israel Appeal (UIA) and the Council of Jewish Federations (CJF) – but also took aim at redirecting funds to bolster Jewish identity in a process that empowers US-based local federations and gives them greater say over spending in Israel. To a large extent the assembly was a culmination of a decade-long debate on 'Jewish Pluralism'.[118] The Israeli daily *Ha'aretz* reported that Reform and Conservative representatives were 'trying to take advantage of the assembly to define the aspiration towards religious pluralism in Israel as one of the major goals of American Jewry, with all the implications this would have for the allocation of funds'. Orthodox representatives, on the other hand, protested against 'the significant place allocated to the events of the Society for Humanistic Judaism'.[119]

## CONCLUSIONS

The Jewish-American Diaspora is the largest, most active and most significant for Israeli politics and society. Moreover, issues of ethno-religious identity are more prominent (highly controversial and dynamic) between American Jews and Israel than between Israel and other diasporic kin. The reality of America allowed most American Jews to become an integral part of their adopted country, rather than 'sojourners' awaiting their 'redemption' and return to the homeland. While Jews living in the former Soviet Union, Morocco, Argentina or even France have recognized the clear duality of their national existence, most American Jews feel that they have the unequivocal right to call America home, and that a fully 'normal' Jewish life can be led in the United States, not just in Israel. Yet those of them who wish to remain 'affiliated Jews' cannot relegate the historic homeland to the periphery. They continue to affirm their attachment and commitment to the State of Israel, and are nourished by its Jewish images. Thus, non-religious Israeli holidays, such as Independence Day and Jerusalem Day, became part of the calendar of celebrations for non-Orthodox American Jews. For many of the Orthodox, the creation of the State of Israel was perceived as the dawn of Jewish redemption. Even for ultra-Orthodox American Jews, for whom the creation of the modern Jewish nation-state was a premature and sinful act, the fact that it is governed by Jews has compelled their involvement in Israeli matters in a way that strongly challenges their original animosity to Jewish nationalism.

Indeed, while members of other faiths in the United States may find themselves under duress – mostly as ethnic groups or as religious minorities – or may be associated with other countries (or cultures) in ways that may compromise their standing inside America, they cannot be considered 'diasporas' in the same way as Jews are. For Jews, a diasporic condition is almost endemic (conceptually speaking) once they reside outside the Land of Israel. Since the boundaries of Judaism are within the realm of *The Homeland*, they act as a constant barrier to the quest of belonging to another nation-state. This reality has created many tensions of 'dual loyalty' for the Diaspora.

As early as 1885, the blueprint of American Reform Judaism declared that Reform Jews did not consider themselves a nation and therefore did not anticipate a return to Palestine. More than a century later, although Reform Judaism continues to sound the blessings of church–state separation and of pluralism in the United States as the most conducive conditions for the realization of Judaism, the movement no longer ignores the centrality of Jewish political autonomy. In 'A Statement of Principles for Reform Judaism' adopted at the 1999 Pittsburgh convention, Reform moved beyond embracing 'religious and cultural pluralism as an expression of the vitality of Jewish communal life in Israel and the Diaspora', to affirming 'the unique qualities of living in *Eretz Yisrael*, the land of Israel', and to encourage *aliyah*.[120]

In 1977, Charles Liebman, a leading scholar of Diaspora–Israel relations, observed that 'because Israel is a symbol, its particular policies are not very important to American Jews'.[121] He qualified this statement by arguing that only the Orthodox were willing to expend energy and money to influence Israeli affairs since 'unlike virtually every other Diaspora group, [they] have a clear image of what Israel should be like and a sense of religious obligation to translate the image into specific policies'.[122] Liebman's assertion that Israeli 'Jewish content' is more relevant to the Diaspora Orthodoxy than to non-Orthodox denominations is built on the assumption that the latter's version of Judaism is loose and ephemeral. According to him the questions of Jewish-Israeli identity are secondary to Reform and Conservative Jews and the prospects of intervention 'fall outside the boundaries of [their] legitimate activity'.[123] He could only envisage Jewish-American Orthodox interventions to restrain Israeli Zionist attempts to erode the state's 'Jewish content'.

As we have seen, the growing involvement of committed American Jews of liberal religious persuasions (Conservative, Reform and Reconstructions) in Israeli affairs challenges Liebman's thesis. As they have become more cognizant of the centrality of Israel to their own Jewish-American identity, these movements have challenged the cosy relationship between the orthodox rabbinate and the state in Israel by engaging directly in a struggle to redefine Israel's identity in their own image. This undertaking – which for political and socio-cultural reasons was unimaginable two decades earlier – has provided these movements with a new focus for organizing and constructing Jewish identity in America. Indeed, non-Orthodox American-style religious denominations and their religious practices have grown significantly in the last decade throughout Israel.[124] The tacit assumption of many Jewish-Americans is that the Diaspora has

much to teach its benighted Israeli cousins. Living in a heterogeneous environment, American Jews – so the argument runs – have
learned the blessings of diversity, and accept the legitimacy of many
different forms of religious Jewish expression. Moreover, thanks to
constitutional guarantees of church/state separation, American
Judaism is not demeaned by the kinds of electoral horse-trading to
which Israeli religious parties must inevitably stoop. In short,
American Jews and American Judaism have flourished in an atmosphere of pluralism and tolerance, and Israeli Jews would do well to
learn from their example.

In February 1999, an organization tentatively titled the North
American Coalition for the Advancement of Religious Freedom in
Israel adopted its first mission statement, protesting against the
current 'Orthodox monopoly' that 'has circumscribed the right of
complete religious expression in Israel in matters of personal
status...We support the right of full religious expression and
worship for all streams of Judaism at public religious sites such as
the Western Wall in Israel.' Some 18–25 major Reform, Conservative
and non-denominational religious and non-religious North
American Jewish organizations are expected to join the coalition,
which would represent an estimated 2.5 to 3 million North
American Jews, perhaps 80 to 85 per cent of all affiliated Jews there.
Their aim is to educate and mobilize on these issues among North
American Jews in order to have an impact on Israeli society. As one
organizer (Mark Seal, Jewish Reconstructionist Federation) put it,
'People are concerned, people are talking about it, and I think it's a
question of: where's the society going, where's the culture going?'.

In the last few years Israeli governments have been assessing the
Conversion Law in the hope of bridging gaps and healing wounds.
This process invigorated Conservative and Reform forces inside
and outside Israel. The most striking development is perhaps the
fact that the Conservatives are gradually being recognized by
significant segments of moderate orthodoxy as legitimate partners
in a dialogue on Jewish identity. Although the moderate Orthodox
have made efforts to distinguish between the Reform and
Conservative streams, it is evident that current debates have helped
to further legitimize a more pluralistic approach to religion, Jewish
conversion, separating the sexes in synagogue, and qualifying
women as rabbis. It is my assertion that the Conservative and
Reform movements have made the first step in providing non-
Orthodox Israeli Jews – the majority of whom still profess a belief

in God and in Judaism – a means of reconnecting with their Jewish identity and history in ways which are more compatible with their modern way of life, and in times of a serious crisis in traditional Zionism.

Contrary to the thesis about the growing separation between Israel and the American Diaspora, one can see nascent signs of change in the direction of infusing traditionalist Israeli Judaism with liberal American Judaism as an alternative middle way between an aggressive ultra-Orthodoxy and unqualified secularism, in a process that draws Diaspora and Israeli Judaism closer. This process is nourished by the growing complexity of Israeli society, especially since about 25 per cent of the more than 800,000 immigrants who have moved to Israel from the former Soviet Union over the past decade are non-Jewish according to *halacha*. Yet most of these immigrants have come to Israel legally in accordance with the Law of Return, which allows citizenship 'to any Jew who expresses his will to live in the State of Israel', and are exploring non-Orthodox ways to become Jewish. Under the current law, non-Jews with at least one Jewish grandparent may also come to Israel.

The fact that the Diaspora is taking an active role in Israel's difficult process of forming its Israeli/Jewish character can become a source of spiritual empowerment for Judaism in the Diaspora, and may breathe new life into the Diaspora's connection with the homeland. Indeed, this process is intertwined with American Reform's own efforts to halt their growing distance from traditional Judaism. In Israel, this process may yet reawaken and bring new dimensions to the lives of many who have seen themselves as traditionalists, yet have grown alienated from Jewish practices in the absence of liberal components owing to ultra-Orthodox imposition and Orthodox political extremism. Perhaps this process may bring into being Zionist thinker Ahad Ha'am's vision of turning the Land of Israel into a spiritual centre embedded both in liberalism and in the fundamental teaching of Judaism.[125] Indeed, from the point of view of US-based Reform and Conservative Judaism, their labour to transform Israeli Jewish identity corresponds closely with the general diasporic dynamic whereby US-based diasporas 'market the American creed' to their homelands in a way that transforms both their kin abroad and promotes their own identities within the United States.

NOTES

1. Earlier drafts of this paper were presented at the International Conference on National Identity of New States at the Yitzhak Rabin Centre for Israeli Studies, Tel Aviv University, 2–4 March 1998, the annual meeting of the American Political Science association, Atlanta, 2–5 September 1999, and the International Conference on Diasporas: Transnational Identities and the Politics of the Homeland at the University of California, Berkeley, 12–13 November 1999. I wish to thank Avi Ben Zvi, Aharon Kleiman, Roni Bart and Tamar Wittes for their helpful comments and criticism.
2. Deborah Sontag, *New York Times*, 11 September 1999, p. 5.
3. J. J. Goldberg, *Jewish Power: Inside the American Jewish Establishment* (Reading, MA: Addison-Wesley, 1996), p. 340.
4. David Landau, 'Who Is A Jew: A Case Study of American Jewish Influence on Israeli Policy' (New York: American Jewish Committee, March 1996).
5. Abraham Ben Zvi, 'Partnership Under Stress: The American Jewish Community and Israel' (Jaffe Centre for Strategic Studies, August 1998), p. 35.
6. When on 29 March 2000, Judaism's Reform movement declared that gay relationships were 'worthy of affirmation' and gave its support to Reform rabbis who decided to officiate at same-sex ceremonies, some rabbis expressed concern that the decision would undermine the efforts of the movement to expand its presence inside Israel. Rabbi Uri Regev, the head of the Reform movement in Israel, declared that 'Israeli society is not as progressive yet as we would like to see…but at the same time, it is certainly opening up to understanding of the rights and the plight of homosexuals in a way that is gratifying'. See Gustav Niebuhr, 'Reform Rabbis Back Blessing of Gay Unions', *New York Times*, 30 March 2000, pp. 1 and 21.
7. Tamara Hausman, 'US Demographer: New Criteria Needed for Defining Jewishness', *Jerusalem Post*, 22 October 1999.
8. Naftali Rothenberg, 'Jews in Israel and the United States: Diverging Identities', in Ernest Krausz and Gitta Tulea (eds), *Jewish Survival: The Identity Problem at the Close of the Twentieth Century* (New Brunswick, NJ: Transaction, 1999), pp. 166–7.
9. Will Herberg, *Protestant–Catholic–Jew: An Essay in American Religious Sociology* (Chicago: University of Chicago Press, 1983), p. 193.
10. Seymour Martin Lipset and Earl Raab, *Jews and the New American Scene* (Cambridge, MA: Harvard University Press, 1995), p. 117.
11. Jack Wertheimer, *A People Divided: Judaism in Contemporary America* (New York: Basic Books, 1993), p. xix.
12. Ibid., p. xvii.
13. Steven M. Cohen, 'Israeli–Diaspora Relations: A Survey of American Jewish Leaders' (Tel Aviv: The Israeli–Diaspora Institute, December 1989), p. 1.
14. Ibid., p. 37.
15. Ibid., p. 43.
16. Alan M. Dershowitz, *The Vanishing American Jew: In Search of Jewish Identity for the Next Century* (Boston: Little, Brown, 1996), p. 242.
17. A survey of post-Soviet immigrants who came to Israel between 1989 to 1999 found that only 8 per cent of them identified as Israelis, 47 per cent as Russians and 45 per cent as Jewish, *Jerusalem Post*, 20 January 2000.
18. Baruch Kimmerling, 'Between Hegemony and Dormant *Kulturkampf* in Israel', in Dan Urian and Efraim Karsh (eds), *In Search of Identity: Jewish Aspects in Israeli Culture* (London: Frank Cass, 1999), p. 67.
19. The quotes appear in Antje Kohler, 'Orthodox Domination of the Religious Councils and the Exclusion of Reform and Conservative Jews', unpublished paper, Tel Aviv University, 1999.
20. Yosef Dan, a leading Israeli scholar of Judaic studies, has argued that the hostility of many Israelis towards Orthodox politics has led them to abandon Judaism altogether, thereby downgrading the validity of Jewish pluralism and Jewish cultural aspects and unintentionally legitimating the ultra-Orthodox religious hegemony. This process has contributed to the decline of Judaic scholarship inside Israel, while in the West, Judaic studies have flourished under the new creed of diversity and

multiculturalism. Va'adat Shenhar, a committee appointed by the late education minister Zevulun Hammer to study the decline of Jewish identity among Israelis, has found that the general decline of ideologies, the rise of consumerism and global markets, the politicization of religion and the growing gap between religious and secular Jews, as well as debates over issues of peace with the Arabs (which over the years became imbued with religious significance), have all contributed to the declining attachment to Judaism among non-observant Jews. See Yosef Dan, 'Empty Hands', *Free Judaism*, 11–12 (October 1997), p. 9 (in Hebrew); 'Nation and World, Jewish Culture in a Changing World' ('Am Ve'olam'), Recommendations of the Committee for Investigation into Judaic Studies in State Education, Israeli Ministry of Education, 1994.

21. A 1993 study by the Guttman Institute of Applied Social Research maintains that Israeli society has a strong traditional bent, and, as far as religious practices is concerned, there is a continuum from the 'strictly observant' to the 'non-observant.' See Shlomit Levy, Hanna Levinson, Elihu Katz, 'Beliefs, Observances and Social Interactions Among Israeli Jews' (Jerusalem: Louis Guttman Israel Institute of Applied Social Research, December 1993), p. 2. Asher Arian writes that 'in 1996, the overwhelming majority of Jews identified themselves as "Jewish" and "Israeli." Respondents were given four identities to rank: Jewish, Israeli, their ethnic classification (Ashkenazi or Sepharadi), or religion (observant or secular)...More than 40 percent of the respondents chose each of "Jewish" and "Israeli" as both first and second choice. Ethnic and religious observance identities were left far behind', Asher Arian, *The Second Republic: Politics in Israel* (New York: Chatham House Publishers, 1998), p. 7.

22. Charles Liebman, 'Comment' on Yossi Klein Halevi's essay, in 'Jewish Identities in Post-Rabin Israel' (Institute on American Jewish–Israeli Relations, July 1998), p. 23.

23. The Guttman study quoted above revealed that the 45 per cent of Jewish Israeli respondents were willing to consider Reform or Conservative options to Orthodoxy.

24. See Yair Sheleg, 'Russian Jews Choosing Reform Judaism', *Ha'aretz*, 21 December 1999; Haim Shapiro, 'Melchior Unveils Plan to Convert Immigrant Children', *Jerusalem Post*, 21 December 1999.

25. For reports on the movements' activity inside Israel, see Ephraim Tabory, 'Reform Judaism in Israel' (New York: American Jewish Committee, October 1998); Harvey Meirovich, 'The Shaping of Masorti Judaism in Israel' (New York: American Jewish Committee, January 1999). See also *Ha'aretz*, 21 February 1999, p. 6. For a Reform discussion see 'Is the Legal Struggle the Wrong Way to Go?', Albert Vorspan and David Saperstein, *Jewish Dimensions of Social Justice* (New York: UAHC Press, 1998), pp. 144–5.

26. Efraim Karsh and Dan Urian, 'Introduction' in Urian and Karsh (eds), *Jewish Aspects in Israeli Culture*, p. 4.

27. For the statement see Shahar Ilan, 'Progressive Jews: "What Synagogue Are We Not Going to?", *Ha'aretz* (English edition), 21 February 1999, p. 6.

28. Cited in Rabbi G. Hirsch's keynote address, published in the *Electronic Newsletter of the World Union for Progressive Judaism*, Special Convention Issue, 11 March 1999, p. 5. The writers were vehemently attacked by secular Israelis who argued that by endorsing Reform and Conservative Judaism and by calling on Israelis to join these movements they were undermining the vision of a secular/humanistic Jewish–Israeli movement. For A. B. Yehoshua's response to these charges see *Free Judaism*, 14 (April 1999), p. 38 (in Hebrew).

29. 'What Do American Jews Believe?', *Commentary*, August 1996, p. 30.

30. See 'Reform Judaism Creates Its Own Israeli Identity', ARZA/World Union, North America (http/rj.org/arzawuna/st/st2.html). The journalist Yossi Klein Halevi has articulated a similar vision of how Israel should develop a new, indigenous Judaism which builds on American diasporic innovation. See his essay in 'Jewish Identities in Post-Rabin Israel', Institute on American Jewish–Israeli Relations, July 1998.

31. The 1998 Annual Report of the New Israel Fund is entitled 'The New Israel: Mosaic Identities'. Its grants inside Israel are listed in the following categories: Safeguarding Civil and Human Rights, Bridging Social and Economic Gaps, Fostering Tolerance and Religious Pluralism, Advancing the Status of Women,

Promoting Jewish and Arab Equality and Coexistence, Pursuing Environmental Justice.

32. While the Orthodox rebuked the appeal as jeopardizing the unity of the Jewish people, the president of the American Jewish Congress considered the action in line with American democratic values: 'What we find wanting in America – the imperfections of Democracy that we recognize and seek to correct – must also be considered faulty and in need of correction in Israel'. Interestingly, the prime minister welcomed the appeal 'as not an interference by an alien body, but an indication that the Jewish world lives Israel's problems... what affects Israel, affects them', cited in S. Zalman Abramov, *Perpetual Dilemma: Jewish Religion in the Jewish State* (Cranbury, NJ: Associated University Press, 1976), pp. 375–6.

33. Charles S. Liebman, *Pressure Without Sanctions: The Influence of World Jewry on Israeli Policy* (Cranbury, NJ: Associated University Press, 1977), p. 212.

34. While fewer than 10 per cent of American Jews are Orthodox they comprise over 80 per cent of American immigrants, Yair Sheleg, 'The North American Impact on Israel Orthodoxy' (New York: American Jewish Committee, October 1999).

35. With the exception of the Lubavitch Hasidic sect of New York. See ibid., p. 6.

36. Largely because of the liberal Zionist reluctance to carry on the vision and struggle for a 'Greater Israel'. The fracture is compounded by Orthodox cultural criticism of what they consider the Israeli abandonment of its Jewish content.

37. While upholding *halachic* theology modern Orthodox Jews also allow for Western-democratic norms and values in their daily life, pp. 11–12.

38. When a group of Orthodox undergraduates at Yale University filed a lawsuit to change Yale's policy 'requiring all freshman and sophomores to live in a mixed-sex dormitory' thereby 'forcing them into an environment whose mores were sharply at odds with their strict [religion]', they were denounced by liberal segments in the Jewish community 'for seeking to establish a 'ghetto-Judaism' on an Ivy League campus', Jack Wertheimer, 'The Orthodox Moment', *Commentary* (February 1999), pp. 18–24.

39. George M. Marsden, *Religion and American Culture* (San Diego, CA: Harcourt Brace and Jovanovich, 1990), pp. 219–20. See also Bernard Susser and Charles S. Liebman, *Choosing Survival: Strategies for a Jewish Future* (Oxford: Oxford University Press, 1999), p. 44.

40. Interview with Rabbi Ammiel Hirsh, 29 December 1999.

41. Sidney Goldstein, 'Profile of American Jewry: Insights from the 1990 National Jewish Population Survey', in David Singer and Ruth R. Seldin (eds), *American Jewish Year Book 1992*, Volume 92 (New York: American Jewish Committee, 1992), pp. 12–132.

42. Zvi Gitelman, 'Language and Ethnic Identity: Yiddish in the Soviet Union', unpublished paper, University of Michigan, 1999.

43. David Vital, *A People Apart: The Jews in Europe 1789–1939* (Oxford: Oxford University Press, 1999), pp. 366–7.

44. Perhaps this is why a recent volume on 'transnational religion' overlooked the contemporary Jewish experience altogether. See Susanne Hoeber Rudolph and James Piscatory (eds), *Transnational Religion and Fading States* (Boulder, CO: Westview Press, 1997).

45. The 1985 platform's authors proclaimed: 'We consider ourselves no longer a nation, but a religious community, and, therefore, expect neither a return to Palestine... nor the restoration of the laws concerning the Jewish state'. See 'Reform Judaism and Zionism: A Centenary Platform', *CCAR Journal* (Spring 1998), p. 10.

46. Yosef Gorny, *The Quest For Collective Identity* (in Hebrew) (Tel Aviv: Am Oved ,1986), pp. 141–60.

47. Vorspan and Saperstein, *Jewish Dimensions of Social Justice*, p. 137.

48. *Electronic Newsletter of the World Union for Progressive Judaism*, WUPJ News-issue 9, 11, March 1999.

49. See Harvey Meirovich, 'The Shaping of the Masorti Movement in Israel' (New York: American Jewish Committee, January 1999), p. 6.

50. David Schoenbaum, *The United States and the State of Israel* (Oxford: Oxford University Press, 1993), pp. 58–62. For a discussion on the Jewish-American role in

President Truman's decision to accord recognition to the State of Israel, see Alexander DeConde, *Ethnicity Race and American Foreign Policy: A History* (Boston, MA: Northeastern University Press, 1992), pp. 131–6.

51. Peter Novick, *The Holocaust in American Life* (New York: Houghton Mifflin, 1999).
52. The Council for Judaism was at the time the only distinctively anti-Israel organization.
53. Cited in Samuel C. Heilman, *Portrait of American Jews: The Last Half of the 20th Century* (Seattle, WA: University of Washington Press, 1998), p. 17.
54. Ibid., p. 56.
55. Gil Merom, 'Israel National Security and the Myth of Exceptionalism', *Political Science Quarterly*, 114, 3 (fall 1999), p. 412.
56. Schoenbaum, *The United States and the State of Israel*, p. 63.
57. Charles S. Liebman and Eliezer Don-Yehiya, *Civil Religion in Israel* (Berkeley, CA: University of California Press, 1983), p. 90.
58. Arthur Hertzberg, 'Israel and the Diaspora: A Relationship Reexamined', *Israel Affairs*, 2, 3–4 (spring/summer 1996), p. 172.
59. Menahem Kaufman, 'Envisaging Israel: The Case of the United Jewish Appeal', in Allon Gal (ed.), *Envisioning Israel: The Changing Ideals and Images of North American Jews* (Jerusalem: Magnes Press, 1996), p. 224.
60. Nathan Glazer, *American Judaism*, p. 115.
61. Wertheimer, *A People Divided*, p. 4.
62. Jonathan D. Sarna and David G. Dalin, *Religion and State in the American Jewish Experience* (Notre Dame, IN: University of Notre Dame Press, 1997), p. 246.
63. Ibid., pp. 245–61.
64. Glazer, *American Judaism*, p. 116.
65. Cited in Abraham Ben Zvi, *Decade of Transition: Eisenhower, Kennedy and the Origins of the American–Israeli Alliance* (New York: Columbia University Press, 1998), pp. 56–7, 96. On 2 November 1956 President Eisenhower wrote to Edward E. Hazlett: 'I gave strict orders to the State Department that they should inform Israel that we would handle our affairs exactly as though we didn't have a Jew in America', cited in DeConde, *Ethnicity, Race, and American Foreign Policy*, p. 136.
66. Ibid. See also Robert J. Lieber, 'Domestic Politics and Foreign Policy: Making Sense of America's Role in the Middle East Peace Process', *World Affairs*, 161, 1 (summer 1998), p. 5.
67. Stuart E. Eiszenstat, 'Loving Israel – Warts And All', *Foreign Policy*, 81 (winter, 1990–91), p. 92.
68. Stephen Warner, 'Work in Progress toward a New Paradigm for the Sociological Study of Religion in the United States', *AJS*, 98, 5 (March 1993), p. 1067.
69. Sarna and Dalin, *Religion and the American Jewish Experience*, p. 262.
70. On this point see the brilliant essay by Hayim Soloveitchick, 'Migration, Acculturation, and the New Role of Texts in the Haredi World', in Martin E. Marty and R. Scott Appleby (eds), *Accounting for Fundamentalisms: The Dynamic Character of Movements* (Chicago, IL: Chicago University Press, 1994), pp. 206–7.
71. Cited in O'Brien, *American Jewish Organizations and Israel*, p. 10.
72. Peter Novick, *The Holocaust in American Life* (New York: Houghton Mifflin, 1999).
73. Cited in Jonathan Kaufman, *Broken Alliance: The Turbulent Times Between Blacks and Jews in America* (New York: Scribner's, 1988), p. 208.
74. Alan Dershowitz, *Chutzpah* (New York: Simon and Schuster, 1991), p. 80.
75. Cited in Kaufman, *Broken Alliance*, p. 202.
76. Marshall Sklare, *America's Jews* (New York: Random House, 1971), p. 216.
77. Kaufman, 'Envisaging Israel: The Case of the United Jewish Appeal', p. 222.
78. Max Beloff, 'The Diaspora and the Peace Process', *Israel Affairs*, 1, 1 (autumn 1994), p. 33.
79. David Vital, 'Diplomacy in the Jewish Interest', Occasional Paper No. 1 (Tel Aviv University, 1983), p. 4.
80. Reform leaders were warmly received by the Israeli government and the press, and Prime Minister Eshkol stressed the movement's potential as messengers of change in Israel's religious landscape. The Israeli Orthodox, however, attacked the movement as 'enemies of Zion' and frustrated their scheduled mixed-gender service at

the Western Wall. Although Reform leaders cancelled the service – for 'fear of physical violence to others, and, even more, of the possibility of political repercussions
reflecting on Israel's rights in the Holy Places' – they gained public sympathy and
were able to put the question of religious pluralism on the Israeli agenda. See
Abramov, *Perpetual Dilemma*, pp. 370–4.
81.  Marsden, *Religion and American Culture*, p. 221.
82.  Paul Berman, 'The Other and Almost the Same', *New Yorker*, 28 February 1994, p. 68.
83.  Melvin I. Urofsky, *We Are One: American Jewry and Israel* (Garden City, KS: Anchor
Press, 1978), p. 374.
84.  Cited in ibid., p. 376.
85.  Kenneth D. Wald *et al.*, 'Reclaiming Zion: How American Religious Groups View the
Middle East', *Israel Affairs*, 2, 3–4 (spring/summer 1996), pp. 147–66; Leo Ribuffo,
'Religion and American Foreign Policy: The Story of a Complex Relationship',
*National Interest* (summer 1998), p. 45.
86.  J. J. Goldberg, *Jewish Power: Inside the American Jewish Establishment* (Reading, MA:
Addison-Wesley, 1976), p. 175.
87.  Ibid., pp. 174–80.
88.  Charles S. Liebman, 'Israel in the Mind of American Jews', in Eliezer Don-Yehiya
(ed.), *Israel and Diaspora Jewry: Ideological and Political Perspectives* (Jerusalem: Bar-
Ilan University Press, 1991), p. 34.
89.  Alan Cowell, 'Prominent U.S. Jews, Visiting Israel, Voice Unease', *New York Times*, 2
March 1988; Linda Feldman, 'US Jews in Turmoil over Violence in Israel', *Christian
Science Monitor*, 4 March 1988.
90.  Landau, 'Who Is a Jew?', pp. 10–11.
91.  Roth, p. 81
92.  Eisenstat, 'Loving Israel', p. 93.
93.  Aaron S. Klieman, *Israel and The World After 40 Years* (Washington, DC: Pergamon-
Brassey's, 1990), p. 178.
94.  David Vital, *The Future of the Jews: A People at the Crossroads* (Cambridge, MA:
Harvard University Press, 1990), p. 136.
95.  Ibid.
96.  Cited in Ron Zohara, 'Ethiopians in the Ghetto of Los Angeles' (in Hebrew), *Ha'ir*,
31 December 1993, p. 57.
97.  *Boston Globe*, 14 February 1996, and *Newsweek*, 12 February 1996.
98.  *Yediot Ahronot*, 24 July 1996.
99.  Although a majority of Orthodox respondents in a 1995 public opinion survey
opposed the peace process. See 'American Jewish Attitudes Toward Israel and the
Peace Process', conducted for the American Jewish Committee by Market Facts,
7–15 August 1995.
100. See Caryle Murphy, 'Reform Jewish Leaders Urge Support', *Washington Post*, 11
January 2000; Shlomo Shamir, 'Reform Jews Try Rallying for Peace', *Ha'aretz*, 10
January 2000.
101. Amy Dockers Marcus, 'Burden of Peace: American Jews Grapple with an Identity
Crisis as Peril to Israel Ebbs', *Wall Street Journal*, 14 September 1994, pp. 1, 6.
102. Thomas L. Friedman, 'Mischief Makers', *New York Times*, 5 April 1995.
103. In a 1998 bestseller in Israel, *The Messiah's Donkey*, author Seffi Rachlevsky fero-
ciously scorned the growing ultra-Orthodox power in Israel. His analysis of the
ultra-Orthodox abuse of the Israeli state system further galvanized secular Israeli
anxiety and, according to one observer, contributed to the 'secular counterrevolu-
tion that brought Prime Minister Ehud Barak to power in May 1999'. See a review
of the book by Micha Odenheimer, *Foreign Policy* (fall 1999), pp. 144–7.
104. For an excellent analysis of the dynamics of the ultra-Orthodox economy, see Eli
Berman, 'Sect, Subsidy and Sacrifice: An Economist's View of Ultra-Orthodox Jews',
unpublished paper, Boston University, National Bureau of Economic Research,
March 1999.
105. David Vital, 'Israel and the Jewish Diaspora: Five Comments on the Political
Relationship', *Israel Affairs*, 1, 2 (winter 1994), pp. 184–5.
106. Soloveitchik, 'Migration, Acculturation, and the New Role of Texts in the Haredi
World', p. 223.

107. Vital, 'Israel and the Jewish Diaspora', p. 185.
108. Soloveitchik, 'Migration, Acculturation, and the New Role of Texts in the Haredi World', p. 221.
109. Heilman, *Portrait of American Jews: The Last Half of the 20th Century* (Seattle, WA: University of Washington Press, 1995), p. 146.
110. Ibid., pp. 154–5.
111. Ibid., p. 154.
112. I am indebted to Mark Stern of the American Jewish Congress for this observation. For the relatively poor ultra-Orthodox community, especially Hasidic Jews like the Satmar sect of New York Kiryas Joel, the livelihood of their day schools and *yeshivot* is more central to their continued existence than the somewhat vague church–state question that preoccupies other mainstream American Jews. Some in the Conservative movement, which saw a dramatic growth of its day schools, argue that 'in pluralistic America, where there are constitutional guarantees against the establishment of any *one* religion and where the prevailing ethos ordains that Judaism is one of the "three religions of democracy", the strengthening of parochial school would not endanger the Jewish status for all citizens. What endangers Judaism is ignorance and all-pervasive secularism.' This opinion was expressed as early as 1970 by Rabbi Seymour Siegal, a professor at the Jewish Theological Seminary. See Sarana and Dalin, *Religion and State in the American Jewish Experience*, pp. 268–9. On the landmark case of Board of Education of Kiryas Joel Village School District v. Grumet 114 s. Ct. 2481 (1994) see David M. O'brien, *Constitutional Law and Politics Volume Two: Civil Rights and Civil Liberties* (3rd edition) (New York: W. W. Norton, 1997), pp. 702–13.
113. For this idea I am indebted to Avi Ben-Zvi, who writes that 'the "special relationship" paradigm…comprises a broad cluster of predispositions, sentiments and attitudes toward Israel in American public opinion, which are permeated with sympathy, support and affection'. See his *Decade of Transition*, p. 4. See also Yossi Shain, *Marketing the American Creed Abroad*, p. 202.
114. *International Herald Tribune*, 20–21 September 1997, p. 1.
115. Jonathan Broder, 'Netanyahu and American Jews', *World Policy Journal*, 15, 1 (spring 1998), pp. 89–98.
116. Cohen, 'Israel Diaspora Relations', p. 43.
117. Financial support from American Jewry is no longer the make-or-break revenue source it was in Israel's early years. At around $500 million per annum, it represents but a small fraction of the Israeli economy, the GNP of which is approaching $70 billion. However, the way in which the money that is given is directed is increasingly important to Israel. While in the early days of state-building, different variants and interpretations of Jewishness were no more than a marginal factor in determining how diasporic funds were distributed, in recent years there has been a perceptible shift in the nature of the recipients of diasporic money within Israel, with civil and political society becoming increasingly significant in determining issues pertaining to homeland identity. Questions of internal composition ('Who is a Jew?'), of external conduct (relations with outside entities in the international system, including the debate on the universalist vs particularist paradigms of international affairs), and regime characteristics (particularly the debate over religion and liberalism in domestic political affairs) are major foci of diasporic interest and money. See Yossi Shain and Martin Sherman, 'Diasporic Transnational Financial Flows and Their Impact on National Identity', forthcoming. See also the special informative report of the American Jewish Committee, *Ha'arez* (Hebrew edition), 12 March 1999.
118. Marilyn Henry, 'GA Ends with United Body, Divisive Issues', *Jerusalem Post*, 21 November 1999.
119. Nitzan Horowitz, 'Historic Assembly to Be a Melting Pot, as U.S. Jewish Organizations Merge', *Ha'aretz*, 17 November 1999.
120. See statement by the Central Conference of American Rabbis, May 1999.
121. Liebman, *Pressures Without Sanctions*, p. 202.
122. Ibid., p. 206.
123. Ibid., p. 213.

124. For a list of the activities and institutions of the movements in Israel see Harvey Meeirovich, 'The Masorti Movement in Israel' and Ephraim Tabory, 'Reform Judaism in Israel' as well as the movements' publications.
125. Ahad Ha'am was an advocate of 'spiritual' Zionism and a leading critic of the absence of Jewish content in Herzel's Zionist thinking. For a similar assessment see Alan Dowty, *The Jewish State: A Century Later* (Berkeley, CA: University of California Press, 1998), p. 252.

# 17 Weaving the Future of Israel

## YEHEZKEL DROR

### FRAME

Zionism is one of the greatest success stories in human efforts to weave the future.[1] Within 50 years it produced a large and thriving Jewish society in the Land of Israel, and the State of Israel has become a viable political entity. Furthermore, despite pronounced differences, Israel's main features approximate the original visions of Zionism much more so than in the case of other revolutionary transformations. However, at present the evolutionary potential of Israel remains wide open, with both extremes, or alternative futures – decline and ascendance – constituting distinct possibilities.

'Rise and decline' are an implied major interest of David Vital, as expressed in his studies on the history of Zionism, his thoughts on the future of the Jewish people and his work on small states. It is therefore fitting to devote this essay to a prescriptive exploration of possibilities for weaving the future of Israel so as to (a) decrease the probabilities of decline; (b) increase the probabilities of thriving; and (c) gear for the unforeseeable.

Developing and implementing operational policies for weaving the future is a challenge that requires outstanding statecraft supported by a well-equipped 'central brain of government'. Therefore, I also propose to outline institutional redesigns directed at upgrading Israeli capacities to engage in deliberate future-weaving. Such redesign is all the more essential given that Israeli choice-making faculties are declining in quality at the very same time as Israeli power resources and historic opportunities are improving. This results in a paradox that may well become a tragic trap unless salient political and governmental institutions are drastically reformed. Avoiding precisely such a trap while augmenting Israeli future-weaving capacities is the main thrust of this essay.[2]

FACING CROSSROADS INTO THE FUTURE

Israel's predicament can best be summed up in a metaphor by the classical Chinese Confucian scholar Xunzi: 'As Yang Zhu once lamented at a crossroads: if a man makes an error of half a step in the wrong direction, when he awakens to the fact, he will have made a blunder of a thousand li'.[3]

Many alternative possibilities open to Israel are not determined by single choices, but by decision chains enabling possibilities for changing, and not only reversing, directions. Still, the metaphor fits well, both because Israel does face fateful critical choices that are largely irreversible, as in the Middle East peace process, and because decision chains, too, pose critical choices, though in a more extended sense.

The evolutionary potentiali[4] of Israel within the next 30 to 50 years[5] in its three-tiered regional, Jewish diasporic and global settings is extensive, and includes contradictory possibilities. The following are alternative pathways to the future:

- Prospective relations with other Middle Eastern states can be either peaceful and cooperative, or conflictive, escalating to mass killings.
- Internally, Israel can deepen its character as a distinctively Jewish state, with cultural autonomy for its non-Jewish minorities. Or it may become a multi-ethnic, integrated and secularized 'normal' state. Or it may evolve into a divided society with acute conflict, extending to domestic violence between Jews and non-Jews on the one hand, and between different Jewish sectors on the other.
- Israel may become predominantly a 'knowledge economy' within a 'knowledge society', with higher standards of living for all, combined with an increasingly multi-dimensional and society-wide quality of life. Or it could develop into a stratified economy, with hi-tech high-income and low-tech low-income parts, high unemployment, underemployment and intense socio-economic conflict.
- Culturally, Israel can be a centre of pluralistic creativity of Jewish and universal significance. Or it may become a rather mediocre society in cultural terms, dominated by the global mass media and external standards.

This sketch of alternative futures for Israel may seem banal, until three further considerations are inserted into the equation:

a) Owing to relatively recent global and regional developments some of the main alternative futures are realistic within the given time span of 30 to 50 years. Thus, only since the 1979 peace with Egypt and the collapse of the Soviet Union have regional peace and stability in the Middle East become a feasible contingency. And only globalization, combined with the growing importance of high technologies, has opened up the scenario for Israel's becoming a knowledge-economy.

b) Israeli society is characterized, much more so than nearly all other democracies, by intense and widely held ideologies on desired futures. Various images of Israel as a secular, Jewish–Zionist, Zionist–religious or ultra-orthodox society and state are held and propagated by main social actors. True, there seems to be some erosion of ideological fervour in parts of the population, who long for 'normality' – but this itself is a future-driving belief and motivation. Therefore, it is correct to continue characterizing Israel as the most ideological of all democracies. This, in turn, provides potent future-driving energy and will, thus making the necessity for choice among alternative futures much more of a social issue than in other countries.

c) Israel faces concrete decisions that are of great portent. This is obvious with respect to Arab–Israel peacemaking, but applies to other choices, such as land use, water desalination, immigration and defining 'being a Jew', employment, education, weapon-systems development, the political system and more.

At the deeper level of historic processes, the radical nature of alternative futures facing Israel results from the lack of a stable history which might normally dictate at least some main lines to the future. Granted, Judaism and the Jewish people have a long history, yet the enlightenment, the Holocaust, the establishment of the State of Israel and the leap into new existential Diaspora realities together constitute a fundamental hiatus in history. Also, modern Zionism, the State of Israel and, very uniquely so, the Jewish population and society in Israel,[6] are relatively new. Therefore, while Judaism, the Jewish people and the idea of a Jewish State in the Promised Land provide a sense of continuity and condition some aspects of the future, the unfolding of Israel is relatively under-determined by 'long-term historic processes'.[7]

When the impact of global and regional transformations is taken into account, then indeed the future of Israel should be viewed as wide open. Certainly, relatively rigid factors and processes impose constraints, but some of these, too, may be more elastic in Israel than in other countries. This is illustrated by (a) any number of possibilities (though these may close soon) regarding the future borders of Israel; and, more importantly, (b) its immigration-dependent Jewish population.

The idea of a crossroads and of crossroads-chains implies choices a society is free to select, which can make a big difference to the future. In the case of Israel, many of the variables determining the future are exogenous. This is well illustrated by the single most important development for the future of Israel since the peace with Egypt, namely the collapse of the Soviet Union, with the resulting large-scale, high-quality Jewish immigration and the resulting transformation in geo-strategic dynamics of the Middle East. Internal changes in Middle East and West Asian countries, domestic politics in the US and the European Union, global economic developments and crises – these are but a few non-linear[8] factors strongly influencing the future of Israel yet beyond the control of its policy instruments.

This said, from an external perspective and without taking into account domestic decision-making constraints,[9] it seems quite clear that Israel still retains significant future-weaving resources. First, Israel is more powerful than ever, in terms of its human capital, economic resources and military capabilities, and external political support. Second, our global economic and technological environments offer innumerable opportunities for using Israeli knowledge-resources to achieve socio-economic prosperity. Third, large parts of the Middle East are in transition, providing Israel with windows of opportunity for influencing – though not shaping – their future interfaces with Israel.

This estimation in no way presents a voluntaristic view according to which Israeli 'will' can freely shape its future. In many respects possibilities are strictly limited. Thus, for example, a Palestinian state is almost inevitable; there is little probability of achieving peace with Syria without relinquishing nearly all of the Golan Heights; there is no effective way to prevent potentially hostile states from acquiring or developing nuclear weapons; global economic pressures limit Israeli social-policy choices. But even in such spheres Israel can nevertheless exert some degree of influence. Thus, relations with states acquiring nuclear weapons can be improved and hostile acts on their part deterred; while Israel can adopt taxation and social policies of its own choosing without necessarily damaging international competitiveness; and so on.

Therefore, my initial conclusion is that Israel faces profoundly significant crossroads, in time providing 'objective' opportunities for choice between alternative pathways leading into quite different futures.[10] However, maximizing this potential hinges on two further, partly overlapping conditions: that domestic conditions do not over-determine choices and thus close options and opportunities; and that Israeli choice faculties are of sufficient high quality to produce good, even optimal decisions.

## REALISTIC NIGHTMARES AND VISIONS

The importance of realistic visions as compasses for decision-making, in addition to their functions in consensus-building and as a motivational device, is well recognized in modern management practice and literature.[11] Democratic governments, however, run into difficulties in using realistic visions because their utilization as electoral tools spoils their function as policy compasses and because consensus-building is served by ambiguous statements and general slogans of little subsequent use in concrete policy-making. Most important of all, widespread rejection of the very idea of weaving the future and, instead, reliance on market forces and civil society as arbiters of a better future all but erase the very basis on which realistic visions must stand as policy compasses and guidelines.

Leaving aside the implications of these fallacious views and practices in other countries, clearly the situation of Israel is different, both in terms of social values and high-risk and high-hope crossroads which require collective choice. Israel needs sober, realistic visions as policy compasses.[12] However, realistic visions depend on contentious values. Quite obviously, realistic visions based, respectively, on ultra-orthodox, secular Zionist or post-Zionist values must differ in important respects, just as a realistic vision based on values of the Arab minority will differ from those of the Jewish majority.

To cope with this difficulty I recommend, first of all, constructing a realistic nightmare as a 'negative' policy compass that can serve as the frame for policies reducing the probability of decline and catastrophe. Avoiding 'the bad' is a major policy goal that must always precede striving to achieve more of 'the good'. An additional advantage is the greater ease of achieving consensus on ills to be avoided rather than concrete, positive values to be realized.

The realistic nightmare vision which I propose is grounded in a revised version of non-religious, but Judaism-based, Zionism,[13] while the proposed realistic nightmare is relatively less dependent on disputed values. Readers with other values are invited to adjust the realistic vision to their own norms. But I hope that most of its features will be accepted by the vast majority of Israeli Zionists.

The essence of a realistic nightmare for Israel for the next 30 to 50 years can be summed up as follows:

- oscillation between armed conflicts and partial peace, with growing traumatization of Israeli society and strong disagreement on whom to blame;
- slow economic growth, growing endemic unemployment, increasing disparities in income and the material quality of life;
- deepening social disagreement leading to violent conflicts concerning relations between religion and state;
- explosive tensions between Jews and Arabs within Israel proper;
- a Jewish population diminishing to less than 65 per cent of the total population, the result of differential birth rates and net emigration of Jews, including high-tech professionals;
- erosion of relations with the Jewish people as a whole, with Israel's 'centrality' for Jewish existence disputed;
- cultural imports dominating the mass media, with indifferent local artistic and literary creativity;
- a regime that is democratic, but whose national politics are fragmented and dominated by narrow interests, with low-calibre governments, public apathy and cynicism, and a weak capacity to govern;
- all in all, Israel as a mediocre Western state including a mix of many Middle Eastern elements.

This realistic nightmare is not presented as a bogey image, as is often the case in demagogic literature, and in the presentations of well-intended but non-professional brain-stormers and 'think-tanks'. Nor is this nightmare a 'worst-case' doomsday scenario. In my estimation of Israel's evolutionary potential, the nightmare presented here is 'realistic'. It is not only 'possible', but also 'quite likely' in the absence of counteracting deliberate interventions with history because a number of present developments, policies and default decisions actually lead towards this plausible if undesirable direction.

Therefore, in serious policy-thinking and policy-planning, this and similar realistic nightmares must be analysed as a basis for designing and implementing *counter-policies*. But this is not a task for this chapter. Instead, I turn to the alternative realistic vision.

Again, limiting myself to major items, the essence of a more upbeat, realistic vision for Israel for the next 30 to 50 years, based on Jewish–Zionist secular values, can be summed up as follows:

- a Jewish majority of at least 70 per cent, with significant net immigration from the Diaspora;
- deepening of the Jewish nature of the state in pluralistic modes, together with cultural autonomy for the minorities;
- relatively stable peace with Middle Eastern and West Asian countries, together with superior Israeli military capacities and the socio-economic ability to prosper despite conflicts and threats of war;
- significant Jewish pluralistic creativity coupled with Israel's central position for world Jewry and intense involvement in global Jewish affairs;
- economic prosperity thanks largely to a knowledge and information economy, together with near-full employment combined with extended leisure activities;
- reduced social disparities;
- 'unity within plurality', with 'creative tensions' between various sectors, including continuous debate over the desired nature of the State of Israel, especially with respect to religion and state, but non-violent in nature and aimed at promoting mutual respect in the midst of principled disagreement;
- evolution towards a 'learning' and 'high-culture' society;
- high-quality democracy combining informed discourse and participation with accountable power élites in order to facilitate weaving the future;
- all in all, Israel as a unique country based on Jewish and human values, striving for cultural and social excellence while increasingly enjoying higher global standing as a state to be emulated.

This realistic vision is emphatically not utopian. It takes fully into account the limits of possibilities within the one-generation time frame of 30 to 50 years. Therefore, it is offered as a guide to policy-making, with concrete implications for critical choices and choice-chains to be faced by Israel in the near future, to which I now turn.

## POLICIES AND CRITICAL CHOICES

Policies are principles guiding and integrating various decisions synchronically and diachronically. Critical choices and choice-chains are selections between pathways posed by crossroads and crossroads-chains leading into the future. Both are modalities for weaving the future by developing and applying policy instruments to historic processes so as to divert them, within the evolutionary potential of a given entity, from nightmares and decline towards visions and prosperity. However, since situations, processes and the very meanings of 'decline' and 'prospering' change with time, policy-making and critical choices are continuous processes. Constant adjustments are accepted as being essential, especially in periods of rapid change, as the twenty-first century is sure to be characterized.

Given this model, to which institutional components will be added later, I am now 'leaping' into examples of future-weaving policies and critical choices and choice-chains derived from them. I do so without detailed analysis and reasoning, which require at least a book. Hopefully, the reader will discern the links leading from what has been said to the policy and critical choice examples.

I proceed by presenting three procedural policy-making guidelines, dealing with policy-making as a whole, and five substantive policy guidelines, dealing with specific domains.

## POLICY-MAKING – GUIDELINE ONE: LONG-TERM CONSIDERATIONS SHOULD RECEIVE GREATER WEIGHT IN CURRENT POLICY AND DECISION-MAKING

There is no doubt about the commitment of senior Israeli decision-makers to the long-term future of the state. However, Israel is increasingly becoming a populist mass democracy, with the satisfying of public opinion as expressed in polls displacing more and more weaving of the future. The weakness of institutional arrangements for taking a longer-term look and applying it to current choices further aggravates the situation.

This pathology is shared by all contemporary democracies, some more so and some less so. But Israel is rapidly becoming one of the most afflicted, whereas its existential needs require more long-term policies than most other democracies. Therefore, the policy-making system and its political and social settings and the machinery of government in part must be transformed, so as to increase the weight given to long-term considerations and their quality, as required by the evolutionary potential of Israel between nightmares and visions. Ways for doing so will be proposed in a sub-chapter below.

## POLICY-MAKING – GUIDELINE TWO: ADVANCING THE PEACE PROCESS MUST BE COMBINED WITH SERIOUS ATTENTION TO OTHER FUTURE-SHAPING DOMAINS

Peace and war are a crucial element of realistic nightmares and visions. But they are not the only element, or necessarily the single most important one. While peace and war interact with the other elements of thriving or decline, there is no simple linear relation. Thus, peace does not assure the overall thriving of Israel in terms of Jewish–Zionist values. Nor does non-peace necessarily prevent the overall thriving of Israel, and it must not be permitted to do so. Therefore, any sequential approach is terribly misguided if it insists upon deferring action on future-shaping until such time as the peace process is consummated. Holding progress on other fronts hostage to resolving the regional conflict is all the more serious a mistake as the success of the peace process, or its failure, will prompt social traumas which will have a serious negative impact on other crucial future-shaping issues – unless, that is, preparatory policies are adopted and effectively implemented.

## POLICY-MAKING – GUIDELINE THREE: STRIVING FOR AN EXEMPLARY, HIGH-CULTURE AND EQUITABLE SOCIETY, BASED ON JEWISH AND HUMAN VALUES, SHOULD BE AT THE CENTRE OF POLICIES AND OF CRITICAL POLICY CHOICES

This guideline is anathema in part to post-Zionist views and to some versions of liberal democracy. It certainly stands in opposition to widely accepted views on the limited functions of the state and of collective action as a whole. Also, it increases policy disagreements, given differences of opinion over the desired social future. Nevertheless, the need for 'societal architecture' in Israel is clearly implied in the realistic vision and in its underlying normative bases. If 'normalization' of Israel as a mediocre state is to be avoided, Israeli society must engage in active 'self-production',[14] with governance fulfilling a central role. Indeed, societal architecture is pivotal for the second phase of Zionism and state development towards which Israel and the Jewish people are moving.[15]

However, this societal architecture must be 'soft' and democratically flexible in contrast to 'command societies'. Networking with non-governmental action groups, equitable distribution of costs and benefits, participatory decision-making, facilitating rather than enforcing – all these characterize the desired societal architecture I have in mind. Still, a degree of 'creative destruction'[16] and enforcement of democratic choices against resisting groups is unavoidable in order to advance Israel's prosperity. This, to be sure, raises difficult issues concerning selective use of the authority of the state and of force – issues that require separate discussion.

Let me now proceed to a number of policy blueprints and critical choices grounded in the policy-making guidelines as well as in (a) the realistic nightmares and (b) no less realistic visions. Policy guidelines on the institutional implications of this will be discussed later.

## POLICY GUIDELINE ONE: THE JEWISH MAJORITY SHOULD BE INCREASED

In many respects, this may well be the single most important factor shaping the future of Israel. If the Jewish population declines below a critical level, say around 70 per cent, realizing the realistic vision becomes very doubtful, making any of the nightmare visions that much more plausible. On the other hand, were the Jewish population to increase to about 80 per cent, that would provide a solid foundation for realization of the realistic vision. Hence, the need to make critical choices designed to meet this policy guideline.

*Critical choices:* Resources should be devoted to increasing Jewish immigration. The Law of Return should not be amended, but conversion and social integration of immigrants of doubtful Jewish status should be given highest priority. The number of foreign labourers becoming permanent residents *de facto* without being integrated into the Jewish people should be strictly controlled, and in fact reduced. Similarly, peace agreements should definitely not permit the return of Arab refugees in more than symbolic numbers.

## POLICY GUIDELINE TWO: THE JEWISH PLURALISTIC NATURE OF ISRAEL SHOULD BE DEEPENED, WITH CULTURAL AUTONOMY FOR THE COUNTRY'S MINORITIES

The guideline to deepen the Jewish nature of Israel derives directly from both realistic nightmares and realistic visions. Less obvious, however, are the other two main elements of the proposed policy guideline, namely pluralism and cultural autonomy.

The guideline for promoting Jewish pluralism has four bases. It is normatively implied in democratic values. It is a *Realpolitik* condition for deepening the overall Jewish nature of Israel and the fuller integration of Israel into the Jewish people, just as, thirdly, pluralism is a main stimulus for creativity, which in turn is an essential part of the realistic vision and a precondition for realizing its other parts. And, fourthly, it is deeply rooted in the cultural and spiritual history and traditions of Judaism and the Jewish people.

Moving to cultural autonomy for the minorities, it is impossible in the long run to deepen the Jewish nature of the state as a whole – while maintaining democracy and a minimum of overall social cohesion – without recognizing the right of minorities to deepen their own cultural identity and facilitating it. Hence, the recommendation to promote cultural autonomy of the minorities: the faster the better, but also subject to safeguards against subversive misuse.

This one policy guideline leads to many critical choices, including some opposing actual decisions that have been made.

*Critical choices:* Recognition should be granted to all streams of Judaism. Jewish studies in schools should be completely reformed to fit the interests and needs of pupils while helping them to form their own autonomous Jewish identity. Public symbols and rituals should be revised to fit Jewish traditions and values. Efforts to impose Jewish symbols and studies on the minorities should be replaced by recognition of their own symbols and studies in combination with state symbols and shared subjects. Authentic, non-politicized cultural deepening in the minorities should be respected and actively supported.

### POLICY GUIDELINE THREE: SOCIAL EQUITY CONSIDERATIONS SHOULD BE GIVEN FAR GREATER WEIGHT IN ECONOMIC POLICIES

One of the more ominous developments in Israel is indiscriminate adoption of 'free market' dogmas and policies without adequate efforts to integrate them with Jewish values of social justice and equity. A clear symptom is the growing income gap and its acceptance as 'good' by many top-level decision-makers, without any serious counter-measures being taken. The decline of the Kibbutz movement, without any other social justice-seeking forms of sub-societies emerging, is another symptom of the decline of social values in Israel. The increasing political power of monied interests further propels momentum in a 'nightmare' direction. The dominance of economists in policy-making, without any real counter-weights, both illustrates the slippery slope on which Israel is headed in this matter, and makes it that much more slippery.

The lack of recognized 'critical choices' in this socio-economic domain only further characterizes the situation, making development of innovative options a must.

*Critical choices:* Social-policy thinkers and professionals should be put into high policy-making positions so as to offset overinfluence by economists. The minimum wage should be raised. An active employment policy should be adopted, with emphasis on training and mobility. Provision of equal-life chances should be assured through the education system, including for the minorities. National ownership of land reserves should be maintained. Taxation should be made more progressive. Social experimentation with new forms of communes and cooperatives should be encouraged.

### POLICY GUIDELINE FOUR: ISRAEL SHOULD BE ADVANCED TOWARDS A LEARNING, POPULAR, HIGH-CULTURE AND KNOWLEDGE SOCIETY

In the abstract, all will agree with this policy guideline. But, in fact, very little of significance has been achieved, despite some cultural policy plans recently prepared by the Ministry of Culture, Education and Sport (a ridiculous hybrid in itself!) and some think-tanks. Educational policies are conservative and focus on secondary matters, such as matriculation examinations. Mass sports receive far more resources than cultural activities. Research budgets are inadequate. And very little is done to advance learning as a main activity by those with unprecedented leisure time on their hands.

Here, too, critical choices are not even on the agenda, and need, first of all (a) development and (b) explication. Still, some can be provisionally identified for the moment to illustrate applications of this fourth policy guideline.

*Critical choices:* Resources should be transferred from mass sport facilities to educational and cultural ones. Computer, environment-based learning and remote learning should be advanced rapidly in schools, colleges and society as a whole to increase study-time productivity and diffuse individualized learning opportunities. Cultural activities should be subsidized to a larger extent, in respect of both popular (not 'mass'!) culture[17] and high-culture, in the pluralistic senses of those terms. Significant portions of mass media programmes should be reserved for learning and cultural programmes, including many more locally produced ones.

## POLICY GUIDELINE FIVE: IDEOLOGICAL DIVISIONS AND DEEP DIFFERENCES OF OPINION SHOULD BE ACCEPTED AS 'NATURAL' TO ISRAEL, WITH EFFORTS CONCENTRATING ON BUILDING MUTUAL RESPECT AND UNDERSTANDING, AND ON CONTAINING VIOLENCE

In the policy space at which this guideline is directed, the situation is paradoxical. Chimerical options with no existence in reality receive much attention, while critical options that do happen to be quite real are overlooked entirely. In my opinion, far too much public discourse and too many government measures are wasted on marginal issues and choices that do not make a significant difference simply because of a mistaken conception of what 'critical' means for a nation.

Ideological divisions and differences of opinion are natural to the Jewish people and to social processes taking place in Israel. Present 'divisions' are in no way more serious than earlier ones: in the Jewish people, in pre-state Israel and in earlier state periods.

Furthermore, divisions and differences of values and views, however sharp and intense, are if anything conducive to cultural and spiritual creativity as highlighted in the realistic vision. Besides, according to my reading of the dynamics, no 'value architecture' can or should be expected to make any real difference in value disagreements within the next 30 to 50 years.

Looked at correctly, ideological divisions and differences of opinion are not only prevalent in the Jewish people and Israel but are never 'resolved' with any sense of finality. Thus, they are best left to organic historical processes, with government action limited to setting down 'rules of behaviour' for preserving social cohesion and especially for preventing violence. This should not be read as meaning that important choices are not to be faced or should not be developed, but that they should be less radical than many of the imagined ones.

Accordingly, the proposed critical choices here are quite different from those included in public discourse and on the political agenda.

*Critical choices:* The most important suggested 'critical choice' is to avoid many suggested critical choices. Thus, it is better that no constitution presuming to set down definitive norms and rules on relations between state and religion be drafted and pushed through to ratification at all costs.

Moving to less critical but still important choices: acceptability of state institutions by all citizens should be advanced by drawing different groups into political activities and setting up a 'Constitutional Court' overlapping the Supreme Court but more 'representative'. Military and national service by all should be advanced in ways acceptable to 'outside' groups such as the ultra-orthodox and the minorities, rather than imposed on them. Educational and mass media autonomy should be facilitated on the condition that shared core themes are included. Private initiatives to build bridges and increase mutual understanding and respect should certainly be supported. A 'Joint Council' should be set up by public law, but it should be consultative in nature and without the authority to make obligatory decisions. All streams of Judaism should receive recognition, as already mentioned. In respect of 'hot' issues, such as personal status and Sabbath laws, the status quo should be maintained and problems should be coped with *ad hoc* and pragmatically. Comprehensive, 'once-and-for-all' solutions are best avoided as neither necessary nor possible.

All these and other policy-making guidelines, policy guidelines and critical choices are provisional and subject to serious policy contemplation, discourse, research and development. But this requires institutional capacities, which are lacking at present. Hence, the real need for engaging in institutional redesign as a precondition for the effective weaving of the future of Israel, to which I now turn.

## INSTITUTIONAL REDESIGN

Let me start with three overall guidelines for institutional redesign directed at upgrading future-weaving capacities. All three differ from prevailing views on regime and governance reforms in Israel.

a) In dealing with issues of regime and governance, the necessity to assure high-quality democratic capacities to govern and weave the future should receive serious attention. This is instead of overdoing legalistic architecture, doubtful ideological discourse on 'what is more democratic', and an exclusive preoccupation with the rights of individuals now living, in glaring contrast to the gross neglect of (i) public needs, (ii) individual responsibilities and duties, and (iii) the rights of future generations.

b) Israel's uniqueness as a Jewish state and its relations with the Jewish people, in its normative aspirations and ideological commitments, and in its precarious geo-strategic situation must be fully taken into account. This requires much greater caution and discrimination in importing ideas and institutions from other countries and learning from their experience; it also requires greater originality in institutional design reflecting this uniqueness.

c) The habit of dealing *ad hoc* in a piecemeal fashion with institutional issues as needs and ideas arise is disastrous for the quality of politics and governance in Israel: one day – primaries; the second day – direct elections of the prime minister; the third day – 'Norwegian' resignations of ministers from the Knesset; a day earlier – direct elections of city mayors; a day later – institutionalization of referenda; and so on. This constant quest for *ad hoc* improvisations – a myopic preoccupation with repairing holes without paying prior attention to the overall fabric – leads unavoidably to system demolition in general.

What is really needed in order to progress towards quality democracy and adequate weaving-the-future capacities is a comprehensive reconsideration of the Israeli political and governance system as a whole. Therefore, a recommendation of critical importance calls for setting up a 'blue ribbon', public–professional commission to prepare alternative political and governance reform proposals.

Several tentative personal ideas for institutional redesign on the regime level to be considered by such a commission include:

- Reducing political fragmentation by introducing a higher threshold for entry of parties into the Knesset.
- Increasing the power of the prime minister by enabling him to call once for new Knesset elections without himself resigning, subject to his being confirmed in office by the newly elected Knesset.
- Setting up a 'Second Chamber' with consultative and law-delaying powers, composed of individually appointed personalities not active in party politics.
- Setting up of a 'Constitutional Court', the majority of its members Supreme Court judges, but with the addition of personalities who possess invaluable knowledge and accumulated experience in social and public affairs to be selected by a special committee.

In the absence of a public commission, there is no choice but to proceed with these and other proposals as critical choices that need to be adopted. Still, it is far preferable to set up the commission, as proposed above, and to freeze all structural regime changes. This reservation does not apply, however, to incremental improvements and reforms in the machinery of Israeli government that are meant to upgrade integrated longer-term policy development – especially professional policy-planning units operating from within the prime minister's office capable of applying broad perspectives to the critical, strategic issues.

The difficulties encountered in undertaking the first steps in this direction perfectly illustrate the built-in resistance to improved policy-making reforms and procedures within the existing Israeli policy-making establishment. Thus the National Security Council finally created in 1999[18] has experienced extreme difficulty in defining its position, carving out its 'turf' and consolidating its position and role within the apparatus of executive government. Similarly, initiatives aimed at setting up a planning authority, likewise inside the prime minister's office, were frozen at the start of the new century because of resistance within the Barak coalition. These difficulties ought to be overcome, with the National Security Council developing into a major long-term policy-planning unit having assured opportunities to input its studies and recommendations into ongoing decision processes, and the badly needed National Planning Authority duly empowered. These two staffs ought then to be encouraged to work closely together, *inter alia* in profiling operational realistic visions and nightmares for Israel for the year 2025.[19]

## WHAT ABOUT SOCIETY?

Moving away from decline towards prospering within rapidly changing twenty-first-century environments requires the extensive restructuring of Israeli society.[20] Democratic governance can facilitate societal learning and adjustment by soft societal architecture as suggested above. But Zionism was not fully realized by statehood alone and bringing about a thriving Israel is only a state function in part. It is largely up to a variety of social and non-governmental actors to move society towards its future. Providing such support for governmental action is a prerequisite without which democratic weaving of the future is impossible.

A separate essay is required to focus on upgrading the will and capacity of the Jewish society in Israel to evolve towards the kind of prospering depicted in the realistic vision, or towards any other vision that has the potential for gaining broad, enthusiastic public support. This in turn requires, for instance, discussion of the crucial roles of élites and of ways to develop élites able to fulfil societal guidance functions on the social and governance levels alike. However, as noted, this is a matter for another occasion, essential though it may be for completing the analysis and proposals worked out in this essay.

## TALKING, ACTING, THINKING

At both open and closed meetings of senior Israeli policy-makers, a standard phrase is 'we should stop talking and start acting'. It is very unusual to find the prior need – thinking profoundly – mentioned. This, I am afraid, is not only a matter of habit of speech but it reflects a very disturbing reality. Thinking on policy issues is certainly widespread in government and non-governmental élites. But, with few exceptions (such as defence R&D), deep, long-term, comprehensive and high-quality policy cogitation is not wide-spread in Israeli governance, to put it mildly. Even worse, the absence of a 'central brain of government' is not even noted as a serious omission by top decision-makers, who do little to repair this lacuna.

This is not the place to dwell on the causes of this dangerous omission. But, in closing, let me enumerate some of them so as to demonstrate the many barriers which impede adequate thinking on weaving the future in Israeli politics and governance: as already mentioned, the descent into populist, mass-media democracy, shared with other countries; dogmatic stances; the pressure of current issues; the requirements of coalition maintenance; a neo-feudalistic division of policy domains between ministries and parties. Add to this list the non-professionalism of the senior civil service; fear of leaks; unwarranted self-confidence on the part of top decision-makers; a governmental culture of anti-intellectualism; and more.

If the thriving or decline of Israel were predetermined by rigid historic processes, then in the long run the weaknesses of future-weaving capacities would not matter. However, this is not the case. As I try to show in this chapter, the future of Israel is as yet open and undetermined. The country and nation are poised precariously between prospering and decline, with the actual course over the next 30 to 50 years and beyond very much dependent on the poli-cies that Israel develops and implements at present, and the strategic choices it makes now.

Therefore, likely errors in the estimates and recommendations of this chapter can be passed over. What really matters is the validity of the larger thesis: first, that Israel's futures depend extensively on Israel itself; second, unless averted in time, default processes that are essentially dysfunctional could well lead to national decline. It follows, therefore, that radical improvements in Israeli policy-thinking and action are imperative in order to avoid nightmares and approximate realistic visions. Failing in this great national enterprise because of our own shortcomings, including shortsight-edness, as well as stubbornly holding on to outmoded policy and

critical choice-making, would be a historic tragedy brought about
by what can only be regarded as the highest, most egregious of all
political sins.

NOTES

1. The metaphor of 'weaving the future' is taken from *Plato's Statesman*. For a recent
   version in English, see Plato, *Statesman*, edited by Julian Annas and Robin Waterfield
   (Cambridge: Cambridge University Press, 1995).
2. As presented in four books in Hebrew by the author, on the dynamics of Israel, state-
   building, grand-strategic security issues and refounding of Zionism.
3. John Knoblock, translator and annotator, *Xunzi: A Translation and Study of the
   Complete Works* (Stanford, CA: Stanford University Press, 1990), Vol. II, p. 161.
4. For this concept see C. R. Hallpike, *The Principles of Social Evolution* (Oxford:
   Clarendon Press, 1988).
5. Taking into account the time cycles of socio-political processes on one hand and the
   limits of foresight on the other, 30 to 50 years is the appropriate period to be taken
   into account in policy-making on main future-shaping domains. Because of uncertainty, long-term policies constitute fuzzy gambles and require constant revision in
   the light of actual developments. But this does not negate the necessity to consider
   seriously the long-term implications of main choices as long as one does not run into
   much 'inconceivability'. See Yehezkel Dror, 'Statecraft as Fuzzy Gambling with
   History', *Futures Research Quarterly*, 9, 3 (autumn 1993), pp. 95–107; and Yehezkel
   Dror, 'Beyond Uncertainty: Facing the Inconceivable', *Technological Forecasting and
   Social Change*, 62, 1 and 2 (August/September 1999), pp. 151–3.
6. A major difference between Israel and other new states is that Zionism planned and
   brought about, with the help of other historical events, a movement of people
   producing the Jewish majority of Israel. This effect of the Zionist revolution is
   unique.
7. Therefore, the application of Fernand Braudel's long-term historical approach to the
   State of Israel may provide important insights on continuity of Jewish ideas and
   beliefs and help us to understand some features of Israel, but it is unable to explain
   most of the dilemmas and alternative futures facing the state. As a whole, it is impossible to understand contemporary Israel on the lines of Braudel's history of France.
   See Fernand Braudel, *The Identity of France*, Vol. I: *History and Environment* (London:
   Collins, 1988), and Vol. II: *People and Production* (London: Collins, 1990).
8. Very relevant is Courtney Brown, *Serpents in the Sand: Essays on the Nonlinear Nature
   of Politics and Human Destiny* (Ann Arbor, MI: University of Michigan Press), 1995.
9. For the distinction between 'internal' and 'external' views of decision-making, see
   Michael E. Bratman, *Intention, Plans, and Practical Reason* (Cambridge, MA: Harvard
   University Press), 1987.
10. Relevant, in a broad sense, is the large theoretical and monographic literature deal-
    ing with the rise and decline of nations and 'grand strategies'. To limit myself to a
    few illustrations: in terms of general theory, especially relevant is Roberto
    Managabeira Unger, *Part I of Politics, a Work in Constructive Social Theory: False
    Necessity – Anti-Necessitarian Social Theory in the Service of Radical Democracy*
    (Cambridge: Cambridge University Press, 1987); and his book *Plasticity into Power:
    Comparative–Historical Studies on the Institutional Conditions of Economic and Military
    Success* (Cambridge: Cambridge University Press, 1987).
        On the monographic level, the case of the Dutch Republic is of much interest as a
    historical metaphor for Israel. The best treatments of this subject are Jonathan I.
    Israel, *The Dutch Republic: Its Rise, Greatness, and Fall 1477–1806* (Oxford: Clarendon
    Press, 1995); and Karel Davids and Jan Lucassen (eds), *A Miracle Mirrored: The Dutch
    Republic in European Perspective* (Cambridge: Cambridge University Press, 1995).
        On the levels of philosophy of history and models of reality, my approach is based
    on views such as these presented, respectively, in Geoffrey Hawthorn, *Plausible*

*Worlds: Possibility and Understanding in History and the Social Sciences* (Cambridge: Cambridge University Press, 1991); Niall Ferguson (ed.), *Virtual History: Alternatives and Counterfactuals* (London: Picador, 1997); and Storrs McCall, *A Model of the Universe: Space–Time, Probability, and Decision* (Oxford: Clarendon Press, 1994).

11. See, for example, Gary Hamel and C. K. Prahalad, *Competing for the Future* (Boston, MA: Harvard Business School Press, 1994).

12. Also needed are utopias, to serve as normative grounding for realistic visions. The absence of modern Israeli utopias may well be a symptom of the lack of serious normative concern with its internal futures, all the more pronounced when contrasted with the visions presented on its external futures in a peaceful Middle East. See, for example, Shimon Peres and Arie Naor, *The New Middle East* (New York: Holt, 1993). The dearth of modern Israeli utopias is all the more pronounced when compared with the significance of utopias in pre-state Zionism. See Rachel Elboim-Dror, *Yesterdays Tomorrow: Vol. I. Zionist Utopias; Vol. II. An Anthology of Zionist Utopias* (Jerusalem: Yad Izhak Ben-Zvi Institute and Bialik Institute, 1993) (in Hebrew, English version in preparation).

13. As presented in my book *Refounding Zionism* (Jerusalem: Zionist Library, 1997) (in Hebrew, English version in preparation).

14. I have borrowed the term from Alain Touraine, *The Self-Production of Society* (Chicago, IL: University of Chicago Press, 1977).

15. A devastating criticism of the pre-state and early state periods on the basis of the neglect of social equity goals is to be found in Zeev Sternhell, *The Founding Myths of Israel: Socialism and the Making of the Jewish State* (Princeton, NJ: Princeton University Press, 1997). His historical judgment is exaggerated because of his underestimation of the difficulties of engaging in state-founding and -building and social architecture at one and the same time. However, the tradition of neglecting societal architecture is very strong and reinforced by many vested interests, entitlements and habits of thought. Hence the paradox that even actors deeply committed to Jewish values, including prophetic ideas of social justice, such as the Zionist National Religious Party, and actors trying to practise in their sub-societies's social justice, such as the Kibbutz movements, pay only minor attention to equity-promoting social policies. All the more needed, and harder to achieve, is societal architecture.

16. As propounded in Joseph A. Schumpeter, *Capitalism, Socialism and Democracy* (New York: Harper & Row, 1942), Ch. 7.

17. Popular culture involves interaction and participation, while mass culture is passive, spectatorial and mainly amusement-oriented. See Michael Kammen, *American Culture, American Tastes: Social Change and the 20th Century* (New York: Knopf, 1999).

18. The formal present name 'National Security Council' is incorrect, and illustrates the incorrect adoption of terms from other countries.

19. The pioneering project '*Israel 2020*': *Master Plan for Israel in the 21st Century*, resulting in 18 volumes of grand scenarios, options and sectoral and overall policy visions and plans (published in Hebrew in 1996), is an important step in this direction. But a more comprehensive, uncertainty-sophisticated and value-sensitive realistic vision, in part classified, is needed – to be prepared by in-house governmental policy staffs together with a network of university institutes, think-tanks, policy-thinkers, professionals, etc. Realistic nightmares are much more sensitive. They should be prepared in the main in select staff units in government on a highly classified basis, with independent policy-thinking units being encouraged to prepare such images on their own responsibility (as some have done recently).

20. Very relevant is Mancur Olson, *The Rise and Decline of Nations: Economic Growth, Stagflation, and Social Rigidities* (New Haven, CT: Yale University Press, 1982).

# David Vital: Bibliography

*Books*

1. *The Inequality of States: A Study of the Small Power in International Relations* (Oxford: Clarendon Press; Oxford University Press, 1967), pp. 198.
   *reprinted:* 1972
   *reprinted:* Westport, CT: Greenwood Press, 1980
   *Spanish edition: La desigualdad de los estados* (Madrid: Instituto de Estudios Politicos, 1976).
2. *The Making of British Foreign Policy* (London: George Allen & Unwin, 1968; and New York: Praeger, 1968), pp. 119
   *reprinted:* 1971
   *Spanish edition: La elaboración de la politica exterior británica* (Madrid: Instituto de Estudios Politicos, 1977)
   *extracts in:* James Barber and Michael Smith (eds), *The Nature of Foreign Policy: A Reader* (Homes McDougall/ Open University Press, 1974).
3. *The Survival of Small States: Studies in Small Power/Great Power Conflict* (London: Oxford University Press, 1971), pp. vi + 136
   *Hebrew edition (revised): Medinot ketanot be-Mivhan ha-Kiyum* (Tel Aviv: Am Oved, 1972)
   *Spanish edition: La supervivencia de los pequeños estados* (Madrid: Instituto de Estudios Politicos, 1975).
4. *The Origins of Zionism* (Oxford: Clarendon Press; Oxford University Press, 1975), pp. xvi + 396
   *paperback edition:* 1980
   *reprinted:* 1990
   *Hebrew edition (revised): Ha-Mahapekha ha-Zionit*, Vol. I: *Reishit ha-Tenu'a* (Tel Aviv: Am Oved, 1978)

*extracts in:* Yerahmiel Cohen (ed.), *Mekhkarim be-toldot yisrael ba-'et ha-hadasha*, pp. 357–87.

5.  *Zionism: The Formative Years* (Oxford: Clarendon Press; Oxford University Press, 1982), pp. xviii + 514

\*Awarded the *Jewish Chronicle* (London)/Harold H. Wingate Literary Prize, 1982

\*Awarded the Kenneth B. Smilen/*Present Tense* (New York) Literary Prize (for History), 1983

*paperback edition:* 1988

*Hebrew edition: Ha-Mahapekha ha-Zionit*, Vol. II: *Shenot ha-'Izuv* (Tel Aviv: Am Oved, 1984)

*extract in:* Yossi Goldstein (ed.), *Bein zion le-zionut: toldot ha-tenua ha-zionit 1914–1918* (Tel Aviv, 1994), pp. 177–207.

6.  *Zionism: The Crucial Phase* (Oxford: Clarendon Press; Oxford University Press, 1987), pp. xvi + 392

*Hebrew edition: Ha-Mahapekha ha-Zionit*, Vol. III: *Shelav ha-Hakhra'a* (Tel Aviv: Am Oved, 1991).

7.  *The Future of the Jews: A People at the Crossroads?* (Cambridge, MA: Harvard University Press, 1990), pp. xii + 161

*French edition: L'Avenir des Juifs: Un peuple à la croisée des chemins?* (Paris: Calmann-Levy, 1992)

*Italian edition: Il futuro degli ebrei* (Florence: La Giuntina, 1992).

8.  *A People Apart: The Jews in Europe 1789–1939*, Oxford History of Modern Europe series, general editors: Lord [Alan] Bullock and Sir William Deakin (Oxford: Clarendon Press; Oxford University Press, 1999), pp. xviii + 944.

*Academic articles, review articles and reviews, and selected miscellaneous political, literary and dramatic criticism*

**1952**

1.  'Jerusalem Answers Prague', *The Economist* (London), 6 December 1952.

**1953**

2.  'Israel and the Russians', *The Economist* (London), 7 March 1953.

3.  'Synagogue and State', *The Economist* (London), 8 August 1953.

Regular contributions of leading articles and opinion columns on international affairs (usually under the heading 'Marginal Comment') in the *Jerusalem Post*.

## 1954

4. '"Avaz pereh" meulaf' (*review of* a performance of Ibsen's *The Wild Duck*), *Ha-Oomah: shavu'on bilti talui*, 17, 23 December 1954.

Regular contributions of leading articles and opinion columns on international affairs (usually under the heading 'Marginal Comment') in the *Jerusalem Post*.

## 1955

Theatrical criticism in the *Here and Now* weekly (Tel Aviv):

5. 'Modernizing Molière' (*review of* Molière's 'The Miser'), 5 April 1955.
6. 'Americans Abroad' (*review of* a performance of 'The Tea House of the August Moon' by John Patrick), 14 April 1955.
7. 'Beware of Pity' (*review of* 'Come Back Little Sheba' by William Inge), 21 April 1955.
8. 'Lear at Habimah' (*review of* a performance of Shakespeare's 'King Lear'), 28 April 1955.
9. 'Luke-warm Tea' (*review of* 'Tea and Sympathy' by Robert Anderson), 25 May 1955.
10. 'Closed Shop in the Theatre', 1 June 1955.
11. 'New Company Tries Too Hard' (*review of* 'Kilometre 56' by Moshe Shamir), 16 June 1955.
12. 'Didactic review' (*review of* 'The Good Soul of Szechuan' by Bertolt Brecht), 23 June 1955.
13. 'Quixote on the Ole Prairee' (*review of* 'The Rainmaker' by N. Richard Nash), 30 June 1955.
14. 'French Mechanics or American Slickness' (*review of* 'The Conquerors' by P. A. Bréal), 14 July 1955.
15. 'Theatre Without Aim', 21 July 1955.
16. 'Habimah's New Venture' (*review of* 'A Sleep of Prisoners' by Christopher Fry), 4 August 1955.
17. 'Mossinsohn Tackles History' (*review of* 'Cambyses' by Yigal Mossinsohn), 25 August 1955.
18. 'Hell and Damnation' (*review of* 'Eldorado' by Yigal Mossinsohn), 1 September 1955.
19. 'Israeli or Jewish Play?' (*review of* 'The Lady of the Palace' by Leah Goldberg), 22 September 1955.
20. 'Dissatisfaction with Life' (*review of* 'Henry IV' by Luigi Pirandello), 26 October 1955.
21. 'Euripides Bound' (*review of* 'Medea'), 16 November 1955.

22. 'Irish Wit in Tel Aviv' (*review of En attendant Godot* by Samuel Beckett), 30 November 1955.
23. 'Boulevard Theatre' (*review of* 'The Italian Straw Hat' by Labiche and Michel), 7 December 1955.
24. 'Kafka on the Stage' (*review of* 'The Castle' by Max Brod), 21 December 1955.

### 1956
Theatrical criticism in the *Here and Now* weekly (Tel Aviv):
25. 'Romanticizing the Jewish Village' (*review of* 'Pandre the Hero' by Zalman Shneour), 4 January 1956.
26. 'Beauty and the Kibbutznik' (*review of* 'Maayana' by Moshe Politi), 8 February 1956.
27. 'French G. B. S.' (*review of* 'La Parisienne' by Henri Becque), 22 February 1956.
28. 'Hasmonaeans on the Stage' (*review of* 'The War of the Sons of Light' by Moshe Shamir), 4 April 1956.
29. 'Pathetic Little Man' (*review of* 'A View from the Bridge' by Arthur Miller), 9 May 1956.

### 1961
30. 'The Death of Aleksander Mihailovitch' (a story), *Jewish Quarterly*, viii, 4 (32) (autumn, 1961).

### 1966
31. 'Czechoslovakia and the Powers', *Journal of Contemporary History* (London), i, 4 (October 1966).
    *reprinted in:* Hans W. Gatzke (ed.), *Europe Between Two Wars* (Chicago: Quadrangle Books, 1972).

### 1967
32. 'The Meaning of Munich', *Jerusalem Post*, 14 July 1967.
33. 'Light and Levantinism', in M. Mindlin and Chaim Bermant (eds), *Explorations* (London: Barrie & Rockliff for Institute of Contemporary History, 1967).
34. 'On Approaches to the Study of International Relations', *World Politics* (Princeton), xix, 4 (July 1967)
    *reprinted in:* Klaus Knorr and James N. Rosenau (eds), *Contending Approaches to International Politics* (Princeton: Princeton University Press, 1969)
    *reprinted in: Joint Reprint Series*, School of African and Asian Studies, University of Sussex, No. 13
    *reprinted in:* G. S. Masannat and G. Abcarian (eds), *International Politics* (New York: Scribner's, 1970)
    *reprinted in:* Durbin and B. Sanders (eds), *Contemporary International Politics* (New York: Wiley, 1971).

35. *Review of* Ossip K. Flechtheim, *Eine Welt oder keine?*, Philip E. Jacob and Alexine I. Atherton, *The Dynamics of International Organization*, and Herbert C. Kelman, *International Behaviour: A Social-Psychological Analysis*, in *Political Studies*, xv, 2 (1967).

**1968**

36. 'Double-talk or double-think? A Comment on the Draft Non-proliferation Treaty', *International Affairs* (London), xliv, 3 (July 1968).

37. 'The Making of British Foreign Policy', *Political Quarterly* (London), xxxix, 3 (July–September 1968)
    *reprinted:* for use of students and faculty of the National War College, Washington, DC.

38. *Review of* L. W. Martin, *The Sea in Modern Strategy*, in *Political Studies*, xvi, 2 (1968).

39. 'Security for the Non-nuclear?', *Insight*, 2 (summer 1968).

40. 'After the Tanks: Dubček Survives; Czechoslovakia Goes Under' (by David Brno (pseud.)), *Jerusalem Post*, 30 August 1968.

41. *Review of* James E. Dougherty and J. F. Lehman, *Arms Control for the Sixties*, Karl W. Deutsch, *Arms Control and the Atlantic Alliance*, Jeremy J. Stone, *Strategic Persuasion*, Albert Willot, *Désarmement: Les postes d'observation*, and Alexander Glutz von Blotzheim, *Le Plan Rapacki et les propositions Mendès-France*, in *International Affairs*, xliv, 4 (October 1968).

42. *Review of* Walter Laqueur, *The Road to War 1967* and N. Bar-Yaacov, *The Israel–Syrian Armistice*, in *International Affairs*, xliv, 4 (October l968).

**1969**

43. 'The Problem of Guarantees' in C. F. Barnaby (ed.), *Preventing the Spread of Nuclear Weapons* (London: Souvenir Press, 1969).

44. 'The World from the Classroom', *International Journal* (Toronto), xxiv, 4 (autumn 1969).

45. 'Askanim, ha-miflagot ve-da'at ha-kahal', *Ma'ariv*, 8 April 1969.

**1970**

46. 'Mimshal ha-nassi Nixon ve-hasikhsukh ha-'aravi–yisraeli', *Sekira Hodshit*, September 1970.

47. 'The 'Unholy' Assault on Zionism: Four Books of Contemporary History', *Jerusalem Post*, 13 November 1970.

48. *Review of* Leopold Laufer, *Israel and the Developing Countries: New Approaches to Cooperation*, in *Political Science Quarterly*, lxxxv, 3 (September 1970).

**1971**

49. 'Israel and the Arab Countries – An Ethno-national Confrontation', in Stephen L. Spiegel and Kenneth N. Waltz (eds), *Conflict in World Politics* (Cambridge, MA: Winthrop, 1971).

50. The Analysis of Small Power Politics', in A. Schou and A. O. Brundtland (eds), *Small States in International Relations: Nobel Symposium 17* (Stockholm: Almquist and Wiksell; New York: John Wiley, 1971).

**1972**

51. 'Diplomatic Channels', *review of* Michael Brecher, *The Foreign Policy System of Israel*, in *The Times Literary Supplement*, 1 September 1972.

**1973**

52. 'Force and Innocence', *Dispersion and Unity* (Jerusalem), 19/20 (1973).

53. 'Pegisha mekhubedet: ha-tevuna mehayevet et ha-vatikan lehagiya lehesder im Yisrael', *Yediyot Aharonot*, 18 January 1973.

54. 'Ha-daberet shel ha-zameret', *Yediyot Aharonot*, 1 February 1973.

55. 'Ha-sikhsukh ha-yisraeli–aravi be-einei ha-zelav ha-adom', *Yediyot Aharonot*, 12 February 1973.

56. 'Hegayon zevai u-tevuna politit', *Yediyot Aharonot*, 26 February 1973.

57. 'Behirato shel nassi', *Yediyot Aharonot*, 21 March 1973.

58. 'Zionism Revisited: Herzl', *Commentary* (New York), lv, 5 (May 1973).

59. 'Hakamat ha-medina lo patra et ba'ayat kiyumeinu ke-uma', *Yediyot Aharonot* (Independence Day supplement), 6 May 1973.

60. 'A Very Special Case', *Jerusalem Post* (Independence Day supplement), 6 May 1973.

61. 'Hahzarat ha-imun', *Yediyot Aharonot*, 1 November 1973.

**1974**

62. 'Israel after the War – the Need for Political Change', *Commentary* (New York), lvii, 3 (March 1974).

63. 'A Palestine Issue', *review of* Isaiah Friedman, *The Question of Palestine 1914–1918*, in *Commentary*, lvii, 6 (June 1974).

**1975**

64. *Towards a New Polarization of Jewry?*, 19th Noah Barou Memorial Lecture, 10 December 1974 (London, 1975).

65. 'Jewish Power Sharing', *Jewish Chronicle*, 7 March 1975.
66. 'A Comment on Sovereignty', *Australian Outlook* (Journal of the Australian Institute of International Affairs), xxix, 3 (December 1975).
67. 'Ha-dinamika shel ha-kohot ha-po'alim ba-mizraj ha-tikhon', *review of* Yair Evron, *The Middle East: Nations, Super-powers and Wars*, in *Hamizrah Hehadash*, xxv, 3 (99) (1975).

**1976**

68. 'Israel and Jewry: Digging In', *Midstream* (New York), xxii, 9 (November 1976) (revised and expanded version of Barou Lecture, 1975).
69. 'Arzot ha-berit me'azevet mehadash et mediniyuta ba-'olam', *Yediyot Aharonot*, 13 May 1976.
70. 'The Opening of a Field', *review of* Michael Brecher, *Decisions in Israel's Foreign Policy*, in *Government and Opposition*, xi, 3 (1976).

**1977**

71. 'Struggles between States', *review of* Hedley Bull, *The Anarchical Society*, in *The Times Literary Supplement*, 22 July 1977.
72. 'Israel en het Wereldjodendom', Amsterdam, 1977.
73. 'Pierre Boissier' (*in memoriam*), in *Pierre Boissier (1920–1974)* (Geneva: Institut Henry-Dunant, 1977).

**1978**

74. 'Hozeh hagana 'im Arzot ha-Berit – neged: Hozeh temurat hahlashateinu', *Migvan*, 28 July 1978.

**1979**

75. 'Zionism and Israel', in Elie Kedourie (ed.), *The Jewish World* (London: Thames and Hudson, 1979)
    *French edition: Le Monde Juif* (Antwerp: Fonds Mercator, 1980).

**1980**

76. 'The Definition of Goals in Foreign Policy', in A. Arian (ed.), *Israel: a Developing Society* (Assen, Netherlands: Van Gorcum, 1980)
    *Hebrew edition: Israel – Dor ha-Hithavut* (Tel Aviv: Zmora, Bitan, Modan, 1979)
    *reprinted in:* Benyamin Neuberger (ed.), *Diplomatiya be-Zel 'Imut* (Tel Aviv, 1984)
    *reprinted in: Medina, Mimshal ve-Yahasim Beinleumiim* (Jerusalem), 13 (winter 1979).
77. 'Siakh shel Hershim', *Mahbarot le-sufrut la-hevra u-le-bikoret*, 1 (January 1980).

78. 'Shelosha mabatim 'al ha-leumiyut ha-yehudit', *Mahbarot le-sufrut la-hevra u-le-bikoret*, 3 (March 1980).
79. 'Onlookers and Participants', *review of* Bernard Wasserstein, *Britain and the Jews of Europe 1939–1945*, in *Commentary*, lxix, 2 (February 1980).

**1981**

80. 'The Holocaust and Zionism', in *Festschrift in Honor of Dr. George S. Wise* (Tel Aviv, 1981).
81. 'One People?', *review of* Paul R. Mendes-Flohr and Jehuda Reinharz (eds), *The Jew in the Modern World*, in *Commentary*, lxxi, 3 (March 1981).
82. 'Continuity and Change in the Jewish People after the Establishment of the State of Israel', in Shimon Shamir (ed.), *Self-views in Historical Perspective in Egypt and Israel* (Tel Aviv, 1981).
83. 'Divrei yemei ha-zionim ve-divrei yemei ha-yehudim', *Ha-Zionut*, vii, (1981)
    *English version:* 'The History of the Zionists and the History of the Jews', in *Studies in Zionism* (Tel Aviv), 6 (autumn 1982).

**1982**

84. 'For Now There is No Consensus', *Present Tense*, x, 1 (autumn 1982).
85. 'One Man's Doctrine', *review of* Shlomo Avineri, *The Making of Modern Zionism: The Intellectual Origins of the Jewish State*, in *Commentary*, lxxiii, 4 (April 1982).
86. *Review of* William Frankel, *Israel Observed*, in *Middle Eastern Studies*, xviii, 2 (April 1982).

**1983**

87. 'Ha-zionut ha-datit – paradoks?' ('Religious Zionism – a Paradox?'), in *Sugiyot be-Toldot ha-Zionut ve-ha-Yishuv* (Tel-Aviv), 2 (1983).
88. 'The Zionist as Thinker: Ahad Ha-Am and Hibbat Zion', in Jacques Kornberg (ed.), *At the Crossroads: Essays on Ahad Ha-Am* (Albany, NY: State University of New York Press, 1983).
89. *Review of* Rael Jean Isaac, *Party and Politics in Israel: Three Visions of a Jewish State*, in *Middle Eastern Studies*, xix, 3 (July 1983).
90. *Review of* Alan Edelstein, *An Unacknowledged Harmony: Philo-Semitism and the Survival of European Jewry*, in *American Historical Review*, lxxxviii, 4 (October 1983).

**1984**

91. 'The Rites of Zion', *review of* Charles S. Liebman and Eliezer Don-Yehia, *Civil Religion in Israel*, in *Commentary*, lxxvii, 5 (May 1984).

92. 'Zarat ha-yehudim ve-zarat ha-zionut', *Ha-Zionut*, ix (1984)
    *English version:* 'The Afflictions of the Jews and the Afflictions of Zionism', in S. A. Cohen and E. Don-Yehiya (eds), *Conflict and Consensus in Jewish Political Life* (Bar-Ilan University Press, 1986)
    *reprinted in:* Jehuda Reinharz and Anita Shapira (eds), *Essential Papers on Zionism* (New York: New York University Press, 1996).

93. *Review of* Alex Bein, Hermann Grieve, Julius H. Schoeps (eds), *Theodor Herzl: Briefe und Tagebücher*, i, *Briefe und Autobiographische Notizen 1866–1895*, in *Journal of Jewish Studies* xxxv, 2 (autumn 1984).

**1986**

94. *Review of* Richard I. Cohen (ed.), *Vision and Conflict in the Holy Land*, in *Studies in Zionism*, vii, 1 (1986).

**1987**

95. 'Zangwill and Modern Jewish Nationalism', *Modern Judaism* (Baltimore), iv, 3 (October 1984)
    *Hebrew version:* in *Zemanim*, 24 (winter 1987).

96. 'Nationalism, Political Action, and the Hostile Environment', in Jehuda Reinharz (ed.), *Living with Antisemitism: Modern Jewish Responses* (University Press of New England, 1987).

97. 'Leumiyut muvneit – irgun politi u-fe'ula politit' ('Enstructured Nationalism: Political Organization and Political Action), in Shmu'el Almog *et al.* (eds), *Temurot Ba-Historiya Ha-Yehudit Ha-Hadasha* (Transition and Change in Modern Jewish History), Essays in Honor of Shmuel Ettinger (Zalman Shazar Centre, Jerusalem, 1987).

98. 'Founding Father', *review of* Norman Rose, *Chaim Weizmann: A Biography*, in *Commentary*, September 1987.

99. *Review of* Menahem Kaufman (ed.), *Yahadut Zemanenu: Shenaton le-'iyun u-le-mekhkar*, Vol. 3 (1986), in *Studies in Zionism*, viii, 1 (spring 1987).

**1988**

100. 'Diplomacy in the Jewish Interest', in Ada Rapaport-Albert and Steven Zipperstein (eds), *Jewish History: Essays in Honour of Chimen Abramsky* (London: Halban, 1988).

**1989**
101. 'Our Road to Zion: A Memoir', *Commentary*, lxxxvii, 5 (May 1989).

**1990**
101. 'Power, Powerlessness and the Jews', *Commentary*, lxxxix, 1 (January 1990).
    > reprinted in: Fred Schultz (ed.), *Multicultural Education* (Guilford, CT: 1994).
102. 'Ma'azan me'ah shenot historiya yehudit' (One hundred years of Jewish History – a reckoning), in Haim Avni and Gideon Shimoni (eds), *Ha-Zionut u-mitnagdeiha ba'am hayehudi* (Jerusalem, 1990)
    > French version: 'Le Sionisme et ses opposants: le bilan d'un siècle d'histoire juive', *Pardès* (Paris), 11 (1990).
103. 'Ahad Ha-'Am as the Sage of Zionism', *Jewish History*, iv, 2 (autumn 1990).
104. The Toughest Subject', *review of* Lucy S. Dawidowicz, *From that Place and Time*, in *American Scholar* (winter 1990).

**1991**
105. 'After the Catastrophe: Aspects of Contemporary Jewry', in Peter Hayes (ed.), *Lessons and Legacies: The Meaning of the Holocaust in a Changing World* (Evanston, IL: Northwestern University Press, 1991).
106. 'European Jewry 1860–1919: Political Organization and Trans-state Political Action', in Paul Smith (ed.), *Non-Dominant Ethnic Groups in Inter- and Trans-State Relations* (New York University Press for the European Science Foundation, 1991).

**1992**
107. 'Bread Upon the Waters: The Legacy of the British in Jewish Palestine' and 'When It Began in Earnest', *The Times Literary Supplement*, 5 June 1992.
108. 'A Prophet in Israel', *review of* Yeshayahu Leibowitz, *Judaism, Human Values and the Jewish State*, in *The Times Literary Supplement*, 23 October 1992.

**1993**
109. 'De la diaspora à l'Etat d'Israel: fondamentalisme ou pragmatisme', *M*, 61–62 (May–June 1993).
110. 'De l'identité israélienne', in *Pardès*, 18 (1993).
111. 'Az Allam es nemzet', *Múlt és Jövó* (Budapest), 4 (1993).
112. 'The Trials of Self-Restraint', *review of* Anita Shapira, *Land and Power*, Henry Near, *The Kibbutz Movement*, Vol. I, and Aryeh

Fishman, *Judaism and the Modernization of the Religious Kibbutz*, in *The Times Literary Supplement*, 4 June, 1993.

113. 'At the Crossroads of History: Is there a Future for the Jewish People?', *Jewish Quarterly* (London), 1993.

**1994**

114. 'Some of the Forks in the Road', in Efraim Karsh and Gregory Mahler (eds), *Israel at the Crossroads* (London and New York: British Academic Press/Tauris, 1994).

115. 'Israel and the Jewish Diaspora: Five Comments on the Political Relationship', *Israel Affairs* (London), 2 (1994).

116. 'A Hawkish Cuckoo', *review of* Yaron London, *Kishon: du-siakh biografi*, in *The Times Supplement*, 21 January 1994.

**1995**

117. 'Irreversible Loss', *review of* Robert S. Wistrich (ed.), *The Terms of Survival*, in *The Times Literary Supplement*, 5 May 1995.

118. 'No More Prophets in Israel: A Transatlantic Reading of Jewish History', *review of* Norman Cantor, *The Sacred Chain*, in *The Times Literary Supplement*, 24 November 1995.

119. 'Izrael és a diaszpóra', *Múlt és Jövó* (Budapest), 4 (1995).

**1996**

120. 'The Flight from Jewry', *review of* Bernard Wasserstein, *Vanishing Diaspora*, in *The Times Literary Supplement*, 16 February 1996.

121. 'Ha-am ha-yehudi u-demuto ha-'atida be'einei hogei ha-zionut be-reishita', in Yisrael Gutman (ed.), *Temurot yesod ba-'am ha-yehudi be-'ikvot ha-shoah* (Jerusalem, 1996)

>    *English version:* 'The Future Image of the Jewish People as Envisaged by the Ideologues of Early Zionism', in Yisrael Gutman (ed.), *Major Changes Within the Jewish People in the Wake of the Holocaust* (Jerusalem, 1996).

122. 'A Prince of the Jews: The Legacy of Herzl's *Der Judenstaat* to Modern Israel', *The Times Literary Supplement*, 7 June 1996.

123. 'Towards a New Concert of Powers?', in Werner Bauwens *et al.* (eds), *Small States and the Security Challenge in the New Europe* (London and Washington: Brassey's, 1996).

124. 'They Came from the East', *review of* Geoffrey Wheatcroft, *The Controversy of Zion*, and Raphael Patai, *The Jews of Hungary*, in *The Times Literary Supplement*, 23 August 1996.

125. 'Al leumiyut ve-leumiyutam shel ha-yehudim', in Dina Porat *et al.* (eds), *Sefer Yovel le-Daniel Carpi* (Tel Aviv, 1996).

**1997**

126. 'From Curiosity to Remorse: The Struggle to Establish the Truth about the Holocaust', *review of* David S. Wyman, *The World Reacts to the Holocaust,* in *The Times Literary Supplement,* 7 March 1997.

127. 'Minor Power/Major Power Relations and the Contemporary Nation-State', in E. Inbar and G. Sheffer (eds), *The National Security of Small States in a Changing World* (London: Frank Cass, 1997).

128. 'How Herzl Took the Lead', *The Times Literary Supplement,* 29 August 1997
    *Hungarian version:* 'Hogyan vette át Herzl a vezetést?', *Múlt és Jövó* (Budapest), iv (1997).

**1998**

129. 'Israele: Da stato di fatto a stato di diritto', *Rassegna Mensile di Israel* (Rome), lxiv, terza serie (1998).

130. 'Il sionismo: rivoluzione o rivolta?', in *Nuova Storia Contemporanea* (Rome) (May 1988), pp. 21–30
    *Hebrew version:* 'Ha-zionut ke-mahapekha? Ha-zionut ke-merida?', in Aharon Amir (ed.), *Keshet: Kovets le-tsiun yovel* (Tel Aviv, 1998)
    *English version:* 'Zionism as Revolution? Zionism as Rebellion?', *Modern Judaism,* 18 (Johns Hopkins University Press, Baltimore), pp. 273–83.

131. 'The Cost of Leaving Vilna', *review of* Dan Jacobson, *Heshel's Kingdom,* in *The Times Literary Supplement,* 6 March 1998.

**1999**

132. 'Dreyfus in the Hexagon', *review of* Pierre Birnbaum, *Le moment antisémite,* in *The Times Literary Supplement,* 5 March 1999.

133. 'Israel Expects: The Israel Elections 1999', *Jewish Chronicle,* 21 May 1999.

134. 'From "State within a State" to State' (*an amended English version of No. 129*), *Israel Affairs,* v, 4 (summer 1999)
    *reprinted in:* Efraim Karsh (ed.), *Israel: The First Hundred Years,* Vol. I (London: Frank Cass, 2000), pp. 32–42.

135. 'Ha-ma'amad ha-politi ha-yisraeli u-shemo ha-tov shel ha-'am' (The Israeli Political Class and the Honour of the Nation), *Mifne,* xxviii (November 1999).

**2000**

136. 'Ha-zionut ke-mahapekha? Ha-zionut ke-merida?' (*No. 139*), *reprinted in:* Anita Shapira *et al.* (eds), *Eidan ha-Zionut* (Jerusalem, 2000).

137. 'Quit You Like Men', *review of* Andrea Dworkin, *Scapegoat: The Jews, Israel, and Women's Liberation*, in *The Times Literary Supplement*, 1 September 2000.

138. 'Not Single Spies but in Battalions: Espionage Uncovered in France, Russia, Britain and the US', *review of* Jacques Baud, *Encyclopédie du renseignement et des services secrets*, Bertrand Warusfel, *Contre-espionnage et protection du secret: Histoire, droit et organisation de la sécurité nationale en France*, William E. Duff, *A Time for Spies: Theodore Stephanovich Mally and the Era of the Great Illegals*, and Stuart A. Herrington, *Traitors Among Us: Inside the Spy Catcher's World*, in *The Times Literary Supplement*, 1 December 2000.

# Index